A NOTE TO THE READER

I hope this book will help you find comfort and personal strength from the most beloved collection of poetry in the Christian and Jewish traditions. You will notice that my approach to the psalms has several distinctive aspects. It proceeds in sequence from Psalm 1 to Psalm 150—through the whole book. By reading one page of this book each day along with the assigned psalm text, you will discover the concerns and themes of the psalmists of old. You might be taken aback by the unrestrained emotion—depression, anger, rage, and exuberant happiness—that you find, or even by a poem celebrating the marriage of a king and his bride (Psalm 45). You also will come to recognize the various forms of the psalms, noting especially the frequency of laments and hymns. Reading the psalms in the biblical sequence can be a rewarding and enlightening spiritual exercise for the year.

I make an effort to avoid personal and autobiographical anecdotes that are only loosely related to the actual text before us. I concentrate instead on what appears to be the stark reality of the psalmist's world and, when possible, on how a particular psalm functioned in ancient Israelite worship. As such, this book can serve also to open the door to more scholarly and historical study of the psalms.

Problems of interpretation are occasionally identified (see also "A Short Introduction to the Paslms, p. 368). What should we do with the so-called cursing psalms, in which the psalmist prays for God's wrath on the psalmist's enemies? Is there a specifically Christian way to read such psalms? Moreover, I show how various ethical issues arise for readers today. For example, Numbers 25:6–13 reports that Aaron's grandson Phinehas drove a spear through a man and a woman, and yet, according to Psalm 106:30–31, this action was "reckoned to him as righteousness."

In many cases I compare a topic or term in the psalm with its use in other biblical passages so that you will become familiar with central concepts in the Bible as a whole. Several of these terms are listed in the index in the back of this book.

A knotty issue for anyone who writes about the psalms is the choice of pronouns in referring to the psalmists. Were there any women psalm writers? Of the more than 250 prayers in the Bible (including the 150 psalms),[1] only about one dozen—none of them in the book of Psalms—are attributed to women. The best known of these are the songs of praise by Hannah (1 Samuel 2:1–10) and Mary (Luke 1:46–55), which are closely related in content. Considering the fact that women and men were segregated at liturgies at the temple in Jerusalem, and considering also that the superscriptions of several subgroups of psalms attribute them to guilds of male temple singers, in this book I generally use masculine pronouns to refer to the psalmists.

I suggest that you establish a daily routine for this reading of the psalms. There is no substitute for reading the assigned psalm verses in a good translation (unless otherwise indicated, I use the *New Revised Standard Version*). Compare your own experience with that of the psalmist. Conclude with the prayer sentence, adding your own personal petitions.

PSALMS
through the Year
Spiritual Exercises for Every Day

M ARSHALL D. J OHNSON

Augsburg Books
MINNEAPOLIS

PSALMS THROUGH THE YEAR
Spiritual Exercises for Every Day

Large-quantity purchases or custom editions of this book are available at a discount from the publisher. For more information, contact the sales department at Augsburg Fortress, Publishers, 1-800-328-4648, or write to: Sales Director, Augsburg Fortress, Publishers, Box 1209, Minneapolis, MN 55440-1209.

Library of Congress Cataloging-in-Publication Data
Johnson, Marshall D.
  Psalms through the year : spiritual exercises for every day / Marshall D. Johnson.
    p. cm. — (Lutheran voices)
  Includes bibliographical references and index.
  ISBN-13: 978-0-8066-5332-7
  ISBN-10: 0-8066-5332-9 (pbk. : alk. paper)
  1. Bible. O.T. Psalms—Devotional use. 2. Bible. O.T. Psalms—Criticism, interpretation, etc.
I. Title.
  BS1430.54.J64 2007   2006028951

Cover design by Kevin Vanderleek; Cover photo © New York Public Library/Art Resource, NY. Used by permission.
Book design by Becky Lowe

The paper used in this publication meets the minimum requirements of American National Standard for Information Sciences—Permanence of Paper for Printed Library Materials, ANSI Z329.48-1984.

Manufactured in the U.S.A.

11   10   09   08   07   1   2   3   4   5   6   7   8   9   10

CONTENTS

A NOTE OF THANKS

Although writing is a solitary activity, book publishing is a team effort. I am grateful to all those at Augsburg Books who have made this project possible, including persons in acquisitions, marketing, design, proofreading, production, and manufacture. I am especially indebted to senior publicist Bob Todd for his prodigious labors, and to senior editor Gloria Bengtson and production editor Michelle Cook for their shepherding of the project. Thanks also to our daughter Jennifer, an expert in the Queen's English, and to my wife, Alice Joy, for putting up with my reclusive labors.

ADVICE FOR THE NEW YEAR

*T*he turn of the year is a transition for everyone, a time to reflect on *what has been* and to anticipate (or fear) *what might be* in the coming months. Resolutions—both superficial and serious—are made, most to be quickly forgotten and perhaps a few to lead to healthy changes in lifestyle. Psalm 1 offers sound advice at this turning point.

The book of Psalms opens with a "wisdom psalm," part of a group that has close affinities to the books of Proverbs and Ecclesiastes. (Some manuscripts of Acts 13:33 call *Psalm 2* "the first psalm," indicating that Psalm 1 was added as the introduction to the entire book during its final editing.) Wisdom literature aims at fostering virtues and manners that make for a peaceful, prosperous, and happy life. It often takes the form of contrasts between the wise and the foolish, the wicked and the righteous, the rich and the poor, etc. Psalm 1 first describes the righteous (verses 1–3) and then the wicked (verses 4–5), and it concludes with a summary that contrasts the two.

The psalmist urges us to avoid the "advice of the wicked" and the "seat of scoffers" by giving heed to "the law [*torah*, instruction] of the LORD" (verses 1–2), presumably all or part of the first five books of the Old Testament. Just as Paul encouraged his converts to "pray without ceasing" (1 Thessalonians 5:17), so the psalmist encourages unending meditation on the instruction of the LORD.

The person who seeks to follow God's will is like a tree with roots that reach to a constant water supply, so that it will not wilt in the summer heat but bear good fruit. Such a person will flourish even during the stressful times that will certainly come. At the beginning of another new year, let us examine the principles and assumptions by which we live. Take care how your life is rooted.

O God, in this new year increase in me the desire
to seek your will and to mediate on it. Amen.

WHEN LIFE TURNS TO CHAFF

$\mathcal{F}$ew persons today have seen chaff—or even know what it is. Along with straw, it is what's left after grain is threshed—the hulls and beards of the heads of grain. On the West Bank of Palestine, threshing is still done today as it was in biblical days. The ripe grain stalks are gathered at a threshing floor (a clean, hard outdoor surface) and then tossed up into the air so that the wind blows away the chaff. A century ago in America, threshing machines did the job, blowing the straw and chaff out of the back of the machine into a huge pile while the grain came through a chute out the side into a grain wagon. Today the job is done by air-conditioned combines, machines that drive through the field, pick up the grain, and thresh it in one operation.

"The chaff that the wind drives away" is not worth much—even less than the straw, which can be used for bedding animals. So little rooted and so little valued, says the psalmist, are the wicked, those who scoff at moral values and God's law. The psalmist, certain that the LORD abandons the wicked to their ways, thinks that they should be excluded from the worshiping congregation. Psalm 1 presents an overly simple, black-and-white contrast between the "righteous" and the "wicked," without any shadings in between. It nonetheless reminds us that human lives can be wasted by thoughtless or evil actions and decisions.

The content of the righteousness spoken of here is not spelled out. That will come in subsequent psalms. But we know that it centers on the basic values of the psalms: justice, mercy, and faithfulness. Those who seek moral values such as these are "happy" or "blessed," as Jesus called them in the Beatitudes (Matthew 5:3–12).

Lord God, during the coming year lead me in the paths
of justice, mercy, and faithfulness. Amen.

EARTHLY PLOTTING AND HEAVENLY LAUGHTER

*P*salm 2 is the first example in this book of "royal psalms," which were composed for the enthronement of the king in Jerusalem.

During the interval between the death of the king and the enthronement of his successor, the rulers of the neighboring kingdoms plot to take advantage of this time of vulnerability for Jerusalem and free themselves from Judah's domination. In heaven, however, God laughs (God laughs also in Psalms 37:13 and 59:8)—not in good humor and certainly not with a chuckle, but in derision. God announces, "I have set my king on Zion, my holy hill" (verse 6). The machinations of the petty kingdoms will come to nothing. The time of insecurity for God's people is over.

The kings "take counsel together, against the LORD and his anointed" (verse 2). The Hebrew word for "anointed" is "messiah." After the Davidic line of kings was abruptly ended by the Babylonian destruction of Judah in 587 B.C., the term "anointed" came to refer to the hope for an ideal king of the future, a "messiah," and many royal psalms then were reinterpreted along these lines. Not surprisingly, early Christians often assumed that these psalms refer to Jesus.

The image of God laughing in derision is hardly comforting, even if we think the objects of this derision are our enemies. It is an expression of wrath, and it should cause us to engage in self-reflection. Are there aspects of our national life at which God would respond in derision? Do we use our great power wisely and with justice? Do we dare to plan policy based on justice and liberty for all? Do we work for freedom and justice for all?

O God, grant me wisdom, grant me courage
for the living of these days. Amen.

DIVINE PATERNITY
AND THE WRATH OF WAR

*T*he king now speaks in verses 7–9. He recounts God's promise to him of victory over the nation's enemies, and the psalm concludes with a warning to the "rulers of the earth" to submit themselves to God and to his agent, the king in Jerusalem. If they do not submit, they will be mercilessly broken with an iron rod and dashed to pieces like a broken pot (verse 9). This psalm is remote from modern democratic ideas. We no longer subscribe to the idea of the divine right of kings, and we look askance at those who think they know God's choice in a political election. We can scarcely imagine the horrors of war that afflict so many in other parts of the world. But we cannot give up striving to increase justice within our nation and between nations.

These verses are a clear example of how an ancient text could be reinterpreted as the decades and centuries rolled on. The king in Jerusalem could be called a son of God (see 2 Samuel 7:14 and Psalm 89:26–27). What would happen to Psalm 2 when the monarchy came to an end? It was not simply discarded but instead came to be read as applying to the future king, the messiah. It is therefore not surprising that verse 7, "You are my son; today I have begotten you," is used to interpret the resurrection of Jesus as the beginning of Jesus' divine sonship in Acts 13:33 and Romans 1:4 (there are also possible allusions to this verse in the account of Jesus' baptism in Mark 1:11 and of his transfiguration in Mark 9:7). Similarly, in Hebrews 1:5 and 5:5, Psalm 2:7 is taken to refer to Jesus' uniquely divine sonship, indicating his superiority to angels.

Christians honor Jesus as the Son of God in a unique sense—not as a leader in battle but as the model of the ideals of peace and justice among nations.

O God, cure your children's warring madness, and make me
to be an instrument of your peace. Amen.

THE SOURCE OF DELIVERANCE

*P*salms 3–7 are the first examples of the lament, the most numerous category in the book of Psalms. A lament will often include the reason or occasion for the plea (see verses 1–2), an expression of confidence in God's protection (verses 3–6), and a passionate plea for deliverance (verse 7). (The superscription of Psalm 3 attributes the poem to David when he fled from his son Absalom, but such headings are not part of the original composition and therefore should not be assumed to indicate the historical occasion.)

The meaning of "Selah," as after verses 2, 4, and 8, is unknown; it probably indicates the place in the singing when an instrumental interlude should be played. This psalmist refers to "many" foes rising up against him, taunting him, saying that God will not come to his help. The psalmist has fled to the "holy hill," the temple in Jerusalem, where, according to fairly common practice, he has apparently spent the night (verse 5) in a prayer vigil to God (such prayers are sometimes referred to as "incubation psalms"). After intense prayer, he is emboldened to cry to God, "Rise up" and "deliver me," for "deliverance belongs to the LORD" (verses 7–8).

This prayer gives voice to everyone throughout the ages who has endured suffering and persecution. It invites the hopeless to take refuge in the confidence of God's judgment. We all experience crises and anguish in this life. Such experiences can rob us of joy and lead to deep despair—or they can make us stronger and more compassionate human beings. Happy are those who can turn to human friends or family for comfort and redress in times of crisis. But the psalmist knows that true deliverance belongs to the LORD, from whom all blessings flow.

*God of all comfort, be with me when trouble comes
and hope fades away. Amen.*

WHEN HONOR DISSOLVES IN SHAME

*T*he poet in this lament uses language familiar to those who are falsely accused. The sufferer in the past has felt claustrophobic distress, but God has given him "room," that is, freedom from his accusers and space for relief. Now, again, lies have been told about him, apparently in public. It might have involved a legal accusation, for the psalmist addresses "God of my right" (verse 1), that is, the one who will demonstrate his innocence. The upshot is that his "honor" has turned to "shame" (verse 2).

Honor and shame are powerful emotional realities common to all humanity, not least among the peoples of the Near East. Honor refers to feelings of self-worth, value, and dignity. Shame is the public loss of such feelings, and is often accompanied by feelings of being confined, pent in, and straitjacketed. Can there be a more damaging experience? Shame differs from guilt. You can feel guilty without anyone knowing about your fault. Shame refers to "loss of face" and therefore always involves how you think you are viewed by others.

What can you do when you feel shamed? Do not neglect the human help and comfort that are available to you—counselors, pastors, legal advisers, support groups, friends, and family. But also, "know that the LORD has set apart the faithful for himself"; "the LORD hears" (verse 3). Psalm 4 gives witness to the security that comes from the experience of God's comfort in the face of all defamation and enmity.

O Lord, I call on you in my time of need;
give me room when I am in distress. Amen.

PEACE THAT COMES FROM TRUST

*I*n the midst of public shame and false litigation, the psalmist reminds himself not to respond in kind. "When you are disturbed, do not sin" (verse 4); instead, ponder your situation in privacy and in silence. How often in life do we react to insult and injury by seeking revenge that can only disrupt relationships and bring us further shame! It is all too easy to burn our bridges behind us. But the psalmist has found the path to inner peace: "I will both lie down and sleep in peace; for you alone, O LORD, make me lie down in safety" (verse 8).

There is profound wisdom in the adage of Alcoholics Anonymous, "Let go, let God!" This calls us to give up our claim to be the absolute masters of our lives and to give up also the demand that our personal honor be immediately vindicated, whatever the consequences for others. There are times in life when we must go through the dark valley of hopelessness before we are able to let God be God for us. It can be a terribly wrenching ordeal. Perhaps the psalmist symbolically entered this darkness by meditating all night at the temple (see verse 8) but, in any case, his heart was eventually gladdened by the assurance that there is but one secure object of trust and but one source of true peace and safety.

The words of the psalmist find an echo in Paul's powerful words in Romans 8:34–39: "Who is to condemn?" If God provides righteousness, what hostile power can prevail?

Be with me, O God, in the dark passages of life,
and lead me to peace and safety. Amen.

BOASTS, LIES, AND DECEIT

Strange and bad things can happen when a person feels unloved, loses self-esteem, and becomes insecure. One person shrinks back in depression from social contact. Another erupts in a torrent of self-congratulatory boasting. Another speaks ill of friends in the false hope of thereby enhancing his or her standing. And a few lash out in violence against family members or complete strangers. As we have learned, violent criminals—including some leaders of nations—often have experienced personal trauma and rejection early in life.

Psalm 5, a lament, gives a list of such antisocial behavior: "the boastful . . . those who speak lies . . . the bloodthirsty and deceitful" (verses 5–6). The psalmist himself has experienced injury from these kinds of wickedness: He pleads his case before God as he prepares a sacrifice in the morning (verse 3) and cries out with sighs (verse 1) that will not stop until justice is done.

Many psalm writers were closely connected with the temple in Jerusalem. So also, this psalmist enters the temple with full confidence in the "steadfast love" of the LORD. Steadfast love is a dominant motif in the psalms, referring to the unchangeable, persistent goodwill of God toward the faithful people. God, the psalmists insist, is reliable and benevolent and will not abandon those who suffer unjustly.

We can live with the same confidence. Saints throughout all the ages have known that the heart of God is not wrath but enduring grace—steadfast love.

Lord God, save me from my own insecurity and keep me
mindful of your steadfast love. Amen.

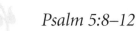

RIGHTEOUS RELATIONSHIPS

*T*his lament continues with a contrast—perhaps an over-simple contrast—between the wicked and the righteous. The wicked are devoid of truth, have hearts of destruction, and flatter with their tongues while their throats are in reality open graves (verse 9). They have guilt. By contrast, the righteous, who love the name ("Yahweh," verses 11–12), appeal to God's righteousness (verse 8) and flee to God for refuge (verse 11).

The psalmist also gives expression to a sentiment that—lamentably—is all too common among persons of faith. He asserts that in acting deceitfully to *him* the wicked have rebelled against *God* (verse 10). He identifies his own self-esteem and values with those of God. We would do better to leave to God the ultimate judgment of others, including our enemies and opponents.

Verse 8 speaks of "righteousness," a significant motif in both Testaments. Old Testament writers refer to God's righteousness as God's rule through the covenant with Moses in fellowship with the people. It is thus primarily a term of relationship. In the psalms the term often suggests God's vindication of the people or the individual sufferer, a meaning close to that of salvation. Ideas of mercy, truth, faithfulness, and steadfast love are closely associated with the term. The psalmist prays for the demonstration of God's righteousness in his own life.

As God is righteous, so also we are to practice justice in our relationships with others. As God's righteous acts lead to songs of joy (verse 11), so human acts of righteousness can bring healing and joy, even in situations of conflict.

God of righteousness, make me aware of my own ego needs
and mindful also of the needs of others. Amen.

FACING THE THREAT OF DEATH

*T*his psalm is the first of seven "penitential psalms" in traditional church liturgy (Psalms 6; 32; 38; 51; 102; 130; 143). But it really is not so much a cry of repentance as it is the anguished utterance of a gravely ill person who faces the extremity of death. The language is powerful and excruciating, expressing what is almost inexpressible: he is "languishing," his "bones are shaking with terror," and his "soul"—his very being—is likewise "struck with terror" (verses 2–3). Like the ancient Israelites generally, he is not hopeful about what lies beyond death. "In death there is no remembrance of you; in Sheol who can give you praise?" (verse 5). "Sheol" is neither heaven nor hell but the abode of the dead, a shadowy existence with only a faint semblance of life. The poet appeals to God for release from this fate, so that he can again praise God with full consciousness.

The depths of despair stem from the psalmist's certainty that he stands under the wrath of God (verse 1). He is sure that God has turned away from him and cast him off. In other words, he assumes that guilt and illness are inseparably connected and cannot think that bad things happen to good people. Powerful protests against such assumptions, however, come from the book of Job and from Jesus' teaching that blessings and tragedy fall upon all, without regard to their deserving (see, for example, Luke 13:1–5).

In the midst of his fear of wrath, the despairing person appeals to the LORD's "steadfast love," God's unswerving works of righteousness, to save his life (verse 4). That aspect of his experience we can follow.

Save me, O God, from the time of trial,
and be with me in the end. Amen.

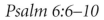

A NIGHT OF WEEPING, A MORNING OF ASSURANCE

The psalmist does not reveal the sickness from which he suffers, but his eyes are sore with weeping, and tears have fallen on his sickbed. As in many psalms of lament, he struggles with insomnia. The suffering is profound—and almost unfathomable.

In verse 8, however, a great change takes place. The sufferer summons strength, suggesting that he has heard the word of the LORD, who has answered his plea. Like Job, he expels those who attribute his illness to his own misdeeds. "Depart from me, all you workers of evil, for the LORD has heard the sound of my weeping . . ." (verse 8). (Jesus' quotation of this verse in Matthew 7:23 and Luke 13:27 has an entirely different context, namely, that of a false confession of faith.)

This powerful psalm can serve only with qualification as a reading at a sickbed. On the one hand, it graphically communicates the anguish of sickness and facing death. It describes the shallowness that we often exhibit when we try to respond to extreme suffering.

On the other hand, however, it is not good pastoral practice to enforce the anguished person's association of guilt and suffering, of God's wrath and the fear of death. Neither is it helpful for the sufferer to spend hours of the day praying for the comeuppance of the enemies. Fasten your attention instead on the steadfast love of God (verse 4), which makes earnest prayer effective.

Remain with me, O God, through sickness and health.
Give me comfort and hope in time of distress. Amen.

IS IT I?

*P*ersecuted by adversaries, the psalmist has fled to the temple, affirming his innocence and appealing to the LORD for protection and judgment.

The situation presupposed in this lament is precisely what is prescribed in 1 Kings 8:31–32: "If someone sins against a neighbor and is given an oath to swear, and comes and swears before your altar in this house [the temple], then hear in heaven, and act, and judge your servants, condemning the guilty by bringing their conduct on their own head, and vindicating the righteous by rewarding them according to their righteousness."

The God of the Bible is preeminently the God of justice, who accomplishes deliverance for the poor, the persecuted, the helpless, the falsely accused, and the oppressed. The righteous sufferer knows this and therefore cannot withdraw into silent self-pity but must always join the struggle for truth and justice, even if it involves justice for oneself.

Before seeking our own justification, however, it is well for us to examine ourselves. The psalmist opens his desperate plea with self-examination and a challenge to God: If he has done harm to his friend or has unjustly attacked his foe, then let God's judgment come upon him in the form of destruction by his enemy. Let us see whether there is a log in our own eye before we attempt to pluck the splinter from our neighbor's (compare Matthew 7:3; Luke 6:41).

Search me, O God, and see if there
is any wicked way in me. Amen.

JUSTIFICATION OF THE RIGHTEOUS

*A*s with other laments of the falsely accused or persecuted, Psalm 7 is concerned with the justification of the *righteous*—not, as in Paul's letters, with God's justification of the *sinner* through sheer, undeserved grace. The psalmist does not ask for mercy or grace but instead issues a gripping plea for redress, for correcting a gross injustice.

The psalmist acknowledges that God judges the nations with equity, and he now asks that God do the same for him as an individual. He is righteous, he has inner integrity (verse 8), and he is willing to undergo examination by a court of the people (verse 7). Doing justice to the suffering, by the same token, involves punishment for the wicked oppressor, who has "deadly weapons" and conceives evil (verses 13–14). Justice will involve turning their violence on their own heads (verse 16).

There is little in this life that is so difficult to accept as injustice—especially when we are its victims. And there are few things that are so commonly experienced. Some persons in our society are victims of violent crime. But many more are victims of gossip or slander, with the painful result of ostracism. In such circumstances it is entirely appropriate to follow the example of the psalmist: present your case before God; offer yourself to God's scrutiny; and urgently appeal for justice. It will do no one good if we fail to defend our integrity in the struggle for truth. By the same token, we should also come to the defense of others who are in desperate need of justice.

Whether we are victims or are helping others, always we remember to give thanks when justice is made a reality in our world (verse 17).

God of justice, establish justice in my life
and in my community. Amen.

OUR PLACE IN THE MAJESTIC SWEEP OF THE UNIVERSE

*P*salm 8 belongs to the category of "hymn," the sole purpose of which is to glorify God. Unlike laments, hymns generally avoid references to the emotional state of the psalmist. Hymns often address God directly, using the second-person pronoun. Some psalms give praise for God's actions in history, while others, like Psalm 8, reflect on God's majesty in the natural world.

Anyone who has lived in a remote area of the countryside has stood in wonder gazing at the brilliance of the stars, especially on a moonless night—an experience that residents of our cities and large towns no longer have. The effect must have been awe-inspiring to the ancients, who lived before electricity or even gaslight lit the night.

When beholding the majesty of the night sky, the psalmist is overwhelmed by the puniness and insignificance of the human being in the vast sweep of things. Are we mere ciphers on a speck of dust floating in a vast cosmic ocean? How can the creator of the earth and the heavens be concerned about the welfare of such transient characters as we? Read further in Psalm 8 for the answer.

Verse 2 has always perplexed readers. How has the LORD "founded a bulwark" against his foes "out of the mouths of babes and infants"? Whatever the meaning, the psalmist is sure that God can break the power of his foes by the voice of weak children.

We often hear criticisms of persons who say they can worship God in the natural world, in parks, forests, mountains, and beaches. Our psalmist would demur: The created world and the human being are works of God, whose majesty can become apparent as we consider the vastness of space and the uncounted galaxies of the universe.

I thank you, Lord of heaven and earth,
that you are mindful of my life. Amen.

THE GLORY
OF HUMAN BEINGS
IN THE NATURAL WORLD

*I*f human beings seem insignificant in comparison with the majesty of the natural world—and especially the vast sweep of the heavens—how astounding that God has given us a place of preeminence over all other created beings! The LORD has made humans "a little lower than God." ("God" here translates the Hebrew word *elohim*, in plural form, the generic Hebrew term for God or any kind of gods or divine beings.) This suggests that humankind ranks above all creatures, not only on earth but also the heavenly host of angels.

Psalm 8, especially verses 6–8, can be considered Genesis 1 set to music. The psalmist certainly has Genesis 1:26–31 or some form of it in mind. God gave human beings "dominion" over all other creatures in land, sea, and sky. Such assumptions are compatible with the methods of natural science and technology that have been such a blessing (and, in some cases, a bane) for Western civilization. Such assumptions also have led to environmental pollution and exploitation of other creatures for human comfort and enjoyment. This psalm does not remove our obligation to exercise dominion over nature responsibly and without the arrogance of a privileged species.

Psalm 8 reflects the perspective of a vast universe. On the level of individual life, however, we can't always share the confident joy of the psalmist. There are times when life overwhelms us with unexpected difficulties, loss, and suffering. But we too should find comfort in the knowledge that the LORD of the universe cares for us and would crown our lives also with honor.

O Lord, our God, how majestic
is your name in all the earth. Amen.

JANUARY 16   *Psalm 9:1–6*

EXULTING AT THE FALL OF THE ENEMY?

*I*n the original Hebrew, Psalms 9 and 10 constitute one poem. It is written as an acrostic; each second verse begins with the successive letter of the Hebrew alphabet. The alphabetical structure partly explains the difficulty we have in following the sequence of thought, which is seen also in the mixing of the forms of the lament and the song of thanksgiving.

The psalmist speaks both of personal enemies (verse 3) and of God's rebuke of the "nations" and their cities, which lie in "everlasting ruins" (verses 5–6). This reflects the common human tendency to exaggerate the importance of those who we think have injured us and to generalize from our experience with individuals to the larger groups to which they belong. Such a train of thought can both lead to thoughts of revenge and also to foster prejudice (the word literally refers to judgment in advance of learning the facts) against groups of people. What the psalmist experiences here is not *Schadenfreude*, unspoken satisfaction at the misfortune of our colleagues, but overt exultation at the destruction of enemies. Another unfortunate human tendency given voice in this psalm segment is common among religious folks, namely, to assume that our enemies are also enemies of God.

It is unhealthy to deny or suppress our feelings of anger and enmity. But to deal responsibly with such feelings requires that we give attention also to those psalms that speak of guilt, repentance, and forgiveness.

> *O God, help me to foster justice and mercy*
> *in all my dealings. Amen.*

GOD'S JUSTICE
AND HUMAN OPPRESSION

Of one thing the psalm writers are certain: God's justice is not arbitrary, and it will ultimately prevail over the entire earth. "He judges the peoples with equity" (verse 8). The psalmist knows that God's justice might well be at odds with our human assumptions about guilt and punishment, but he is certain that he can rely on the fairness of God as judge.

The psalmist offers pastoral advice to all who are oppressed. God's justice will be for them a fortress in the time of trouble. This is not a theology of glory or wealth or national dominance but rather a pointer to the secure source of hope and comfort, that is, to the LORD who "sits enthroned for ever" (verse 7). Although the LORD is enthroned on the temple mount in Jerusalem, the "stronghold for the oppressed," God's judgment encompasses the entire world, all peoples (verse 8). Yahweh is neither a tribal god nor a religious symbol of a nation's identity but the all-encompassing principle of justice in the cosmos, especially for the oppressed and troubled (verse 9).

Does justice prevail in this life? Is life fair? We know from experience that the answer is both yes and no. Innocent persons have been executed for murders they did not commit. Other persons who have been falsely accused are eventually vindicated. The psalmist does not deal with these difficult issues of justice denied and justice delayed. He is concerned with the way we respond to hostility, false accusations, or personal injury. It is appropriate that we demand justice and vindication. In doing so, however, we also recognize that our demands are subjective and possibly one-sided. Let us seek honest self-evaluation and then appeal to the justice of God, who decides with equity for the oppressed and the oppressor alike.

Give me, Lord God, a vision of your justice, and grant me
strength to live justly in an unjust world. Amen.

THE HOPE OF THE POOR

*T*he psalmist has been rescued from "the gates of death" (verse 13) and now gives thanks to God in the temple precincts in Jerusalem. He identifies himself as belonging to the "poor" and "needy" (verse 18), certain that the LORD is especially inclined toward and watchful over the welfare of the underprivileged, the handicapped, and those without adequate legal protection.

The idea that the poor have a special claim on God's protection goes back to the ancient period of Israel's history. Israel's identity was shaped in the exodus from Egypt, with the deliverance of a legally helpless people from a powerless situation. The psalmist knows that the helpless and defenseless have only one refuge and hope: the Lord God. But this hope is secure and sure: "The needy shall not always be forgotten, nor the hope of the poor perish for ever" (verse 18).

Jesus also spoke of a blessing for "you poor" (Luke 6:20) or "the poor in spirit" (Matthew 5:3). All of us can relate to these designations. There are times when we too feel that we have approached the "gates of death" (verse 13). Let us at such times, with the psalmist, bring our grief to the one secure and certain source of hope.

"Joy of the desolate, light of the straying,
    Hope of the penitent, fadeless and pure!
Here speaks the Comforter, tenderly saying,
    "Earth has no sorrow that heaven cannot cure."[2]

God of all comfort, when I approach the gates of death,
be with me in comfort and sustain my hope. Amen.

GOOD THINGS SEEM TO BE HAPPENING TO BAD PEOPLE

The psalmist has run across some truly unpleasant types: they are arrogant, they devise wicked schemes, they are greedy, they curse Yahweh, and they have no fear of God because they are practical atheists, saying, "God will not seek it out," and thinking, "There is no God" (verses 2–4).

The psalmist continues the complaint: out of their mouths come cursing words full of iniquity. They wait in ambush to murder the innocent and helpless and seize the poor in their nets (verses 7–9). And they are confident that their arrogance and dominance will last for generations (verse 6) because God—if there is God—"has hidden his face, he will never see it" (verse 11).

The most despairing thing for the psalmist, however, is that the ways of the wicked "prosper at all times" (verse 5). Good things are happening to really bad people. Why? How? Where is God?

We need to retain this kind of biblical realism in our world. Injustice and evil exist, both on the national and the personal level. The arrogant use of power still wreaks havoc in the lives of the powerless. And we must admit that God at times seems hidden.

Yet we know that despair and anguish are not the end of the matter. The psalmist brings his complaint to one who can and will address the wrong. Men and women of faith live in hope.

Out of the depths I cry to you, O Lord.
O Lord, hear my cry. Amen.

Psalm 10:12–18

A CRY FOR THE RESTORATION OF JUSTICE

*L*ift up your hand . . . see . . . take it into your hands." The psalmist grippingly appeals to God's justice, which he finds lacking in a society where power is held by arrogant, deceitful, and greedy plotters. The agitation of the speaker is clear from the pleas that God "break the arm of the wicked and evildoers" (verse 15).

The divine intervention that the psalmist seeks is not only inward spiritual comfort but also God's visible action experienced in real life. Redress is needed for "the oppressed" (verses 12, 18), "the orphan" (verses 14, 18), and "the meek" (verse 17) within the psalmist's society—an emphasis frequently found in the message of the great prophets.

The psalm ends with a hymn of assurance that God will indeed intervene on behalf of the suffering (verses 15–18). Yahweh is king forever; true power is God's. Ultimately—at some point—God's kingdom and rule will become effective over the entire cosmos. Then—but perhaps not before then—"those who strike terror" will be able to do so no more.

Biblical writers are acutely aware of human anguish, and the recurring emphasis on God's concern for the poor, oppressed, and underprivileged groups in society is an important legacy inherited also by the church. But, at the same time, these writers also are supremely confident in the ultimate implementation of God's justice and rule over creation.

I praise you, O God, as the Lord of justice
and the source of true hope. Amen.

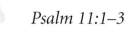

"WHAT CAN THE RIGHTEOUS DO?"

*P*salm 11:1, which we might classify as a "song of trust," recalls for many the haunting Spanish folk song, sometimes sung at religious services or funerals to the following words:

> *Flee as a bird to the mountains, you who are weary of sin;*
> *Go to the clear flowing fountain where you may wash*
> *   and be clean.*
> *Fly, for th'avenger is near you, call and the Savior will hear you;*
> *He on his bosom will bear you, you who are weary of sin.*[3]

"Flee like a bird to the mountains"—such was the advice given by friends to one who was seeking refuge from persecutors. In Jerusalem and its environs there were—and are—many options in the rugged and deserted wilderness of Judea or in more settled areas in the hill country for someone who wanted to flee to the mountains to escape pursuers. In the Christian church of the first few centuries, many fled into the desert from what they considered to be a corrupt society; monasticism began as withdrawal from the world.

But wait! The psalmist wants to stay put—in the Jerusalem temple. That is where one can take refuge in the LORD (verse 1). There are the "foundations" of his life, and if they are destroyed, where else can "the righteous" find secure refuge (verse 3)?

Our lives need firm foundations. We need the support of family, friends, and the social safety net. Without such underpinnings, there is no security. But we can rest assured: The God of justice is our refuge.

In you, O Lord, I take refuge. Amen.

Psalm 11:4–7

THE EYES OF GOD
AND THE CUP OF WRATH

*I*n these verses the psalmist reflects powerful images of God that are found in several biblical passages:

Although the Lord's throne is in heaven, in a special sense God resides "in his holy temple" (verse 4; see also Psalm 9:11; Psalm 132; 2 Samuel 6; and 1 Kings 8), more specifically, in the "holy of holies."

God's "eyes" are continuously fixed on humankind, testing both the righteous and the wicked, with special abhorrence of those who create violence (verse 5). Job, thinking that God was unjustly tormenting him, complained bitterly that God's scrutiny allows him not even to "swallow his spittle" (Job 7:19). For the psalmist, however, the righteous will find refuge from persecution and violence, while "the wicked" will experience such things as befell Sodom and Gomorrah, namely, "coals of fire and sulfur" and "a scorching wind" (verse 6).

God pours out a "cup," a striking image that was familiar to ancient Israelites. It can be a "cup of salvation" (Psalm 116:13), but here it is a cup of wrath (as in Isaiah 51:17, 22; Lamentations 4:21, 32, 33; and elsewhere). Jesus also, in the garden of Gethsemane, referred to his fate as his "cup" (Mark 14:36).

It is natural for us to feel and think that our actions have consequences. When we err, we might experience either shame or guilt—or both. But God is just, and God's watchful eye can be also a source of comfort and blessing.

Eternal God, watch over me
and lead me in right paths. Amen.

HAVING A DOWN DAY

*E*ven the best among us have days in which we think everything is getting worse fast, and there is no hope that things will get better. The ancient Greek Diogenes went about the streets of ancient Athens with a lantern in broad daylight looking for one good person. In an oddly similar account, the prophet Jeremiah went about the streets of Jerusalem looking for one person who acted justly and sought truth (Jeremiah 5:1).

The psalmist in this lament has hit bottom. "There is no longer anyone who is godly; the faithful have disappeared from humankind" (verse 1). The evidence of this is the lack of personal morality: "They utter lies," they flatter, they boast (verses 2–3). But there is also social immorality: They despoil the poor and needy (verse 5).

It is not difficult to find signs of decline in any society. Religion is perverted into dangerous fanaticism. Politics turns to character assassination. Military atrocities are committed in the name of national self-interest or even religion. Businesspersons rob their companies of millions—or billions—of dollars while the whistleblowers are punished instead of rewarded.

The psalmist becomes convinced of a way out of this downward spiral. The Lord God will "rise up" (verse 5); God's promises are sure and pure (verse 6); the Lord will protect the defenseless, even as "vileness is exalted among humankind" (verses 5–8). The person of faith cannot remain a pessimist.

Save me from debilitating depression, O God,
and give me a renewed hope in your promises. Amen.

WHEN WILL IT EVER END?

*T*he psalms of lament often raise the plaintive cry, "How long, O LORD, how long will you hide your face from me?"—as here in verse 1. Those who experience chronic suffering, whether physical, mental, or spiritual, often feel that it will never end. Conversely, the conviction that it *will* end is necessary for us to survive the ordeal.

Although the psalmist speaks in anguish about "pain in my soul and . . . sorrow in my heart," he seems to think that he is very near death: "Give light to my eyes, or I will sleep the sleep of death" (verse 3). There is no hint of the nature or cause of his suffering, of which we learn only that it is both acute and of long duration. The psalmist feels forsaken by God, and this is the primary and worst agony (see also Psalm 22:1). "Where is God in my suffering?" is the question raised over the centuries and millennia by countless men and women of faith, including Jesus' dying words, a quotation of Psalm 22:1, "My God, my God, why have you forsaken me?"

Suddenly and unexpectedly, the psalmist changes the focus from his own pain to the steadfastness of God: "my heart shall rejoice in your salvation" (verse 5). The psalmist and Job (see Job 42:5–6) found that a firm trust in God's steadfast love (here, verse 5) or even God's bare presence in the midst of suffering was more than enough to sustain hope in the midst of anguish and suffering.

Be with me, O God, in times of anguish and pain;
show me the light ahead. Amen.

FOLLY THAT LEADS TO CORRUPTION

*T*his psalm combines features of the lament form with thoughts from wisdom literature (like the book of Proverbs). The "fool" is typically contrasted in Proverbs with wisdom. The term includes the ideas of both deficient intellect and corrupt morality. It is only such a person who could think in his heart, "There is no God" (verse 1). This is a kind of practical atheism, the idea that God is not present to intervene to punish injustice and evil but remains hidden from human life. Such a person lives as though there is no God.

As in Psalm 11:4, "The LORD looks down from heaven . . . to see if there are any who are wise, who seek after God" (verse 2). But there is none, not one. "They have all gone astray" (verse 3). And the irreligion of the foolish has again led to the oppression of the poor (verse 6). For biblical writers as a whole, failure to acknowledge God leads to moral corruption—and such is the paradigm of folly.

The apostle Paul, in the letter to the Romans, emphasizes two basic thrusts of Psalm 14. He insists, first, that even Gentiles have a natural knowledge of the oneness of God (Romans 1:18–23), but their failure to honor God as such leads to moral corruption (Romans 1:24–32). Second, he comes to the conclusion that all human beings, both Jews and Gentiles, have fallen short of God's glory and are enmeshed in sin (Romans 3:9–20).

In different ways, however, both Paul and the psalmist look forward to the time when "the LORD restores the fortunes of his people" (verse 7). To be a person of faith is to live with hope.

Help me, O Lord, in my doubts and questionings to rely on your promise of the ultimate restoration of all things. Amen.

BLAMELESS
IN THE SANCTUARY

$\mathcal{P}$salm 15 is a liturgy for entry into the temple in Jerusalem. Some Christians might call it an introit or opening prayer or processional. The "holy hill" is the temple mount in Jerusalem, and the word "tent" used here of the temple recalls the early period of Israel's history, when worship was centered in the tent sanctuary (see 2 Samuel 7:6; Psalm 61:4; Isaiah 33:20).

Who may approach and enter the temple area? the psalmist asks. The extended answer is not what we might expect. No ordination ceremony, no ritual acts, no purification rites are mentioned, but only a list of moral virtues. The general requirement is righteousness ("what is right") and having basic inner integrity ("speak the truth from their heart," verse 2). Specific examples then follow: avoid slander, treat friends and neighbors with respect, honor the God-fearers instead of the wicked, stand by your promises, and avoid financial wrongdoing (verses 3–5). Psalm 15 thus inserts the strong moral values of the prophetic tradition into a cultic act, procession into the temple precincts. There is no tension between the moral and the ritual, between the prophetic and the priestly components of spirituality.

For Christians—no less than for Jews—true worship presupposes and requires righteousness. Not that we on our own can attain moral perfection or "walk blamelessly," but in purity of heart we put our trust in the source of true integrity and justice.

Create in me a clean heart, O God,
and renew a right spirit within me. Amen.

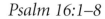

MY CUP, MY LOT, MY GOODLY HERITAGE

*T*his song of trust (see page 371, below) is filled with joyous confidence in God as the only source of all good things.

The LORD God is the psalmist's "chosen portion," "cup," "lot," and "goodly heritage" (verses 5–6)—terms that were associated with the distribution of the land of Canaan as described in the conquest under Joshua (Joshua 13:23; 14:4; 15:13; 17:5; and elsewhere). This is a graphic way of acknowledging God rather than oneself as the cause and font of life's blessings. The psalm singer is not a self-made person.

The psalmist has received advice and counsel from God "in the night," an intriguing expression that makes us wish to know more about the manner in which this took place. The prophets received the word of Yahweh, sometimes after periods of waiting (see, for example Jeremiah 42, especially verse 7) and sometimes after sleeping on the question. Did our psalmist keep vigil or "incubate" at a shrine throughout the night?

In any case, the singer of Psalm 16 gives thanks for the nearness of God in the midst of the threatening dangers of life. His personal life is blessed by God's bestowal of a goodly portion—a life of blessing and goodness.

Like the psalmist, we believe that we have a "goodly heritage" (verse 6). The fortunate among us have inherited from past generations a viable faith that can sustain us in our passage through life. Let us preserve and transmit this heritage.

I too give thanks, O Lord, for life, for health,
and for the abundance of blessings. Amen.

THE JOY OF DELIVERANCE

*A*mong the numerous psalms of lament and complaint, it is refreshing to read words from one who is overfilled with joy and gratefulness. The psalmist speaks of a glad heart, a rejoicing soul, and a secure body (verse 9).

The occasion for this outpouring of gladness is the psalmist's experience of deliverance from an immediate and acute threat of death. "Sheol," also called "the Pit," is the shadowy realm of the dead in early Hebrew thought. The psalmist's recovery allows him to remain in the presence of God, in whom there are "fullness of joy" and "pleasures for evermore" (verse 11).

The application of verse 10 in Acts 2:31 (Peter's sermon on the day of Pentecost) and Acts 13:35 (a sermon of Paul's) to the resurrection of Jesus raises an important issue in the interpretation of the book of Psalms generally. The two citations in Acts presuppose (1) that David wrote Psalm 16 (on the superscriptions of the psalms, see pages 369 and 378, below) and (2) that he was making a prediction about Jesus' resurrection after crucifixion. We need to let the psalm text retain its integrity; the psalmist wrote several centuries before the time of Jesus and was speaking of himself. We properly understand the citations of Psalm 16 in Acts not as "fulfillment" of predictions but as parallels between Old Testament passages and the Christian experience of the risen Jesus.

In all cases, we rejoice with those who rejoice, especially in recovery from a life-threatening experience.

Be with me, O God, in the extremities of life and keep alive
for me the joy of your salvation. Amen.

THE STEADFAST LOVE OF THE LORD

*I*n this plea for vindication from false accusations, the psalmist presents his case before the LORD. With what appears to be unseemly self-vaunting, he insists that there is "no wickedness" in him; his mouth "does not transgress"; he avoids the "ways of the violent"; his feet "have not slipped" (verses 3–5). What accounts for this unabashed boasting?

The answer comes in verse 7: "Wondrously show your steadfast love, O savior of those who seek refuge from their adversaries." "Steadfast love" is at once a frequent and an amazing attribute of God in the Old Testament. The inner core of God, so to speak, is not to be seen in wrath against the wicked nor in the exercise of power but rather in loyalty to God's promises to the people, especially as contained in the law codes of the Torah. The psalmist boldly presents his innocence to God, claiming God's promise to vindicate the righteous. This is a prayer that God's steadfast love be made real in the actual life of the psalmist.

Like the psalmists of old, we often struggle with the apparent absence of God in the midst of human suffering and injustice. To lay a claim on God because of our presumed uprightness would be an act of hubris and presumption. We should think twice before doing so. Much better it is to give voice to our distress and to appeal to God's mercy, knowing that it is unmerited on our part.

Show your steadfast love, O Lord,
to all who seek refuge in you. Amen.

Psalm 17:8–15

MAKING IT THROUGH
THE NIGHT

$\mathcal{T}$he writer gives us several hints about what is going on in this psalm. He would be hid "in the shadow of your wings" (verse 8), that is, under the wings of the cherubim in the holy of holies of the Jerusalem temple. (A cherub is a winged sphinx. There were two carved cherubim hovering over and guarding the Ark of the Covenant in the holy of holies.) He would spend the night there, presenting his plea and his lament before the special dwelling place of the Lord. (Some commentators refer to this practice as "incubation" or night vigil, praying through an entire night at a holy place.)

The enemies are described: They are pitiless, they pursue and surround the victim, and, like a lion, are ready to tear him to pieces.

The appeal is equally striking. "Guard me as the apple of the eye" (that is, the pupil of the eye). The psalmist does not shrink from leveling a lasting curse on his enemies; they are to be destroyed, and also their children (verses 13–14). Although God is characterized as having an abundance of "steadfast love," the psalmist displays little of such sentiment to those who seek his ruin.

Several psalmists suffered from insomnia, and it is a debilitating experience for many even today. But the one who prays will indeed make it through the night: "When I awake I shall be satisfied, beholding your likeness"—sensing God's presence in the temple and assured of God's deliverance. Making it through the night darkness could be a terrifying prospect in the years before our well-lighted culture. Even now the dark of night be can a source of dread.

Through the terrors of the night be with me,
Lord God. Amen.

SNATCHED FROM THE SNARES OF DEATH

*T*his psalm occurs also in 2 Samuel 22, where it also is presented as David's song of thanksgiving after having defeated "all his enemies" (see the superscription of this psalm and also 2 Samuel 22:1, 50). Verses 37–45 confirm that the psalm did indeed originally celebrate a great victory or victories of a king over his enemies.

The opening verses include common but powerful biblical metaphors for God as well as for the human experience of dire threat. God is "my rock, my fortress . . . my shield, and the horn of my salvation" (verse 2). The metaphor of "rock" and "fortress" might be ultimately derived from the holy mount in Jerusalem, on which the temple was built. God as "shield" goes back to an early period; in Genesis 15:1 the LORD confirms to Abram (Abraham), "Do not be afraid, Abram, I am your shield. . . ." And the "horn of my salvation" can refer to military strength and victory; military defeat can be described as the cutting off of the nation's horn (Jeremiah 48:25). Luke 1:69-72 takes up this phrase, presumably as applied to Jesus, with reference also to rescue from "our enemies" (verse 71).

In verses 4–5 the king uses metaphorical language to describe the military threat he faced: "cords of death . . . torrents of perdition . . . cords of Sheol . . . snares of death." The battle would be one of physical survival. But the king goes to the temple to present his prayer for strength and victory, and he assures his people that God heard him (verse 6).

It is common in battles for each side to pray for victory, and sometimes they pray to the same God (see verse 41). This also is a form of military madness. For most of us most of the time, it is best to let God's justice straighten things out.

Be for me, O God, my rock and my fortress
in time of peril. Amen.

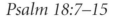

A TERRIFYING DISPLAY OF DIVINE GLORY

$\mathcal{S}$everal Old Testament texts describe the special, overpowering revelation of God's glory in narrative poetry. Such passages are known as theophanies (from the Greek word for "manifestation of God"). A theophany typically includes thick darkness being penetrated by dazzlingly brilliant light (like flashes of lightning), booms of thunder, hail, falling balls of fire, and the quaking of the earth—all of which the onlookers know to be the approach of the holiness of God's majesty. (Examples of theophanies are Exodus 19:16–20; Judges 5:4–5; Isaiah 30:27–28; Habakkuk 3:3–16.)

Psalm 18:7–15 combines details from a thunderstorm with those of a volcanic eruption and earthquake: The mountains tremble, emit smoke and glowing coals, and quake (verses 7–8). The LORD, around whom are "thick darkness" and clouds (verses 9, 11) descends on a cherub (two of which guarded the Ark of the Covenant in the holy of holies in the temple). Hailstones and coals of fire break through the darkness, and lightning flashes like arrows (verses 12, 14). In the peals of thunder the Most High utters his voice (verse 13). The terrifying experience is like the laying bare of the foundations of the world (verse 15).

Unlike the desire of many in the twenty-first century to depict God as the kindly bestower of worldly success, biblical men and women were acutely aware of the holiness and majesty of God. God is not to be trifled with or to function simply as a character in our consumer-oriented church services. The psalmists knew better: God is to be worshiped.

Lord God, heavenly king, almighty God and Father:
I worship you, I give you thanks. I praise you
for your glory. Amen.

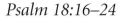

HUMAN INNOCENCE AND DIVINE DELIVERANCE

*T*his portion of Psalm 18 raises difficult questions of human innocence and divine reward. Can we claim reward from God on the basis of our good living? The king in Psalm 18 seems to do so unabashedly: He is "righteous," has "clean hands," and has "kept the ways of the LORD," including "his ordinances . . . and his statutes" (verses 20–22). He is "blameless," and without guilt (verses 23–24). If this is David speaking (see the superscription of this psalm), we might wonder how, in view of the many difficulties that follow his adultery in 2 Samuel 11, he was able to make such assertions. Is this the same psalm singer who, according to the superscription of Psalm 51, poured out his heart in confession of guilt over his adultery? Can any human being claim perfect righteousness in the presence of God?

Clarity emerges when we notice the reference to "ordinances," "statutes," and "clean hands" and remember that this psalm is being prayed in the temple. "Who shall stand in his holy place?" asks Psalm 24:3. The answer: "Those who have clean hands and pure hearts" (24:4). Participation in temple ritual required conformity to the Torah (Israelite laws like those in Deuteronomy or Leviticus, which included prescriptions for purification from sins). The psalmist has prepared himself by following the Torah's requirements.

As a result, this warrior was drawn up from the threat of being overwhelmed by "mighty waters" (verse 16) and delivered from powerful enemies. It is appropriate to give thanks to God for successes that come from beyond our own strivings, but let us give credit to whom credit is due.

*Lord God, lead me to an honest
and realistic self-appraisal. Amen.*

THINGS WILL BALANCE OUT

*F*rench writer Jules Renard (1864–1910), in his journal for December 1906, asserted, "There is a justice, but we do not always see it. Discreet, smiling, it is there, to one side, a little behind injustice, which makes a big noise."[4]

Such a sentiment is common in the psalms as well as in many other parts of the Bible, and we often hear similar thoughts from those who suffer. Even when the most horrible things happen to apparently decent and innocent people, we can't believe it is by sheer chance and without any purpose. Persons who have lost a family member by murder or who have been treated for cancer are often asked by interviewers on television whether the experience has caused them to doubt their faith. Invariably they say that their faith has seen them through the ordeal.

The psalmist says that God shows himself as loyal to those who are loyal, as pure to those who are pure, but as perverse to those who are crooked. This is not to say that we invent God in our own image, but that, with God, justice ultimately holds sway. Verse 27 confirms that the humble are delivered and the haughty brought low. God's way is "perfect," and the LORD's promise "proves true" (verse 30).

Christians also believe that in the end the will of God will be fully implemented in all of creation. Much of what we experience in this life appears to be sheer chance and accident. But we anticipate the day when God's rule will be effective in all reality.

May your will be done, O Lord, on earth
as it is now being done in heaven. Amen.

WAR AND PEACE
AND THE JUSTICE OF GOD

$\mathcal{E}$very man thinks God is on his side. The rich and powerful know that he is." Such was the opinion of Jean Anouilh (1910–1987) in his play *The Lark* (1953). How often have we heard of opposing armies in war praying for victory to the same God? Even more strange—if not blasphemous—is the spectacle of opposing high school football teams praying for victory before a game.

This portion of Psalm 18, however, seems to support such practices. The king attributes his military victories to the action of God, who "made my enemies turn their backs to me, and those who hated me I destroyed" (verse 40, but the idea permeates verses 31–42). The enemies were annihilated and "cast . . . out like the mire of the streets" (verse 42). The king even says of his enemies, "They cried to the LORD, but he did not answer them." Were both sides in the struggle groups within Israel? And why would God answer the prayer of one king and not the other, when both pray to the same God?

Poems that depict military victories and the power of the king must be read alongside those of the prophets' denunciations of the abuse of power and the blessedness of peacemaking. The world over the past century—and even now—is replete and over-replete with genocide and war crimes. Can we overcome jingoistic nationalism and seek ways to get beyond the idea that the human race consists exclusively of the righteous and the evildoers?

Free our people, O God, from national hubris
and lead us in the path of peace. Amen.

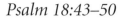

HOW DO WE DEAL
WITH SUCCESS?

$\mathcal{M}$artin Luther King Jr. (1929–1968) wrote, "What is needed is a realization that power without love is reckless and abusive and that love without power is sentimental and anemic. Power at its best is love implementing the demands of justice. Justice at its best is love correcting everything that stands against love."[5]

Psalm 18 as a whole is a highly exuberant song of military victory by a king, a thanksgiving for astounding victories over enemies, and a paean of praise uttered in the Jerusalem temple to God for these triumphs. In the closing lines, the psalmist summarizes the completeness of these victories and the international reputation the king has gained from them. Foreigners cringe before his power (verse 45). The psalm ends with repeated statements that it is the LORD who has wrought these things.

Persons who have found themselves at the peak of success after long and arduous struggles often lapse into depression—which seems strange to those who have not had that experience. They wonder whether the success was deserved, and they might wonder about what to do next. Feelings of emptiness might sweep over them. Can you survive success?

It is certainly proper for us to find satisfaction in a job well done and to rejoice over it. But such feelings must be tempered when our success comes at the expense of others. "Power without love is reckless and abusive."

In joy and in sorrow, in success and in failure, O God,
I am yours. Amen.

WORDLESS SPEECH FROM THE HEAVENS

*A*s seen both in the meter and the content, Psalm 19 is composed of two originally separate psalms. Verses 1–6 are in the form of a hymn (see page 369, below), and verses 7–14 are a poem in praise of the law (Torah).

Psalm 19:1–6, like Psalms 8; 104; and 148, praises the work of God as creator. The poem begins with words of great majesty that are familiar from Joseph Haydn's *Creation*: "The heavens are telling the glory of God. . . ." The "glory" (*kabod*) of God is revealed in "the works of his hands" (so reads the Hebrew). God's *kabod* is God's holy presence, especially in the Jerusalem temple (see 2 Chronicles 7:2).

Striking in this psalm is the assertion that "the heavens" and "the firmament" are constantly issuing wordless speech. It reminds us of the concept of the "harmony of the spheres" of medieval times. But the thought is perhaps closer to the idea of "natural revelation," the conviction that the natural world, apart from any written or oral communication, provides evidence of—or at least a sense of—God's glory (compare Paul's assertion in Romans 1:18–23). In verses 4b–6 the psalmist, in words similar to some ancient Near Eastern poems to the sun, reflects on the sun emerging each day from the heavens as an illustration of God's glory breaking through to the sphere of human existence.

The psalm's concept of wordless speech that breaks through from the heavens is reflected in the writings of the early Christian bishop Ignatius (martyred in Rome in A.D. 117) when he speaks of Christ as God's "Word [Greek: *logos*] proceeding from silence" (Letter to the Magnesians 8:2). For Ignatius, the Christ or Logos (the divine aspect of Jesus) is the word of God among us that speaks to us of the steadfast love of God.

I acknowledge your glory, O God,
in the things that have been made. Amen.

THE RULE OF LAW

*L*ike Psalm 119, Psalm 19:7–10 centers on the "law of the LORD" (*torah* of Yahweh). The psalmist praises the Torah, listing its various components: "decrees" (verse 7), "precepts" (verse 8), "commandment" (verse 8), and "ordinances" (verse 9). The word *Torah* sums up all aspects of God's will for human behavior.

The psalmist's response to Torah is positive and exuberant: the Torah "revives the soul," "making wise the simple," "rejoicing the heart," and "enlightening the eyes." Its prescriptions are "sweeter . . . also than honey." There are several reasons for this great praise. In its ordinances and commandments, the Torah reveals the path of wisdom and right living (verse 7). But the Torah is much more than laws. It includes also various kinds of instruction and numerous promises of God that bring hope to the individual and to the nation (this is especially the case for the form of the Torah in the book of Deuteronomy).

References to the "wise" and "simple" in verse 7 and the statement in verse 9 that "the fear of the LORD is pure" point to connections between these verses and wisdom books like Proverbs (compare Proverbs 1:7, "The fear of the LORD is the beginning of knowledge").

Christians have often had a negative view of Torah, using the concept as a foil to show the superiority of the "gospel." But Jesus himself affirmed the validity of the Torah (Matthew 5:17–20 and elsewhere), and Christians of all generations have recognized the need for moral instruction. The "rule of law" in human societies does not always coincide with God's will; it can be skewed by political ideology and partisan machinations. Thank God for the Torah of true justice.

Keep me steadfast, O Lord, in your word.
Give me wisdom. Amen.

Psalm 19:11–14

HIDDEN FAULTS AND ACCEPTABLE WORDS

$\mathcal{T}$he psalmist takes the Torah as his guide for life. Its prescriptions "warn" God's "servant" of wrong paths and convey the knowledge of good and evil. But may there not be faults of which the psalmist is unaware? What about unintentional failures?

Old Testament law codes do in fact distinguish between intentional and unwitting infractions (see, for example, Leviticus 4:2, 22, 27; Numbers 15:22, 27–31; Joshua 20:3). Moreover, the basic premise of many of the legal prescriptions in the Torah is that the punishment must fit the degree of culpability. Was the killing intentional, accidental, or due to carelessness? Several Christian liturgies also mention both sins of omission and sins of commission.

In addition to the ambiguity that often attaches to legal cases, we know how difficult it is to come to a realistic self-appraisal. It is therefore fully appropriate that we pray to be cleansed of our "hidden faults" (verse 12). We do not know ourselves as God know us.

There is a hopeful note here as well. According to Psalm 19, the word of God contains not only demand but also encouragement. "This word is the place where God himself as the Creator meets human beings in life-giving and life-sustaining fidelity." [6]

The psalm ends in verse 14 with words often used by preachers before they begin the sermon, but which are appropriate for all of us as we begin our day:

> *Let the words of my mouth and the meditation*
> *of my heart be acceptable to you, O Lord,*
> *my rock and my redeemer. Amen.*

YOUR HEART'S DESIRE

*T*his psalm appears to be a prayer that was uttered during or after sacrifices at the temple in Jerusalem. In the prayer the priests (and other worshipers) beseech God for the king's victory in battle. The "name of the God of Jacob" (verse 1) is Yahweh, and the name is present in a special way in "the sanctuary" (verse 2), the temple.

The idea of the LORD as a God of battles is an ancient one in Israel (see the ancient poem in Habakkuk 3; also Deuteronomy 20:4; 1 Samuel 17:47; Isaiah 13:4; Psalm 24:8; and elsewhere). Praying and sacrificing before battles are common among many ancient peoples. The Greek historian Thucydides, in his magnificent *History of the Peloponnesian War*, describes ritual preparations before the battles between Sparta and Athens. The idea of God protecting and blessing our nation is much alive in the United States at the beginning of the twenty-first century. Nonetheless, after the disaster of September 11, 2001, two prominent American evangelists offered the bizarre opinion that God had removed his protection from America, allowing the unjust killing of more than 2,700 persons. Civil religion—secular religion—in the United States is alive and flourishing. Any talk of removing religious symbols and words from national objects and ceremonies produces an emotional outcry.

We most certainly should pray for protection for those who face the violence of battle. We pray also for protection for our country. But most of all we pray for the time when nations study war no more and there is no longer any need for battle.

Grant us peace, O God, with justice and harmony;
keep hope alive among us. Amen.

OUR PROPER PRIDE

Those who are praying at the temple in Jerusalem express assurance that "the LORD will help his anointed," that is, the king, and give him "mighty victories" (verse 6). And the final verse puts the same thought in the form of a plea: "Give victory . . . O LORD; answer us when we call" (verse 9).

The psalmist then draws a contrast between two kinds of boasting. The enemies boast or "take pride" in chariots and horses, "but our pride is in the name of the LORD our God" (verse 7). This thought is fully in line with verses 1–5, in which the "name" of God will provide protection and give victory to the people.

But the psalm also reminds us of the futility of the arms race and of military buildups such as that of the early twentieth century that led to the disasters of World War I and its sequel, World War II. Where there are stockpiles of weapons, there is a good chance that they will be used. And if they are used, there will be great waste of human life and resources. Faith based on the justice of God can lead us from such folly.

Martin Luther linked Psalm 20 with Psalm 33:16–17: "The entire psalm . . . wants to make the point that a prince of the peoples should not be confident in any strength, should not trust in any resources, should not depend on any plans of his own, as that passage in Psalm 33 says, 'A king is not saved by his great army; a warrior is not delivered by his great strength. The war horse is a vain hope for victory, and by its great might it cannot save.' But let him await help from heaven, let him know that victory comes from above, let him hope alone in the name of the Lord. . . .'"[7]

Give our national leaders wisdom and a desire
for justice, Lord God. Amen.

THE BLESSED RULER

*I*f Psalm 20 is the king's prayer before battle, Psalm 21 is the king's thanksgiving after achieving a victory in battle. The king's prayers have been granted: He rejoices in "rich blessings" (verse 3); his life has been preserved; and he has gained glory, splendor, and majesty (verse 5).

The victory is due to the action of the LORD, in whom the king trusts. The "Most High" has "steadfast love" for the king (verse 7)—just as God had promised to David in 2 Samuel 7:15.

With Psalm 21 we meet issues of interpretation common to many of the "royal psalms" (see also the comments for January 4 and for February 12). A crisis of interpretation arose for ancient Israelites when the Davidic monarchy came to an end in 587 A.D., after descendants of David had reigned in Jerusalem for some four hundred years. Gradually the ancient priests and scribes came to read the royal psalms as referring to the "messiah," the future ruler who would restore the Davidic monarchy and Israelite (Judean) independence.

Christians from the earliest period called Jesus "the Messiah," and they naturally interpreted many of the royal psalms as prefiguring or even predicting the kingship of Jesus. Originally, however, the royal psalms celebrated the power and activities of the kings in Jerusalem.

A nation is personified in its leader, and none more so than in a monarchy. Even today Europe's royal families draw the attention of the tabloids. Most blessed, however, is the nation whose leader trusts in the steadfast love of the Lord and works for justice in the land.

Lord God, keep us steadfast in the search for truth and give us humility and compassion in the use of power. Amen.

EVIL PUT TO FLIGHT

The second half of Psalm 21 reflects in multiple ways on the destruction that the LORD had wreaked on the king's enemies. They were "swallowed up" in the wrath of the LORD as in a fiery furnace (verse 9). The defeat was so complete that the next generation among the enemies was likewise destroyed from the earth (verse 10). The annihilation of the enemies reminds us of "holy war" in the book of Joshua and elsewhere.

We live in a radically different political system from that of the psalmist, one in which the national government is forbidden to establish any privileged religious sect. What meaning can we derive from a poem that reflects the ideas of the divine right of kings? Has the passage of time rendered the psalm irrelevant?

In the early years of the third millennium A.D., however, the tendency toward theocratic political systems (in which a religion or a religious group holds national power) is found not only in Muslim countries but also elsewhere. In the United States—and, to a lesser degree, elsewhere in the West—we pray to God for blessings and protection on our country. Ordinary citizens desperately want to believe that the "founding fathers" of the United States were conservative Christians, when in fact many (like Thomas Jefferson) were anti-Trinitarian deists.[8] Fortunately for us all, they successfully argued that church membership should be completely voluntary.

As the old saying has it, "Scripture must be interpreted with scripture." Christians will read the forthright and honest vituperations against the enemy in light of teachings on mercy that we find in the prophets and in the teachings of Jesus.

Save us, O God, from jingoism; increase in us respect
for all the children of earth. Amen.

Psalm 22:1–5

NO ANSWER

This poignant lament is the most frequently quoted psalm in the New Testament, especially in accounts of Jesus' death (Matthew 27:35, 39, 43, 46; Mark 15:29, 34; John 19:23–24, 28). Some readers have thought that the psalmist was referring to crucifixion. Others are convinced that the psalm in several ways "predicted" the crucifixion of Jesus. But a basic premise of biblical interpretation is that the text must have had *some* meaning in its original context. Originally, therefore, the psalm referred neither to Jesus nor to a coming messiah (the idea of a suffering messiah is foreign to pre-Christian Judaism). Nonetheless, several details in the psalm have curious *parallels* in the narrative of Jesus' death.

According to Matthew and Mark (see above), Jesus himself quotes the opening verse of the psalm, the "cry of dereliction," "My God, my God, why have you forsaken me?" This is consistent with what the Gospels' picture of Jesus wrestling with his fate in the Garden of Gethsemane, praying that this "cup" would be removed from him (see Mark 14:36).

There is no more unfathomable grief than feeling forsaken and utterly abandoned by God in a time of crisis and dire distress. This is no mere intellectual wondering about the justice of God; it is a cry from the depths when persistent prayers go unanswered.

The psalmist does not inform us of the occasion for this experience of the pits of despair. But, in extreme anguish, he reminds God that his forebears put their trust in God and were delivered. Why not now?

If you have experienced such an extreme situation, you can still utter "*My* God" as a statement of faith, and you might find that the path leads upward after you hit bottom. If you have not plumbed such depths of despair, blessed are you.

Do not abandon me, O God, in the pits of despair. Amen.

Psalm 22:6–13

THE FAITHFUL SCORNED

*T*he psalmist presents to God some examples of his suffering. He has lost his humanness ("I am a worm, and not human," verse 6); indeed, he has lost all respect from his contemporaries, who scorn and despise him (verse 6). They mock him and taunt him to ask God to "rescue the one in whom he delights" (verse 8). Did the enemies think that the psalmist was parading his piety? Could these be the words of the suffering prophet, Jeremiah (see Jeremiah 20:7–12)?

The psalmist asserts that his life has been in the hands of God since his birth. He has not deserted God, but God has seemingly deserted him at a time when disaster looms (verses 9–11). Enemies, strong as the famous bulls of Bashan (the area east and northeast of the Sea of Galilee) and ravenous as roaring lions, have encircled him (verses 12–13).

Although several biblical books (notably, Deuteronomy, the historical books, and Proverbs) uphold the idea that there is justice in this life, with rewards for piety and punishments for evildoing, there are also many examples in the Bible of the apparent failure of this principle in real life. Harold Kushner famously wrote about how bad things can happen to good people, and we all have seen compelling examples of this.

Psalm 22 brings us face-to-face with biblical realism. Not all believers become millionaires and live happily ever after. There are times when we have nowhere to turn but to God—the source of our life.

Keep me steadfast, O God, when I pass
through the extremities of life. Amen.

THE ANATOMY OF DESPAIR

*T*he psalmist experiences physical agony. Verses 14–15 describe fever and ague with the consequent feeling of dehydration. We all have suffered such debilitating effects during influenza. All strength leaves the body, the bones ache, and the victim feels that death would not be difficult to endure.

Onlookers surround the victim like a pack of wild dogs, while the victim wastes away so that he can count his ribs (verses 16–17). So certain are the onlookers of the victim's approaching death that they already begin to divide his property among them (verse 18).

Seldom can we find in literature—whether ancient or modern— such graphic descriptions of a combination of physical, spiritual, and emotional grief. It is understandable that Christians often have thought of a crucified victim and that some have sought here a pre- figuring of the death of Jesus. The psalm does not predict things to come; it describes the real suffering of a real person in the real time of the worshiping community. It should be read as an expression of the agony of all those who face the extremities of life—prisoners of war, the person on the deathbed, accident victims, the person caught up in debilitating depression, and many others. The psalmist gives voice to the plea of all such sufferers. It is appropriate to lament when the occasion calls for it.

But then the psalmist appeals to the secure source of comfort and help: "But you, O LORD, do not be far away!" (verse 19). Even in the midst of dire distress we can turn to God.

In the agony of pain and suffering,
be near me, O God. Amen.

AFFLICTION TURNED TO PRAISE

*I*n a remarkable turnaround, the psalmist ends his agonizing lament and abruptly turns to thanksgiving. Amazingly, he uses the past tense: "You have rescued me" (verse 21b). Either the rescue has already taken place or else it should be understood as an expression of unflinching trust in the LORD's response. The past tense is used also in verse 24: "He did not despise or abhor the affliction of the afflicted. . . ." But in verses 20–21 the sufferer reissues his plea for deliverance: "Deliver my soul from the sword, my life from the power of the dog!"

At any rate, so certain is the suffering of the LORD's response that he announces that he will tell of God's name (that is, Yahweh) to the congregation (verses 22, 25), and he will fulfill his vows (offerings) there (verse 25).

The sufferer counts himself among "the poor" (verse 26; the term is translated "the afflicted" in verse 24). Whether this refers to financial poverty or to the idea that the sufferer is poor in the presence of God is not certain. In any case, those who humbly and with trust seek deliverance from God shall be satisfied and shall then praise the name of the LORD.

The persistence of hope in the midst of dire straits is a common biblical motif. Hope is not necessarily a guarantee of a blessed outcome, but it is a necessary component of life and a corollary of faith in the God of the Bible.

Keep hope alive, Lord God, in the extremities of life,
that I may bless your name. Amen.

THE UNIVERSAL GOD

*P*salm 22, the most terrifying of all laments in the book, ends with a magnificent acknowledgment of the universal dominion of God. This praise has three aspects:

1. Not only Israel but "all the families of the nations" shall worship before the LORD. Although we might wonder whether God was originally perceived by the Hebrews as a tribal deity—one among many others, although the only one to be worshiped—for the psalmist there *is* no other God. The LORD, Yahweh, is God of every tribe and nation.

2. Not only the living but also the dead—that is, persons of the past—shall bow down before the one God. Other psalms presuppose an insurmountable gulf between the dead and Yahweh; the dead cannot praise God (see Psalms 6:5; 88:10–12). This psalmist affirms that not only the living but also the people of the past will eventually come to acknowledge the lordship of God.

3. Those who will praise God are not only persons from the past and persons still living but also those of future generations. Knowledge of God will be transmitted to those still unborn, so that ultimately all persons ever born into this world will bow down before the universal God.

When reflecting on this psalm, Christians will be reminded of the Christ-hymn in Philippians 2:6–11, which speaks of every creature "in heaven and on earth and under the earth" "bowing the knee" (verse 10). We think also of Paul's assertion in 1 Corinthians 15 (see the argument leading up to verse 28) that, in the end, God will be all in all.

Great are you, O God, and greatly to be praised,
now and through all eternity. Amen.

FEARLESS THROUGH THE DARKEST VALLEY

*A*lmost everyone has a story about how this most beloved of all psalms has had an impact on his or her life. It is not surprising that more than a dozen hymns are based on this psalm.

This psalmist reflects the experience of real danger. Verses 1–4 present an unforgettable contrast between passing through the "darkest valley," the "valley of death's shadows," and a calm, sunny, green pasture alongside of fresh water. Good pasturage and a watering place are two of the main concerns of the shepherd in a land of heat and scarce water. Sometimes, however, in order to reach such places we must pass through the valley of the shadow of death. In antiquity the bottom of a ravine was a place of danger and threat, especially in the darkness of night (see Genesis 32:22–32). The shepherd leads the flock in the "right paths" (verse 3) to reach the goal.

It was commonplace in the ancient Near East that the king is the shepherd of his people. For the Israelites, the Lord is king and therefore also shepherd. The Lord protects the people in danger and leads them to security in time of threat and sustenance in time of hunger. In this psalm, however, the focus is on the individual's thanksgiving more than that of the community. To confess that "my shepherd is the Lord" is much more than a romantic, pastoral image. It indicates the source of the psalmist's—and our—confidence in the real experience of threat and danger in our lives.

Good shepherd, be with me
in the darkest valleys of my life. Amen.

BLESSINGS THROUGH ALL THE DAYS OF MY LIFE

A new scene emerges in verse 5 of this psalm. The Lord, the good shepherd, now appears as the host at a lavish banquet in which the guest is anointed and his cup overflows. The psalmist may be thinking of a thanksgiving meal at the temple in Jerusalem, offered in gratitude for preservation from enemies, who are to take note of the source of the psalmist's protection by the Lord.

The psalmist's association with the temple is confirmed by the final verse: "I shall dwell in the house of the LORD [the Jerusalem temple] my whole life long." This for him is the ideal life.

Psalm 23 says important things about the past, the present, and the future. The LORD has led, guided, and protected the psalmist in the past, even through the dangers of darkness and evil. In the present the LORD prepares a banquet, offering the psalmist table fellowship and rich blessings. And the grateful worshiper is certain that the "goodness and mercy" he has experienced from the LORD will follow him in the future, through the entire course of his life.

Fewer Westerners than ever before now live in a rural setting. But even city dwellers can sincerely confess that "my shepherd is the LORD," and we all can rejoice in the confidence and assurance of well-being toward which this beautiful psalm points.

For goodness, mercy, and your table of fellowship
I give thanks, O Lord. Amen.

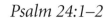 *Psalm 24:1–2*

WHOSE WORLD IS IT?

Like us, the biblical writers look at the world sometimes with wondrous awe and at other times with debilitating despair. The pessimistic attitude is found most clearly in the writings of John, where, in spite of the statement that "God so loved the world . . ." (John 3:16), we find the assertions that the devil is "the ruler of this world" (John 14:30) and that "the whole world lies under the power of the evil one" (1 John 5:19).

The psalmist will have none of this. "The earth is the LORD's and all that is in it." God willed the universe into existence, and what God wills is good. There is nothing in Psalm 24 about the corruption of the world, although the psalmist does refer to corrupt acts on the part of humans (verse 4). This is not the attitude of "God is in his heaven and all is right with the world," but the psalmist has no doubt that God is the prime cause of the natural world and all the life within it, including ours, and that God will watch over this handiwork.

Can you personally confess that "the earth is the Lord's and all that is in it"? For most of us, life is a struggle between hope and despair. We cannot fully control our own course through life. Biblical faith, however, and not least the testimony of the psalmists, urges us to keep hope alive because, in the end, God will be all in all.

Lord God, you have given me the breath of life,
and I have enjoyed the blessings of your creation.
I give you thanks. Amen.

UNADULTERATED PRAISE

*M*any composers have set to music the majestic words of Psalm 24, which Christians often use as an "introit" or call to worship. The psalmist speaks of a twofold entry into the temple precincts in Jerusalem—that of the people in verses 3–6 and that of the LORD, the true king, in verses 7–10.

The people who enter for worship are reminded that hypocrisy has no place among the people of God. Worshipers are to have "clean hands and pure hearts" (verse 4) that is, both worthy deeds and guileless thoughts. They seek "vindication from the God of their salvation" (verse 5), acknowledging that God, the creator of all that is, will keep them and protect them in times of threat and trouble. Such are they who worship God in spirit and truth. (This psalm does not specify what we need to do when we sin. That is the subject of the penitential psalms, like 6; 32; 38; 51; 102; 130; and 143).

The people shout for the opening of the temple gates and doors, that the "King of glory" may enter into the midst of the worshiping congregation. The word "glory" can refer to the presence of God in the temple (see Psalm 26:8; 2 Chronicles 7:2), especially in the book of Ezekiel. Who is this King of glory? It is the "Lord of hosts," Yahweh Sebaoth, the God of creation and the God of history who is "mighty in battle."

This psalm is full of confidence, joy, and dignified celebration. Blessed are we when we have the sense of glory and wonder in our worship.

Give me, O God, the assurance of your blessing
and your salvation. Amen.

YOUTHFUL SINS
AND GOD'S FAITHFULNESS

*I*f this lament seems to shift abruptly from one thought to the next, there is a simple reason: in the original Hebrew it is arranged in acrostic form, each verse beginning with the successive letter in the Hebrew alphabet. There is nonetheless much wisdom and worthy teaching in it.

The psalmist turns to God in trust (verse 2), confident that his prayer will be answered. Unlike those who are treacherous (verse 3), the psalmist seeks truth and the LORD's paths (verses 4–5), appealing to the God's mercy and steadfast love, which "have been from of old" (verse 6).

These thoughts lead to the main petition of this section of the psalm: the psalmist acknowledges the sins and transgressions of his youth and begs God not to remember them (verse 7). How different from the psalms of vengeance and those in which the psalmist boasts of or protests his innocence before God! The psalmist appeals to what we might call God's better nature: mercy, steadfast love, goodness, uprightness, and faithfulness.

Few persons indeed can make the transition from puberty to adulthood without guilt, and some are burdened with thoughts of adolescent sexual experimentation or other difficulties for an entire lifetime. How important it is, then, to have a sense of the mercy of God. Like the psalmist, when we are weighted down by guilt for events from the past, we can appeal to the goodness of the LORD and to God's faithful and steadfast love.

According to your steadfast love, remember me,
O Lord. Amen.

GUILT AND FORGIVENESS

Like most of us, the psalmists lamented and complained more than they thanked or confessed. But Psalm 25 reveals a realistic awareness of the persistent inner workings of guilt. Guilt dominates the psalmist's thinking (it "is great," verse 11), and it produces loneliness and affliction (verses 16, 18). The poet feels constricted, confined, caught in a net (verse 15), and claustrophobic (this is the meaning of "my distress" in verse 17). Guilt has removed the joy of living and has become an obsession. We learn nothing about the cause of this guilt or the wrong that the psalmist has done, but he presents all this anguish to the LORD, confident that God will consider his distress. The psalmist prays for pardon (verse 11) and forgiveness (verse 18), which will bring relief from the debilitating effects of living with guilt.

The psalmist knows that God can bring relief to the one who fears God and is intent on following the right path. He not only confesses his guilt but expresses reverence to God and hopes to experience a renewal of "the friendship of the LORD" (verse 14).

What does it mean to forgive or to be forgiven? The Hebrew word translated "forgive" in verse 18 means simply "to take up" or "take away, remove" but the Greek word in the New Testament means "to give up," "to let go." It is helpful to think of forgiveness not as a change of attitude on the part of the one who forgives but as the sufferer's release from the obsession of guilt. To be forgiven is to be released from life-choking guilt.

Consider my affliction, O Lord, and, from the abundance
of your mercy, forgive my sins. Amen.

DEALING WITH VIOLENT HATE

One of the most frequently occurring themes in the psalms is the reference to threatening enemies. As with many of us, danger drove the psalmists to beseech God for protection and deliverance. This psalmist has faced "violent hatred" from "many foes." America in the early twenty-first century is witnessing an abundance of violence and hatred. As a society we are learning to live with color-coded threat levels. But the reference in Psalm 25 to the fear of being "shamed" (verse 20; see also verse 2) suggests that this particular threat was not so much one of physical violence as a threat to one's social status that came from slander.

Biblical scholars in recent years have reminded us of the importance in ancient societies of the concepts of honor and shame. It was not simply a matter of "looking good" or "keeping up appearances" but of a sense of personal dignity and personal worth that is necessary for a healthy life—for us as much as for the ancients.

The psalmist points to two elements that are required for personal honor, integrity, and uprightness (verse 21). The person of integrity cannot act from duplicity or double-mindedness, which reveal a fractured life and are incompatible with honor.

Where can the psalmist go to avoid the threat from the foes? He takes refuge in the God of Israel, a mighty fortress.

In our violent world, O God,
be my refuge and strength. Amen.

STANDING BEFORE GOD

*A*lthough at first glance this psalm might appear to be full of self-righteous boasting, a closer look reveals that it is written by one falsely and maliciously accused. The petitioner flees to the temple, where the "glory" of the LORD resides. There he submits to God's scrutiny and makes a poignant appeal for vindication and redress—a procedure described in 1 Kings 8:31–32.

The psalmist is certain that he does not deserve the attack of the evildoers. He has integrity and unwavering trust in the LORD (verse 1), he is faithful (verse 3) and innocent (verse 6), and does not consort with the hypocrites and wicked (verses 4–5). In the temple he undergoes a ritual of affirmation: he washes his hands before the altar of the LORD, declaring his innocence (verse 6; compare Deuteronomy 21:6–7 and Pilate's action in Matthew 27:24).

The psalmist's assertion that he loves "the house in which you dwell, and the place where your glory abides" (verse 8) suggests the possibility that he was a priest or Levite who served at the Jerusalem temple. In any case he assumes that justice will prevail, assured by the righteous Judge of the whole world.

We are rightly appalled at news stories of individuals who have been in prison on death row for years, only to have their innocence proved by DNA tests. What can be more unjust? And we are deeply hurt when we become the objects of gossip and slander. What can we do at such times? Let us follow the example of this psalmist, who flees to the presence of God, presenting there his heartfelt petitions, relying on God's justice finally to prevail.

Merciful God, I pray for those who are unjustly imprisoned.
Give them courage and hope, and give us strength to work
for justice for all. Amen.

CONFIDENT IN GOD'S LIGHT AND SALVATION

*T*he first section of Psalm 27 is an impressive, beautiful, and comforting song of trust that precedes the lament of the falsely accused in verses 7–14.

The Lord is the psalmist's "light," "salvation," and "stronghold." Isaiah also refers to God as "the light of Israel" (Isaiah 10:17), and the designation of God as salvation and stronghold or fortress is frequent in the prophets and the psalms.

The anonymous petitioner, like the one in Psalm 26, has fled for refuge to the temple, the "house of the Lord," where he would prefer to remain for the rest of his life (verse 4). There he "inquires," pleads for redress and justice, and exults in beholding the "beauty of the Lord." The psalmist finds blessed peace in the midst of the magnificence of the temple. So also, when we sit in silence in the nave of a great cathedral, a sense of well-being and comfort—and of the presence of God—can flood over us. In the temple the psalmist expresses assurance that the "evildoers," "adversaries," and "foes" who, like wild animals, seek to devour his flesh (verse 2), will stumble and fall and come to nothing.

God will shelter the faithful person on the day of trouble and set him above his enemies, producing a feeling of joyous relief. Let us also on the day of trouble turn to the one who is the stronghold of our life (verse 1).

*Lord God, be my light and salvation in threatening times
and in times of well-being. Amen.*

FACE TO FACE

*W*e can discern much from the expressions of a face—a whole range of emotions from elation to grief. We respond instinctively to each situation. The Bible has numerous references to the "face" of God, and God's face also evokes in the responder an appropriate reaction.

The prophets often speak of God "hiding his face" from the people's evil deeds. Jeremiah has God say, "I have set my face against this city [Jerusalem] for evil and not for good"; "I have hidden my face from this city" (Jeremiah 21:10; 33:5; see also Isaiah 8:17; Ezekiel 15:7). And the psalmists cry, "How long will you hide your face from me?" (Psalm 13:1; see also 69:17).

Conversely, there is blessing when the Lord turns his face toward us. "The upright shall behold his face" (Psalm 11:7). "Restore us, O God; let your face shine, that we may be saved" (Psalm 80:3). "Let your face shine upon your servant" (Psalm 31:16). And, most familiar, Aaron's benediction, "The LORD make his face to shine upon you, and be gracious to you" (Numbers 6:25).

In Psalm 27 the petitioner pleads, "'Come,' my heart says, 'seek his face!' Your face, LORD, do I seek. Do not hide your face from me" (verses 8–9).

All of these utterances are simply a prayer for assurance that God is for us and will not abandon us—that God will come to our aid in time of distress and suffering. There are times when each of us needs to pray in such a way—times when we need to sense the shining face of God.

Hear, O Lord, when I cry aloud; be gracious to me. Amen.

THE GOODNESS OF GOD IN THE LAND OF THE LIVING

*I*n many respects our lives seesaw between pessimism and optimism, between disappointment and blessing. In our down days we might think that we have no hope unless there is an afterlife. But, as the psalmist says, we usually find that joy returns in the morning (Psalm 30:5), when the new day dawns, and our thoughts and our energies can again be directed to life in the here and now.

Ancient Israelites prayed to "see the goodness of the LORD in the land of the living" (verse 13), that is, in their earthly life. At least in the earlier periods of their history, the Israelites seem not to have had a clear conception of what to expect after death; Sheol for them was a shadowy existence, not by any means a full life. Their religion was literally down-to-earth.

For Christians the resurrection of Jesus requires (or at least allows) more of an emphasis on the hereafter and of the ultimate restoration of what is now out of kilter. But Christians—no more than Jews—cannot write off the here and now. "The earth is the LORD's and all that is in it," says the psalmist (Psalm 24:1), and we therefore have no right to treat creation with abuse or contempt. If things at the moment seem to be spiraling downward, be patient and wait for the LORD (verse 14). Give thanks for your blessings and honor the Creator.

O God, grant us wisdom, grant us courage,
for the living of these days. Amen.

SPEAKING PEACE AND DOING EVIL

*I*n this lament the psalmist has a gripping fear that he will die if he does not find deliverance from the LORD. "If you are silent to me, I shall be like those who go down to the Pit" (verse 1). The "Pit" is Sheol, the place of the dead, a condition of shadowy survival near the grave graphically portrayed in Psalm 88:3–7 (see also Psalm 115:17).

The threat of death apparently comes from personal enemies who "do not regard the works of the LORD but "speak peace . . . while mischief is in their hearts" (verse 3). Jeremiah also fulminated against those who "have treated the wound of my people carelessly, saying, 'Peace, peace,' when there is no peace. They acted shamefully . . . yet they were not at all ashamed, they did not know how to blush" (Jeremiah 6:14–15; 8:11–12).

Political leaders often use well-planned public relations maneuvers to accomplish their objectives, sometimes blatantly calling their programs the opposite of the effect they will have. A plan for relaxing the rules for industrial polluters might be called the "Clean Skies Program." "Employment Opportunities Program" might be a plan to "outsource" jobs to foreign countries. The temple singers pray that the LORD would repay those who engage in "double-speak."

The psalmist calls for inner integrity, a wholeness of personality that brings our talk into harmony with our thoughts and actions. This can be a difficult and long process. But it is an important part of what we mean by "salvation."

Cleanse my thoughts and my deeds, O Lord,
and make me whole. Amen.

GIVING THANKS IN SONG

*T*he Lord has heard the psalmist's plea, and the psalmist now breaks forth in song: "I am helped, and my heart exults, and *with my song* I give thanks to him" (verse 7).

The entire book of Psalms has sometimes been called "the hymnal of the temple" in Jerusalem. No doubt many of the psalms were sung on specific occasions as liturgies in the temple—processionals, thanksgivings, national laments, coronations, and others. What we can know of the details of such temple music is sketchy with respect to the instruments, the musical forms, and the composition of the singers. The final two verses of Psalm 28 seem to be an addition to this psalm to make it more appropriate for public worship.

But the body of the psalm speaks to the experience of an individual who was sorely threatened by enemies who then sought help from the Lord and found deliverance. He joyfully blesses God and expresses firm trust in God's protection. An important component of the response is the psalmist's song. Robert Lowry (1826–1899) expressed a similar sentiment in his hymn "How Can I Keep from Singing?"

No storm can shake my inmost calm,
while to that rock I'm clinging.
Since Christ is Lord of heaven and earth,
how can I keep from singing?

Give me voice to sing your praise;
give me hope to live my days. Amen.

GLORY IN THE STORM

*I*n this powerful hymn, the glory of God is revealed in the crashes of thunder during a mighty storm that moves from north to south over the Holy Land. Both the form and the content of the psalm are carefully wrought. This means that it should be read and considered as a unity (see also pages 369–370, below).

With respect to form, verses 1–2 (the prologue) are balanced by verses 10–11 (the conclusion). In between there are six groups of lines (stanzas or "strophes"), each introduced by the words "the voice of the Lord" (*qol Yahweh*).

Thunder, "the voice of the Lord," breaks out over the Mediterranean Sea ("over the waters," verse 3), moves to the land over Lebanon (verse 5), then turns south to end up in the Negev desert ("the wilderness of Kadesh," verse 8). Along with booming thunder, there is hail ("he makes Lebanon skip like a calf," verse 6), and lightning sweeps across the sky ("flames of fire," verse 7).

The worshipers in the temple respond to this awesome drama with one word: "Glory!" The Hebrew term here, *kabod*, points to the specialized presence of God in the holy of holies in the temple.

Ancient Israelites believed that "the earth is the Lord's" (Psalm 24:1)—not ours and not that of some evil power. Therefore it is appropriate for us to find a sense of the glory and majesty of God in the forces of nature and in the handiwork of creation.

For the wonders of nature, O God of creation,
I praise you. Amen.

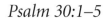

JOY IN THE MORNING

*C*an you resonate to the song "Help me make it through the night," or are your thoughts more like "Help me get up in the morning"? There are night persons and there are morning persons.

In this song of thanksgiving, the psalmist has been drawn back from the very maw of death ("Sheol," "the Pit," verse 3) and restored to health. We are not told of the specific nature of the trouble, but the reference to healing (verse 2) and the sudden change of situation during the wee hours of the night suggest a physical aliment. The psalmist had experienced this malady as linked to God's anger (verse 5). The ancient Israelites, believing in both the power and the justice of God, had no alternative than to attribute suffering to the will and action of God.

The sufferer had spent the night in weeping. Some ancient Israelites pressed their case before the Lord by spending the night in prayer at the temple precincts. Anyone who passes the night hours in grief, unable to find sleep, knows how miserable insomnia can be. But, with the rising sun, relief and healing came to the psalmist; "joy comes with the morning" (verse 5). The psalmist praises God, whose anger is for a moment but whose "favor is for a lifetime" (verse 5).

No matter how desperate our situation might be at a given time, we can be certain that God is slow to anger and abiding in steadfast love. That is our hope when the night is long.

Keep me steadfast in my trust in you, O God. Amen.

FROM MOURNING
TO DANCING

*I*t is easy to see why interpreters have often called Psalm 30 one of the most attractive in the entire collection. It has a light and flowing poetic style and is full of joyous thanksgiving. It gives a thematic overview of one person's life, and it has a happy ending.

The psalmist engages in retrospection. He looks back to the time before the trouble, when he felt as secure "as a strong mountain" (verse 7), prosperous and enjoying the favor of the Lord. But then trouble came—perhaps a debilitating illness. God's face was hidden (see the comments for February 27, above), and the psalmist was dismayed. In his distress he called to the Lord: "What profit is there . . . if I go down to the Pit? Will the dust praise you?" (verse 9). In line with the common ancient Israelite tradition, he believes that the dead cannot praise God. He presents his suffering to God, appealing to God's grace.

Then his mourning is turned to dancing, and his sackcloth to joy. In his exhilaration he promises to praise God forever. Life is precious, and we should give thanks for each new day.

It is good to give joyous thanks when we have experienced a unique blessing, but it is even more admirable to remember our blessings when things take a turn for the worse. Remember that, whether we live or die, we are the Lord's.

I rejoice in the blessings I receive from you, O God. Amen.

MY ROCK AND MY FORTRESS

*T*ravelers in the Holy Land can understand why ancient Israelite poets and hymn writers so often spoke of rocks and fortresses. The great mountain fortress of Masada near the shores of the Dead Sea, built by Herod the Great and used by the Zealots battling the Romans, was only with great difficulty captured by the overwhelming force of the Roman army in A.D. 73.

Rock in the Old Testament is a symbol of dogged firmness and stability. The LORD tells the prophet Ezekiel to be firm in pronouncing judgment on his people: "Like the hardest stone, harder than flint, I have made your forehead; do not fear them . . ." (Ezekiel 3:9). Most often, however, the symbol is applied to God, suggesting utter reliability and steadfastness. The image of Hannah's prayer, "There is no Holy One like the LORD, no one besides you; there is no Rock like our God" (1 Samuel 2:2) is repeated over and over in the Psalms (for example, Psalms 18:2, 31; 62:2–7; 71:3; 94:22; 144:1–2).

In Psalm 31, a lament, God is a mighty fortress, a "rock of refuge" that saves. This salvation is the result of God's righteousness (verse 1). Although in this psalm salvation means deliverance from foes, Martin Luther, in part following Paul's reading of psalms, found it to mean that human salvation is the *bestowal* of God's righteousness on humans who do not merit it. Christians look to experience salvation in this life and in the life to come.

You, O Lord, are my rock and my fortress;
for your name's sake lead me and guide me. Amen.

LIVING THROUGH GRIEF, SCORN, AND TERROR

*T*he contrast in Psalm 31 between the buoyant confidence of verses 1–8 and the depths of dread and despair of verses 9–13 could hardly be greater. These two sections might have originally been separate compositions, although a lament often does contain both expressions of confidence and graphic utterances of grief.

The psalmist's eyes are sore from weeping (verse 9). His suffering is chronic and has drained the strength out of his body (verse 10). Worse yet, the victim has become a pariah. His enemies scorn him, his neighbors and acquaintances react with horror, and many whisper behind his back, plotting to take his life (verses 11–13). He is avoided by those who see him in the street and feels as useless as a broken pot at the side of the road (verse 12). If the references to the eye, body, and bones suggest a physical ailment, the allusions to the psalmist's social ostracism point toward slander and personal threats.

The similarity of these verses to the laments of the prophet Jeremiah (his "confessions," Jeremiah 11:18—12:6; 15:20–21; 17:14–18; 18:18–23; 20:7–13; 10:14–18) is startling. Consider the following: "I hear many whispering: 'Terror is all around! Denounce him! Let us denounce him!' All my close friends are watching for me to stumble" (Jeremiah 20:10). Did the psalmist, like Jeremiah, arouse violent hatred because of his preaching of repentance and divine judgment? Did Jeremiah compose this psalm? We cannot know.

One thing we learn from this psalm is that it is appropriate for us to lay before God our innermost despair and fear. There is a reason why this psalm begins with the image of God as rock and fortress before describing the terror of life. In times of dark despair we can turn to our faithful God.

Do not forsake me, O God, in the depths of despair. Amen.

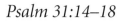

"MY TIMES ARE IN YOUR HAND"

*P*ausing after his excruciating lament in verses 9–13, the psalmist returns to the expression of trust in the Lord and a renewed plea for deliverance from his enemies.

"You are my God" means for the psalmist, "My times are in your hand" (verses 14–15). If we indeed trust that the Lord is our God, we should not be oppressed by thoughts that our times are corrupt and that our society is going to hell in a handbasket. Trust in God does not ensure that we will be exempt from the troubles of this world, but it does assure us that in the end all things will be restored to what God originally intended.

The psalmist's petition includes familiar—albeit graphic—details. He prays that God's face will shine on him (see the comments for February 27, above), revealing God's steadfast love (verse 16). He fears being "put to shame"—an almost universal dread among ancient Mediterranean peoples—and prays that his enemies experience that fate and that they "go dumbfounded to Sheol" (verse 17), which will mean the end of their "lying lips," their insolence, their pride, and their contempt (verse 18).

There is much to fear in this life—and much that needs change both in our society and in our lives as individuals. It is comforting to know that our insurance company keeps us "in good hands." But to know that our times are in God's hand is much greater comfort.

Keep me safe in your steadfast love, O Lord. Amen.

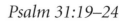

ABUNDANT GOODNESS

*T*o judge from the psalms, social relations in biblical times were as difficult as they are now. In today's verses we read of "human plots" and "contentious tongues," of being "beset as a city under siege," and of those who act haughtily. Earlier verses in Psalm 31 reflect a condition of dire distress. It is true that we, like the ancient psalmists, are most apt to turn to God in prayer when we experience such oppression.

But our petitioner now prays in hymn form (see page 369, below) in the midst of such an experience. He praises the abundant goodness of God, gives thanks for "the shelter of [God's] presence," and expresses trust that these blessings will continue into the future.

One of the real tests of faith comes when tragedy or suffering enters our lives. Do we respond with anger against other people—or perhaps against God? Do we sink into unrelieved depression? Or do we doubt the very goodness of God? Such emotions can at times actually have positive effects, but the one thing that is nonnegotiable for persons of faith is the essential goodness of God. This is the foundation for the hope that we keep alive in the midst of sorrow and despair.

The unshakeable assurance of the goodness of God enables the psalmist to give us this sound advice: "Be strong, and let your heart take courage, all you who wait for the LORD" (verse 24).

I bless your name, O God, for your steadfast love for me,
even in the midst of sorrow. Amen.

BLESSED FORGIVENESS

*T*his remarkable thanksgiving psalm reveals profound insight into the effects of guilt on both the human psyche and the human body. But it communicates an equally strong experience of the assurance of forgiveness as blessed relief. Its understanding of the need for repentance is unusual in the book of Psalms.

The psalmist uses three Hebrew words in verses 1–2 to refer to the cause of his guilt feelings. "Transgression" refers to the revolt of the human will against the divine will. "Sin" denotes failure or missing the mark. And "iniquity" is the concept of distortion or perversion, a "twisting." The psalmist is aware of the actions or thoughts that produced the guilt, and he takes full responsibility for them.

The effects of guilt are graphically described. Before confessing ("while I kept silence," verse 3), his body was "wasting away," a psychosomatic symptom and not (as some readers have thought) a physical ailment. He groaned day and night, his strength dried up as a desert scene in midsummer. The life was sucked out of him.

Then came the turning point: the guilty person acknowledged—did not hide, but confessed—his sin, his iniquity, and his transgression. He opened his life to God and then experienced the blessed relief of forgiveness, the "covering" of his sin (verses 1, 5).

The forgiven sinner is pronounced "happy," *ashrey* in Hebrew, which in Greek is translated *makarios*, the word used by Jesus in the Beatitudes ("Blessed is . . ."). This is unbounded happiness, blessed happiness that comes from blessed forgiveness.

Grant me awareness of my failures, O God; forgive my sin and give me the blessed assurance of forgiveness. Amen.

A LIFE-CHANGING EXPERIENCE

*T*his part of Psalm 32 consists of three distinct sections of two verses each. The psalmist first calls all the faithful to follow his example—to look to the LORD in times of distress, as he had done when overcome by guilt. To describe the distress he uses the gripping image of "the rush of mighty waters," a great tsunami that cannot reach those who flee to their "hiding-place," the LORD (verses 6–7).

A shift takes place in verses 8–9. Here the speaker is the LORD (such utterances, usually in poetic form, are called oracles), and the message is like that of the wisdom psalms. God will instruct, teach, and counsel those who are teachable (unlike a stubborn horse or mule that requires a bit and bridle). This guidance will prevent further excruciating experiences of guilt.

Finally, in verses 10–11, comes an expression of praise and joy for the steadfast love that surrounds those who trust in the LORD. The psalmist has had a life-changing experience, and nothing can diminish the joy of forgiveness.

There are times in our life when we are overcome with regret—whether for embarrassment or guilt for a wrongful deed. We might say (or think), "I wanted to sink through the floor." When such negative feelings are not neutralized, they can cripple your personality. Therefore, happy indeed are those whose transgression is forgiven.

You are a hiding place for me, O God;
you preserve me from trouble. Amen.

THE JOY OF JUSTICE

*I*n form, Psalm 33 is acrostic; each of its twenty-two lines begin with the successive letter of the Hebrew alphabet. As to content, it is a hymn, concentrating not on the subjective state of the worshiper but on the glory and steadfast love of the LORD.

Verses 1–3 are a hymnic introit that calls on the righteous to rejoice and praise the LORD with stringed instruments and singing. The "new song" (see also Psalm 96:1; 98:1) is probably not a change in musical style but rather an outburst of praise for a new blessing. We would like to know more about the music performed in the Jerusalem temple, but it is clear that it could often be exuberant and uninhibited with the sounds of instruments and voices.

The attributes of God occupy verses 4–5. The "word of the LORD" is parallel to "his work," both of which are upright and done in faithfulness. Among the praiseworthy attributes of God are righteousness, justice, and steadfast love—terms all frequently used of God in the Old Testament. The gods of the peoples of the ancient Near East, Greece, and Rome typically act capriciously and exhibit all the petulant emotions of human beings. By contrast, the LORD is not capricious but predictably just and righteous. God is steadfast in justice but also in love. God wills for us—as for the ancient Israelites—nothing but good. And for this we respond with joy.

I praise you, O God, for your justice and steadfast love.
Reveal your righteousness in my life. Amen.

THE CREATIVE WORD

*B*y the word of the Lord the heavens were made" (verse 6). In Genesis 1 God creates by speech, by *word*. "Let there be light . . . (Genesis 1:3). Our psalmist acknowledges that God's word is powerful, bringing into being the heavens and all the host of heaven, the angelic beings whose function is to praise God. God's command established the limits of the oceans, as a person might constrain water in a bottle (verse 7a), and God created underground water that can gush forth in a spring (verse 7b). God's powerful word should inspire fear and awe on the part of the peoples of the earth (verses 8–9).

God's word was not only active in creation but is operative also in the historical affairs of the nations. "The Lord brings the counsel of the nations to nothing . . ." (verse 10). Wise rulers will therefore submit to the will of God, who directs history to its proper end. Blessed, therefore, is the nation whose God is the Lord (Yahweh, verse 12).

Old Testament writers found occasion to praise the glories of God both in nature and in history. Christians also can find traces of the work of God in natural phenomena—the beauty of a forest, a canyon, a brook, a sunset—and in examples of progress in history for the increase of human welfare. But we can also find nature to be "red in tooth and claw," and history brings not only blessing but also disaster and untold suffering. Both history and the natural world need to "be set free from . . . bondage to decay" (Romans 8:21). Christians have therefore looked to Jesus as the ultimate Word of God, who prefigures our redemption as well as that of the natural world itself.

Unleash your liberating word
in our turbulent world, O God. Amen.

A VAIN HOPE

The twentieth century was a time of incredible new weapons of war—the tank, the airplane, rocket-propelled missiles, napalm, and the nightmare of atomic bombs. Much of the world lived through many years of tension and apocalyptic fears during the "cold war," which involved standoffs between the major powers. Destructive missiles were called "peacemakers," and a popular slogan was "peace through strength." Massive firepower, however, proved to be unable to stop the terrorists of the early twenty-first century.

During the struggles of the second half of the twentieth century, stirring voices called for nonviolent change—among them Mohandas Ghandi in India, Martin Luther King Jr. in the United States, and Nelson Mandela in South Africa. These individuals were able to accomplish great improvements in human societies, but they were not able to still the voices that called for continued development of military power.

Great armies, warriors, and war horses —one of the mightiest of military forces in the ancient Near East—were prized by rulers in Old Testament times. But the psalmist knew that the nation's security was not ultimately in the hands of the military forces. "The war horse is a vain hope for victory" (verse 17).

What can make our country great and keep it so? Weapons of war—however necessary they might be in this dangerous world—are not enough. If we would seek to please God in our nation, we will work for implementing justice—economic and social—in all levels of society.

Help all of us, O God, to love kindness, seek justice in our
midst, and walk humbly with you. Amen.

THE EYE OF THE LORD

*T*he reverse of the "Great Seal of the United States" is located to the left of the green side of the U.S. one-dollar bill. The "all-seeing eye" is at the top of a pyramid, above which are the Latin words "Annuit coeptis," which means something like ". . . has favored our undertaking." The designers of this seal probably had in mind that "Providence" or God favored the undertaking of the founding fathers of the United States.

The all-seeing eyes of God are frequently mentioned in the Old Testament. "The eyes of the LORD are in every place, keeping watch on the evil and the good" (Proverbs 15:3; see also 22:12). The eyes refer to God's omniscience and therefore can be either an ominous symbol or a sign of grace and favor. Because of his righteousness, "Noah found favor in the eyes of the LORD" (Genesis 6:8 RSV), and "David did what was right in the eyes of the LORD" (1 Kings 15:5 RSV). God's eyes look for truth (Jeremiah 5:3), and Habakkuk says, "Your eyes are too pure to behold evil" (1:13). But another prophet conveys the word of the LORD against those who fail to do justice, "I will fix my eyes on them for harm and not for good" (Amos 9:4). And Job complains that God's scrutinizing eye will not let him alone even to swallow his spittle, and he hopes for the time when "the eye that beholds me will see me no more; while your eyes are upon me, I shall be gone" (Job 7:8).

The psalmist took comfort in knowing that "the eye of the LORD is on those who fear him, on those who hope in his steadfast love" (verse 18), because God had delivered him from death. Let us strive for the wholeness that allows us to think of God's eye as comforting rather than threatening.

Let your steadfast love, O Lord, be upon me. Amen.

THE CRY OF THE POOR

*P*salm 34 is a song of thanksgiving in acrostic form (the first letters of lines follow the sequence of the Hebrew alphabet). The content also is reminiscent of wisdom psalms.

The first ten verses of this psalm have three parts: in verses 1–3 the psalmist sings the praise of the LORD; verses 4–6 describe the psalmist's experience; and verses 8–10 are a commendation of God's help to others in need.

It is often frustrating to modern readers that we are not given more specific information about the difficulty the psalmist refers to. In a prayer God does not need to be reminded of the particulars. Most often the psalmist has been falsely accused by foes or suffers from some physical ailment. In this case, however, we might think of a situation of economic poverty. The psalmist describes himself as "this poor soul" (verse 6) and says that those who fear God "have no want" and "lack no good thing" (verses 9–10). He cried to the LORD, and was saved. Again we would like to know more precisely how he was delivered from need. But the psalmist felt that he was surrounded by "the angel of the LORD," who protected and delivered him.

The Bible as a whole depicts God as having a special concern for the poor and humble. In Psalm 34 they are "the humble" (verse 2), the "holy ones" (verse 9) who fear God. This emphasis continues in the New Testament, where Jesus pronounces blessing on the poor (Luke 6:20) and directs his attention mainly to people in need. Whether in prosperity or in need, let us also trust in the goodness of the LORD.

I will bless the Lord at all times; his praise shall continually be in my mouth. Amen.

"NEAR TO THE BROKENHEARTED"

*T*he greatness of the psalms is seen in many ways, not least by their realism about human life on this earth. The psalmists complain, beg, curse, give advice, and praise. In the brief midsection of Psalm 34 a wisdom teacher offers advice about the desire for a long life (verse 12), deceitful speaking (verse 13), evildoers (verse 16), the righteous (verse 17), and about the brokenhearted and those crushed in spirit (verse 18). These themes are well known from the book of Proverbs and other wisdom literature.

One of the qualities of being human is the ability to sense when others suffer. The word sympathy means "to suffer with." Even when we see on television an image of mother weeping over the untimely death of a child, our spirit may be crushed. And when someone close to us suffers, our own hurt may be so great that we don't know how to say a word of comfort or hope to the victim.

The psalmists knew that the Lord is full of compassion. God has the attribute of sympathy. "The LORD is near to the brokenhearted" (verse 18). It is like saying that the universe is ultimately not unfeeling and unfriendly but redemptive. We may not understand many of the statements about God in the Bible, but we can be sure of God's unfailing sympathy in our suffering and that God is near to all the brokenhearted.

As you, O God, are full of compassion,
help me to show comfort to those in need. Amen.

AFFLICTIONS OF THE RIGHTEOUS

*W*hy bad things happen to relatively good people has bothered and perplexed human beings since the dawn of time—even long before the writing of the book of Job. We assume that things should balance out, that goodness should be rewarded and evil punished. The question is especially acute for those who believe in the justice and power of God. God's justice presumes the *desire* to set things straight, and God's power presumes the *ability* to do so. But we know from experience that justice often is not implemented in this world.

The psalmist acknowledges that good behavior in itself does not bring an untroubled life of good fortune. "Many are the afflictions of the righteous" (verse 19); they can be "brokenhearted, and ... crushed in spirit" (verse 18), their trust in life shattered. Such an experience, however, can lead the despairing person to a profound realization of the nearness of God in the midst of depression. The LORD is there to rescue and to redeem the life of his servants—not to condemn them (verse 22).

In a striking phrase, the LORD "keeps all their bones; not one of them will be broken" (verse 20). Their physical life is protected from assaults of their foes. The expression reminds us of Exodus 12:46, which forbids the breaking of the bones of the sacrificed Passover lamb, and the Gospel of John cites the verse in referring to the unbroken bones of the crucified body of Jesus (19:36).

We can know peace when we accept the ambiguities of life, even while holding firmly to our trust in the goodness of God.

Keep me, O God, under the shadow of your wing. Amen.

DELIVERANCE FOR THE WEAK AND NEEDY

*P*salm 35 belongs to a frequently occurring subtype of the personal lament. This subtype is variously called "the cursing psalms," "imprecatory psalms," or "psalms of vengeance." In these psalms the poet freely expresses revulsion, disgust, and the desire for revenge against those who have injured or attacked him. These psalms often depict the aggressors as enemies not only of the psalmist but also of God (see "The Cursing Psalms," pages 380–382, below).

Psalm 35 consists of two laments (verses 1–10 and verses 11–28), each of which concludes with a statement of assurance of God's help in time of desperate trouble.

This psalmist is certain that he has been falsely attacked: "Without cause they hid their net for me; without cause they dug a pit for my life" (verse 7). In rage he calls on the LORD to take up arms—shield and buckler, spear and javelin—on his behalf (verses 1–3). He desires nothing for his enemies except "shame and dishonor" and that they be "turned back and confounded" (verse 4), pursued by "the angel of the LORD" (verse 6). This, the psalmist thinks, would be sweet revenge. When the enemies fall into the pit that they have devised for their victim, the psalmist "shall rejoice in the LORD, exulting in his deliverance" (verse 9).

As the wisdom writer says, there is, indeed, "a time to love, and a time to hate" (Ecclesiastes 3:8). It does little good to bottle up our hostility, pretending it isn't there. We should admit our hostilities, face up to them, and deal with them in a nonviolent way that does not perpetuate or even heighten the tension. Bring them to the Lord, who is willing to share our griefs and burdens.

Be with me, O God, in my anger; give me strength
and courage to rise above my indignation. Amen.

SCHADENFREUDE: "THEY GATHERED IN GLEE"

*T*he useful German word *Schadenfreude*, coined by Friedrich Nietzsche in 1895, has no exact equivalent in English, even though it refers to an almost universal human tendency. It is an emotion that nobody wants to own up to—the feeling of satisfaction over someone else's misfortune, especially that of a person we don't especially like or who has injured us in some way. The literal meaning of the word, "shameful joy," suggests that the feeling is a mixture of pleasure and guilt. We know that it is not right, but it arises within us nonetheless.

The lamenter in Psalm 35 has been falsely accused (verses 11, 20), mocked and reviled (verse 16), and his good efforts have been repaid with evil deeds (verse 12). Worst of all, however, he had to witness his enemies gathering "in glee" at his "stumbling" (verse 15). In treachery they rejoice over his plight, winking their eyes (verse 19), and arrogantly gloating (verse 21). Those who gloat have perhaps gone beyond *Schadenfreude*, making no attempt to conceal their glee but rather taking delight in rubbing salt into the victim's wounds.

Schadenfreude obviously affects personal relationships ("There but for the grace of God go I"; "Thank God it didn't happen to me"), but it is seen also on the larger scale of groups and nations. How can we rejoice over high "body counts" of the slain enemy or over the humiliation of conquered peoples? The psalmist was the object of the *Schadenfreude* of others. When we feel this emotion coming over us, we can do no better than to think of the Golden Rule: Do to others as you would have them do to you. Put yourself in the other's place.

God of grace, increase in me the ability to suffer
with those who suffer. Amen.

VINDICATION FROM GOD

*T*he two parts of this psalm (verses 1–10 and verses 11–28) exhibit typical components of the personal lament. These include graphic descriptions of the occasion (vicious attacks by personal enemies) and the cry, "How long, O Lord, will you look on?" (verse 17). Now, in verses 22–26, there is an extended, desperate plea to God for vindication and for deliverance from the taunts and plots of the enemies: "Do not be silent! . . . "Wake up! . . . Vindicate me, O Lord, my God. . . . Let those who rejoice at my calamity be put to shame and confusion." The psalm ends with a promise of praise to God that would follow the expected act of divine justice: "My tongue shall tell of your righteousness and of your praise all the day long" (verses 27–28).

When a well-known televangelist calls for the murder of a foreign leader who has done no harm to his people, we are taken aback. In our supposedly civil society we are embarrassed at overt and explicit calls for revenge, even when we might agree that the object of such feelings deserves no good. People in the biblical world had fewer scruples about such things. It was a culture dominated by the tension between honor and shame. The psalmist had been acutely shamed by vicious attacks and mockery. He brought his complaint to God, begging for the restoration of his honor and for shame on his enemies.

When responding to personal attacks, we, like the psalmist, can bring it to the Lord in prayer. In our prayer, however, we can include a petition that we be *freed* from the strangling desire for vengeance— which is what the word "forgiveness" basically means.

Deliver me from evil, dear God, and help me
to overcome thoughts of vengeance. Amen.

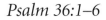
HUBRIS AND HYPOCRISY

*P*salm 36 is a mixture of wisdom words (verses 1–4), classic words from Hebrew prophecy in a hymn (verses 5–6), and a lament (verses 10–12).

The psalmist acknowledges the influence of leaders who flatter themselves, arrogantly thinking that their evil plots to gain power by character assassination and various kinds of mischief will never be exposed and brought to justice. They spend night and day thinking how they can suppress any and all opposition to their plans to enrich themselves and their friends at the expense of the poor. They might attend worship services and make a pretense of piety. But, in reality, "deep in their hearts, there is no fear of God before their eyes" (verse 1).

But the psalmist draws on the powerful imagery of the prophets to assure us that God's steadfast love operates on earth and in heaven, on land and on sea, and for humans and animals alike. (On God's care for animals—a rather rare sentiment in the Bible—see Psalms 104:14, 21, 27; 147:9.) This steadfast love manifests itself in "righteousness," just judgments, and saving acts (verses 5–6). The time will come when the evil plots of hypocritical leaders will backfire, and justice will once again prevail in the land.

At some points in their lives, most individuals face hostility on a personal level. Potentially more destructive, however, are national leaders with an inflexible ideology that seeks enrichment of the powerful at the expense of those who struggle for the necessities of life, all the time using deceptive slogans to neutralize critics and whistleblowers. But, the psalmist assures us, God's justice will ultimately prevail.

Your steadfast love, O Lord, extends to the heavens.
Your righteousness is like the mighty mountains. Amen.

LIGHT AND LIFE

*D*rawing on several classic images, the psalmist reiterates the praise of God's providence and protection and then concludes with a plea that God will continue these blessings in the future.

For the psalmist, God's protection emanates from the temple in Jerusalem, "your house" (verse 8). There, in the holy of holies, the priests envisaged the God of the universe enthroned above the wings of the cherubim, which were outstretched over the Ark of the Covenant. "All people may take refuge in the shadow of your wings" (verse 7). And there they might feast on the fat and flesh of sacrificed animals (verse 8). And there in the temple area—at least symbolically—is the "fountain of life" (verse 9; Jeremiah 2:13 refers to "the fountain of living water"), another image for the presence of God among the people.

Finally, the petitioner acknowledges that "in your light we see light" (verse 9). Light, the first thing created in Genesis 1, is one of the most central aspects of God in the Bible. For the ancients, without electricity or any other good means of nocturnal illumination, the darkness of a moonless night was profound, even though the starlight could be amazingly beautiful (something not many North Americans in the twenty-first century experience). Darkness would continue to be associated with death for centuries to come, and the classic text of Christian requiems includes the prayer for "light everlasting" for those who have died.

The light of God is "the light of your face" (Psalm 4:6; 89:15), the assurance of divine presence in the midst of our sorrows. This brings with it the certainty of God's eventual triumph over all manifestations of evil. No matter what comes our way in this world, we can do no better than to invest our hope in the grace of God.

O God, make your face to shine upon me. Amen.

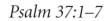

ON TRUST
AND PATIENT STILLNESS

*T*he rather lengthy Psalm 37 consists entirely of wisdom sayings such as can be found in the book of Proverbs. These proverbs—arranged in acrostic form—have been collected by a man advanced in years who has had wide experience of life (see verse 25). Patient trust in God's ultimate defeat of evil is the theme that pervades the entire psalm.

Verses 1–2 advise godly persons not to fret over the wicked or be envious of them. Do not let sinners negatively affect your inner life—even if they have power over your outward existence. The psalmist is certain that sin will have its consequences, and the wicked will certainly wither like grass in the hot summer sun.

Verses 3–4 stress the positive attitude that the pious should cultivate: "Take delight in the LORD and do good"—that is, trust and obey, have faith and do good.

Verses 5–7 encourage the godly to "commit your way to the LORD . . . wait patiently for him." These verses inspired the great hymn writer Paul Gerhardt, in the midst of war and personal tragedies in 1656, to write the hymn "Commit Thou All that Grieves Thee" (*Befiehl du deine Wege*):[9]

Commit thou all that grieves thee and fills thy heart with care
    To him whose might and glory the starry skies declare.
Possess thy soul in patience, be firm in God's employ,
    And thou in radiant beauty shall see the Sun of joy.

The psalmist's advice is summed up in contemporary form in the prayer attributed to Reinhold Niebuhr:

O God, grant me the serenity to accept things I cannot change,
    courage to change things I can,
    and wisdom to know the difference. Amen.

ANGER THAT LEADS TO EVIL

*T*he psalmist displays an acute understanding of the psychological workings of anger. There is a moral risk in continuing to fret over the wrongful deeds of others. Do not fret—it leads only to evil (verse 8). If we cannot let go of anger at those whom we think intend to injure us, our indignation—even if righteous—can unwittingly put us in the same place as those who sin against us.

Almost every day we learn in our news media of violent acts committed by persons who are filled with anger—anger at individuals over specific, perceived wrongs like teenagers being bullied at school or anger at the general injustice of the world. It is not only terrorist types or religious fanatics who operate from anger but also ordinary people in our midst. Anger management has become a cottage industry.

How can we deal with anger that wells up within us? First, remind yourself that anger usually hurts us more than the object of our anger; it can cause both mental anguish and physical illness. Then direct your attention to physical or mental activities that take your mind in other, more healthful directions. Finally, as the psalmist reminds us in speaking of the LORD's derisive laughter (verse 13), when we keep in mind that God will eventually overcome all forms of evil, we are able to "let go and let God." The New Testament word for forgiveness literally means "let go." Those who learn to let go are the meek who shall inherit the land (verse 11), as Jesus promised in the Beatitudes (Matthew 5:5).

*Forgive me my sins, O Lord, as I forgive those
who sin against me. Amen.*

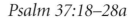

"THE LORD LOVES JUSTICE"

The psalmist tells us, "I have been young, and now am old, yet I have not seen the righteous forsaken" (verse 25). On the basis of personal experience, he insists that the blameless will abide forever (verse 18) and that the wicked will perish and vanish "like smoke" (verse 20). The righteous are blessed with model families, and their children never have to beg (verses 25–26). These repeated assertions might seem to us in the twenty-first century to be a bit hollow. We have seen too much injustice, too many innocent victims of violence, and too many martyrdoms. Even our psalmist acknowledges that the righteous might have down days ("though we stumble, we shall not fall headlong," verse 24).

At the heart of verses 18–28, however, is a basic biblical principle: "the LORD loves justice" (verse 28a). For our psalmist, as for the book of Proverbs, God's justice requires that goodness be rewarded and evil punished. This conviction is the basic interpretive device throughout the historical books of the Old Testament. But the prophets, the book of Job, and the teachings of Jesus suggest a different approach. They acknowledge the reality and the force of injustice in this world, and they commiserate with those who suffer unjustly. They know that bad things can happened to good people, even though they cannot understand why this is the case. In the midst of injustice they work for the increase of justice, knowing that "the LORD loves justice."

God's justice is to be mirrored in our concern for the welfare of the poor, the widow, the orphan, the hungry, those who mourn, the sick, the dying, and all those who face the extremities of life. We hope for the ultimate triumph of justice over injustice. In the meantime, we seek to make our faith active in works of righteousness.

*O God, may your will be done on earth, as it now is being
done in heaven. Amen.*

"WAIT FOR THE LORD"

*H*ere again we find a sharp contrast between "the righteous" and "the wicked." While the wicked have hatred so strong that it leads to thoughts of murder (verse 32), the righteous "utter wisdom" and "speak justice," because "the law of God is in their hearts" (verses 30–31; Jeremiah 31:31–34 speaks about the future, when the law would be written on the heart). For the pious Israelite, the concept of the law (*torah*) of God is the basis of all true spirituality. The law (the Pentateuch as a whole? Deuteronomy in particular?) includes promises of protection from enemies (verse 33) and the inheritance of land (verse 29), among other things. These two promises recur in verse 34, and they are the reason for the psalmist's advice, "Wait for the LORD."

Many who read verse 34 will think of the solo in Felix Mendelssohn's oratorio *Elijah*, which includes the words, "O trust in the Lord, wait patiently for him. . . ." This counsel comes during a time of great conflict in the history of Israel, namely, the attempt by Queen Jezebel to replace the worship of the LORD with her native Phoenician worship of the Baals. Although utterly despondent and despairing over the persecution unleashed by Jezebel, Elijah retires to the holy mountain where the law was given to Moses, there to remain in isolation until God provides renewed strength and confidence.

Sometimes, in the midst of turmoil and uncertainty, what is most difficult to do is to do nothing. To be sure, it is not always good to respond in this way. But part of maturity is to recognize when we have done all that we can and then to leave the rest to God. This is a central component of what it means to have faith.

*Merciful God, increase my trust and strengthen
my inner being for the trials of life. Amen.*

THE SOURCE OF SALVATION

Some persons have read Psalm 37 as though it were a theoretical statement justifying the ways of God in this world. God punishes the wicked and rewards the righteous; there is no such thing as innocent suffering. A few readers have called this idea "faith in retribution." It is easy to find such thoughts in this psalm, which includes typical contrasts between the wicked and the righteous that we find in wisdom literature.

A close look at verses 35–36, however, reveals that something much simpler might be involved here. The psalmist does not articulate a general theory of justice but rather reflects on what has happened to specific individuals known to him. He has seen arrogant persons oppressing others who were later brought to nothing—who simply vanished. Conversely, he has seen peaceful individuals blessed by descendants (verse 37). The knotty and unsolvable problem of innocent suffering is not brought to the fore.

In any case, the psalmist is certain of the source of his refuge and strength. "The salvation of the righteous is from the LORD; he is their refuge in the time of trouble" (verse 39). Although he uses the third person plural pronoun "they," the psalmist speaks for himself; he gives his personal testimony to the providence of God, as he has done throughout the psalm.

There are times in our lives when we turn to God by default. When you are in deep anguish, suffering a tragic loss, you are not in the mood for philosophical speculations on the question of justice. You need to know where to find consolation. In such times, echoing the words of the old gospel song, you ask "Where can I go but to the Lord?"

O Lord, you are my refuge in time of trouble;
save me from the time of trial. Amen.

DEPTHS OF DESPAIR

*A*s in Psalms 6 and 22, the psalmist lays bare the agony of his body and the anguish of his soul over a dreadful illness. Arrows have sunk into him (verse 2), there is no soundness in his flesh or bones (verse 3), his heart throbs (verse 10), and the light has gone out from him (verse 10). The references to his wounds festering and growing foul (verse 5) and to the burning of the flesh (verse 7) suggest that the man was suffering from leprosy. This would also explain why his friends, companions, and neighbors "stand aloof . . . far off" from him (verse 11). The torment of his illness is compounded by social ostracism.

Like many who undergo extreme suffering, the psalmist expresses the feeling of being pushed down, crushed, with a heavy weight on him (verses 3, 4, 6). Perhaps worse than this mental depression is the feeling that he is being punished by God for his sins: "My iniquities have gone over my head" (verse 4; also verses 1–2, 5). The assumption that sickness is punishment for sin—a view held both by the psalmist and by his acquaintances (verse 11)—was widespread at the time. The victim who holds this view suffers not only from a dreadful physical illness, mental depression, and social ostracism, but also from overpowering guilt.

When faced with personal tragedy, we think, "What did I do to deserve this?" We don't want to think that life doesn't make sense. But wait. Didn't Job protest the idea that his suffering was the result of his sin (Job 3–31)? And didn't Jesus say that God sends sun and rain on the wicked and the righteous (Matthew 5:45; see Luke 13:1–5; John 9:2–3)? In the depths of despair, let us turn to the true source of comfort.

> *O Lord, all my longing is known to you;*
> *my sighing is not hidden from you. Amen.*

CONFESSING INIQUITY

We now learn that the sufferer is not only socially ostracized but also the object of evil plots by enemies who seek his ruin. So strong is this threat and so debilitating his illness and depression that he is "ready to fall" (verse 17).

But, like the servant of God in Isaiah 53:7, the victim steels himself to be deaf and mute before his oppressors. He pretends not to hear them and refuses to respond to their taunts. Instead, he turns inwardly to God for rescue (verses 15–16). In his desperate plea the psalmist confesses his sin, giving voice to the traditional idea that his personal sin is the cause of his suffering. This repentance, he believes, will remove an obstacle that hinders God's action on his behalf. He ends his lament with the plaintive words, "Do not forsake me, O LORD; . . . make haste to help me, O LORD, my salvation."

In traditional church liturgy Psalm 38 is one of seven "penitential psalms" (Psalms 6; 32; 38; 51; 102; 130; 143), that is, poems in which the psalmist acknowledges and expresses sorrow for his sins. In this case the repentance is motivated by the thought that his sin has caused the traumas he is undergoing and that, when the sin is covered or removed, his life can be restored. Better it is to acknowledge our sins of omission and commission simply because that is the right thing to do—without regard to the hope for reward for our confession.

Do not forsake me, O Lord; O my God,
do not be far from me. Amen.

LIFE IS BUT A DREAM

*A*s a teenager I smiled when I heard my 93-year-old grandfather comment about the brevity of life (he lived another ten years). As the years pass, however, his remark becomes less amusing. Popular songs dwell on this theme: "Is that all there is?" "Life is but a dream." Blaise Pascal asked, "What is man within the natural world? A nothingness in the presence of infinity" (*Pensées* 2.72). Some ancient Israelites had the proverb, "Let us eat and drink, for tomorrow we die" (Isaiah 22:13).

The shortness of life is a common lament among the sages and psalmists of ancient Israel. Job complains that "A mortal, born of woman, few of days and full of trouble, comes up like a flower and withers" (Job 14:1–2.) The prophet laments that "All people are grass . . . ; the grass withers, the flower fades . . ."(Isaiah 40:6–8). See also Job 9:25–26 and the comments below on Psalm 90:5–6, 10.

Psalm 39 laments that life is "fleeting," "a few handbreadths," "a mere breath," "like a shadow" (verses 4–6). There is a slight note of sarcasm in verse 5, "My lifetime is as nothing in your sight." Job also complained about the shortness of life, but then he said, almost blasphemously, that his death would be an escape from God's scrutiny: "For now I shall lie in the earth; you will seek me, but I shall not be" (Job 7:21).

We cannot live well constantly thinking about death. But the knowledge that we are here temporarily, as sojourners, should focus our minds on what is important and not on the petty annoyances of life. Yes, "this is the first day of the rest of your life." Let us thank God and make the most of it.

I bless you, O God, for life and for the good things
that enrich my days. Amen.

"WHAT DO I WAIT FOR?"

The Worldly Hope men set their Hearts upon
Turns Ashes—or it prospers and anon,
Like Snow upon the Desert's dusty Face,
Lighting a little Hour or two, is gone.
>—Edward Fitzgerald, *The Rubáyát of Omar Khayyám* (1859)

He who has a *why* to live can live with any *how*.
>—Victor Frankl, *Man's Search for Meaning*

*T*heologians remind us of the need to distinguish between ultimate concerns and those that are penultimate. Our psalmist asks—rhetorically—"And now, O Lord, what do I wait for?" Of course, he knows what is the ground of his future: "My hope is in you" (verse 7). Part of the reason for his expression of hope is the fact that he is convinced that God is the cause of his sickness (which he does not specify): "It is you who have done it" (verse 9). His hope therefore is that God will "remove your stroke from me" (verse 10), and bring healing.

We would do well to make a list on paper, putting our hopes in descending order. The hope to win the lottery would be far down on the list, as would ideas on how to keep up with the neighbors. Higher on the list should be opportunities to improve relationships, work for justice, and find ways to encourage children and youth to develop into mature and compassionate adults. At the top of the list, our psalmist would urge, would be our confidence in our creator and sustainer.

> *And now, O Lord, what do I wait for?*
> *My hope is in you. Amen.*

TO AVERT GOD'S SCRUTINY

*T*he psalmist accuses God of punishing a person's sins by destroying what is most precious to a person—health and life itself. It is not that the punishment is undeserved, but that it is severe and destructive. God, he says, is like a moth consuming what a person holds dear. He follows this complaint with a triple plea that God act: "Hear my prayer . . . ; give ear to my cry; do not hold your peace . . ." (verse 12).

The final lines of the psalm consist of two remarkable thoughts. (1) The psalmist claims to be a "passing guest, an alien, like all my forebears" (verse 12b). We might think that he was a foreigner who attached himself to Israel. But we find this same thought in Psalm 119:19. Most striking is the close parallel in the Chronicler's formulation of David's last prayer: "For we are aliens and transients before you, as were all our ancestors; our days on the earth are like a shadow, and there is no hope" (1 Chronicles 29:15). Does the Chronicler's prayer have a literary connection with Psalm 39?

(2) The downward spiral of the psalm continues to the end. The final words are an unexpected and shocking request for God to leave him alone!—quite different from the plea in verse 12a for God to hear. "Turn your gaze away from me, that I may smile again, before I depart and am no more" (verse 13). This reminds us more of Job (see Job 7:19) than of one who trusts in God's providence. But anyone who has gone through the valley of the shadow of death will resonate with the honest emotion of this psalm. Sometimes we must go through the depths before we can speak of light and hope.

O Lord, I am a guest and a sojourner in this life.
Give me hope in the midst of despair. Amen.

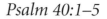

FROM MIRY BOG TO NEW SONG

Compared with the pessimism of Psalm 39, how refreshing and how welcome is the change of tone in the first verses of Psalm 40! After a long period of patient waiting and pleading, God gave this psalmist a "new song . . . a song of praise to our God" (verse 3). It is as though the LORD pulled him up out from the mud on the bottom of a well and set him on solid rock (verse 2). The prophet Jeremiah was thrown into a cistern after predicting—in the presence of the national leaders—the destruction of his nation: "Now there was no water in the cistern, but only mud, and Jeremiah sank in the mud" (Jeremiah 38:6).

The "new song" will lead many to trust in the LORD (verse 3), and that will increase the well-being of the community. So the poet turns in verse 5 from the first-person singular ("O LORD *my* God") to the first person plural ("your wondrous deeds and your thoughts towards *us*"). Our prayers deal with our personal welfare, but they continue on to importune God regarding the common good of our neighbors.

The "new song" in the mouth of the psalmist is not some new musical style but rather the melody of joyous celebration that contrasts with the "old song" of lament and woe. It is not a boastful song but one that centers on the community of faith to which the psalmist belongs. Johnson Oatman Jr. (1856–1922) put the psalmist's testimony of verse 2 into poetic form in his gospel song:

> *Lord, lift me up and let me stand,*
> *By faith, on heaven's table land,*
> *A higher plane than I have found;*
> *Lord, plant my feet on higher ground. Amen.*

NOT SACRIFICE,
BUT DOING GOD'S WILL

*T*he book of Leviticus includes laws requiring various sacrifices and offerings, each of which has a different function: burnt offerings (1:1–17); cereal offerings (2:1–16); peace offerings (3:1–17); sin offerings (4:1—5:13); and guilt offerings (5:14—6:7). These—some of them bloody—were overseen by the priests and offered at the temple in Jerusalem, where also most of the psalms were sung.

It is therefore striking that Psalm 40:6 asserts not only that God does not desire these offerings but also that God has not required them. Similar statements were made by several prophets (Isaiah 1:10–14; 66:3; Jeremiah 7:21–22; Hosea 6:6; Amos 5:21–25; Micah 6:6–8). This verse proves that there was not an unbridgeable gulf between the prophets' version of true worship and that of the temple singers in Jerusalem. Both Jeremiah and Ezekiel were from priestly families.

If the grateful worshiper is not to make a sacrifice or offering to God, what should he do? Instead of an animal or gift of cereal, he is to present himself: "Then I said, 'Here *I* am . . .'" (verse 7). What does the LORD require? Not sacrifices, but the whole person—a sentiment expressly stated by Paul in Romans 12:1: "Present your bodies as a living sacrifice, holy and acceptable to God, which is your rational worship" (adapted).

The "book" the psalmist refers to (verse 7) is probably not a written song of thanksgiving that he presents in the temple but rather the "book of the law" (see 2 Kings 23:8–13) that was current in his day. The psalmist delights to follow the precepts in this book (verse 8) and tells of his great deliverance in the midst of the worshipers (verse 9).

I worship you, O God, with my thoughts,
words, and deeds. Amen.

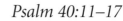

HAVING A BAD DAY

*W*hen someone says to an acquaintance of mine, "Have a good day," he responds with tongue in cheek, "I have other plans."

Our psalmist has been caught in a downward spiral; he has hit bottom. The evils that encompass him are "without number," corresponding to the number of his iniquities, which are "more than the hairs of my head" (verse 12). His lament reminds us of the "confessions of Jeremiah" (for example, Jeremiah 20:7–18), who also was cast into a cistern, the bottom of which was muddy and stinky (see verse 2 of this psalm: "the desolate pit . . . the miry bog").

But hitting bottom sometimes is the beginning of new life. The sufferer in desperation turns for help to the LORD (verses 13, 16–17), pleading also for vindication in the face of his enemies (verses 14–15). One of the slogans of the twelve-step program associated with groups like Alcoholics Anonymous is, "Let go, let God." Let go of your futile attempts at self-healing, let go of your pride and attempts to save face, and let go of your attempts to blame others for your troubles. Sometimes hitting bottom is necessary before renewal can begin. Turn, then, to the God of all mercies, who understands our motivations and our childish need to look good. Lay yourself bare before the God of all comfort, renouncing your pride, and discover again the unconditional grace of God, where we find solace and restoration.

Let your steadfast love, O God, keep me safe forever. Amen.

PREFERENCE FOR THE POOR

*T*alk about going against popular opinion! Our psalmist pronounces the poor and the sick happy, asserting that the LORD protects them and sustains them during illness. In everyday reality, however, we know that poverty is anything but a blessing. A Swahili proverb asserts, "When poverty crosses the threshold, love flies out the window." Poverty is not sought but endured.

The psalmist does not pray to become destitute. His words reflect his personal experience. Although not wealthy, he has experienced the blessings of God, being sustained on his sickbed and delivered from a debilitating illness. His words come close to irony: God shows partiality toward the poor; even they—perhaps *especially* they—know the blessings of God in daily life.

The prophets and Jesus also repeatedly proclaimed God's preference for the poor: "Blessed are you who are poor, for yours is the kingdom of God" (Luke 6:20). These words reflect a deep-seated hope that justice will ultimately prevail for human beings and throughout the cosmos. It is not yet a reality in our societies, but people of faith can devote their energies to examine the causes of poverty and also to relieve the suffering that poverty brings to uncounted multitudes in industrial countries as well as in the developing world. Mother Teresa is an admirable model. Her life centered on a simple belief: "The poor are our brothers and sisters . . . people in the world who need love, who need care, who have to be wanted" (1975).

Help me, O God, to empathize with those who struggle
for bread, and keep me from condescension
when I am able to help. Amen.

AN UNFAITHFUL FRIEND

$\mathcal{P}$salm 41:13 is not an original part of this psalm but rather the conclusion of the first "book" in the collection of psalms (see page 377, below). Verses 4–12 are a lament that centers on the shunning of a man who was desperately ill.

The psalmist in verses 1–3 had spoken of God's care and blessing of the poor and those in deep distress. He now turns to his own case ("As for me . . ." verse 4), and his case is one of extreme despair. In his prayer for healing he acknowledges his sinfulness (verse 4), even as his enemies anticipate his death and the eradication of his memory (verse 5). They "utter empty words" and "whisper together about me," phrases that suggest that they engage in a kind of sorcery against him. They are sure that the victim will die.

Much worse, however, was the desertion of his "bosom friend in whom I trusted, who ate of my bread" (verse 9). There are few experiences in life more debilitating than that of shunning, especially by someone who you thought was a loyal and faithful friend. Jeremiah experienced this (Jeremiah 20:20; 38:12), and Psalm 41:9 is quoted in John 13:18 with regard to Judas's betrayal of Jesus.

The victim writes his lament after experiencing healing, which he attributes to God's blessing (verses 11–12). Not all victims of shunning will have such a happy outcome. But where can we go in our despair but to the LORD? God's grace is the ultimate word for every one of us.

O Lord, be gracious to me, and raise me up. Amen.

THIRSTING FOR GOD

Commentators agree that Psalms 42 and 43 form a unit (note the refrain repeated in 42:5, 11 and 43:5). The two psalms are a lament by one whose pilgrimage to the Jerusalem temple has been prevented by illness.

The initial image in the psalm is that of a deer desperately looking for water in a riverbed in the dry season, a riverbed called in Palestine a "wadi." The image fits the hilly area of northern Galilee. Thirst is a powerful biological drive. Without water a person can die within a very few days. Our psalmist thirsts for God. His "soul" (*nephesh*, inner being) "longs" for God, especially to "behold the face of God" (verse 2). The metaphorical language suggests that the lamenter had planned to journey to the temple in Jerusalem, where, he believed, God's presence was particularly localized.

At the moment, however, this thirst was not quenched. Tears have come both day and night, and his unnamed acquaintances taunt him, "Where is your God?" (verse 3). Why does God not come to his aid? Why does God prevent him from journeying to the holy place in Jerusalem?

At some critical times in our lives, when we desperately long to sense the presence of God, we experience only God's absence. Those are the times when we need to concentrate on past blessings and on the certainty that God's inner essence is nothing but grace. What is more satisfying than a cool cup of fresh water to a parched mouth? And what is more life-renewing than a sense of God's shining face?

My soul thirsts, O God, for you; my soul longs for you. Amen.

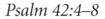

THE RENEWAL OF HOPE

*T*he psalmist lived in the north, in "the land of Jordan and of Hermon, from Mount Mizar" (verse 6). The Hermon mountain ridge is often snow-capped; it lies about twenty-five miles west-southwest of Damascus and thirty miles south-southeast of the Sea of Galilee. On the slopes of the verdant mountain, cataracts thunderously descend (verse 7) to form the Jordan River. The precise location of Mount Mizar is unknown, although it probably refers to one of the peaks on the Hermon ridge.

From this scenic location the poet recalled how he had gone with throngs of pilgrims to a festival at the temple in Jerusalem, "the house of God." There he experienced the presence of God, and he joined the great multitude in "shouts and songs of thanksgiving" (verse 4).

During his lament, the psalmist pauses to have a conversation with himself (verse 5), a refrain that recurs in 42:11 and 43:5: "Why are you cast down, O my soul, and why are you disquieted within me? Hope in God; for I shall again praise him." He directs his plea to "the God of my life" (verse 8), and this is the fount of his hope. His sickness—so he hopes—is not unto death; he will recover and he "shall again praise him" (verse 5), presumably in the Jerusalem temple.

The life of most people consists of the alternation between despair and hope, even though each person will have a unique balance between the two. "Into each life some rain must fall," as the old song has it. But we have some control over how we respond to our experience of the depths. Let us do all that we can and leave the rest to the grace (the "steadfast love," verse 8) of our God.

My soul is cast down within me, and therefore
I remember you, O God. Amen.

Psalm 42:9–11

"WHY HAVE YOU FORGOTTEN ME?

*T*he frequently occurring biblical image of God as rock recurs here (verse 9). This is consistent with the thoughts of cataracts in the rocky slopes of Mount Hermon (the top ridge of which reaches up to 9000 feet), the area where the tribe of Dan settled (verse 7). But the poet complains, "Why have you forgotten me?" (verse 9). He is in dire straits. He appears to have a "deadly wound" in his body; verse 10 could also be translated, "While my bones are being crushed. . . ." He fears that he is in a life-threatening situation.

In addition to his physical suffering, however, the petitioner is mocked, taunted, and oppressed by his enemies, who never tire of asking him, "Where is your God?" (verses 9–10). The enemies assume that the poet's illness has come from God, and the poet himself cannot think otherwise. God, he assumes, has forgotten him (verse 9).

Almost every person of faith has experienced the absence of God in times of despair. Even Jesus on the cross, quoting Psalm 22:1, cried out that he was forsaken by God (Mark 15:34). When we sink into despair, we can and should turn to friends and, at times, professional counselors. But through it all, let us repeat the psalmist's refrain: "Why are you cast down, O my soul? . . . Hope in God." Let us turn to our help, our rock, and the object of our hope.

Be with me, O God, when I am
disquieted and cast down. Amen.

LIGHT AND TRUTH LEAD TO GOD'S PRESENCE

*P*salm 43, the final stanza of the poem now separated into Psalms 42–43, begins with the demand for vindication "against an ungodly people . . . who are deceitful and unjust" (verse 1). Vindication in this context would mean recovery from sickness, interpreted as intervention by God.

The psalmist continues to hope to make a pilgrimage to the temple mount in Jerusalem, where God's presence is localized—"to your holy hill and to your dwelling" (43:3). He would approach the altar in front of the building, where animals were sacrificed, and there "praise you with the harp" (verse 4). (His musical talents are not mentioned elsewhere in Psalms 42–43.)

In order to accomplish this pilgrimage the poet prays that God would "send out your light and your truth; let them lead me; let them bring me to your holy hill" (verse 3). Light is the essential character of the creator, the first act of creation (Genesis 1:3), a symbol of God's presence. The appeal to God's truth or, differently translated, "faithfulness," is a claim on God's promise of deliverance to the pious sufferer.

The beautiful poem (Psalms 42–43 as a unit) concludes with the familiar refrain, "Why are you cast down, O my soul?" (verse 5).

This ancient poet is a model of piety for us. He does not shrink from complaining about misfortune. He begs and pleads with God. But he interrupts his lament with a thrice-repeated refrain in which he reminds himself that if he hopes in God he need not be cast down or disquieted within himself.

Send out your light and your truth, O God;
let them lead me. Amen.

THE ACTION OF GOD IN THE AMBIGUITY OF HISTORY

*A*lthough Psalm 44 is a lament, it begins much like a hymn that celebrates God's actions in past history, especially the Israelite conquest of Canaan. God has driven out the nations and planted the psalmists' ancestors in their land (verse 2). The invasion succeeded, so the psalmist asserts, not because of the power of the Israelites' weapons but because of God's mighty act of deliverance (verses 4–8). The psalm singer reminds God of these acts of deliverance in the past and pleads for God to act now after a humiliating defeat at the hands of enemies (see verses 9–16).

The psalmist expresses no trace of concern about the morality of the conquest of Canaan—the use of the sword to seize the territory of other people—or any sense of the suffering caused by the invasion. He takes for granted that the conquest was a gracious and saving act of God.

Persons of faith have always sought evidence of God's actions in history. We are accustomed to speak of "divine Providence" and to think that the will of almighty God must certainly be evident in what happens on Earth. But some, like Martin Luther, believed that history is at best an ambiguous revealer of God. We usually find in history only the hidden God, traces and tracks of God's presence. The essence of God, said Luther, is most clearly revealed not in the sweep of history but rather in the work and fate of Jesus, who for Christians is the revealer of God par excellence.

Deliver us as a people, O God, from self-righteousness,
and let us find our security in you. Amen.

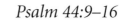

NATIONAL DISGRACE

*G*raphic images of military disaster in Psalm 44:9–16 convey a sense of extreme despair. The army retreated in the face of the enemy ("turned backed," verse 10) after suffering a slaughter. The foes looted their possessions, took hostages, and sold the survivors into slavery among various foreign peoples (verses 11–12). Added to the death and destruction was the shame and disgrace that fell on the Israelites: they were the objects of taunting, derision, and scorn, and they became a laughingstock among the neighboring peoples (verses 13–16).

Our psalmist assumes without any doubt that God has caused the military disaster, and he does not shrink from hurling startling accusations against God: "You have not gone out with our armies. . . . You made us turn back. . . . You have sold your people for a trifle . . . (verses 9–12).

Although some fundamentalist leaders in the United States wondered whether the horrors of 9/11 were allowed by God because of supposed moral lapses on the part of a few Americans, Western persons no longer so quickly assume that military or natural megadisasters are "acts of God." Our world is not perfect, and we can never find an adequate explanation as to why human beings and other living creatures sometimes die in catastrophes of mass proportion. We can only pray that, whatever falls our way in this life, God will be with us and, in the end, will triumph over all forces of destruction.

Open my eyes, O God, to the suffering of our time;
strengthen my hands to help. Amen.

GOD'S HIDDEN FACE

*A*ll of us seem to be born with the feeling that if we are good persons we do not "deserve" to experience severe suffering. This is especially true if we believe that God *wants to* intervene and also that God *is able to* help.

Our psalmist bitterly protests God's silence during a military tragedy that befell his people. "All this has come upon us, yet we have not forgotten you . . . our heart has not turned back, nor have our steps departed from your way" (verses 17–18). Even more bluntly, the psalmist asserts that it is God who has caused the horrifying defeat of the army in a desert place ("the haunt of jackals," verse 19): "Because of you we are being killed all day long, and accounted as sheep for the slaughter" (verse 22; Paul in Romans 8:36 applies this verse to the persecution of Christians).

The petitioner demands to know, "Why do you hide your face?" (verse 24). God remains aloof from the people's suffering as they "sink down to the dust" (verse 25). The psalm ends with the piteous cry, "Rise up, come to our help. Redeem us for the sake of your steadfast love" (verse 26).

The question of God and human suffering has tormented the minds of Jews and Christians for many centuries. Unspeakable tragedy has led some to take the path of agnosticism. Many more, however, remain confident that the steadfast love of God will always be the basic principle of the universe, and this conviction sustains them through all the trials of earthly life.

Redeem me, O God, for the sake of your steadfast love. Amen.

APRIL 14 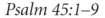 *Psalm 45:1–9*

A RIGHTEOUS RULER

On the occasion of a royal marriage this "royal psalm" praises the virtues and attributes of the king (verses 2–9) and his bride (verses 10–15). The psalmist begins and ends this song of joy with a note of personal delight ("my heart overflows") in singing their praises (verses 1, 17).

Exuberance and exaggeration characterize the descriptions of the king. He is "most handsome of men," with a notable gift for diplomatic discourse (verse 2) and for prowess in battle (verse 3). He is full of gladness, being clothed in wondrously scented garments, listening to beautiful music in ivory palaces, and being served by daughters of foreign kings (verses 7–9). Most important, however, the king fights for truth, justice, equity, and righteousness. Because his priorities are straight, God has anointed him, and the king's line will therefore endure forever (verse 6), a thought that harks back to the reign of David (see Nathan's words in 2 Samuel 7:16).

Verse 6, "Your throne, O God, endures for ever and ever," might reflect the ancient tendency to apply titles of divinity to the king (compare Isaiah 9:6, "Mighty God"). Or we might translate, "Your throne! It is of God, forever and ever."[10] (Hebrews 1:8 transfers the words to Jesus.)

Why should a royal marriage poem be included among the Psalms? Two considerations are important: (1) The ancient Israelites never thought of separating religion and politics—or religion and economics or religion and any part of culture. The rule of God encompasses the whole of the people's lives. (2) The king, like his people, stands under the rule of God, and the king therefore must work for justice, truth, and equity among his people. It is not enough that he claim to have a religious experience or be able to say the right things. He too must walk the walk.

Lord God, give us faithful leaders who work for justice
for all the people. Amen.

105

A ROYAL WEDDING

*W*ith these verses we have an inside glimpse into the life of the palace as the bride is carefully prepared to meet her bridegroom, the king.

She is mentally prepared: The bride is a princess of Tyre, a leading city of Phoenicia just north of Palestine, the homeland of Queen Jezebel. (The first line of verse 12 is difficult to translate, but the Hebrew refers to the "daughter of Tyre.") She is to forget her father's house and direct her allegiance and subservience to her mate, her new king (verses 10–11). She will receive magnificent gifts from the wealthy of the world (verse 12).

She is personally groomed and dressed, with gold-embroidered, many-colored robes and attended by a bevy of virgins, and she then finally enters the palace of the king (verses 13–15), who looks forward to becoming the father of children (verse 16).

Jews and Christians of prior centuries have at times puzzled over the fact that the Bible includes poetry that celebrates the union of man and woman, most notably in the Song of Songs ("Song of Solomon"). Some Jewish interpreters have insisted that such erotic poems are to be read as allegories of the love of God for Israel, and Christian allegorists have suggested that they refer to the love of Christ for his church. There is no need to engage in such flights of fancy. Ancient Israelites usually had a healthy respect for marriage and the raising of children. We do well to rejoice in good relationships between husband and wife and between parents and children.

Keep me steadfast and honorable, O God,
in my relationships with those I love. Amen.

A MIGHTY FORTRESS

*T*he mountains shake, and more than two hundred thousand people perish in an earthquake of devastating scope. The waters of the sea roar and foam, and whole cities are wiped off the face of the earth in a gigantic tsunami. At the same time, nations are in an uproar and tyrants topple.

In the midst of unspeakable natural disasters and calamitous wars, the psalmist lifts his eyes to the distant future—to an ideal society, a city of God, where a peaceful stream flows and where God dwells. There is in Jerusalem the brook Kidron, which flows during the winter rains, and there is the Gihon spring that runs into Hezekiah's tunnel, but the psalmist imagines a glorious, restored, and re-created city—a new Jerusalem. This psalm is thus a "song of Zion" (see Psalm 137:3), a hymn that praises the presence of God's glory in the holy city, Jerusalem. Isaac Watts expressed the psalmist's confidence:

> Let mountains from their seats be hurl'd
> > Down to the deep, and buried there,
> Convulsions shake the solid world—
> > Our faith shall never yield to fear.[11]

"God is in the midst of the city" (verse 5), and God will therefore help it, even when the nations are in an uproar. God utters his voice, and "the earth melts" (verse 6). For the psalmist and his fellow worshipers, therefore, "God is our fortress and strength" (verse 1, literally translated; see also verse 7, "the God of Jacob is our fortress"). This image is famously set to poetry in the words of Martin Luther:

> A mighty fortress is our God,
> > A sword and shield victorious;
> He breaks the cruel oppressor's rod
> > And wins salvation glorious.

Be for me, Lord God, a very present help in trouble. Amen.

JUDGMENT AND A TIME TO DESIST

$\mathcal{T}$he psalmist invites us to imagine the distant future—the ultimate "works of the LORD" (verse 8), the final judgment. God makes an end of all warfare and causes total disarmament of the nations (verse 9). The poet envisages much more than the small kingdom around Jerusalem; it is a picture of universal scope, presided over by the God of the nations—not just of Israel.

And what is the role and task of the worshipers of God during this world-historical upheaval? We are to "be still and know that [Yahweh] is God" (verse 10). This is not a time for the talking heads of think tanks to devise political-military schemes for nation building. It is not a time for hand-wringing and desperation. Nor is it a time for hopeless withdrawal. It is a time to recognize the work of God in bringing an end to human misery. It is a time to desist from our frenzied attempts at good works and to praise God, the creator of universal peace (not only in the holy land), who is then "exalted among the nations" (verse 10).

Violence has characterized the human race since the time of Cain and Abel (or the cave men, if you prefer). Tribalism, competition, fratricide, and war have plagued our species to an extent greater than that of many lesser animals. But the best among us have drawn our attention to a better world, one in which wars cease to the ends of the earth and a peaceful humanity recognizes that God is exalted among the nations. Until that becomes a reality in our world, we rejoice that God is our fortress (verse 11).

O God of Jacob, be for me a mighty fortress. Amen.

THE UNIVERSAL KING

*W*ith no object other than that of rendering praise to God, Psalm 47 is an "enthronement psalm," a hymn that glorifies the LORD as king over all the earth. This claim of God's universal sway is repeated several times ("all you peoples," verse 1; king over "all the earth," verses 2, 7; "king over the nations," verse 8; and to him belong "the shields of the earth," verse 9).

There is, however, a nationalist strain here as well. The hymn is sung by Israelites, and they rejoice that God has given them the land ("he chose our heritage for us," verse 4) by military conquest ("he subdued peoples under us, and nations under our feet," verse 3). And the poet looks forward to the time when all the world's leaders will join the Israelites in recognizing the true God, the God of Abraham: "The princes of the peoples gather as the people of the God of Abraham" (verse 9).

How do we balance universalism and particularism, nationalism and humanitarianism? How can we hold our most profound beliefs in a pluralistic culture, in which we cannot expect that everyone will join our church or accept our beliefs? Thinking that our denomination, our political party, or our nation has a unique claim on God's good pleasure is no longer convincing. The age of triumphalism is no more. The best course is to express our convictions, thank God for our many blessings—including our religious freedom—and let God worry about the rest.

With joy, O Lord, I look forward to your universal reign
of peace and justice. Amen.

THE BEAUTIFUL CITY

*P*salm 48 is a song of praise for Zion, the holy city, Jerusalem, "the city of our God" (verse 1). The most curious statement is that its location is "in the far north" (verse 2), even though Jerusalem is actually located in the southern part of Palestine. Many commentators believe that the psalmist has taken over a widespread belief among the Canaanites and Phoenicians, that Zaphon (which means "north") was the "mountain of the gods." Israelites in northern Palestine would have viewed with awe the lofty range that included Mount Hermon to the north, almost always snow covered.

But our psalmist speaks of Mount Zion, a hill in Jerusalem that came to be also an image used for the entire city. (That Jerusalem is intended is clear from the mention of the temple in verse 9 and Judah in verse 11.) This holy hill is "beautiful in elevation"; it is the "joy of all the earth"—the center of the earth, as later Jewish writers would have it; and it is "the city of the great King" (verse 2). As such, many Jerusalemites believed, it was invincible from foreign attack. And so the psalmist, in a piece of rhetorical bravado, imagines foreign kings assembling for war and approaching Jerusalem. As soon as they see beauty and strength of the city, they fall into panic and flee away trembling (verses 4–7).

Alas, we know from history that Jerusalem—like all the cities of the world—was not impregnable. In horrendous slaughter it was taken by the Babylonians in 587 B.C. and again by the Romans in 70 A.D.—to list only two. We have on earth no lasting city, but we look for the new Jerusalem, our eternal habitation.

Great are you, O Lord, and greatly to be praised. Amen.

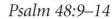

THE JOY OF WORSHIP

*T*he psalmist continues his ode to Jerusalem, concentrating especially on the temple (verse 9) and the defenses of the city (verses 12–13). In the temple the worshipers reflect on God's steadfast love—God's unconditional grace toward the people (verse 9). They especially praise his sacred name, Yahweh, usually translated as "the Lord" (see verse 1).

The worshiper urges everyone to take a walking tour of the city—probably not a liturgical procession but an inspection of the city's defenses. "Count its towers, consider well its ramparts; go through its citadels" (verses 12-13). These military fortifications, the psalmist asserts, are evidence of God's protection of the city throughout the generations (verses 13–14).

Unlike most areas of the world, we in North America have been spared the horror of foreign invasion of our territory and the destruction of our cities. (The tragic events of 9/11, so incredibly shocking and world-changing for us, did not result in the occupation of our land.) Military invasion was an ever-present threat in the ancient Near East, and Palestine lay as a buffer between the great empires of Egypt and Mesopotamia (present-day Iraq). It is therefore not surprising that the psalmist in Jerusalem praises God for the towers, rampart, and citadels of his city.

Military threat in our time is of a vastly greater scope than the ancients could imagine. The arms race squanders the wealth of the nations, and small countries vie for the acquisition of nuclear weapons. How much more should we put our trust not only on our defenses but on the steadfast love of God, whose grace reaches beyond one people to all peoples and all nations (verse 10).

I ponder your steadfast love, O God; let it overcome
the hatred and violence among tribes and nations. Amen.

LIFE IS BEYOND PRICE

*R*eferences to "wisdom," "meditation of my heart," proverbs, and riddles (verses 3–4) make it quite clear that Psalm 49 falls into the genre of wisdom literature. The speaker is not God nor someone speaking in the name of God but a wisdom teacher who wishes to transmit what he has learned through the difficult and varied experiences of real life.

The sage begins by summoning his audience, "all inhabitants of the world, both low and high, rich and poor" (verses 1–2). He then announces the theme: Why should you fear rich and powerful men, even when they set out to persecute you? Their wealth cannot save them from the Great Equalizer, namely, death. They cannot ransom their life and avoid going down to "the Pit" (verse 9, translated in the New Revised Standard Version as "the grave"). They can't take their wealth with them.

No human society in the history of the world has experienced such a glut of worldly goods as we have in North America today. Many families are not satisfied with only two automobiles for their "McMansions," and they need extra garage space for their "toys." We live in a consumer society and are urged to think that our inner needs can be filled by acquiring more and more things. And we are able to ignore the masses of humanity who go to bed hungry and work for one dollar a day.

Our psalmist's thoughts are similar to the word of Jesus, "Take care! Be on your guard against all kinds of greed; for one's life does not consist in the abundance of possessions" (Luke 12:15).

Keep me, O Lord, from the shallowness
of living for things. Amen.

FACING DEATH

*T*he similarities between Psalm 49 and the book of Ecclesiastes are striking. Death comes to the wise and the fool alike (verse 10; compare Ecclesiastes 2:12–16). Every human being, no matter the status, perishes like animals (verse 12; compare Ecclesiastes 3:19: "The fate of humans and the fate of animals is the same; as one dies, so dies the other . . ."). Those who are self-satisfied in this world will be like sheep whose shepherd is death; their eternal home is Sheol, the realm of shadows associated with the grave (verse 14).

But then comes verse 15—an enigmatic ray of hope in a dismal context. "God will ransom my soul from the power of Sheol." "Soul" (*nephesh*) is not an immortal component of our humanness but the life-force that expires at our last breath. The psalmist is not referring to his automatic survival of death. What then?

The phrase "for he will *receive* me," uses the same Hebrew verb as in Genesis 5:24, "Enoch walked with God; then he was no more, because God *took* him." Did our psalmist believe that, as Enoch was taken to the presence of God, so also he would be "received"? We think also of the prophet Elijah at the end of his life ascending to the presence of God in a chariot of fire (2 Kings 2:11).

Our psalmist expresses the faith—and the hope—that God will seize his life-force from the maws of Sheol and take him into the divine presence. Even death and Sheol cannot remain in the face of God's steadfast love for his own.

We who live on the after-side of Easter confess that Jesus also was taken up by God. And we confess that such is the ultimate fate of all those who put their faith in God.

When my last hour comes, O God, receive me
into the eternal habitation. Amen.

Psalm 50:1–6

JUDGMENT

*P*salm 50 does not fit the major genres of psalms (see pages 369–373, below). The body of the psalm, verses 7–21, is in the form of a prophetic oracle (God is the speaker), sandwiched between verses 1–6, a theophany, and verses 22–23, a concluding admonition to the worshipers.

Some of the most majestic passages in the Bible depict the overpowering manifestation of God's glory and majesty to human beings—a literary form called theophany. Such texts often refer to natural phenomena such as fire, earthquakes, lightning, thunder, darkness, and the human response of dread and awe. God's appearance to Abram in Genesis 15:12–17 involved "deep sleep," "terrifying darkness," "a smoking fire-pot and a flaming torch." The making of the covenant at Mount Sinai involved a thick cloud, trumpet blasts, the mountain being wrapped in smoke, and the appearance of "the glory of the LORD . . . like a devouring fire" (Exodus 19:16–25; 24:15–18). See also Isaiah 6 and Habakkuk 3.

Our psalmist prepares the people for words of judgment by appealing to the overpowering glory of God: God comes like "a devouring fire, and a mighty tempest all around him" (verse 3). God comes for the purpose of judging his own people, his "faithful ones, who made a covenant with me" (verse 5).

All biblical writers assert that God is just. Abraham asked God, "Shall not the Judge of all the earth do what is just?" (Genesis 18:25). Ancient persons, fearing punishment, sometimes found this to be a terrifying truth. But others realized that God accomplishes justice primarily in saving events, destroying evil and creating the conditions for redemption and renewal. God paradoxically reveals his justice by acting in grace toward finite and erring humans. Thanks be to God!

Help me, O God, to balance justice
and mercy in all my doings. Amen.

THE DESIRED SACRIFICE

*T*here are great differences between the priestly and the prophetic approach to spirituality. In general terms, priestly religion centers on liturgical acts, impressive forms of worship, and properly conducted rituals. Prophetic religion centers on implementing the will of God for justice and humanity in everyday life. Our psalmist today speaks of the relative value of the worship of God by means of animal sacrifices.

The ancient Israelites developed and practiced several kinds of animal and cereal sacrifices, each with a specific function. Some of them were thank offerings, some were to expiate sin, and others seem to have the main function of fellowship among the worshipers and between them and God. These sacrifices are described in Leviticus 1—7. No one knows why the ancients first practiced animal sacrifice. (Genesis 8:21 and Leviticus 1:17 crassly assert that the Lord smelled the "pleasing odor" of the sacrificed animals.)

Unlike the prophets (Isaiah 1:10–17; Amos 5:21–24; Micah 6:6–8), our psalmist does not call for the abolition of animal sacrifice (verse 8). But he does ridicule the practice. "If I were hungry, I would not tell you. . . . Do I eat the flesh of bulls or drink the blood of goats?" (verses 12–13). What then does God require of us? Micah insists it is to "do justice, and to love kindness" (Micah 6:8). Our psalmist mentions two things: (1) render thanks to God from your whole being (verse 14) and (2) bring to God your troubles and concerns; rely on the goodness of God for your ultimate well-being.

Take my life and let it be consecrated, Lord, to thee. Amen.

THE DESTRUCTIVE POWER OF WORDS

*A*ccording to the old proverb, slander always sticks—if it is repeated often enough. The victim can never get rid of all of its traces. Anyone who has been the object of slander or gossip knows that words have the power to destroy, and the effects are long-lasting.

Out psalmist draws a contrast between the words of God and the malicious words of the wicked. The wicked recite God's statutes (verse 16). Which statutes? The psalmist mentions three of the Ten Commandments: stealing, adultery, and false witness (verses 18–20). Yes, the wicked are able to recite the commandments accurately, but they have not allowed them to guide their conduct. Instead, they have "cast my words behind you" (verse 17).

Ignoring the words of God, the wicked have given their "mouth free rein for evil," (verse 19) even slandering their own sibling (verse 20). They have spoken in deceit (verse 19), seeking to elevate themselves at the expense of their brother.

God had remained silent during their gossip sessions, but "now I rebuke you, and lay the charge before you" (verse 21). The justice of God might seem slow in coming, says the psalmist, but it will come. And it comes in two forms: for those who forget the commandments that they have memorized "there will be no one to deliver [them]" (verse 22). But those who engage in proper worship and "go the right way" will see the "salvation of God" (verse 23). Let us not only talk the talk but also walk the walk.

> *On my heart imprint your image, O God, that my life*
> *might reflect your goodness. Amen.*

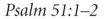

INVOCATION: OVERCOME BY GUILT

*P*salm 51, a personal lament, is the most profound analysis of sin and renewal in the Old Testament. It consists of an invocation, a confession, a supplication, and a dedication.

The invocation, verses 1–2, is a cry for mercy. The psalmist three times appeals to the character of God: (a) "Have mercy" suggests the image of a young camel being weaned and taken away for training; the mother is in a state of frenzy; she refuses food and tries to break her bonds. (b) "Steadfast love" (*hesed*) refers to God's faithfulness to the covenant promises. (c) The term translated "abundant mercy," from the Hebrew noun for "womb," suggests motherly love. Hebrew expressions of divine love often are drawn from terms for maternal emotions.

The psalmist, overcome by guilt, uses three synonyms to describe his condition: "transgression," willful rebellion against the law; "iniquity," a state of distortion or bending; and "sin," missing the mark, falling short of the goal. Corresponding to this are three synonyms for pardon: "blot out, "wash," and "cleanse."

The psalmist is in an acute state of disorientation. He desperately longs for wholeness, and he knows that this requires cleansing. He does not identify the sin he has committed, but it has come to be an obsession, dominating his thought day and night. He knows what he has done, but he knows also that the God he worships is a God of mercy and steadfast love. No human comforter, no matter how solicitous, can renew his life. It must come from God.

Lord, have mercy. Amen.

CONFESSION: SIN AGAINST GOD

$\mathcal{T}$he psalmist attempts no evasion of responsibility whatever. Although he knows what he has done, he does not inform us: "I know my transgressions. . . ." This feeling of guilt has become an obsession; he cannot get rid of it: "My sin is ever before me" (verse 3).

The confession, "Against you, you alone, have I sinned," does not indicate that he had committed a cultic offense that did not involve other human beings. It is instead similar to David's confession after committing adultery with Bathsheba: "I have sinned *against the* LORD" (2 Samuel 12:13; the superscription of Psalm 51, which asserts that this psalm is David's confession at that occasion, is remarkably apt). Sin is a transgression of a command from God, and thus all sin is against God, whether it has injured another human being or not.

"Truth in the inward being" (verse 6) also includes recognition of just penalty. "You are justified in your sentence" (verse 4, quoted in the same sense by Paul in Romans 3:4–5). When we stand before the ultimate Judge, we can offer no excuses.

Theologians have had a field day with statements like verse 5: "Indeed, I was born guilty, a sinner when my mother conceived me." But the psalmist is not articulating any theory of original sin nor of the supposed evil of the act of procreation. His overwhelming sense of guilt causes him to admit that his entire life has exhibited a tendency to rebel. His thought reminds us of Job's lament: "How then can a mortal be righteous before God? How can one born of woman be pure?" (Job 25:4; compare Job 14:1, 4; 15:14).

How can such a weight of guilt be removed? The psalmist knows (see the following verses).

In my finitude and weakness, O God, allow me a glimpse
of what I can be. Amen.

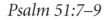

SUPPLICATION: THE JOY OF FORGIVENESS

*I*n a series of petitions alternating between negative and positive, the guilt-obsessed person now turns to the sole hope for renewal and restoration. Verses 7, 9, and 11 are negative, while verses 8, 10, and 12 are positive.

Graphic images from ritual practices are used. "Purge me with hyssop" (verse 7)—probably a clump of marjoram, used in the ritual cleansing of lepers or of those ceremonially polluted by contact with a corpse. Forgiveness means purification.

"Wash me"—lustrations of various kinds are prescribed in the book of Leviticus for the removal of ritual impurity. Snow is a recurring image for purity in Old Testament poetry (see, for example, Isaiah 1:18), although it was a rare occurrence except for the higher elevations, like Mount Hermon.

The psalmist's guilt so permeated his being that he speaks of it as the crushing of his bones (verse 8). (Jeremiah's compulsion to speak the words of Yahweh was "something like a burning fire shut up in my bones; I am weary with holding it in, and I cannot," Jeremiah 20:9.) In desperation, the psalmist pleads that his guilt be hidden and blotted out—expunged as from a criminal record (verse 8). That would be the way to joy and gladness.

Guilt and shame are two debilitating emotions. While shame is the fear of what others think about you, guilt is the awareness that you have acted contrary to your own principles. If you are to regain a productive life, guilt must be removed.

When my shortcomings overwhelm me, Lord God,
show me the way once again to joy and gladness. Amen.

A CLEAN HEART

Philosophers have debated whether human nature is perfectible. Is the human race gradually becoming morally better? Are we evolving toward a species superior to what we now are? Our psalmist thinks otherwise, and the gruesome history of the past one hundred years suggests that he was right. What is needed is not improvement but replacement, the creation by God of "a clean heart" within us (verse 10).

The prophets looked forward to the time when God would accomplish a change of heart among the people. Jeremiah knew that "the heart is devious above all else; it is perverse" (Jeremiah 17:9) and that God one day would write his law on the human heart, assuring that God's will would then be kept without training and struggle (Jeremiah 31:33). And Ezekiel, in an echo of the words of our psalm, conveys this promise of God: "A new heart I will give you, and a new spirit I will put within you" (Ezekiel 36:26).

The psalmist's prayer for a clean heart and a new spirit reflects the belief that not only salvation but also the possibility of good moral life should be considered a gracious gift of God. He prays to be infused with the holiness of God's very spirit so that he can once again know the joy of "salvation," that is, the gladness that accompanies the sense of fellowship with God.

In the midst of disorientation let us pray for a new orientation so that we too can regain a sense of the presence of God and the joy of salvation.

Restore to me the joy of your salvation, O God,
and sustain in me a willing spirit. Amen.

DEDICATION: TESTIMONY TO SINNERS

*I*f God would blot out the offender's iniquities, then he can turn his attention to others. In the community he will proclaim his new-found salvation and invite others also to bring their guilt before the Lord. Personal salvation leads to concern for the community.

The request "Deliver me from bloodshed, O God" (verse 14) juts into the context. The Hebrew term translated "bloodshed," if read with different vowels (the original Hebrew text has no vowel indicators), can be translated "silence," so that the meaning would be, "Deliver me from dumbness, and enable me to sing aloud of your deliverance." This makes good sense in the context of the stanza.

But it is possible also that the psalmist has committed an act that deserved capital punishment. Once again the superscription of the psalm, which identifies it as David's confession of sin after his adultery with Bathsheba, is strikingly appropriate. David arranged for the military death of Bathsheba's husband, Uriah the Hittite. He was guilty of bloodshed. According to the narrative in 2 Samuel 12—19, David's sin brought temporal punishment. The child born from the adulterous union died, and David and his family experienced severe tragedies, including a civil war fomented by his son Absalom. According to 2 Samuel, God nonetheless continued to bless the errant king.

Whichever way we translate the text, it is a powerful reminder that God's mercy has no end, and renewal always remains a possibility. The natural response of such experience of grace is to rejoice and "sing aloud of your deliverance" (verse 14).

When I am bowed down in guilt and despair,
keep me mindful, O God, of your grace. Amen.

PRAISE, NOT SACRIFICE

*W*hat form should our thanksgiving to God take? The psalmist was familiar with the variety of sacrifices and offerings—of animals, birds, cereal grains, or libations— at the temple in Jerusalem. Some of the sacrifices were for thanksgivings. Others, like the burnt offering (verse 16) were for atonement of sin and guilt (see Leviticus 1, especially verse 4). But the psalmist, like the poet of Psalm 50:8–15, knows that these rituals—however impressive or bloody—were not enough to please God. Such practices might be used in the futile attempt to manipulate God. Instead, "the sacrifice acceptable to God is a broken spirit" (verse 17). (Verses 18–19 are generally thought to be an appendix added to soften the anti-sacrifice language.)

Renewal takes place when we realize who we are and what we have done—when we confront our failures and bring them in contrition to God. A magnificent service of worship, perhaps with the powerful music of J. S. Bach, can move us toward faith. But true piety can never be complete when we have constructed our liturgies or composed our creeds most carefully. Purity of heart is required.

The prophets never tired of calling us from outward expressions of religious piety to inner integrity and a life of justice. Isaiah asserted that "bringing offerings is futile," but "learn to do good; seek justice, rescue the oppressed" (Isaiah 1:13, 17). Amos issued a classic protest: "Even though you offer me your burnt-offerings and grain-offerings, I will not accept them. . . ." He then gets to the heart of the matter: "But let justice roll down like waters, and righteousness like an ever-flowing stream" (Amos 5:22, 24). Such prophetic words are fully in line with Paul's advice, "Present your bodies as a living sacrifice, holy and acceptable to God, which is your spiritual worship" (Romans 12:1).

*Heal me, O God, from my brokenness, and let my life
be a thank offering. Amen.*

BOASTING BEFORE THE FALL

Complaining about braggarts is a tricky business; it can backfire. Our psalmist bitterly vituperates against a powerful evildoer (verses 1–5), and he looks forward to the downfall of the presumptuous boaster when the righteous will rejoice and mock (verses 6–7). But then the psalmist proceeds to boast about his own piety—and has the audacity to present his boast to God! It reminds us of the comment by Alexander Pope in his *Essay on Criticism* (1711):

> Of all the causes which conspire to blind
>> Man's erring judgment, and misguide the mind,
> What the weak head with strongest bias rules,
>> Is Pride, the never-failing vice of fools.

Is the psalmist's certainty of the downfall of the boaster well founded? The relation between pride and power in Western politics in recent years has resulted in much damage to the common good. Politicians of all stripes use half-truths, innuendo, and character assassination to gain positions where they can affect the well-being of millions of people. The psalmist's complaint about someone whose "tongue is like a sharp razor," who works treachery, and who loves "evil more than good, and lying more than speaking the truth" (verses 1–2) seems like part of a political campaign. As with the psalmist of old, we cry out, How long, O Lord?

Pride often goes before destruction (Proverbs 16:18). But sometimes the "vice of fools" persists far too long.

Cleanse my thoughts and my words, O Lord. Amen.

Psalm 53:1–3

HUMAN FOLLY

*T*his poem is almost identical to Psalm 14, except for parts of verse 5 and also that the divine name Yahweh, translated "the Lord," occurs in Psalm 14 but not in Psalm 53. This poem was apparently transmitted in two traditions.

In ancient Israelite thought, *theoretical* atheism was not a real option. That God stands over the universe was not questioned. But *practical* atheism—living *as though* there is no God—was perhaps just as common then as it is now. Many are the examples in biblical tradition of persons who thought in their hearts that they could avoid God's scrutiny or could escape God's judgment. Such persons, asserts our psalmist, are fools (verse 1).

Like Paul in Romans 1:18–32, our psalmist suggests that the refusal to recognize God's rule leads to moral corruption. Bad theology produces bad morals (verse 1).

More striking, however, is the assertion that this condition afflicts the entire human race: "They have all fallen away; they are all alike perverse; there is no one who does good, no, not one" (verse 3). Are all, then, fools? Does the psalmist exempt himself? More likely he is thinking as did Diogenes of ancient Athens, who went around with his lantern, looking for one honest person, or perhaps of Jeremiah, who looked in each block of the city of Jerusalem to see whether he could find "one person who acts justly and seeks truth" (Jeremiah 5:1).

We tire of hearing bad news. But we know that, in the end, there is God, and at the end therefore we will celebrate the joy of salvation.

Let me seek wisdom, Lord God, to discern the path
of truth and justice. Amen.

JUDGMENT ON THOSE WHO MALTREAT OTHERS

One of the difficulties we have in reading the Bible is the great distance in time and in culture between the authors and their communities, on the one hand, and our twenty-first century Western life, on the other. Letter writers refer to specific problems and situations that both parties were aware of but which we have to reconstruct. So also we are not informed of the specific occasion for the complaint in many of the psalms of lament.

Psalm 53 refers to "evildoers, who eat up my people as they eat bread, and do not call upon God" (verse 4). Who are they, and what are they doing? We cannot know for sure, but they seem to be Israelites preying on their own people. The psalmist thinks that they should be calling on God, and he asserts that God has already rejected them (end of verse 5). Their retribution will bring great terror that involves military disaster: "God will scatter the bones of the ungodly [or 'the aggressor']" (verse 5).

This psalm combines features of wisdom literature and the tradition of the prophets. If the evildoers had any knowledge, they would call on God for deliverance in the face of military threat. But they have none. As the prophets did in their time, so the psalmist accuses the leader of the nation of abusing those in their charge (verse 4). This would indeed be a strange but powerful part of the liturgy for a temple service.

A society's ruling class can become so corrupt that reform does not suffice and divine action is required. Our psalmist concludes with a fervent prayer that things would change, that deliverance would come from Zion, with God restoring the fortunes of the people (verse 6). We also pray for honest and just leaders.

Lord God, raise up for our nation honest and faithful servants
of the public good. Amen.

THE NAME OF GOD UPHOLDS MY LIFE

*T*he psalmist in this lament appeals to the power of God's name, which, according to verse 6 in Hebrew, is "Yahweh," usually translated "the LORD" (see note 5). One of the Ten Commandments forbids us to take this name in vain (Exodus 20:7, "the name of Yahweh your God").

The divine name is associated with power ("might," verse 1) and "faithfulness" (verse 5). The prophet Jeremiah praises God's name with strikingly similar words: "There is none like you, O Yahweh; you are great, and your name is great in might" (Jeremiah 10:6; the same thought occurs in 16:21). This power is what the petitioner needs as a defense against the "insolent" who have risen against him; they are "ruthless" (verse 3). And—most especially—"they do not set God before them" (end of verse 3), which means that their impiety, their ignoring of God, is the cause of their evildoing.

The psalmist, however, is so certain that the LORD will come to his aid that he sings of the defeat of the enemies as though it has already happened: the LORD "has delivered me from every trouble, and my eye has looked in triumph on my enemies" (verse 7).

There might have been a touch of magic in the ancient Israelite's reverence for the name of God. But, certainly, Western culture has gone much too far in the other direction. We have grown accustomed to vulgar language in our popular culture and in everyday conversation. Although good manners cannot be equated with religious piety, we know that becoming sensitive to our use of language can have an effect on the quality of our lives. Words have power, and language affects behavior.

Hallowed be your name, O Lord. Amen.

THE WINGS OF A DOVE

Yet again we read of a person hard beset and in dire distress. The "clamor of the wicked" (verse 2) has resulted not only in severe emotional distress but also in physical symptoms for the petitioner. The psalmist cries out, "My heart is in anguish within me. . . . Fear and trembling come upon me, and horror overwhelms me" (verses 4–5). Compare Jeremiah: "My anguish, my anguish! I writhe in pain! Oh, the walls of my heart! My heart is beating wildly; I cannot keep silent" (Jeremiah 4:19).

This man is in a tunnel and cannot see the light at the end. His city is raging with violence and strife, and the wicked who have seized control of the city walk about on its walls (verses 9–10), looking for anyone who would threaten them. Is the writer thinking of Absalom's capture of Jerusalem from his father, David (2 Samuel 15—17)? We cannot know. In any case, the ruin of the city is imminent; depravity, oppression, and fraud have gained the upper hand in its midst.

What is one to do? Our psalmist would flee to the wilderness and find shelter from the raging wind and tempest (verse 8). "O that I had wings like a dove! I would fly away and be at rest. . . . I would lodge in the wilderness" (verses 6–7).

Such is the cry of everyone who feels trapped in an irreparable, hopeless situation. It then seems as though the only rational thing to do is to give up, drop out, and let destruction run its course. But the person of faith cannot leave the world to its deserts. Even when hope is fading, let us remember that the earth is the Lord's, and all that is in it.

Give ear to my prayer, O God; consider my plea
and renew my hope. Amen.

BETRAYED BY A FRIEND

Of all experiences in life, betrayal by a trusted friend is one of the most difficult to bear.

Because of his preaching of judgment, Jeremiah found himself increasingly isolated until finally his close friends turned against him, seeking his downfall (Jeremiah 20:10). Similarly, our lamenting psalmist describes an intimate friendship: "my equal, my companion, my familiar friend, with whom I kept pleasant company" (verses 13–14). They had worshiped together in the house of God, but now the friend has joined the enemies. From his enemies he could hide (verse 12), but how can he deal with treachery?

Betrayal by a close friend is devastating. It produces a feeling of worthlessness for having trusted an untrustworthy person. It foments anger and depression. It raises questions about our judgment. Because of the intimate friend's knowledge of our situation, such betrayal has great potential for further damage.

The betrayed psalmist turns to God, but with what language! He curses them to "go down alive to Sheol" (verse 15). In ancient Israelite thought, Sheol was the grave, around which might hover the specters or shadows of the dead. But here the thought perhaps includes also the idea of punishment for the "evil [that] is in their homes and in their hearts" (verse 15). So also, Jeremiah prayed that his enemies "will not succeed" and that "their eternal dishonor will never be forgotten" (Jeremiah 20:11).

Can we do better, even in the extremity of betrayal by a friend? We can perhaps not rid ourselves of our negative emotions, but we can keep in mind that revenge is counterproductive. The word "forgiveness" in New Testament Greek means to "let go"—not necessarily to have a change of emotion. If we can let go of such experiences we can move beyond the betrayal.

Help me, Lord God, to let go of the hurts that have
come my way. Amen.

"CAST YOUR BURDEN UPON THE LORD"

$\mathcal{F}$elix Mendelssohn, in his oratorio *Elijah*, addresses the comforting words of Psalm 55:22 to the despairing prophet:

Cast thy burden upon the Lord, and he shall sustain thee.
He never will suffer the righteous to fall:
>he is at thy right hand.
Thy mercy, Lord, is great and far above the heav'ns:
Let none be made ashamed that wait upon thee.

The psalmist was betrayed by his closest friend, violating a relationship of trust—a covenant—using deceptive and misleading talk, "speech smoother than butter, but with a heart set on war" (verse 21). To whom could he now go?

The betrayed person turns to the LORD in round-the-clock complaining and moaning (verse 17). He expresses confidence that God will hear and save him and at the same time cast his enemies "into the lowest pit" (verse 23).

Of the large number of laments in the book of Psalms, it would be interesting to know how many of the sufferers were vindicated—how many were rescued from their suffering. Even today many pious persons believe in Providence, certain that their prayers will have their desired effect. Experience teaches us that such is not always the case. Bad things do happen to good people, even to people of faith. Because we can never know why this is the case, we can do no better than to cast our burdens upon the Lord and, with the psalmists, pray for God's sustaining presence.

In the day of trouble, sustain me, O God,
with your presence. Amen.

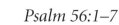

BE NOT AFRAID

*A*s with many others, the superscription of this psalm specifies the tune to which it was to be sung: "The Dove on Far-off Terebinths" (or "The Dove of Silence, Far Off"). We know little about the melodies of ancient Israel, but they had a well-developed music tradition. The meaning of the Hebrew word *Miktam* is uncertain, although it probably indicates a kind of psalm to be sung softly, as a murmur.[12]

This lament has two parts, verses 1–7 and verses 8–13, with a similar refrain in the middle of each (verse 4 and verses 10–11).

The psalmist uses many verbs to describe his enemies' behavior: they trample, oppress, fight against, seek to injure, stir up strife, lurk, watch his steps, hope to have his life (verses 2–6). All their thoughts are against him for evil (verse 5). But neither the identity of the enemies nor the specific cause of their hostility is indicated.

The psalmist puts on a brave face: "I am not afraid; what can flesh do to me?" (verse 4). "Flesh" in the Old Testament refers not to the body in contrast to the soul but to the frailty of human existence in contrast to the glory of God. There is no undue exaggeration of the power and cunning of the enemy. They are human and participate in human weakness.

When we walk through the storm, it might not be enough to hold our head up high and whistle in the dark. The poet appeals to the grace of God (verse 1). That is also our refuge.

Be gracious to me, O God, in the midst of distress. Amen.

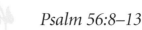

TEARS IN A BOTTLE

The petitioner finds some comfort from the thought that God remembers. The torments the psalmist has suffered are preserved by God in the scroll of life ("your record," verse 8; compare this concept in Job 19:23; Psalm 69:29; Malachi 3:16, "book of remembrance"). This means that, even if his sufferings become a "cold case," it is possible that he can eventually be vindicated. God has "kept count" of his tossings and, in a poignant phrase, has "put my tears in your bottle" (verse 8).

God remembers our sufferings and God cares. One day, so the psalmist asserts, God will act on his behalf and his enemies will retreat (verse 9). So certain is he of this outcome that he is prepared to make a thank offering for the deliverance of his soul from death. The psalmist, to quote Samuel Terrien, has

> the firm hope of walking in the constant presence of the divine deliverer. From then on, human existence becomes a life unspoiled by darkness. It is illuminated by a light without tenebrous horror. . . . The elation of the hero leads him not to flee a pursuer but to march on, to step up, and presumably to grow.[13]

Some of the days of our life are bright with optimism, joy, and hope. On others life seems to be a vale of tears. The psalmists knew both, and they did not flinch from bringing their trouble to the Lord.

Remember me, O God, and keep my feet from falling,
so that I may walk before you in the light of life. Amen.

"THE SHADOW OF YOUR WINGS"

*S*everal things are distinctive in this psalm compared with other individual laments.

The petitioner makes no protestations of innocence or claims of being falsely accused. He does not presume that God owes him something.

Most striking, there is no demand that God destroy the enemies, but only the calm assurance that God will do so (verse 3).

The psalmist uses imagery from nature to describe both his attackers and also God's protection of him. His enemies are like devouring lions, piercing with sharp teeth and hurling insults and obscenities like sharp swords (verse 4). In another image, a destroying storm passes by, but the poet takes refuge "under the shadow of your wings" (verse 1). (The image is not drawn from the wings of the cherubim in the holy of holies in the temple, which was a place of total darkness—no shadows—and does not fit the image of a storm.)

God is "Most High" (*Elyon*), a name that points to God's supremacy over the natural world (verse 2). Moreover, the refrain (verse 5), in poetic parallelism, speaks of God's glory over the heavens and all the earth.

In this compelling lament, the psalmist is certain of the effectiveness of God's "steadfast love and his faithfulness" (verse 3). God knows our needs before we ask. God has promised to stand by the faithful, and, so the psalmist asserts, God does not need to be reminded of promises made to the believer.

Let me be assured, O God, of your steadfast love
in the difficult times of life. Amen.

"AWAKE, MY SOUL, GIVE THANKS"

*T*his second stanza of the psalm ends with the same refrain as that of the first (verses 5, 11). Note also that the Hebrew word *Selah* occurs in both parts, and in both it marks a statement about the inevitable downfall of the attackers (verses 3, 6). Although the meaning of this word is uncertain, we can imagine that at these two points there would be a musical interlude in the performance of this psalm in the temple; it emphasizes the change of fortune.

The poet has a touch of humor—or at least irony. The enemies have dug a pit to capture the victim but they have fallen into it themselves (verse 6)! Again the past tense is used, so certain is the poet of the outcome of the struggle.

These verses are full of joy and confidence. The poet's heart is not palpitating; it is steady. He breaks into song and plays both harp and lyre through the night until the dawn (verse 7). He would then express thanks to God among the surrounding peoples (verse 9). The psalm ends by returning to terms and themes from the first stanza: steadfast love, faithfulness, and the refrain (verses 10–11).

We might think that this poet had read Norman Vincent Peale's classic book, *The Power of Positive Thinking*—a work that was often unjustly lampooned. Positive thinking is a tremendous asset in our course through life. It is quite different from Pollyanna saying, "All is for the best in this best of all possible worlds." It is based on confidence in God's steadfast love and faithfulness.

I give thanks to you, O Lord, for your faithfulness;
increase my faith. Amen.

ANATOMY OF ANGER

*W*hen you read this psalm you *should* be shocked. If you are not, read it again. This prayer for violent retribution on evildoers exhibits not a trace of mercy. The poet is clearly in a highly agitated state of mind. He asks God to "break the teeth in their mouths . . . let them vanish like water that runs away . . . let them be like the snail that dissolves into slime . . . like the untimely birth that never sees the sun" (verses 6–8). Then "the righteous," presumably including the psalmist, "will rejoice when they see vengeance done; they will bathe their feet in the blood of the wicked" (verse 10). (This reminds us of the general massacre that took place when the Crusaders captured Jerusalem in 1099 A.D.) Who is able to rejoice while standing up to the ankles in the blood of opponents?

The identity of the evildoers hinges on the way we translate verse 1. The Revised Standard Version and New Revised Standard Version both have, "Do you indeed decree what is right, you gods?" (changing the Hebrew *'elem*, "silence," into *'elim*, "gods"). But the original Hebrew text makes more sense: "Do you render justice by silence?" The psalmist has been (or knows someone who has been) the victim of grossly unjust treatment at the hands of a local judge. Instead of waiting to cool off, he wrote about unfair treatment from those who devise wrongs, deal out violence, speak lies, and play deaf like an adder.

Some commentators object to labeling this a "cursing psalm" and prefer to call it a wisdom psalm. But where in the Bible can you find more graphic cursing? The poet has a remarkable gift for cursing. We need not whitewash the language or turn it into something that it is not. This poet reminds us of Paul's words, "We do not know how to pray as we ought" (Romans 8:26).

Grant me, O God, a true vision of your justice;
help me to let go of bitterness. Amen.

ON DEALING WITH ENEMIES

*T*his lament has two parts, and each ends with a similarly worded refrain (verses 6–9 and 14–17).

The petitioner is sure that he is under a death threat (verse 3) from bloodthirsty, powerful persons (verses 2–3), even while he asserts that he has done nothing to deserve their wrath (verses 3–4). The enemies prowl around the city at night like packs of dogs (verse 6), thinking that no one will hear their howling (verse 7). Because the address of God as "Lord God of hosts" (*Yahweh, Elohim Sebaoth,* verse 5) is typical of the language of the temple in Jerusalem, it is clear that Jerusalem is "the city" of verse 6.

The psalmist appeals to God—and what does God do? God laughs at them (verse 8). Three times in the book of Psalms (and nowhere else in the Bible) we read of God's laughter, and each time it is a laugh of derision at the folly of powerful humans who think they are above the law (Psalms 2:4; 37:13; and 59:8). (Attributing human emotions to God—anthropomorphism—is a prominent feature of early narrative material, like Genesis 2—3, and of Hebrew poetry.) The psalmist anticipates the time when he will look in triumph on his enemies (verse 10).

The question of justice in our society as well as in our personal lives is generally less clear-cut than it appeared in the psalmist's vision of things. Is our nation's foreign policy pleasing to God? How can we be sure? Do I have pure motives in my treatment of coworkers, family members, and acquaintances? The psalmists offer a black-and-white world of right and wrong, but they sometimes miss the ambiguous nature of human existence.

O Lord, my strength, I will watch for you;
for you, O God, are my fortress. Amen.

WHEN WE CALL FOR VENGEANCE

*W*hen someone commits a vicious crime, there often is a heated discussion about capital punishment in our news media. Some folks wonder whether life imprisonment in a maximum-security institution would be a harsher punishment than death by lethal injection.

Our psalmist is so beset that he prays that his enemies not be killed immediately. They should be kept alive, at least for a while, so that what they have done will not soon be forgotten by the inhabitants of the land (verse 11). They can then receive their just deserts by being chased about ("totter," verse 11) in the wilderness, "trapped in their pride," consumed in wrath, and then, finally, slain (verses 12–13). All this would be a compelling and gruesome demonstration of God's rule over Jacob (verse 14).

In verses 14–17 the psalmist returns to the refrain. The enemies, the howling pack of dogs prowling through the city, will terrorize him no longer, for God is his fortress and refuge, and God's loving protection will remain steadfast.

The lamenting psalmists often needed to find a balance between their demand for vengeance and the larger scale of justice. But the prophets as well as Jesus call us to examine ourselves before we issue our call for vengeance. Life is ambiguous and confusing, and, in our passage through life, we learn that the larger virtues, like justice and truth, can be as hard to define as they are to implement.

O God, grant me a vision of what justice means in my life
and in my society. Amen.

PLEA TO THE LORD
OF NATIONS

The occasion for this national lament was a major military defeat of the Israelites—probably at the hands of the Edomites, to judge from the words of the king in verse 9, "Who will lead me to Edom?" The lengthy superscription of this psalm refers not only to the tune to which it was to be sung in the temple but also to the occasion, "when Joab," David's army general, "killed twelve thousand Edomites in the Valley of Salt." (This seems at odds with the statement in 2 Samuel 8:13 that David killed "*eighteen* thousand Edomites in the Valley of Salt.")

The military disaster is pictured in cosmic terms: "You have caused the land to quake"; there are cracks on the surface, and the land totters over the abyss (verse 2).

The psalmist appeals to God's promise for Israelite domination not only over the traditional Israelite region (Ephraim and Judah west of the Jordan River and Gilead and Manasseh in the "Transjordan") but also the neighboring lands of Moab across the Jordan, Edom to the south, and Philistia on the southern coast (verses 6–8), lands over which David and Solomon had ruled. The people wonder: Has God rejected Israel and reneged on promises? In the end, however, the worshipers in the temple express confidence that God will turn to help the people and "tread down our foes" (verse 12).

One commentator suggests that Psalm 60 offers "religious justification of real-estate patriotism,"[14] that is, a divine claim to territory belonging to other peoples. This kind of triumphalism was denounced by the prophets, especially Amos and Jeremiah, even though the same attitude was now and again taken over by Christendom. Patriotism is a virtue, but the attitude "My country, right or wrong" can never be a legitimate form of piety.

I pray for blessings on my country, O Lord, and I remember
those in other lands as well. Amen.

"THE ROCK THAT IS HIGHER THAN I"

*P*salm 61 begins as a lament but then includes a prayer for the king (verse 6)—an element of a royal psalm. It has two parts, the first beginning with "Hear my cry, O God," and the second with, "For you, O God, have heard my vows" (verses 1, 5).

The psalmist cries to God "from the end of the earth" (verse 2), that is, from the point when the landmass ends and falls precipitously to the deep. He has reached the end of his rope. The petitioner would find higher ground—"the rock that is higher than I" (or "too high for me," verse 2, end). The poet then speaks as a pilgrim traveling to the temple in Jerusalem (using the ancient expression, "your tent"), where he would seek shelter under the outstretched wings of the innermost room in the sanctuary (verse 4). The temple precincts stood on a rocky prominence, perhaps the "rock that is higher than I." There he would honor the sacred name, Yahweh (verses 5 and 8).

The prayer for the king intrudes suddenly, causing readers to wonder whether verses 6–7 are inserted here from a previously separate poem. The Jerusalem sanctuary was closely associated with the royal line, and many psalms take the form of prayers for the king. But the combination of personal lament and royal psalm is nonetheless surprising. For the psalmist, the success of the king assures protection against his enemies.

Christians have composed songs and hymns that look to Jesus as "the rock that is higher than I." That is fully in line with the early Christian concept of Jesus as the new temple (as in John 2:19–21).

> *Lead me to the rock that is higher than I,*
> *for you are my refuge, O God. Amen.*

"ROCK . . . SALVATION . . . FORTRESS"

*P*salm 62 is a song of trust, with elements of lament, hymn, and wisdom mixed in. "According to Jeduthun" (in the superscription) is found also in the superscriptions of Psalms 39 and 77. It refers to a guild of temple singers (2 Chronicles 5:12; 1 Chronicles 25:1) and here probably indicates a specific tune.

The psalmist apparently was a prominent person in the community (verse 4) who was the victim of political dirty tricks (with which we are abundantly familiar in current American society). Rivals plot to bring him down by double-speak: "They bless with their mouths, but inwardly they curse" (verse 4). But the psalm singer is not unduly perturbed, because, as he twice asserts (verses 1–2 are almost identical with verses 5–6), God—and God alone—is his rock, his salvation, his fortress. His entire being, his "soul" (verses 1, 5) waits in patient silence for deliverance.

The hardness of rock (stone) is a frequent image in the Old Testament for the steadfast protection God offers the people. God is "the Rock of Israel" (Genesis 49:24), "the Rock of . . . salvation" (Deuteronomy 32:15), and, in words attributed to David, "my rock, my fortress, and my deliverer" (2 Samuel 22:2). Rock suggests permanence, security, and reliability. The psalmist knows that his honor, attacked by the deceptive words of his political rivals, depends entirely and solely on the protection of God (verse 7).

We too use rock as a symbol of strength and stability. The Rock of Gibraltar is an image of an insurance company. Think also of "the Rock" of Alcatraz, or "the Rock" (an athlete). The object of faith is firm and secure, even when our faith is less steadfast.

O Lord, you are at my side; I leave it to you to order
and provide. Amen.

A BREATH AND A DELUSION

*T*his interlude could have come from the wisdom books of Ecclesiastes or Proverbs. All the "sons of Adam" (New Revised Standard Version: "those of low estate") are "a breath" (*hebel*), and the "sons of man" (New Revised Standard Version: "those of high estate") are "a delusion" (*kazab*). So also the "Preacher" in the book of Ecclesiastes announces, "Vanity of vanities! All is vanity" ("a breath," *habel*).

So much like a puff of air is the human race that it weighs almost nothing on the scales. The balance scales (verse 9) are a frequent metaphor in the wisdom literature and in the prophetic books, and they can be used to refer to God's judgment on humans (see Job 31:6; Proverbs 16:11; Daniel 5:27).

The only vain ambition the psalmist mentions is the desire for riches—one of the good things in life, according to the wisdom literature. The psalmist, however, knows persons who are willing to use unethical means in their effort to gain wealth. Even those who gain wealth honestly are to realize that the striving for riches should not be an ultimate concern for any human being—who must remain aware of being but a breath in the larger sweep of things.

Like us, the psalmists and other biblical writers could alternate between a pessimistic view of life (as here) and the conviction that all of life is a great blessing from God, and that each individual's life is worth more than the whole world. It is perhaps good that we recognize our minute place in the cosmos while at the same time trusting in our ultimate value in the sight of God.

In a world of consumption and striving, my confidence
is in you, my Creator and Redeemer. Amen.

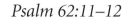

JUST DESERTS?

*O*nce" and "twice" (verse 11)—the psalmist says. "I've told you and I'm telling you again." (This kind of language is typical of the wisdom writers, for example, Job 33:14; 40:5; Proverbs 6:16.) And what is this repeated message? It is the simple yet profound announcement that God wields power in the cosmos and that this power is implemented by steadfast love. Quite a combination it is: power and love! *Power* is required for God's will to become effective, and *steadfast love* is what causes our trust in God to spring to life.

The combination of power and love in the heart of God has a significant implication for the psalmist: "You repay to all according to their work" (verse 12). That God judges justly is a common theme in the Old Testament and also in the New. It is especially prominent in the "Two Ways" teaching of the book of Deuteronomy, which promises land, posterity, and material blessings for those who follow God's commands but the loss of these things for those who do not (see the brief summary in Deuteronomy 30:15–20). Judgment on the basis of works and deeds is found also in the teachings of Jesus (for example, Matthew 7:21–23; 25:31–46), in the writings of Paul (for example, Romans 2:12–16), and in the letter of James (see 2:14–26).

Are we to understand these biblical texts to be in opposition to the venerable Christian doctrine of justification by faith through grace? It is more helpful to realize that our relationship to God is established when we respond to grace with a believing heart, but that this relationship leads to the "works" according to which we shall be judged.

For your steadfast love, O God, I give thanks; let me show
the fruits of this love in my life. Amen.

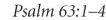

LIFELONG PRAISE

*T*his is a beautiful song of trust (if the psalmist had not so power-fully expressed his inner emotional life, we might consider it a hymn). The psalmist begins with the image of parching thirst "in a dry and weary land" (verse 1; compare Psalm 42:2). Anyone who has traveled through a burning desert in the heat of summer can appreciate the power of this simile. The poet desperately longs for a sense of the divine presence, the overpowering sense of the transcendent holy that many have been taken to be the core of the religious experience. Where can one quench this kind of thirst? For the psalmist it was in the Jerusalem temple, "the sanctuary" (verse 2), where, according to ancient Israelite thought, God's glory (*kabod*, "gravitas," "weight") was localized. The psalmist might have been a temple singer; in any case the psalm would be appropriately chanted in a liturgy there.

The psalmist, however, gives praise not only for God's glorious majesty but most especially "because your steadfast love is better than life" (verse 3). The response is one of joy and gratitude much more than of fear and awe in the manifestation of "glory." So he adopts the ancient posture of prayer, lifting up his hands, and then calling on God's name ("Yahweh" presumably is meant; verse 4).

This psalm encapsulates what is most noble in the spirituality of the psalms. There is no mystical union of the worshiper and God because the psalmist retains his identity and responds in exuberant joy to the real sense of the divine presence in the temple. The poet's entire life span is a joyful response to God's steadfast love. For life and breath, for the necessities of life, and for the sense of God with us, we too can respond with lifelong praise.

Because your steadfast love is better than life,
my lips will praise you. Amen.

INSOMNIA AND PRAISE

Some of the psalmists seem to have been troubled with insomnia, to judge from the frequent references to making it through the night, to nocturnal vigils, and, as in Psalm 63, to meditating through the "watches of the night" (verse 6). The inability to find refreshing rest during the night is a great aggravation for many persons. But, if our psalmist has trouble going to sleep, at least he spends the time in joyful praise, reflecting on God's protection. This brings satisfaction and a feeling of well-being.

The praise-giver mentions two images of God: "wings" (verse 7), which might not specifically refer to the wings of the cherubim over the Ark of the Covenant in the inner sanctum of the temple but rather to the protection a mother hen gives to her young. Also God's "right hand" (verse 8) upholds the grateful poet, even if enemies should threaten his life (verse 9).

The introduction of the death threat and the destruction of the enemies in verses 9–10 is unexpected and abrupt. Is this due to the wandering thoughts of an insomniac? In any case the meditation includes the conviction that the perpetrators will go "down into the depths of the earth" (verse 9), namely, to Sheol. The introduction of the king in the final verse is equally abrupt and seemingly unconnected to what has gone before.

When you have difficulty finding sleep and rest, the psalmist is a good model for you. Find a good basis for meditation—whether the Scriptures, a book of poetry, or the music of J. S. Bach—and consider the blessings that have been yours. Then let your lips praise the goodness of God from a heart that is full and well satisfied.

You, O God, have been my help, and in the shadow
of your wings I sing for joy. Amen.

HUMAN PLOTS AND GOD'S ARROW

*P*salm 64 has the basic components of an individual lament: an appeal to God (verses 1–2), complaint against the enemies (verses 3–6), a description of God's intervention (verses 7–8), and the joyful reaction to the imminent deliverance (verses 9–10). Note also the poetic parallelism: "Hear my voice"/"preserve my life"; "secret plots of the wicked"/"the scheming of evildoers"; "whet their tongues like swords"/"aim bitter words like arrows"; and so on.

The psalmist is in dreaded fear of the plots of the enemy, especially of their words (verses 3, 5). Was the lamenter the object of magical curses ("the scheming of evildoers," verse 2) or of witchcraft, which was known throughout the ancient Near East? The enemies plot, lay snares, and aim bitter words—but the psalmist does not specify the nature of their plot, their purpose, nor their motive. In any case God will bring them to naught, wounding them with arrows (poetic justice for those "who aim bitter words like arrows," verse 3). Those who witness their downfall will shudder in horror at the sight (verse 8).

Modern psychology has shed light on the pervasive evil effects of narcissism in personal relationships and, not least, in the business world. Backbiting, slander, attempts to bring down a rival, meanness that results from feelings of shame and inadequacy, turf battles, flattery, screaming tirades, and a creative variety of plots—all these point to the reality behind the psalmist's lament. Is the world redeemable? we ask. The psalm singer points us to the God of justice.

*Help me to grow in integrity, O Lord, and show me
the way to justice. Amen.*

OVERWHELMED BY GOD'S BENEFICENCE

*P*salm 65, especially the latter part, is a thanksgiving to God for a good harvest. Although the superscription does not indicate that this psalm came from a specific guild of temple singers, the psalmist took pride in being a professional at the Jerusalem temple ("to live in your courts . . . satisfied with the goodness of your house, your holy temple," verse 4).

The psalm overflows with praise of God in what seem to be random, stream-of-consciousness outbursts. Praise is due to the God in Zion, to whom vows can be made (verse 1). Not only Israelites but "all flesh" shall come to worship God there (verse 2; see also verse 5: "you are the hope of all the ends of the earth"). The blessings of the land have come in spite of "deeds of iniquity," as a demonstration that God has forgiven the people (verse 3).

God's benevolence is seen not only in delivering the people from danger but also in the creation of the natural world and regulating the powerful forces of nature—"the roaring of the seas" and the cycles of night and day (verses 6–8). These are "signs" of God's might, not only for the worshipers in Jerusalem but even to "those who live at earth's farthest bounds" (verse 8).

Some human emotions, like envy and rage, are repugnant, even when we find them in ourselves. But those who are able to praise God in unrestrained joy reflect an inward beauty that is attractive both to humans and to God.

*Restore to me, O God, the joy of life that results
in true praise. Amen.*

Psalm 65:9–13

THE BOUNTY OF THE EARTH

$\mathcal{A}$nyone who has tried to farm in a semi-arid land knows the exuberant joy of the community when a soaking rain comes just in time to produce a bountiful harvest. Much of the area of Palestine in which the ancient Israelites settled was semi-arid. Annual rainfall ranged from 1–3 inches in the driest area, the Negev Desert in the south, to around 20–25 inches in the hill country of Galilee in the north.

A time of drought could well lie behind Psalm 65. There would have been great fear that a season of famine lay ahead. But the prayers of the community were answered. The hard and caked earth was softened, with rainwater running through the furrows of the fields. The hills turned green, the pastures and meadows were full of flocks, the valleys were heavy with grain, and the harvest wagons full (verses 10–13). The community gathered at the temple to celebrate the crowning of the year with bounty (verse 11).

The palmist refers to the "river of God" (verse 9)—probably not the seasonal brook Kidron in Jerusalem, and probably not any stream in Palestine. It is the "river whose streams make glad the city of God" (Psalm 46:4), an image for the life-giving water that fertilizes the dry earth and brings sustenance to the people.

Giving thanks is not just for one day toward the end of November. It should be a year-round habit, with special celebrations when we receive a bounty of blessings.

For freedom from hunger, and for the bounty that I enjoy,
I give thanks, O God. Amen.

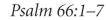

GOD AND HISTORY

$\mathcal{P}$salm 66 combines a hymn, verses 1–12, with an individual's song of thanksgiving, verses 13–20. The two parts belong together, the hymn functioning as the introduction and context for the psalmist's promise to present vows at the temple (verse 13).

The hymn centers on God's deeds in history, specifically the crossing of the sea during the exodus events (Exodus 14—15), a memory that the Israelites remembered as their definitive redemptive act. (A similar watery crossing—of the Jordan River—in Joshua 3 suggests that the beginning of the conquest of Palestine is the culmination of the deliverance at the sea.)

Verses 1–4, addressed to "all the earth," are a summons to a joyful outburst in the temple, one that glorifies God's name, Yahweh, and praises God's powerful deeds. Verses 5–7 specify the redemptive event, the crossing of the sea.

The idea of history is ambiguous, not least to large numbers of contemporary Americans. Henry Ford expressed the typical American sentiment: "History is more or less bunk. It's tradition. We don't want tradition. We want to live in the present and the only history that is worth a tinker's damn is the history we make today."[15] In an essay of 1963, however, Hannah Arendt was closer to the biblical view: "The good things in history are usually of very short duration, but afterwards have a decisive influence over what happens over long periods of time."[16] Jews and Christians over the centuries have looked back to pivotal events in history as foundational and redemptive: for Judaism the exodus from Egypt, and for Christians the life, death, and resurrection of Jesus.

For redemptive moments in history, I give you thanks, O God.
Hasten the day when all creation is made whole. Amen.

WORSHIP AS GRATITUDE

*T*he psalmist admits that the sweep of history brings both tears and blessing. The people have been "tested" and "tried as silver." They have been snared in a net and have had burdens laid on their backs. Other peoples have trodden over them. They had to pass through fire and water (verses 10–12). Yet, in spite of everything, God has preserved them, kept them alive (verse 9), and brought them "to a spacious place" (verse 12). It is clear that this is a poetic allusion to the trials of the exodus wanderings and the difficulties the Israelites had in gaining a foothold in Palestine.

The recollection of past history through the lens of God's providence leads the psalmist to reflect on his own experience as an individual. Like the nation, he has been in trouble (verse 14) and apparently was rescued. He will express his gratitude by entering the temple precincts and there presenting burnt offerings, paying his vows, and making additional sacrifices (verses 13–15). The abundance of sacrificial animals points to a powerful leader, possibly the king.

Our brief time as individuals in history is also marked by weal and woe. Our lives—as well as the broad sweep of history—are marked by ambiguity. Where can we find the meaning of it all? Is there meaning to be found? Our psalmist shows us a better path than to dwell on such imponderables: Praise God for life and breath and give thanks for the blessings that come our way.

I bless you, O God for the great gift of life and for accompanying me through its trials. Amen.

WORSHIP AS TESTIMONY

*W*orship as gratitude progresses in these verses to worship as testimony in the presence of the community of God-fearers. The leader announces to all, "Come and hear!" He has a message to proclaim. He wants the congregation to know that he has cried aloud to God and has praised God. He joyfully testifies that God has listened, thus demonstrating the petitioner's innocence (verses 17–19).

Walter Brueggemann, noted biblical scholar, has interpreted the whole of Old Testament theology in terms of Israel's testimony regarding God.[17] He describes Israel's "core testimony," "counter-testimony," "unsolicited testimony," and "embodied testimony." This descriptive approach to understanding the message of the Old Testament allows the text to speak without assumptions imposed from the outside and thereby to retain its authenticity and integrity. In this work Brueggemann uncovered a basic characteristic of biblical texts of all varieties: There is always a story to be told, a message to be proclaimed, a case to be argued, a truth to be defended, and a gospel to be preached.

This psalmist, like so many others, had presented his case—his testimony—to God (verse 17), and now he gives his testimony to the gathered congregation (verse 16). So it is for us. If worship begins with unbounded gratitude for past blessings, it then leads to a joyful verbalization, a testimony to the awesome deeds of God (see verse 3).

> *I will speak of your steadfast love, O Lord,*
> *in the congregation of the faithful. Amen.*

GIVING THANKS
FOR SUSTENANCE

*T*his joyful song of thanksgiving for a bountiful harvest has often been set to music. The structure is determined by the repeated refrain, "Let the peoples praise you, O God; let all the peoples praise you" (verses 3, 5), which results in three brief stanzas (verses 1–2, 4, and 6–7).

Verse 1 is derived from the "Aaronic benediction" of Numbers 6:24–26: "The LORD bless you and keep you; the LORD make his face to shine upon you, and be gracious to you. . . ." God has wondrously blessed the nation by a rich harvest of the fruits of the earth (verse 6).

Two things stand out in Psalm 67. The first has to do with the fact that the Canaanite religion, sometimes called Baalism, was an agricultural cult, the purpose of which was to ensure the fertility of the soil and good harvests. (This might explain by way of reaction why there are not many harvest psalms in the Old Testament.) Our psalm insists that it is not Baal but the God of Israel who controls the fertility and fruits of the earth.

Second, the psalmist looks beyond the borders of Israel and calls on "all nations" (verse 2) and "all the peoples" (verse 5) to praise Israel's God ("our God," verse 6). God is the universal judge and guide of all nations. The psalmist invites the neighboring nations to acknowledge the true God and share in the resultant blessings. Even though there might be a touch of chauvinism here, the people are invited to broaden their horizons.

It is proper for us to ask God to bless our nation—and other peoples as well—and to give thanks for our great blessings, but we remember that God also is the one who judges all peoples with equity.

O God, be gracious to us and bless us,
and make your face to shine upon us. Amen.

PROTECTION
FOR THE HELPLESS
FROM THE EXALTED LORD

*C*ommentators have considered Psalm 68 the most difficult to inter-pret, both as a whole and in its parts. It is difficult to trace in it a pro-gression of thought, and it gives the impression of being a collection of unrelated fragments. It alternates between speech and narration and includes both lament and hymnic lines.

The psalm begins by quoting an ancient poetic line related to the early wars of the Israelites, Numbers 10:35: "Whenever the ark [of the covenant] set out, Moses would say, 'Arise, O Lord, let your enemies be scattered, and your foes flee before you.'" For our psalm-ist, however, this is a war between the wicked and the righteous, and the Lord fights on behalf of the orphans, the widows, the homeless, and prisoners (verses 3–6). Such oppressed persons can now rejoice in song and be exultant.

The God who accomplishes such a turn of events, a reversal of fortune, is described in powerful, mythic terms, sometimes derived from the images of Israel's neighbors. God "rides upon the clouds" (verse 4), but this is not the God of the Canaanites; God's name is Yahweh (the Lord; verse 4), the God of Israel. It is the God whose "holy habitation" (verse 5) is the temple in Jerusalem, where the wor-shiper community gathers.

This segment of Psalm 68 shows us that the noblest spirituality is a combination of formal worship and social compassion. Let us robustly sing our ancient hymns with their evocative phrases, and then let us turn our attention to those who are excluded from the good things of society.

Give me a sense of your holiness, Lord God, and make me
aware of my neighbor in need. Amen.

HISTORICAL MEMORY

*T*he worshiping community turns its attention to the founding events of the nation, the exodus wanderings and the conquest of Canaan at the time of the Judges. God "went out before [the] people" from Egypt to the place of revelation, Mount Sinai (verses 7–8). The psalm then jumps forward to the gaining of a foothold in Canaan: "you restored your heritage . . . ; your flock found a dwelling in it" (verses 9–10). There was a great victory in the hill country, and a strange sight was etched in the people's memory: snow fell on Mount Zalmon that day (verse 14)!

Although the images cover a vast stretch of time, almost all the phrases have echoes in the book of Judges. Verses 7–8 are a paraphrase of Judges 5:4–5: "Lord . . . when you marched from the region of Edom, the earth trembled, and the heavens poured, the clouds indeed poured water. The mountains quaked before the LORD, the One of Sinai. . . ." Verses 11–14 are based on Judges 5:16, 19. And Zalmon (verse 14) is mentioned elsewhere in the Old Testament only in Judges 9:48 as a mountain near Shechem in the central hills of Palestine. It is abundantly clear that Psalm 68:7–14 recounts an extremely ancient tradition in Israel.

Historical memory has always been a powerful force in shaping society, and it is remarkable how often these memories center on military struggles. The Israelites for centuries kept alive the memory of the friendliness of the Kenite clan at the time of the exodus as well as the treachery of the Amalekites. After almost a thousand years, Islamic societies keep alive the memories of the Crusades, and Serbian nationalism is marked by the memory of a battle with invading Muslims at about the same time.

It is time in the history of the human race to examine our historical memories, legends, and myths in the light of God's justice. Do they preserve hostility, or are they images of restoration and hope?

Save our land from military madness, O God,
in the efforts to protect our people. Amen.

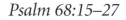

A VICTORY PROCESSION

*T*oday's powerful verses are difficult to interpret. The first stanza speaks of a rivalry between two mountains, "the mount that God desired for his abode," namely, Jerusalem, and the "many-peaked mountain . . . of Bashan" (verse 15). Some readers think that "Bashan" is a cryptic reference to Mount Sinai (see verse 17). Others take it to be a symbol for the highest mountain (like Mount Olympus, the "mountain of the gods"). Still others believe that it alludes to Mount Tabor, an early shrine of the northern Israelite tribes. But Bashan is a territory east of the Sea of Galilee, mostly on the Golan Heights, lying in view of Mount Hermon, the most imposing elevation in the entire area and the site of several non-Israelite shrines. The worshipers in the Jerusalem temple are making a mild jest at rival religions.

The temple singers tell of Yahweh's establishing residence in "the holy place," the Jerusalem temple (verses 17–18). A mighty military procession sets out from Mount Sinai, the foundational site of Yahweh's revelation, and ascends the "high mount" to the holy place, "leading captives in [his] train" (verse 18), to the joyful sounds of singers, tambourine players, and ejaculations of praise (verses 24–26).

The relocation of Yahweh to the holy place, however, is accompanied by blood. "God will shatter the heads of his enemies . . . so that you may bathe your feet in blood, so that the tongues of your dogs may have their share from the foe" (verses 21, 23).

There is a time for patriotism, but there is also a time to resist the call for blood. A pastor during World War II asked the Christian congregation to sing "Praise the Lord and pass the ammunition." Seekers of spirituality cast a critical eye and ear to such bloody victory songs and calls for vengeance, whether in the psalms or in our time.

Show us the way to peace, Lord God,
and deliver us from evil. Amen.

NATIONALISM AND RELIGION

$\mathcal{A}$fter Yahweh was established in the "temple in Jerusalem" (verse 29), the worshipers turned their thoughts to continued protection from everything that threatened their security, whether human or wild animal. They pray that God would scatter and neutralize those who delight in war and look for tribute from conquered nations. They ask God also to "rebuke the wild animals that live among the reeds" (verse 30). Some commentators think this refers to the Egyptians threatening the Hebrews as they attempt to cross the Red Sea ("sea of reeds"). More likely, however, it refers to Leviathan—the crocodile—of Job 41:1; Isaiah 27:1; and Ezekiel 29:3, which ancient Israelites took to be a vestige of the formless chaos that preceded creation. That a "herd of bulls" (verse 30) could bring terror to city dwellers is not surprising.

The God of the temple is ancient. God is the "rider in the heavens, the ancient heavens" (verse 33), an image the Israelites borrowed from Canaanite poetry. God is the God of Israel, who "gives power and strength to his people" (verses 34, 35).

Psalm 68 as a whole is magnificent poetry, evocative of the most ancient of Israelite traditions. Readers today can respond to the graphic and hoary images. But we should also retain a critical eye. Yes, God is with us. We do not worship a tribal god, however, but the creator of all peoples and the one who will guide the entire cosmos toward its ultimate restoration.

> *Send your mighty voice throughout the world, O God,*
> *and make wars to cease to the ends of the earth. Amen.*

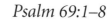

A PANIC ATTACK

*T*his psalmist is like a person being tortured to reveal something that he does not know. He is being dunned to pay back that which he did not steal (verse 4, end). His enemies are more numerous than the hairs on his head and apparently are threatening him with death (verse 4). He does not claim to be innocent (verse 5), but he is being falsely and maliciously accused of things he has not done.

The victim graphically describes the symptoms of anxiety wrought by his attackers. He feels that he is stuck in a deep quicksand where he is unable to gain a foothold; he is about to suffocate. He is hoarse from lamenting to God, and his eyes are sore from crying. The false accusations have brought him reproach and shame, "for your sake," to such a degree that he has been alienated from his family (verses 7–8).

All this is remarkably similar to the experience of the prophet Jeremiah, who was cast into a cistern, where he sank in the mire (Jeremiah 38:6). Jeremiah's faithfulness to God also brought him shame and isolation, even from his own family (Jeremiah 12:6; 15:15–18). It is possible that the psalmist, who has close associations with the temple in Jerusalem, came from the admirers of the prophet (remember that Jeremiah was from a priestly family; see Jeremiah 1:1).

The poet desperately appeals to God, "Lord GOD of hosts," a form of address that recalls the presence of God in the holy of holies of the temple. He awaits a response to his lament.

Many today who experience the suffocating effects of anxiety and panic attacks know precisely what the psalmist is talking about. Blessed are they who have faithful friends who can stand beside them then. There are times when this calls for professional help. In all cases we bring our petitions to God.

Strengthen me, O God, in times of anxiety and stress;
help me to trust in your steadfast love. Amen.

RELIGIOUS PERSECUTION

The psalmist admits to a consuming zeal for God's house, the Jerusalem temple. His fasting there in sackcloth brought insults and mockery, including ribald songs from the drunken louts in the neighborhood (verses 9–12). He called himself a zealot; the mockers view him as a religious fanatic, a crackpot—different words for the same thing. A possible context is the situation in Jerusalem after the Jews returned from exile in Babylon. Around 518 B.C., on the site of the ruined temple, mourners fasted in memory of the destruction of Solomon's temple by the Babylonians some 75–80 years earlier. The prophet Zechariah chastised them, insisting that God desired kindness, mercy, and social compassion instead of ritual observations (Zechariah 7).

The lamenter feels unjustly persecuted—because of his religious piety. Again (see verse 2), he tells God that he is sinking in quicksand, about to suffocate and die and end up in the Pit (Sheol). He begs God to address the situation "at an acceptable time" (verses 13–15).

Psalm 69 is the second most frequently quoted psalm in the New Testament (after Psalm 22). Christians immediately recognize that verse 9 is quoted in John 2:17 regarding Jesus' "cleansing" of the temple: "His disciples remembered that it was written, 'Zeal for your house will consume me'" (the verb is changed to the future tense, suggesting that the author considered the psalm verse to be a prediction). While we know that it was not written as a prediction, as a parallel it is gripping: "Though originally the individual statements in the psalm were not meant to be understood as prophecies pointing to Jesus, this deeply moving testimony to human suffering nevertheless exhibits features which are so characteristic of suffering in general that their relation to [Jesus] . . . forces itself upon any serious consideration of the psalm."[18]

At an acceptable time, O God, in the abundance of your stead-fast love, answer me. Amen.

POISONOUS REPROACH

*W*eighty words in this segment of Psalm 69 convey the desperation of the petitioner. In verse 16 he appeals to Yahweh's steadfast love (*hesed*) and abundant mercy (*raham*, a mother's sympathy). He voices the frequently occurring plea, "Do not hide your face from your servant" (verse 17). He uses a metaphor derived from the legal practice of purchasing one's freedom from debt, from prison, from enslavement, or from confinement by the enemy: "*Redeem* me; *set me free* because of my enemies" (verse 18). The concept of redemption in time would become a leading metaphor for salvation.

He begs for redress—or even mere pity. Enduring shame, dishonor, insults, a broken heart, and despair, there was no one to bring comfort, no one to show pity. His isolation reminds us again of Jeremiah 20:7–12. Instead of pity and comfort, his enemies offer him poisoned food and contaminated drink (verse 21).

The reference to vinegar to drink (verse 21) is alluded to in Matthew 27:34, 48; Mark 15:23, 36; Luke 23:36; and John19:28–29 (only John suggests that Jesus' thirst was "to fulfill the scripture"). It is probable that an actual incident at the crucifixion reminded Jesus' followers of this verse in Psalm 69.

All human beings endure shame from time to time, but the experience is certainly more destructive to some than to others. Before falling into the pit of despair, ask yourself whether the humiliation is commensurate with the situation—the occasion for it, the nature of the ones who shame, and the degree of your culpability. Ask yourself also whether this, too, shall pass. Above all, share your cares and griefs with the God of steadfast love and abundant mercy.

Answer me, O Lord, in the day of trouble;
turn to me in your abundant mercy. Amen.

JUNE 6 *Psalm 69:22–29*

SELF-PITY AND RECRIMINATION

*T*here is such a thing as the art of cursing (think of Johnny Carson as "Carnak the Magnificent" on the old *Tonight* show), but in contemporary American society curses are a matter of tiresome vulgarisms—four-letter words and worse. By contrast, the ancient psalmists displayed a distinct flare for calling down doom on their enemies, and Psalm 69 is a good example.

The enemies offer temple sacrifices and arrange luxurious feasts from the sacrificed animals ("their table," verse 22). They hope for a divine pronouncement of their own "righteousness" (*zedeqah*, verse 27; New Revised Standard Version: "acquittal"). But our psalmist begins his barrage: May their feasts be a trap, like a snare that catches birds (verse 22). May they be blinded and struck with incurable palsy (verse 23). May their assembly become a burned-out camp, with no one left alive (verses 24–25). Instead of being absolved of sin, may guilt be added to their guilt (verse 27). May their names be blotted out of the book of the living (verse 28; see the references to God's book in Exodus 32:32; Psalm 139:16; Malachi 3:16). The vituperation ends with an exhausted cry for protection (verse 29).

Echoes of verses 22–23 are found in Romans 11:9–10, of verse 24 in Revelation 16:1, and of verse 25 in Acts 1:20. Allusions to the "book of the living" in verse 28 are found in Philippians 4:3 and in Revelation 3:5; 13:8; 17:8; 20:12, 15; 21:27.

These curses are utterly serious, with no trace of irony. They are instead full of pathos. In our Western societies such outbursts would be considered unseemly—to say nothing of their questionable morality. We sense the terrible desperation of the petitioner, and we marvel at the unvarnished anger. God help him.

Deliver me, O Lord, from evil without
and from self-deception within. Amen.

THERAPEUTIC THANKSGIVING

*F*inally, after twenty-nine verses of lamenting, moaning, and cursing, the psalmist turns to God in a song of thanksgiving. Did he experience a reversal of fortune that led to this outburst of praise? Or is it merely a literary convention that psalms end on a note of triumph?

Although the poet had undergone a period of fasting at the temple (verses 9–10), he makes no mention of having sacrificed there, even though his enemies apparently had (verse 22, "their table"). And now he insists that his song of praise will please Yahweh more than the burning of animals on the altar of the temple. Was the psalmist an influential leader in the community who aroused fanatic opposition from the priests who oversaw the sacrificial system? At the beginning and again at the end of this strophe, he expresses his devotion to God's name, Yahweh (verses 30, 36). This God, the LORD, hears the pleas of the needy and the oppressed even without their costly donations for sacrifices (verse 33).

The psalm closes with a rapidly broadening horizon: The entire cosmos will praise God for the reconstruction of Judea after the exile and the return of the people to live there (verses 34–36). In this way the suffering and restoration of the petitioner becomes a symbol of the recent history of the people as a whole (like the "Suffering Servant" of Isaiah 53).

Unremitting suffering cannot be borne forever. Even in the midst of the most horrific distress, we must be able to have hope in order to live. Persons of faith can indeed engage in outbursts of protest, but our trust in the God of steadfast love and mercy must eventually trump all defeatism.

I praise you, Lord God, that you hear the prayers
of the needy. Amen.

BULLYING

$\mathcal{P}$salm 70, an individual lament, is almost identical to the final verses of Psalm 40 (see the comments for April 4, above) and has parallels also in Psalms 35 and 71. Most commentators believe that Psalm 70 is the earliest form of this lament and that it was added to Psalm 40:1–11, with verse 12 added as a connecting link. Some Christians will recognize verses 1 and 4 of Psalm 70 as part of their liturgical tradition.

As with most individual laments, there are four characters in this drama: the petitioner, the enemies, those who belong to the community of the petitioner, and God. Each has a specific traditional role to play. The petitioner describes himself as one of the "poor and needy" (verse 5), which can be taken either literally or as referring to his stance in the presence of God. In any case he faces a death threat: his enemies seek his life (verse 2). Either they or their supporters join in vicious mocking at the threatened person. The psalmist prays that the situation would be reversed: let the violent ones be put to shame, confusion, and dishonor. He then calls on the worshiping congregation to praise God's greatness (verse 4), for God is the source of his help.

Bullying is one of the most repugnant and yet common behavior patterns that we find in our elementary schools and beyond. As with some lower animal forms, a victim is selected because of vulnerability and presumed weakness, and the bully or the gang takes pleasure in shaming and often also physically injuring the victim. During the age when the child's selfhood is solidifying, such beastly behavior can have permanent debilitating effects. Persons of faith need to give attention to this problem.

Give me strength, O Lord, to aid those who suffer violence,
especially our children and young persons. Amen.

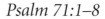

FAITHFUL FROM BIRTH

*T*his mixture of lament and praise comes from an elderly man (verses 9, 17–18) who was accomplished both in instrumental and vocal music (verses 22–23). He most probably worked at the temple, to judge from the wording of the Hebrew text of verse 3, which can be translated, "Be to me a crag into which I can creep, to which I may always come, as you have commanded to help me"[19] (see also the New Revised Standard Version note to verse 3). The "crag" or rocky fortress is the temple in Jerusalem, which was sometimes a literal place of refuge for persons accused of crimes. For the psalmist, the temple was a place of security through the tribulations and blessings of a long life, (verses 5–6).

The psalmist looks back at a long life in several lines of this psalm. The LORD has been his trust "from my youth" and on this God he has "leaned from . . . birth." The statement that "it was you who took me from my mother's womb" (verse 6) has led some to think that his birth was difficult, and that the newborn survived only by the help of God. Reminiscing stimulates the venerable musician to begin a joyous song of praise (verse 8).

The psalmist reminds us of the importance of early childhood training. He would agree with the adage, "Train children in the right way, and when old, they will not stray" (Proverbs 22:6). He required no born-again experience because he had been faithful from birth. It is difficult in our postmodern culture to transmit effectively the good heritage of faith and values that our forebears bequeathed to us. It requires special effort, but the results can be life-changing.

For my predecessors in the faith, I give thanks, O God.
For those who follow, I pray for wisdom and piety. Amen.

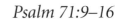

PROTECTION IN OLD AGE

*A*ncient Israelites who survived childhood expected to live to age seventy or perhaps eighty (Psalm 90:10)—not much different from Western societies today. These years can be difficult, with the body gradually weakening (verse 9) and the senses of sight, hearing, and smell that give life its brilliance declining. It should be a time of mellowing, with the passions of youth morphing into easy-going tolerance. But our psalmist feels beset by enemies who seek his life (or are verses 10–11 a boilerplate lament inserted here?).

The psalmist's worst fear is that God will abandon him now that he has reached old age (verse 9; see also verse 18). He believes that his enemies have the same thought: "Pursue . . . that person whom God has forsaken" (verse 11). The fear of divine abandonment is the most severe distress that can befall the human petitioner. Job yearned to sense the presence of God with him: "O that I knew where I might find him, that I might come even to his dwelling!" (Job 23:3), and, at the end, Job repents for no other reason than that God has come to him (Job 42:5–6). In the depths of his suffering the prophet Jeremiah wondered whether God had become for him a seasonal brook that had dried up (Jeremiah 15:18). And Jesus on the cross uttered the cry of dereliction, "My God, my God, why have you forsaken me?" (Mark 15:34).

But the petitioner will not quit hoping. He will remember God's past deeds of salvation and "will come [to the temple] praising the mighty deeds" of God (verse 16). How can one who has spent his life singing, making music, and praising God (see verse 17) give up hope as his body ages? How can we?

Do not forsake me, O God, when my strength is spent. Amen.

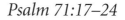

PRAISING GOD IN YOUR GOLDEN YEARS

*T*he aging musician was gifted in playing the harp (*nebel*, which had a large sound box that stood on the floor; this large instrument was plucked with the fingers) and the lyre (*kinnor*, a higher-pitched stringed instrument that was hand-held and plucked with a plectrum).[20] He was also a singer for the temple liturgies (verses 22–23). Now, as he approaches the end of his life, his hair gray and his body weakening, he is intent on continuing this praise in order to transmit the knowledge of God's wondrous deeds to the coming generations. He will tell them not only of the nation's past history but also of his personal life experience, that of plunging to the depths of despair (verse 20) and then of being rescued by the power and righteousness of God (verses 23, 18–19). He would have the next generation know the same kind of trust in God. The psalmist treasured his heritage and was determined to preserve it for his successors.

Aging well is a challenge, even under the best of circumstances. The saying is true: aging is not for sissies. The so-called golden years can bring heartache because of one's own physical decline but even more at the death of a spouse or life-long family members and friends. Many seniors, having quit their profession or the duties to which they have become accustomed, feel that the best has already been. There is only one firm reality that all aging persons can grasp hold of, even up to the end: the grace of God never ends, not even at our death.

Give me strength, O Lord, to praise you all the days
of my life. Amen.

WORTHY GOVERNMENT

*T*his royal psalm takes the form of a prayer to God for the success of the king. It could serve as a liturgy for the enthronement of the king or for an annual celebration of his ascent to the throne. As the superscription, "Of Solomon," might suggest, the repeated themes are drawn from the description of Solomon's reign (as in 2 Kings 3:9; 4:24; 10:10).

In ancient Israel, law and justice come from God, and the implementation is given to the king, the viceroy of God. The policies of the king are supposed to lead to the prosperity of the people and the fruitfulness of the land (verse 3), and the king's administration of justice is to pay special attention to the protection of the poor and oppressed among the people (verse 4). Not least, the king is to work for universal peace (verse 7).

Verses 5–7 express the hope for the *perpetuity* of king's dynasty and for the universal *extent* of his kingdom, from "the River" (the Euphrates) to "the ends of the earth." "Tarshish and the isles" might refer to Phoenician settlements in the western Mediterranean—or even on the Atlantic coast—and Sheba and Seba are probably in the southern Arabian Peninsula, in the area of present-day Yemen.

Western society also has had monarchs who claimed to rule by "divine right," and even in our time there is pressure on religious leaders to announce God's preference in our presidential elections. It is striking that the psalmist prays to God that the king would "judge your people with righteousness and your poor with justice" (verse 2) and that during the king's rule peace would "abound" (verse 7). This is a good test for politicians of any society.

Help me, O God, to work for peace and justice
in my time. Amen.

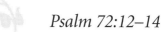

PROTECTOR OF THE NEEDY, POOR, WEAK, AND OPPRESSED

*A*lthough the Bible as a whole exhibits a preference for the poor, this idea is found more explicitly and emphatically in some parts of the Bible than in others. In the Old Testament it is a major motif in Deuteronomy and in the prophets. In the New Testament it is prominent in the teaching of Jesus in Matthew, Mark, and especially Luke, and also in the letter of James. But in the center of this royal psalm, which was presumably chanted in a temple liturgy, we find a surprisingly succinct summary of this theme.

The king "delivers the needy . . . the poor . . . those who have no helper" (as we would say, no ombudsman), the oppressed, and those threatened by violence. The king is more than a legal aid; he functions here as a savior, assuming the functions that elsewhere in the book of Psalms are attributed to God. He not only establishes policies that leave no destitute person behind, but he also will use force to save them from violence; he "redeems their life" because "precious is their blood in his sight" (verse 14). In Psalm 116:15 this is said of God: "Precious in the sight of the Lord is the death of his faithful ones."

The advanced societies of the world have policies that are in line with this biblical ideal. They provide such programs as social welfare nets, universal health care, graduated tax rates, care for the disabled and elderly. Policies that provide additional wealth for the super-rich and cut resources for the education of youth are clearly not what the psalmist had in mind.

Make me a voice for those who have no helper,
Lord God. Amen.

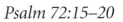

JUNE 14   *Psalm 72:15–20*

ABUNDANT BLESSINGS, ABUNDANT PRAISE

*P*salm 72:18–19 are a concluding benediction for Book II of the present book of Psalms, and verse 20 indicates that this section was originally composed of poems generally attributed to David.

Verses 15–17, beginning with "Long live the king," are a series of blessings on the king that draw on a variety of metaphors and images. "Gold of Sheba," from the land in the eastern part of Yemen, refers to the respect of foreign rulers. The temple worshipers pray that the king's name and fame endure forever, and that the land would bring forth abundantly during his reign. Like Abraham in Genesis 12:1-13, the king is to be a source of blessing for "all nations" (verse 17). The final benediction applies this universalist theme to the Lord: "May his glory fill the whole earth."

Some commentators have thought that the mention of gold as a gift of homage in Psalm 72:10, 15 led to the later Christian identification of the magi from the east in Matthew 2:1-12 as kings.[21] Earlier commentators interpreted the psalm as messianic, as though it referred to the ideal king of the end-time or to Jesus. But "the ideal king of the end-time has no need of the prayers and wishes, least of all of the wish that everything will turn out all right in his kingdom."[22] Psalm 72 was composed as a song of praise to the king, to be chanted in the temple in Jerusalem.

We pray for blessings on our nation, especially for peace and prosperity. But we know that the Lord, whose glory fills the whole earth, will judge us all, both king and people.

Blessed be your name forever, O God,
and may your glory fill the whole earth. Amen.

ENVY AND DOUBT

*P*salm 73 opens Book III of the present collection and begins also a group of "Psalms of Asaph," Psalms 73–83 (along with Psalm 50). Asaph was the ancestor of a guild of temple musicians (see 1 Chronicles 25:1–2), but nothing else is known about him.

Psalm 73 has the marks of an autobiographical wisdom psalm, with some features of the individual lament. The poet is distressed over the apparent unfairness of life. The wicked prosper even as they scoff, and God appears to be indifferent and unheeding.

At the outset, the psalmist acknowledges the common biblical premise that "God is good to the upright, to those who are pure in heart" (verse 1). God is good. But how God's goodness is effected in this world the psalmist does not specify. In fact, he comes close to sliding down the slippery slope into doubt (verse 2) when he sees that the wicked are prospering. "I was envious of the arrogant" (verse 3). This could mean either of two things. He might have begun to doubt the goodness of God *to him*—even if not for the people as a whole. Or he was falling into the sin of envy of the wicked. He saw their prosperity (*shalom*), which God had promised to the upright, the pure in heart.

Envy, the "green-eyed monster," is indeed a destructive emotion. There will always be someone more successful, richer, more handsome, more intelligent, and more popular than I. Should I spend my time agonizing over this "injustice"? Should I doubt the essential goodness of God? Or should I turn my thoughts to productive pursuits and work to increase the effective rule of God over a troubled world?

Purify my heart, O God, and make me mindful
of your blessings to me. Amen.

Psalm 73:4–9

WORLDLY SOPHISTICATES

The psalmist continues his description of the arrogant, wicked persons whom he was on the point of envying. It is a picture of the "beautiful people," the "jet set" who fill the pages of our celebrity magazines and are seen in the best restaurants and country clubs. Unlike the psalmist, who suffered a bodily infirmity of some kind (see verses 14, 26), these worldly sophisticates "have no pain; their bodies are sound and sleek" (verse 4). They can eat what they want and not gain weight. Because they are wealthy, they are not plagued with the troubles of ordinary folk (verse 5). Their pride is just as impressive as their jewelry and clothing (verse 6). They enjoy the "follies" and the good things of life (verse 7). With an assumption of unquestioned entitlement they speak with condescension and malice, and they have the power to threaten others with oppression (verses 8–9).

There are two, somewhat opposing, truths related to these observations. First, the healthiest society by all measurements is one that has a vibrant middle class. Nations in the developing world are cursed by a huge gap between the minute percentage of the population who control almost all the wealth and the masses who—no matter how hard they work—must struggle to find food. Economic injustice is a social evil.

Second, however, pious individuals have often been suspicious of sophisticated persons—and even of highly educated persons. Socially skilled persons are not necessarily evil. Let us allow God to judge the hearts of others, and let us pay attention to the fruits of their actions.

For all that is true, noble, beautiful, and wise,
I thank you, O God. Amen.

PRACTICAL ATHEISM AND THE REWARDS OF PIETY

*A*lthough Psalm 73:10 is difficult to translate, the psalmist seems to suggest that the arrogant snobs described in verses 4–9 are admired by the general population: "the people turn and praise them, and find no fault in them." But the suave sophisticates themselves, although they believe in God, have no fear that God will give them their just deserts. They say, "How can God know?" namely, know what is in their hearts (verse 11). This is practical atheism, living with the assumption that God will not intervene in their lives, living *as though* God did not exist, living with no thought of the justice of God. And so the worldly sophisticates are "always at ease." They "increase in riches," satisfied with themselves and their rightly place at the top of the heap.

By contrast, our psalmist claims, "I have kept my heart clean and washed my hands in innocence" (verse 13). (Public ritual handwashing was a declaration of innocence; see Deuteronomy 21:6–9; Matthew 27:24.) But his piety and his clean living were "all in vain" (verse 13) because he continues to suffer some chronic bodily ailment (the verbs in verse 14 point in this direction). Why, indeed, should the innocent suffer while the arrogant and impious live in self-satisfaction? No matter how hard and how long we search, there is no good answer to this question. Through all the confusions of life, there is only one constant: the steadfast love of the Lord.

Through all the uncertainties of life, Lord God,
be near me. Amen.

JUNE 18   *Psalm 73:15–20*

THE MYSTERY OF INJUSTICE

Simply and straightforwardly, the psalmist raises the question of the book of Job: How does it happen that the self-satisfied prosper while the pious suffer in body and spirit? Is there any reward for piety and doing the right thing? Is there a relation between righteousness and well-being? So vexing was this issue for the psalmist that he toyed with the idea of agreeing with the practical atheism of the wicked who assumed that God would not intervene in their life of entitlement (see verse 11). But that would separate him from "the circle of your children" (verse 15), the community of the faithful, and such a betrayal would be a denial of who he was. Unable to deny his identity, the psalmist wore out his mind puzzling over the problem, unable to find a resolution to this "wearisome task" (verse 16).

In the midst of torturous reflections there came a turning point. In the "sanctuary of God," presumably the temple precincts in Jerusalem (some commentators take the phrase metaphorically, "in mystical communion with the Holy One"), "I perceived their end" (verse 17). In his own mind, the psalmist reached a resolution, albeit a temporary and not entirely satisfactory one, by coming to the conviction that the rich and successful oppressors would have their comeuppance. The conviction was something like the converse of Shakespeare's "All's well that ends well" and more like the saying in the book of Sirach 11:28: "Call no one happy before his death; by how he ends, a person becomes known." The wicked will slip into ruin in a great flood; all that will remain of them will be a bad dream.

There is no theoretical answer to the question of innocent suffering. We can do nothing else than "Let go, let God." But that is more than enough.

Be with me, Lord God, in the bad times
and see me through. Amen.

GOD WITH US THROUGH IT ALL

*L*ooking back on the time before his "conversion" in the sanctuary (see verse 17), the psalmist now feels foolish for his earlier moaning and groaning: "When my soul was embittered . . . I was stupid and ignorant" (verses 21–22). Like Job, he had complained in the bitterness of his heart (Job 7:11) and often. But this, he now sees, was brutish (verse 22) and offensive to God.

The basis of this new confidence is a living sense of the presence of God in the life of the psalmist—almost a kind of mystical communion. The psalmist is "with" God continually; God holds his "right hand" (as God also took the hand of the great Persian emperor Cyrus, Isaiah 45:1), guiding his passage through life, even during the troubles. And in the future God would bring the former complainer to a place of honor (verse 24). The resolution of the vexing problem of suffering is thereby placed in the future, when the principle, "As you sow so also shall you reap," will become effective.

Verses 25–26 are among the great passages of Scripture. They are the essence of every faithful person's confession of faith, embodying pure trust and firm confidence in the eternal God. "My flesh and my heart may fail, but God is the strength of my heart and my portion forever." As these words are uttered, all our envy of the self-important sophisticates of society vanishes (see verse 3).

Whom have I in heaven but you, O Lord? And there is nothing
on earth that I desire other than you. Amen.

Psalm 74:1–11

HORRIFIC DESTRUCTION

*T*his national lament is a graphic response (written about 550 B.C.) to the destruction of the temple in Jerusalem by the Babylonians in 587 B.C. Mount Zion—the temple hill—is in "perpetual ruins" (verse 3). The enemies desecrated it, attacking its trellises with hatchets and hammers before they set it on fire and burned it to the ground (verses 4–7)—this, the "dwelling-place of your name" (verses 7 and 2). The enemies then proceeded to destroy every sanctuary in Judah (verse 8).

The end of Judah was a great turning point in biblical history. The destruction of Solomon's temple in 587 B.C. is still commemorated by religious Jews by fasting on the 9th of Ab (late July or early August). The catastrophe ended the Davidic monarchy and resulted in the exile of the leading citizens of Judah to Babylon. The magnitude of the disaster raised difficult and traumatic questions: Could this be explained as punishment? Had God abandoned his people? How could an Israelite remain faithful to God without a religious center, a functioning priesthood, a state, and a king?

The mourners plead for God to remember the saving acts of the past that led to the establishing of the people in the land (verse 2) and to see what has happened to the central shrine (verse 3). And they can only ask, "How long, O God, is the foe to scoff? Is the enemy to revile your name for ever?" (verse 10).

The events of 9/11 changed the United States in important and long-lasting ways. But the destruction of 587 B.C. was far more life-changing for biblical history. Things would never again be the same, and, at least for many years, the only response that the survivors could make was the lament, "O God, why do you cast us off forever?"

I pray for the day of peace in our world, O Lord.
Make me an instrument of your peace. Amen.

 *Psalm 74:12–19*

CREATIVE ORDER
AND TERRIFYING CHAOS

*L*aments often include an appeal to what God has done in the past. So verses 12–17 of Psalm 74 are much like a hymn or litany in praise of God's actions in creation, while verses 18–19 beg God to "remember" and "not forget" what happened to the people of God in the horrific year, 587 B.C.

The psalmist emphasizes that in creation God was bringing order out of chaos, "working salvation in the earth" (verse 12). "You divided the sea" (verse 13), as in Genesis 1:6, where the firmament separated "the waters [above] from the waters [below]." According to ancient Near East traditions, in this primeval ocean there were vestiges of chaos, like dragons and Leviathan (probably the crocodile, verses 13–14; see Job 41:1–11). God's creative work proceeded by establishing the regularity of the sources of water on the dry land (verse 15), the orderly separation of night and day, the fixed lights, including the sun, stars in the sky, and the predictable course of the seasons of the year (verses 16–17).

But now this orderliness of creation has relapsed into a chaos of unimaginable horror. The lamenter shakes his finger at God: "Remember this, O LORD. . . . Do not deliver the soul of your dove to the wild animals; do not forget the life of your poor for ever." The foreign enemy scoffs, reviling the name of the LORD, and the people pray for the restoration of order.

There are times in the life of a nation (and in the lives of individuals) when it seems that chaos prevails. In such times it does not help to pretend that all is well. But, like the psalmist, we can remind our God that the proper work of God is to avert chaotic ruin and create order.

O Lord, establish justice in all the earth,
and bring order also to my life. Amen.

THE COVENANT REMAINS

Some of those who lived through the fall of Judah to the Babylonians in 587 B.C. wondered whether the tragedy was the result of the breaking of the covenant God made with Moses and the people during the exodus (see Exodus 24:7–8). This covenant included the promise of security in the conquered land of Canaan if the people would keep its demands. The prophet Jeremiah, an eyewitness of the events of 587, boldly asserted that the people had broken the terms of the Mosaic covenant (Jeremiah 31:32), thereby bringing the tragedy upon themselves. Our psalmist, however, asks God to remember the covenant, especially God's promise of security for the people (verse 20). The covenant remained valid throughout the chaos.

The chaos in the land of Judah after 587 B.C. was like the darkness of the caves of the desert regions, filled with danger and unpleasant creatures—and sometimes with violent fugitives (verse 20). The Judahites who remained in the land were "downtrodden" and, both literally and figuratively, "the poor and needy" (verse 21), while the enemy invaders were impious mockers who created a clamorous chaos that never ended (verses 22–23). The psalmist returns to his plea, "Rise up, O God, plead your cause; remember. . . . Do not forget. . . ."

In their desperate suffering, the mourners in the ravaged land of Judah called on God to honor the promises made to the people in the covenant with Moses. Their pleas received an answer some two generations later, when the Persian king Cyrus allowed the exiles of Babylon to return to Jerusalem and there rebuild the temple. We too can stand on the promises of God.

Let it always be, Lord God, that the poor and needy have occa-
sion to praise your name. Amen.

IN GOD'S GOOD TIME

This thanksgiving psalm seems, at first glance, to have an odd theme: praise for God's coming judgment of the earth. Immediately prior to the chanting of this psalm, the congregation heard a recital—either sung or spoken—of God's "wondrous deeds" (verse 1). These deeds might have been God's saving actions in Israel's history, the theme of several psalms. But the references to "the boastful" and "the wicked" (verse 4) suggest that the community was praying for a new act of God's deliverance in the present. To judge from the cosmic language in verse 3—"When the earth totters, with all its inhabitants, it is I who keep its pillars steady"—the wicked in this case are probably not individual opponents but those who threaten the nation.

Unlike what precedes and what follows, verses 2–5 are words attributed to God; that is to say, they have the form of an oracle such as the Old Testament prophets spoke, typically introduced by "Thus says the LORD." And what does God say to the gathered community? God says, in effect, that, in spite of appearances to the contrary, and in spite of many seemingly unanswered prayers, the wicked will indeed be brought to judgment "at the set time," and that this judgment will be just (verse 2). It will affect the entire cosmos (verse 3), and then no longer with the insolent boast and threaten the weak (verse 4–5). This thought reminds us of the words of the sixteenth-century German poet Friedrich von Logau (see note 46, below):

> Though the mills of God grind slowly,
> yet they grind exceeding small;
> Though with patience He stands waiting,
> with exactness grinds He all.

We can take great comfort from the fact that the One who gives us our final evaluation is not a human jury but the God who judges with equity.

We pray, Lord God, for the demonstration of your justice
in our world. Amen.

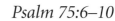

THE CUP

*W*hen Judah, around 600 B.C., was threatened with military invasion by Nebuchadnezzar of Babylon, the leaders looked to Egypt to neutralize the threat. The psalmist knows better: Don't look to the east or west or to the wilderness for your deliverer; "it is God who executes judgment, putting down one and lifting up another. For in the hand of the LORD there is a cup with foaming wine" (verses 7–9).

The image of a cup in the hand of God is surprisingly common in the Old Testament. Sometimes it is the "cup of salvation" (Psalm 116:13 and elsewhere) but especially it functions as a metaphor of judgment (Jeremiah 25:15–28; Ezekiel 23:31–34; Habakkuk 2:15–16; Lamentations 4:21; Zechariah 12:2; and others). Isaiah 51:17–23 sheds light on the meaning of the image: "Stand up, O Jerusalem, you who have drunk at the hand of the LORD the cup of his wrath, who have drunk to the dregs the bowl of staggering. . . ." Those who become drunk from the cup of wrath stagger and fall, so that they are completely unable to continue their insolence. They are rendered helpless and can easily be overcome by their enemies. The same use of the image recurs in the New Testament in Revelation 14:9-10, in which "those who worship the beast . . . drink the wine of God's wrath, poured unmixed into the cup of his anger. . . ."

Biblical images, amazing in their variety, have power to stimulate both emotion and thought. But we see in projects like the "Left Behind" novels what can happen when we forget that they are *images.* Psalm 75 shows us the wisdom of living each day with the One who "will judge with equity."

Give me wisdom, O God, for the living of this day. Amen.

JUNE 25  *Psalm 76:1–6*

THE GOD IN ZION BREAKS THE WEAPONS OF WAR

*I*n 701 B.C. the army of the mighty Assyrian Empire laid siege to Jerusalem, an event narrated in 2 Kings 19 and Isaiah 37. The city was spared from destruction after a plague swept through the Assyrian army, causing them to retreat. The joy that followed this miraculous deliverance is expressed in Psalm 76, which praises the glory of God in the holiest place of the temple in Jerusalem.

Verses 1–3 are in parallel form. This means that we are not to find a separate meaning for "Judah" and "Israel" in verse 1, nor for "Salem" and "Zion" in verse 2. Salem (related to *shalom*, "peace, welfare, health, security") is an ancient Canaanite name for Jerusalem (see Genesis 14:18), and Zion here refers to the temple mount. There God has chosen to dwell, and there his name, Yahweh, is known.

Mount Zion is glorious and majestic (verse 4). It is the site where the enemies were made powerless, deprived of the spoils of war. "They sank into sleep" (verse 5) and their weapons of war—arrows, shields, swords—were destroyed (verse 3). God rebuked the enemy, and "both rider and horse lay stunned" (verse 6).

Two thousand seven hundred years later the human race has not learned the path to peace. We have spurned the prophet's call to "learn war no more" (Isaiah 2:4), and victims of war continue to mount by the hundreds and thousands. Christians, who follow the "Prince of Peace," should be the first to protest military madness.

Save us, merciful God, from the terrors of war.
Show us the path to reconciliation. Amen.

THE FEAR OF GOD

Close to the heart of Judaism is Deuteronomy 6:4–9, the *Shema* (hear): "Hear, O Israel: The LORD is our God, the LORD alone. You shall love the LORD your God with all your heart, and with all your soul, and with all your might. . . ." Jesus identified this as the greatest commandment (Mark 12:29–30). How then are we to understand texts that speak of the *fear* of God, like the recurring motif in the book of Proverbs, "The fear of the LORD is the beginning of knowledge" (Proverbs 1:7; 9:10; 15:33; and elsewhere)?

Fear in the Bible certainly can have a negative sense, referring to the emotion of humans whenever their security is threatened or they expect punishment. Psalm 76:7–12 speaks of the fear that God's wrath causes among the kings of the earth, who engage in military madness but whose wrath is no match for that of God's.

But it is striking that Deuteronomy's command to *love* God is surrounded by commands to *fear* God. Thus: ". . . that you and your children and your children's children may fear the LORD your God all the days of your life . . ." (6:2) and "The LORD your God you shall fear; him you shall serve . . ." (6:13). Such expressions point to the experience of God as the wholly other whose presence evokes awestruck reverence and a sense of the holy. Such fearsome awe is attributed to Moses at the burning bush (Exodus 3:6) and to other biblical figures. This response brings with it trust in God, and it is therefore not opposed to the command to love God. In his Small Catechism, Martin Luther began his explanation of the Ten Commandments with the phrase, "We should fear and love God so that we . . ."

Help me, Lord God, to set my priorities in order—to love
and fear you above all else. Amen.

"HAS GOD FORGOTTEN?"

*T*his lament uses a rich and varied vocabulary, and, as it progresses, it turns into a magnificent hymn. First, however, come the complaints.

Without reminding God of what has gone wrong in his life, the psalmist repeatedly refers to his tormented questionings. He cries "aloud" to God both day and night, often simply moaning because he is unable to find the right words. He is afflicted with insomnia, unable to keep his eyelids closed. All strength is drained from him. There is no comfort (verses 1–4).

His thoughts turn to the past, when, in "the years of long ago" things were so much better (verse 5). And knotty, unanswerable—almost blasphemous—questions arise in his mind: Are the good days gone forever? Have God's steadfast love and God's promises come to an end? "Has God forgotten to be gracious?" Has God's compassion turned to anger? Has the "right hand of the Most High," the work of God in deliverance and rescue (see Exodus 15:6–10), changed and become ineffective (verse 10)?

Over the centuries grieving men and women have uttered the same complaints. "I really didn't deserve this." "This happens only on the nightly news; I didn't think it could ever happen to me." And, if the victim is a person of faith, "Where is God?" "Why do I get no answer?"

Suffering is real. At times life is a vale of tears. But through it all we can raise our complaints to God, reminding God of the promises of old and calling on God to be present in our sufferings.

Reveal to me, Lord God, your steadfast love
in the low times of my life. Amen.

HOLY HISTORY

$\mathcal{T}$he psalmist takes comfort from thoughts of the past. The complaints in verses 1–10 may have arisen from his personal tragedy, but in any case he now turns his attention to God's "wonders" and "mighty deeds" of the past for the people as a whole. (The appeal to the past is typical of the prophets and the priestly tradition but not of the wisdom tradition, the books of Job, Ecclesiastes, and Proverbs.) The Israelite tradition of the exodus from Egypt, the wanderings, and the conquest of Canaan confirm to the psalmist the conviction that God is at heart a God of salvation and deliverance.

God's way—God's trail of events in the course of history—moreover, is "holy" (verse 13), a term not easily defined in any language. "Holy" suggests transcendence and mystery and separation from the mundane. It is the quality that inspires awe and reverence—but also trust in God's ability and desire to save. The question, "What god is so great as our God?" (verse 13b) reminds us of the Song of Moses at the crossing of the sea: "Who is like you, O Lord, among the gods?" (Exodus 15:11; see also 18:11). But the uniqueness of God in our psalm points toward monotheism. The greatest of the "mighty deeds," an act of redemption par excellence, was the deliverance of the people from Egypt under Moses, which is the clear meaning of verse 15. It was "holy," because it inspired awe and reverence.

History can be ambiguous, and we are often hard-pressed to find meaning in it. Being true to our heritage, however, is a good thing, and we should do what we can to transmit the best of our past to our children.

I remember your wonders of old, Lord God,
and I give thanks. Amen.

Psalm 77:16–20

PRIMORDIAL POWER

$\mathcal{V}$erses 16–18 are a hymnic reflection on Genesis 1. As creation begins a "darkness covered the face of the deep, while a wind [or 'spirit'] from God swept over the face of the waters" (verse 2). God separated the waters below from the waters above (verse 6) and then the water from the dry land on the earth (verses 9–10). Our psalmist pictures the conflict that brought order out of chaos: "the very deep trembled" (Psalm 77:16), and brilliant flashes of lightning lit up the dark chaos (compare Genesis 1:3) while the earth shook (verses 17–18). God has unparalleled power to subdue chaotic and destructive forces.

In the concluding verses 19–20, the psalmist turns to the other great Israelite story of the overcoming of watery threat, the Hebrews crossing the sea at their exodus from Egypt. This Israelite memory is indeed ancient, being recounted in poetic form first by the "Song of Miriam" and then the "Song of Moses" (Exodus 15:21; and verses 1–18). It was God who led the people; God's "way was through the sea" (see verse 13 of this psalm). God led his people "like a flock by the hand of Moses and Aaron" (verse 20). (The reference to the "path through the mighty waters" and the statement that "your footprints were unseen" might have been in the mind of those who told the story of Jesus walking on the water of the Sea of Galilee; Mark 6:47–52).

North Americans today often comment that they can worship God in the beauty of the natural world as well as in the established liturgies of "organized religion." The psalmists indeed recognized God's power to bring order into the natural world. But we note that they praised this work of God as they gathered for communal worship at the temple.

I acknowledge your majesty, Lord God, even in the terrifying
powers of nature. Amen.

LEARNING FROM THE PAST

*P*salm 78, the second longest (after Psalm 119), is a poetic summary of Israel's history from the exodus from Egypt to David and the building of the temple. Its form is difficult to classify.[23]

The call to pay attention in verses 1–2 could have come from the book of Proverbs (see there 5:1; also 1:8; 2:1; 3:1; 7:1). It prepares us for the repeated accusations of the people's lack of faith and even rebellion in the historical summary that follows. Evidences of ingratitude and sin in Israel's past might be among the "dark sayings" and parables referred to in verse 2 (Matthew 13:35 applies this verse to Jesus' practice of speaking in parables).

The worshiping community pledges to transmit this heritage— warts and all—to the next generations (verse 6). This tremendous emphasis on childhood education has two purposes. The first is to encourage the children to "set their hope in God, and not forget the works of God" (verse 7). The threat of secularism and the more serious danger of adopting the religious practices of their neighbors were quite real. Recounting God's past acts of rescue and deliverance can serve to strengthen trust in God's help in the present.

The second purpose of the historical recital is to encourage the next generation to "keep his commandments" (verse 7). God had given a law to Israel and had commanded the people to teach it to the children (verse 5; compare Deuteronomy 6:7) so that they "should not be like their ancestors, a stubborn and rebellious generation (verse 8).

Spirituality can be like a perennial plant that bears fruit year after year. Or it can be like a cut flower that delights us for a few days and then wilts. Trust in God requires us to be diligent in the education of our children.

God, bless our religious educators and the children
in their care. Amen.

TREACHERY, A HIDDEN AGENDA, AND ACTS OF DELIVERANCE

*W*inston Churchill once said, "History will be kind to me. I shall write it." Historical memories can be deceptive, and the writing of history often has ulterior motives. History is written by the winners.

Psalm 78:9–11 refers to the defeat of the Ephraimites on the day of battle and that "they did not keep God's covenant" or God's law but forgot "the miracles that he had shown them." The historical allusion is uncertain,[24] but the verses probably recall the Israelite defeat at the hands of the Philistines, when the enemy destroyed the sanctuary at Shiloh and captured the ark of the covenant (1 Samuel 4, especially verses 10–11). Although Ephraim is not mentioned specifically, the name of that tribe, descended from Joseph's son, could by way of shorthand refer to the entire Northern Kingdom (see Jeremiah 7:15; Hosea 4:17). There is a possible hidden agenda here. Verse 67-68 asserts that God "did not choose the tribe of Ephraim; but he chose the tribe of Judah." The Jerusalem community found divine sanction for the centralizing of Israelite worship in Jerusalem, which involved the closing of shrines in the north.

Verses 12–16 recount miracles of the exodus period. These include the ten plagues in the delta region of the Nile River in Egypt, narrated in Exodus 7–12. The crossing of the sea, with the waters standing "like a heap," is told in Exodus 14–15 ("at the blast of your nostrils the waters piled up, the floods stood up in a heap," 15:8). The cloud and fiery light are mentioned in Exodus 13:12 and elsewhere. And the water from the rock recalls Exodus 17:1–7.

We Americans remember best our values of freedom and equality, but we pay less attention to our past failures with respect to racial oppression and our treatment of native peoples. Let us keep our critical faculties alive and our minds open.

Lead me, O God, through the dry periods of life
and give me hope. Amen.

Psalm 78:17–31

COMPLAINTS
IN THE WILDERNESS

*E*xodus 16 and Numbers 11 describe how the Israelites, after escaping from Egypt, complained that God had led them into the wilderness of the Sinai Peninsula to die of hunger. The Lord's wrath was severe against them (Numbers 11:10), but God nonetheless provided them with manna (a substance released from a desert plant when pricked by lice that, when dried on the ground, could be baked or boiled) and large flocks of quail.

Verses 17–31 graphically summarize the narrative in poetic form. The theme of rebellion in the wilderness (verses 17–20) was firmly embedded in the Israelite memory (Psalm 106:24–27; Jeremiah 2:4–6; Ezekiel 20:13; Hebrews 3:15–19 and elsewhere). Even though "when the Lord heard, he was full of rage" (verses 21–22), God "rained down on them manna to eat, and gave them the grain of heaven. Mortals ate of the bread of angels" (verses 24–25). And God raised up winds to drive "winged birds like the sand of the seas" to "fall within their camp" so that "they ate and were well filled" (verses 26–29). The reference to God killing the young men, "the flower of Israel" (verse 31) picks up on the statement in Numbers 11:33 that God's anger caused a plague to break out.

New Testament writers used the images and themes of the exodus in various ways. The long discourse on the "bread from heaven" in John 6:25–50 builds on the theme of manna and the wording of Psalm 78:24–25. And the Epistle to the Hebrews makes much of the wilderness wanderings as a metaphor to the passage through this life of the people of God. Persons of faith today respect God's justice and the references to divine wrath, but our trust in God's grace is the bottom line in everything.

Help me, Lord God, to turn from complaint and rebellion
to gratitude. Amen.

 *Psalm 78:32–41*

IMPURITY OF HEART

Søren Kierkegaard insisted that "purity of heart is to will one thing,"[25] and the author of the Epistle of James warned against being "double-minded" (James 1:7). Our psalmist, in articulating the theme of rebellion in the wilderness, says, "Their heart was not steadfast towards [God]; they were not true to his covenant" (verse 37). The people became accustomed to repenting in time of disaster and rebelling in times of security. This pattern is used as an interpretive device elsewhere in the Bible. For example, in the book of Judges the pattern announced in 2:6—3:6 recurs throughout the entire book: the people rebel, God sends retribution, the people repent, God restores them, the people rebel—and so on through all the "judges." It is a version of "foxhole religion"—the idea that there are no atheists when shots are flying. It reminds us also that Albert Einstein defined insanity as doing the same thing over and over and expecting different results.

Psalm 78:32–39 presupposes this cyclical pattern: God sends military disaster and the people earnestly repent (verse 34). Then they flatter God with lying words (verse 36), only to find themselves in another mess. "They tested God again and again" (verse 41). But here a new thought is inserted: "Yet [God], being compassionate, forgave their iniquity, and did not destroy them" (verse 38). If the people were not "steadfast towards him" (verse 37), God's steadfast love in the last analysis trumped God's wrath.

There are times in our lives when we wonder whether God has turned against us. At such times we might be in danger of becoming double-minded. But the single-minded witness of the Bible is that God's grace ultimately prevails throughout creation.

Clarify my mind, O God, and help me grow in purity
of heart. Amen.

EXODUS SIGNS
AND WONDERS

*T*hese verses reflect on the plagues in Egypt that led to the Hebrew exodus, the miraculous crossing of the sea, and the conquest of Canaan up to the capture of the "holy hill . . . the mountain that his right hand had won," that is, Jerusalem.

The exodus narrative includes a cluster of miracle stories (most of the others in the Old Testament are found in the Elijah-Elisha stories of 1 Kings 17—2 Kings 13). "The fields of Zoan" (verse 43) refers to the eastern part of the Nile delta. Zoan (Tanis in the Greek translation) was earlier known as Avaris. It was the capital of Egypt at the time of Ramses II, the Pharaoh of the exodus.

Seven of the ten plagues are referred to here as "signs" and "miracles," with the sequence of the book of Exodus altered: water changed to blood (compare Exodus 7:17–24); flies (Exodus 8:21–24); frogs (Exodus 8:2–15); locusts (Exodus 10:4–6); hail (Exodus 9:18–26); cattle plague (Exodus 9:3–11); and, finally, the killing of the firstborn of the Egyptians (verse 51 of the psalm; Exodus 11:4–5; 12:29–30). Verse 53 recalls the crossing of the sea and the destruction of the pursuing Egyptians (Exodus 14–15), and verses 54–55 recount the conquest, the apportioning of land among the tribes, and the conquest of Jerusalem.

On July 4 the United States celebrates the Declaration of Independence of 1776. Psalm 78 bears witness to the persistence of the exodus memories in the tradition of Israel. Moses was remembered as the pioneer at the time of the nation's founding, and the events of his lifetime came to be recounted as the greatest historical act of redemption wrought by God for the people of Israel. The exodus means for the Old Testament what the life, death, and resurrection of Jesus means for the New.

When the wild tempests rave, ruler of wind and wave,
do thou our country save by thy great might.[26] *Amen.*

TREACHERY AND DESTRUCTION AT SHILOH

*P*salm 78:56–66 refers to the situation of 1 Samuel 4. In those years, around 1020 B.C., the Philistines, from their territory on the southern coast of Palestine, were threatening the Israelites even in their main settlements in the hill country. (This threat ultimately led the Israelites to establish the monarchy). The main Israelite sanctuary was then located at Shiloh in the central hills (Jerusalem remained a Jebusite city until David captured it shortly after 1000 B.C.).

In 2 Samuel 4, two decisive battles are fought: the Philistines moved from the coast toward the center of the hill country, attempting to cut the Israelite settlements in two. The Philistines scored a major victory, killing some 4000 men (verse 2). The Israelites then brought to the battle the "ark of the covenant of God" (a symbol—and more—of the presence of the LORD). But the Philistines rallied and killed 30,000 foot soldiers (verse 10). What happened to Shiloh is not mentioned in 2 Samuel, but Psalm 78:60 tells us that God "abandoned his dwelling at Shiloh." It was destroyed. The crowning blow, however, was that the Philistines captured the ark (verse 61), and the sons of the priest Eli died (1 Samuel 4:11; Psalm 78:64).

The destruction of Shiloh is corroborated in Jeremiah 7:12–14; 26:6, 9, and the prophet used that event as a warning that God could do to sinful Jerusalem what God had done to the earlier sanctuary. Although the psalm interprets the disaster at Shiloh as punishment for the people's idolatry (verse 58), it is usually difficult to be sure of the work of God in human history. Much seems to happen by sheer chance. But can we learn from the past?

> *Lord God, I pray for the strength and safety*
> *of all persons caught up in the throes of war.*
> *Be with them to protect and save. Amen.*

POLITICAL THEOLOGY

*T*he purpose of this entire psalm becomes clear in its final verses. There were old rivalries between the northern tribes of Palestine, which were descended from Joseph and his son Ephraim (verse 67), and Judah in the south. Tensions existed also between the partisans of King Saul, a Benjaminite, and the Judahite David. The northern tribes had their own religious centers, first at Shiloh and later at Bethel, Dan, and elsewhere. In the context of these north-south tensions, the congregation in the temple in Jerusalem chants a rationale for their own supremacy: God has "rejected the tent of Joseph" (verse 67) and "abandoned his dwelling at Shiloh" (verse 60). God chose instead the tribe of Judah, and built his sanctuary there on Mount Zion, "which he loves" (verses 68–69). Instead of a king from the Joseph tribes, "he chose his servant David . . . to be the shepherd of his people Jacob" (verses 70–71). The building of the temple is mentioned (verse 69)— but not the name of the builder, David's son Solomon.

This so-called David-Zion ideology is pure political theology. There was no possibility of a "secular city" at that time, and the thought of freedom of religion would have been entirely incomprehensible to the ancients.

If we are tempted to read these verses with smugness, however, let us remind ourselves of the Western tradition of the "divine right" of kings—and also of the thin patina of religious piety with which many of our leaders wrap themselves. Remember also that God can always raise up a prophet to remind us that no one is above the law of God.

Open our eyes as a nation, Lord God, that we might see
the right path in a difficult world. Amen.

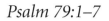

THE EFFECTS OF HORROR

*T*his community lament appears to be an eyewitness response to the greatest tragedy in Old Testament history, the destruction of Judah by the Babylonians in 587 B.C. Although specifics are not given, each verse in this psalm has close parallels in the book of Jeremiah, the prophet of the events of 587 (verse 7 recurs word-for-word in Jeremiah 10:25).[27] Jeremiah personally witnessed the tragedy. "The nations" ("Gentiles" or "pagans"; *goyim* in Hebrew) invaded God's "inheritance." They "defiled your holy temple" and "laid Jerusalem in ruins" (verse 1). So complete was the devastation that there were not enough survivors to bury the dead bodies (compare Jeremiah 8:2; 14:16; 16:4). The *goyim* stood by, mocking the few survivors of the massacre (verse 4, similar to Jeremiah 24:9).

In a lament, the words "How long, O LORD?" typically segue from the complaint to the petition, as here in verse 5. Typically also, the present suffering is attributed to God's anger. But the psalmist now begs that Yahweh's wrath be diverted from the pathetic survivors to "the nations that do not know you" (verse 6).

The horror of 587 was *the* great turning point in ancient Israelite history. Questions about God's justice and power arose in a new literature of despair (for example, the book of Lamentations). The exiles in Babylon had to develop ways to be faithful to their God in a strange land without a temple or a sacrificial system, and a new emphasis on future deliverance emerged.

Unlike people in many other areas of the world, Westerners have only recently had to deal again with the threat of terror, and it has caused much anguish. We readily join our voices with the ancient psalmists and cry out, "How long, O Lord?" Make peace and security a reality in our world!

Our world cries out for redemption, Lord God.
Show us the way to peace. Amen.

THE WAGES OF SIN?

*W*hen tragedy hits us, one question emerges spontaneously: "What have I done?" The psalmist assumed that the fall of the nation in 587 B.C. was the result of sin—but he is not sure whose sin. Verse 8 refers to "the iniquities of our ancestors," while verse 9 begs God to "forgive our sins, for your name's sake."

Ancient Israel indeed was familiar with the idea of inherited guilt. According to the introduction to the Ten Commandments, Yahweh is "a jealous God, punishing children for the iniquity of parents, to the third and the fourth generation of those who reject me" (Exodus 20:5). The prophets of the time were aware of the old proverb, "The parents have eaten sour grapes, and the children's teeth are set on edge" (Jeremiah 31:29; Ezekiel 18:2). But both Jeremiah and Ezekiel negate this idea: "As I live, says the Lord GOD, this proverb shall no more be used by you in Israel. . . . it is only the person who sins that shall die" (Ezekiel 18:3–4). You cannot be punished for the sins committed by others. But, says Jeremiah, bad examples have bad effects: "They have turned back to the iniquities of their ancestors of old, who refused to heed my words" (Jeremiah 11:10).

The idea of inherited entitlements or inherited guilt has run its course. Both aristocracies and caste systems are to be left on the rubbish heap of history. In the great equalization, all humanity stands naked before the God whose judgments are just and whose grace trumps everything.

It's me, O Lord, standing in the need of prayer.
Grant me grace. Amen.

PRISONERS OF WAR

*P*risoners of war in ancient times were no better off than they are in the twenty-first century A.D. Exile was often involved, as in the case of Judah after the Babylonian capture of Jerusalem. Jeremiah 52:30 reports that the total number of the leaders of Judah and Jerusalem who were taken as prisoners to Babylon was 4,600, while 2 Kings 24:14 puts the number at 10,000.

Prisoners and captives are mentioned throughout the Bible. Amos speaks of prisoners of war being led off "with hooks, even the last of you with fish hooks" (Amos 4:2). According to the first-century Jewish historian Josephus, priests were not allowed to marry women who had been captives (because of the fear that they had been raped and might bear children from a non-priestly line).[28] In 587 B.C., when the Babylonians captured Zedekiah, the last Davidic king in Jerusalem, they killed his sons in his presence and then put out his eyes (2 Kings 25:1–7). He was taken as a prisoner to Babylon, where he died (Jeremiah 52:11).

The twentieth century witnessed more victims of war—prisoners, captives, tortured persons, and displaced persons—than any other century in human history. Western churches and other organizations did great work in easing the suffering of millions of such persons. But war continues in our day, and the victims number in the hundreds of thousands. People of faith would do well to support such organizations as The Center for Victims of Torture (St. Paul, Minnesota) and Amnesty International.

Justice demands that we remember the plight of prisoners (Matthew 25:36, 43).

Let the groans of the prisoners come before you,
merciful God. Amen.

GOD'S SHINING FACE

A refrain repeated three times—"Let your face shine, that we may be saved" (verses 3, 7, and 19)—marks the divisions of this community lament. The psalm reflects a particular point in the history of the northern tribes of Israel. Ephraim and Manasseh were the sons of Rachel and Joseph and the core of the Northern Kingdom, while Benjamin was situated between north and south (verse 2). In addition, the references to "Lord God of hosts" (*Yahweh, elohim sebaoth*, verse 4) "enthroned upon the cherubim" of the ark (verse 1) originated in the shrines of the northern tribes and were transferred to Jerusalem when David brought the ark there (2 Samuel 6). Psalm 80 therefore reflects a time of dire crisis in the Northern Kingdom, probably during the invasion by Assyria that led to its destruction in 722 B.C. The people are in great distress, and their neighboring enemies laugh them to scorn (verses 5–6).

In their lament the people beg for salvation from the "Shepherd of Israel" (verse 1, a rare designation of God that appears elsewhere only in Genesis 48:15; 49:24; and Psalm 23:1). "Let your face shine." To sense God's shining face in your life or in the life of your people is the greatest good we can hope for. It is a feeling of blessedness, the assurance of a cosmic yes, an affirmation that all is right. "The Lord make his face to shine upon you, and be gracious to you" (Numbers 6:25) is the best of all possible benedictions.

In times of despair, Lord God, give me a vision
of your shining face. Amen.

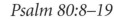

THE VINE

T he images of vine and vineyard for the people of God are found in both Testaments. "Israel is a luxuriant vine that yields its fruit" (Hosea 10:1). But the image could be used also in a negative sense. The "Song of the Vineyard" in Isaiah 5:1–7 complains that, although "the vineyard of the LORD of hosts is the house of Israel," it has borne only wild grapes, not justice but bloodshed. And Jeremiah 2:21 conveys God's words: "I planted you as a choice vine, . . . how then did you turn degenerate and become a wild vine?" For the New Testament, compare Mark 12:1–9 and John 15:1–17.

Our psalmist uses the vine as a historical image. God brought the vine out of Egypt and established it in Canaan, where it finally became so strong under David and Solomon that it reached from the Mediterranean to the Euphrates ("the sea," "the River," verse 11). But now the walls of the vineyard have been broken, and it has been invaded by wild boars who uproot and trample it (verses 12–13), and enemies have burned it with fire (verse 16). In contrast to several other psalms, there is here no thought of the disaster being God's punishment. There is only the plea for God to "turn again" (verse 14), to repent, and to save. The community pledges then to never turn back from God and to call on God's name (verse 18).

The destruction of war is something that we North Americans have not witnessed in our own countries in our lifetimes—for which we thank God. It is hard for us to imagine the horrors of an entire town or city being reduced to rubble and large numbers of persons killed. Let us be peacemakers through all the trials that come, and let us not give up.

O Lord, have regard for the suffering of our time.
I pray for peace and salvation. Amen.

MAKING MUSIC

The opening hymnic verses (1–5) were to be sung at the Jerusalem temple "on our festal day" (verse 3), probably the Feast of Booths, a seven-day harvest festival that commemorated the wanderings of the Israelites after their departure from Egypt (as alluded to in verses 6–10; see also Exodus 23:16). The celebration in Psalm 81 lasted for two weeks, from the new moon to the full moon (verse 3) and culminated in the unmistakable blast of the "trumpet" (ram's horn, *shofar*, verse 3), announcing the beginning of the new year (*Rosh Hashanah*), which followed the Feast of Booths.

The two-week festival was a time of music-making, both choral and instrumental. There were songs to the sound of the tambourine, the "sweet lyre," the harp, in addition to the blare of the *shofar*. There is much we cannot know about music in the ancient Near East, but the books of Chronicles gives names of various guilds of temple singers and musicians. It is not surprising that the book of psalms, closely connected as it is to temple worship, is replete with references both to singing and to instrumental music.

Music has always been prominent in religious worship. The mathematical basis of music—the relationship between the number of vibrations in harmonious notes—reflects a created order in the midst of a chaotic world. But when we make music in church or synagogue, is it to the glory of God (J. S. Bach at the end of his compositions wrote, "To God the Glory") or for ourselves as consumers? Are we interested in what God might want to hear—so to speak—or in what can speak to my personal needs and, at the same time, draw more members into our group?

*I thank you, O God, for the great music of the church
and for those who create and perform it. Amen.*

STUBBORN HEARTS

*A*fter the triumphal music-making of verses 1–5, a priest or prophet speaks in the name of God (verses 6–16). Such oracles are a preferred form for the message of a prophet ("Thus says the LORD. . . .").

Verses 6–10 allude to the events of the exodus and the subsequent wanderings in the Sinai Peninsula. God delivered the people from Egyptian slavery, from "the burden" and the "basket" (apparently for carrying bricks, verse 6). The people called to God in distress for lack of water at Meribah (the story is in Exodus 17:7 and Numbers 20:13), and God answered them "in the secret place of thunder," that is, Mount Sinai (verse 7; the Israelites reached Sinai at Exodus 19:1, and Exodus 19:16 describes the revelation of God there being accompanied by "thunder and lightning, as well as a thick cloud . . . and a blast of a trumpet"). At Sinai God reveals the First Commandment, "There shall be no strange god among you" (verse 9; compare Exodus 20:3) because "I am the LORD your God, who brought you up out the land of Egypt"—words almost identical to Exodus 20:2.

In spite of God's care for the people, they rebelled, and God "gave them over to their stubborn hearts" (verse 12). The prophet-priest then urges the assembled worshipers to walk in the ways of God and thereby enjoy God's blessings: "I would feed you with the finest of the wheat, and with honey from the rock I would satisfy you" (verse 16). The psalm ends with the bottom line for all believers—the priority of God's grace.

Biblical writers can indeed preach fire and brimstone; they can lay down the law; they can pronounce judgment. But, after all has been said and done, there remains only one thing: God's steadfast love. That is our hope.

Lord, keep me in your grace, and let it sustain me
each day of my life. Amen.

A HEAVENLY DRAMA

*T*his psalm is unique, not only because its form does not fit the major categories of psalms, but also because it is a mini-drama set in the heavens. Using the language of Israel's neighbors, the psalmist pictures the council of the gods (the image is found also in 1 Kings 22:19; Isaiah 6:3; 24:21; Job 1–2; Psalms 89:5–7; 103:19). Holding court, God judges the gods (foreign deities, verse 1). They are stupid, without knowledge, and "walk around in darkness" (verse 5). And what is the charge against them? They have caused social oppression by stimulating earthly judges to "judge unjustly and show partiality to the wicked" (verse 2). They should instead have shown justice to the weak, the orphan, the lowly, the destitute, and the needy (verses 3–4). This is more than compassionate conservatism; it is unbounded, compassionate liberalism.

Then comes the denouement: although the gods are "children of the Most High" they shall nevertheless "die like mortals" (verses 6–7). This is a literal, dramatic *Götterdämmerung*, the cataclysmic end of the gods. Their death is due not to some breach of fealty to the Most High God, as we might have expected, but rather to their callous neglect of human need.

If anyone needs to be convinced that the Bible has a preference for the poor, they need read no further than this. It is as though injustice has penetrated the entire cosmos, and now it is being redressed. The gods who tolerated and instigated harsh policies of social oppression are brought to nothing. And so the temple choir sings, "Rise up, O God, judge the earth; for all the nations belong to you! (verse 8).

> *Give me a heart of compassion, Lord God,*
> *for the hopeless and helpless. Amen.*

THE NATIONS CONSPIRE

*T*his psalm includes an impressive catalogue of ancient Israel's enemies, some of whom threatened the survival of the nation even as the lament was chanted in the temple (verses 1–8). Among these are Edomites, descendants of Esau (Genesis 36:1), Ishmaelites, descendants of Abraham and Hagar (Genesis 16:8–11), Moab and Ammon, descendants of Lot by incest with his daughters (Genesis 19:30–38), the Hagrites (1 Chronicles 5:10), Gebal (Joshua 13:5; 1 Kings 4:19), the Amalekites (Exodus 17:8–13; Judges 3:13), Philistia (Judges 3:31; 1 Samuel), Tyre (on the coast north of Israel), and the empire of Assyria (centered in what is now northern Iraq). Israel was completely surrounded by threatening foes.

The remainder of the psalm is a curse on Israel's enemies. They are to be brought down as completely and mercilessly as were the foes of prior history: Sisera and Jabin at the battle won by Deborah in Judges 4–5, Oreb and Zeeb killed by the men of Ephraim at the time of Gideon in Judges 7:25, and Zebah and Zalmunna, killed by Gideon in Judges 8:4–21.

Prayers for the destruction of the enemy in a time of national threat should not surprise us. Psalm 83, however, raises in an acute way the question of "just war." How dare we assume that God is always on our side—even when we engage in a preemptive *blitzkrieg?* How can we define justice during a military struggle? How should we treat enemy combatants? How can we distinguish the truth from propaganda? And most urgently we ask, where is God when thousands of human beings are victims of military atrocity?

Again, O Lord, we pray with Francis of Assisi:
Make us instruments of your peace. Amen.

SING FOR JOY
TO THE LIVING GOD

*A*nyone who has heard Johannes Brahms's glorious choral anthem "How Lovely Is Thy Dwelling Place" will immediately associate it with Psalm 84. A powerful example of the ability of music to elevate the human spirit, its soaring melodic line evokes a sense of spiritual delight in the presence of God.

Anticipation of pure pleasure sustained the pilgrims on their sometimes arduous journey on dangerous and dusty highways leading to Jerusalem (verses 5–6), for they knew that "the God of gods will be seen in Zion" (verse 7). The pilgrim's entire being—"soul . . . heart . . . flesh"—"sing for joy to the living God" (verse 2).

Significant terms are applied to God in Psalm 84. "Yahweh" (verses 2, 11) is the personal name of Israel's God. "Yahweh Sebaoth" ("LORD of hosts," verses 1, 3, 8, 12), an ancient designation, is linked with military might. "The God of gods" (verse 7) reminds us of Psalm 82, in which God presides over a heavenly council of the foreign gods. "God of Jacob" (verse 8) was a favorite designation of God among the northern Israelite tribes of Ephraim and Manasseh, sons of Jacob. "God" (*Elohim*, verses 8, 9, 10, 11) is the general Semitic designation of deity or deities. "King" (verse 3) points to God's ultimate rule in Israel, even though verse 9 refers to the Davidic king in Jerusalem as "our shield . . . your anointed."

At the center of the psalm is "the living God" (verse 2). The psalmist rejoices in God as the source of protection, security, satisfaction, and good fortune—the fullness of life. Happiness, says the psalmist, is to be in the presence of God. "Vaya con Dios," as the Spanish blessing has it. "Go with God" in your life.

O God, I want to live the life I sing about in my song. Amen.

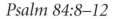

THE JOY OF GOD'S PRESENCE

$\mathcal{V}$erses 8–10 and 12 continue the prayer form, while verse 11 is an appeal to the worshiping congregation. The attraction of the magnificent temple in Jerusalem to Israelites living some distance away was powerful. The psalmist would rather be a doorkeeper there than live anywhere else, no matter how luxurious. Living in proximity to the house of God makes God's blessings all the more palpable. Trusting in the LORD is the source of true and enduring happiness (verse 12).

The effects of what some folks consider to be religion are not always positive. Religious leaders often deal in the guilt business, and their work can be divisive. A prominent television personality once publicly called for the killing of the elected leader of another country. Some have attributed national tragedy to God's wrath on the behavior of segments of the population. Another self-described "Christian" politician reportedly took huge sums of money from Native American casinos to support programs intended to demonstrate that he opposes such vices! Religion can indeed appeal to pathological personalities and be used to evil effect.

Our psalmist, by contrast, is a model of mature spirituality. Here we find no trace of guilt feelings, no desperate pleas for vengeance, no expressions of hatred, and no criticism of those who work for justice. There is nothing but joy and exultation in the thought of coming into the presence of God. That is the source of strength.

My soul longs for the sense of your presence, Lord God.
Be with me through the valleys of life. Amen.

NATIONAL FORGIVENESS

*P*salm 85, a community lament, summarizes the ancient Israelite conception of the relation between God and the nation. Although an individual speaks in verse 8, the first seven verses, in the first-person plural and in parallel form, are well-suited to antiphonal singing in the temple.

The psalm begins with an appeal to God's saving deeds in the past (verses 1–3). The congregation reminds God of God's proper activity—as a preliminary to their plea for rescue in the present (verses 4–7). Two thoughts emerge in the first three verses. First, sin can infect not only the individual but also can pervade society as a whole. The psalmist refers to "the iniquity of your people" and "all their sin" (verse 2). Community structures can perpetuate injustice, as when an aristocracy automatically inherits entitlements even when its members have less than mediocre virtue or talent. Caste systems can permanently prevent large segments of society from any hope of financial or social advancement. Commercial practices can lead to the failure of small businesses, and lack of adequate housing can force some to remain homeless, no matter how hard-working they might be.

Second, the people attribute national disasters to the wrath of God, "your hot anger" (verse 3). This idea of God's wrath is jarringly juxtaposed to the joy in God's presence expressed in the preceding psalm, and it is diametrically opposed to the repeated affirmation of God's steadfast love in many of the psalms and elsewhere in the Bible. We have learned over the centuries that natural disasters are not "acts of God" and that bad things actually do happen to good people. Forgiveness, however, is earnestly to be sought for sins, whether individual or societal.

Let your steadfast love, O Lord, become real in my life
and in the life of my people. Amen.

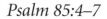

NATIONAL LAMENT

Something has gone terribly wrong—but what? There are hints in verses 11–12 that it had to do with crop failure and the threat of famine ("our land will yield its increase"). Other commentators have suggested that the lament was uttered by destitute Judahites returning from exile in Babylon in the sixth century.

Verses 4–7 function as an A-B-A' stanza. In parallel form, verses 4 and 7 convey the plea for restoration and salvation, while verses 5–6 complain about God's unceasing anger. The nation needs a new revelation of God's steadfast love (verse 7), which is the same as restoration, salvation, and revival.

Old Testament life was basically oriented to this world. The ideal of ancient Israelites was to live in the here and now in joyous and faithful relation with God and in a situation of justice with others. They could speak of a shadowy lingering at the grave, but they generally looked for salvation in the here and now. And this salvation included protection from enemies, daily food, shelter, good family and friends, a just society, and a healthy spirituality.

Christians—as well as Jews—look for God's salvation in the here-and-now as well as in the hereafter. If the earth is the Lord's, then we too can pray with this psalmist:

Restore me, O God of our salvation;
show me your steadfast love, and grant me your salvation
in my passage through life. Amen.

SALVATION AND THE SENSE OF GOD'S GLORY IN REAL LIFE

*A*fter the congregation has pleaded with God for an end to their current suffering, an individual speaks from their midst: "Now I want to hear what God will say." The prophetic voice declares that God has indeed heard the prayers of the people; God will speak peace (*shalom*, salvation, verse 8) "to those who turn to him in their hearts," as in fact the worshipers were doing. God *will* act, so that "his glory [*kabod*] may dwell in our land" (verse 9).

The glory of God is a significant motif in the Bible. It connotes the special, luminous presence of God in a specific locale (see 2 Chronicles 7:2). The prophet Ezekiel spoke of the "glory" of Yahweh leaving the temple in Jerusalem just before it was destroyed by the Babylonians in 587 B.C. (Ezekiel 10) and, in an awe-inspiring vision of the heavenly chariot-throne, he saw God's glory land among the exiles (Ezekiel 1). And the prophet who wrote Isaiah 40:5 spoke about the return of the glory of Yahweh to Judah to be with the returning exiles: "Then the glory [*kabod*] of the LORD shall be revealed," namely, to the people in Jerusalem.

The secularism of the Western world has made it increasingly more difficult to have a lively sense that God is present "in our land" (verse 9) and to live daily with God in mind. Our knowledge of our own mortality, finitude, and inadequacies, however, reflect our need for a sense of transcendence and for the assurance that—in the final analysis and after all is said and done—the last word in the cosmos is "salvation." Such is the faith of the New Testament writer, "For the grace of God has appeared, bringing salvation to all" (Titus 2:11).

Give me a living sense of your glory, Lord God,
your presence, in my life. Amen.

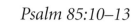

A TREASURY
OF BIBLICAL VALUES

One striking feature of Hebrew poetry is the personification of abstract nouns. A classic example is wisdom speaking as a woman in the book of Proverbs. But we find personification in poetry throughout the Old Testament, as in Psalm 114:3–4, when the sea flees and the mountains skip like rams or, as in Psalm 65:12–13, when the countryside shouts and sings for joy or, as in Joshua 10:12–13, when the sun and moon stand still.

Poetic personifications in verses 11–12 suggest that the occasion for Psalm 85 was a failed harvest: "Faithfulness will spring up from the ground"—as the growing crops—"and righteousness will look down from the sky"—as the falling rain that gives life. Then "our land will yield its increase."

Verses 10–13 of Psalm 85 list four central biblical virtues, values that are attributed to God but that are to be emulated by the faithful people. This prophetic voice asserts that steadfast love and faithfulness [or "mercy and truth"] will meet, and righteousness and peace will kiss each other. When Moses renews the covenant made at Mount Sinai, Yahweh gives this self-description: "The Lord, the Lord, a God merciful and gracious, slow to anger, and abounding in steadfast love . . . keeping steadfast love for the thousandth generation, forgiving iniquity and transgression and sin . . ." (Exodus 34:6–7).

The Apostle Paul urged his converts at Philippi to set their minds on "whatever is true, . . . honorable, . . . just, . . . pure, . . . pleasing, . . . commendable" (Philippians 4:8). We can follow this advice in no better way than to meditate on the four virtues of Psalm 85:10–13: mercy, faithfulness, righteousness, and peace.

Increase in me faithfulness to you and to others, O Lord,
and lead me in the paths of righteousness. Amen.

"IN THE DAY OF TROUBLE"

*A*lthough Psalm 86 appears to be constructed from phrases from a variety of earlier laments, the desperation of the individual sufferer is clearly apparent. The lengthy introduction consists of a series of imperatives: "Incline your ear . . . preserve my life . . . save your servant . . . be gracious to me . . . gladden the soul of your servant . . . give ear, O Lord, to my prayer . . . listen." The petitioner describes himself as "poor and needy" and reminds God of his devotion and trust (verse 2). He then appeals to the better nature of God: "You, O Lord, are good and forgiving, abounding in steadfast love"; "listen to my cry of supplication" (verse 5).

No one can get through this life without days of trouble. But the way we respond to tragedy, misfortune, and sorrow varies greatly from one person to the next. Some are strengthened by the experience of suffering, while others fall into a downward spiral of depression. Some find their way through difficulties by the help of a friendly listening ear, while others require professional counseling. Some persistently ask the unanswerable question, "Why is this happening to me?" while others concentrate on finding answers.

We should not expect a resolution from the blue—as in ancient Greek theater a *deus ex machina*, a god descending from a crane, made things right. But we can and should give voice to our torment in prayer; we can take it to the Lord in prayer, as was the practice of so many of the ancient psalmists.

In the day of my trouble I call on you,
for you will answer me, O Lord. Amen.

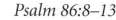

WALKING IN TRUTH

*T*ruth" is an important concept in the Bible. The Hebrew word *emeth* ("truth," verse 11) includes the ideas of firmness, stability, faithfulness, loyalty, and reliability. When applied to God, the word suggests constancy and unchangeableness, so that God can be called a fortress and a rock. God's truth is to be reflected in the life of God's people. Therefore the biblical concept of "truth" can be synonymous with God's commandments or with the whole range of piety and morality, as in verse 11, where the psalmist asks God, "Teach me your way O LORD, that I may walk in your truth."

Yahweh (note the reference to the "name" at the end of verse 11) is incomparable among the gods, having created all the nations, which ultimately shall recognize God's uniqueness (verses 8–9). Indeed, the other gods are nothing (verse 10b). God is "true"—reliable and faithful—and the very heart of God is steadfast love that can bring one up from the depths of Sheol (verse 13). These few verses thereby encompass the heavenly realm of the gods, the sphere of human existence, and the nether regions of Sheol.

When things go terribly wrong, the psalmist has no hesitancy in relying on the ultimate truth and the apex of stability, God's unwavering grace. The proper response to God's faithfulness is to give thanks with your whole heart (verse 12).

Truth is absolutely essential in our spirituality. One of the temptations of religious folk is to engage in wishful thinking. When we read the Bible, should we spend our time trying to link our opinions and desires to a word or two in the text? How much better it is to seek truth instead of confirmation of our own ideas. Don't read your ideas into the Bible. Let the text have its integrity. Most importantly, concentrate on the truth of God, namely, God's faithful and steadfast love.

Lead me into your truth, O God,
and give me an undivided heart. Amen.

"ABOUNDING IN STEADFAST LOVE"

$\mathcal{P}$salm 86:15, like Psalms 103:8 and 145:8, cites the famous introduction to the Ten Commandments: "The LORD, the LORD, a God merciful and gracious, slow to anger, and abounding in steadfast love and faithfulness . . ." (Exodus 34:6). Yes, God's grace always trumps wrath—also in the Old Testament. It is all the more striking that the psalm concentrates on God's mercy when we read that a violent "band of ruffians" and insolent ones are threatening his life (verse 14). The victim asks not for vengeance and judgment on his enemies but only that God show him "a sign of your favor, so that those who hate me may see it and be put to shame" (verse 17). The psalmist's plea is heightened by his self-identification as "your servant" and "the child of your handmaid" (verse 16, RSV), pointing to the piety of his mother, as well.

Although the tyrants of the world might make the headlines, and despite the fact that they evoke fear among the people, the persons we remember most fondly and with the greatest respect are those who act with kindness to others, even when they were the victims of hate and threats. Because it goes counter to our conception of human nature, we are taken aback when a prominent leader forgives his would-be assassin, and when Mother Teresa, because of the necessary condescension involved, asks forgiveness from those whom she helps. So we respond to God not out of terror for God's wrath but in gratitude for divine graciousness.

*Give me strength, Lord God, to refrain from responding
in anger to hateful deeds but instead to think of the beauty
of grace in an imperfect world. Amen.*

"GLORIOUS THINGS"

$\mathcal{J}$ohn Newton (1725–1807), author of many hymns, including "Amazing Grace," wrote a beloved hymn based on Psalm 87 that captures the psalm's sense of wondrous joy:

> Glorious things of thee are spoken,
>   Zion, city of our God;
> He, whose word cannot be broken,
>   formed thee for his own abode.
> On the Rock of Ages founded,
>   what can shake thy sure repose?
> With salvation's walls surrounded,
>   thou may'st smile at all thy foes.
> See, the streams of living waters,
>   springing from eternal love,
> Well supply thy sons and daughters,
>   and all fear of want remove.
> Who can faint when such a river
>   ever flows their thirst t'assuage?
> Grace which like the Lord, the Giver,
>   never fails from age to age.

The psalmist—perhaps a temple singer—watches in rapture as pilgrims throng to the Holy City from Egypt ("Rahab"; see Isaiah 30:7), Babylon, Philistia, Tyre, and as far away as Ethiopia (verse 4). Some of them delight in saying, "I was born here" (verse 5).

Jerusalem, and especially the temple hill there, is the center—the "navel"—of the earth, according to these "psalms of Zion." Its sanctuary shines far above other ancient Israelite worship centers—Dan, Shechem, Shiloh, Gerizim. It is God's own city (verse 3).

Even today first-time pilgrims can be overcome with emotion when they enter Jerusalem. But we know that God is the Lord of the nations and is not limited in time or geography. Our proper worship of the universal God of the cosmos is in spirit and truth.

For the beauty of the earth and for the historical memory of
the place of redemptive acts, we praise you, O God. Amen.

JULY 26   *Psalm 88:1–7*

A CRY IN THE NIGHT

*I*n this, a most graphic lament, we sense the anguish of a man whose depression seems incurable. Like several other lamenters, he suffers from insomnia. Why is it that a person's depression seems to be worst at night? Few Westerners today can imagine what it was like to live without good artificial lighting. Many have not experienced the total darkness of a moonless, cloudy night away from street lights. Although there is great beauty on a starlit night in the wilderness, without moon or stars the nights of the ancient world could be filled with foreboding or even terror. Even today, however, those whose lives are weighed down with anxiety, dread, and hopelessness often find it difficult to make it through the night.

The psalmist's obsession with death leads us to think that he was terminally ill. The core of his being is troubled, and he knows that his "life draws near to Sheol . . . to the Pit" (verses 3–4). There is no help, and he is "like the slain that lie in the grave," no longer remembered by God (verses 4–5). In regions "dark and deep," he feels as though he is struggling far below the waves of the sea (verses 6-7).

One of the most blessed of modern institutions is hospice, an organization devoted to easing the final torments of those facing death. We all know that we are mortal, but we can scarcely understand the dread that comes to many people as they actually face the end. Let us do what we can to make God's grace a reality in the lives of those in the final stages of life.

Bless, O Lord, the hospice workers, and make me
an instrument of comfort to those who face death. Amen.

WHEN HOPE CANNOT
BE FOUND

*E*ven more than in Western societies today, the peoples of the ancient Near East put a high value on friendship. Mutual relationships were to be helpful during all the experiences of life, but especially in times of tragedy and when facing death. The body of the book of Job, chapters 3–37, consists of dialogues between the suffering Job and the friends who come to console him—or perhaps to bring him to repent of the supposed sin that led to his misfortune. Job's friends proved to be singularly unhelpful, and he complained of his social ostracism, even from his family (Job 19:9–22), although, unlike our psalmist, he did not blame God for it (contrast verse 8: "You have caused my companions to shun me").

Desertion by his friends, however, is not the worst. The sufferer fears that his death ("Abaddon," verse 11, the place of ruin and destruction; see Job 26:6; 28:22; 31:12; Proverbs 15:11; 27:20; Revelation 9:11) will be for him the end of God's steadfast love and faithfulness (verse 11). Do God's wonders continue beyond the grave? Can God's salvation reach beyond the "land of forgetfulness? (verse 12). Our psalmist evidently thinks not.

The conviction of renewed life after death emerged only gradually among the ancient Israelites. It took root after the Babylonian exile, when biblical writers were influenced by Persian (Zoroastrian) beliefs. By the time of Jesus, the hope for resurrection was important to the faith of Pharisees and became central to beliefs of all Christians. Our faith in new life cannot divert our attention from our lives in the here and now. But we believe that we will live to praise God forever and ever.

Show me your steadfast love, O God,
now and in the life to come. Amen.

CRIPPLED BY THE FEAR OF DEATH

*T*here is no happy ending for this lament, "certainly the most gloomy words about death in the Old Testament."[29] The prayer peters out with no word of comfort or assurance and with no final plea for help. In retrospect the lamenter concludes that he has been close to death all his life, "from my youth up" (verse 15). Some persons view death is the greatest evil, because it cuts off hope. But Sydney Smith (1771–1845) contended that "death must be distinguished from dying, with which it is often confused."[30] That is, the fear of death can be more difficult to deal with than the actual experience of dying.

Introspective anguish continues in these verses. The sufferer is suffocating beneath a flood of water, and claustrophobia sets in (verse 17). Friends and neighbors shun him, acting out of total ignorance of his situation (verse 18). Worst of all, however, is the lack of any sense of God's loving kindness but instead—at most—only of God's wrath and "dread assaults" (verse 16).

We can learn much from this unrelenting reflection on the problems of death and the absence of God. We cannot deny death by uttering euphemisms or words of false comfort or by acrobatic feats of positive thinking. We must face the fact that we really cannot explain why God is sometimes absent in the midst of human suffering. When pondering the ultimate questions of death and the absence of God, Christians will automatically think of the dying Jesus and his sense of God-forsakenness (Mark 15:34). Sometimes there is nothing we can say, except to protest and issue a challenge to God.

> *O Lord, have mercy on those to whom death draws near,*
> *and bring consolation to those in mourning.*
> *To all grant a measure of your love, taking them into*
> *your tender care. Amen.*

A HISTORICAL PROMISE

*T*his lengthy psalm consists of a hymn (verses 1–18), a royal psalm (verses 19–37), and a lament (verses 38–52). All three sections center on the king in Jerusalem, who reminds God of past promises for the perpetuity of the Davidic line of kings and asks God for victory in the face of threatening enemies.

As in a legal court, verses 1–4 present the opening of the king's case before God. The king echoes the oft-repeated promises that God would show steadfast love and faithfulness to the people of the covenant (among many other passages, Exodus 34:6) and also to the Davidic king. He reminds God "that your steadfast love is established for ever; your faithfulness is as firm as the heavens" (verse 2). What can God say to that?

As a second point in the opening case, the king quotes God's promise to David: "You said, 'I have made a covenant with my chosen one, I have sworn to my servant David: "I will establish your descendants forever, and build your throne for all generations"'" (verses 3–4). A Davidic covenant is mentioned in 2 Samuel 23:5 ("He has made with me an everlasting covenant"); Isaiah 55:3 ("I will make with you an everlasting covenant, my steadfast, sure love for David"); Jeremiah 33:21 ("my covenant with my servant David"); 2 Chronicles 13:5 ("to David and his sons . . . a covenant of salt"); 2 Chronicles 21:7 ("the LORD would not destroy the house of David because of the covenant that he had made with David"). How could God negate all this?

Dare we remind God of past promises when we face threat and danger? Does God need to be reminded? Perhaps it is more appropriate to say that it is our *duty* to bring our troubles to the Lord.

I will sing of your steadfast love, O Lord, forever. Amen.

JULY 30 *Psalm 89:5–18*

OVERCOMING CHAOS

*T*he king tactfully prefaces his case against God in a majestic hymn. He praises God's greatness in the heavenly court, in bringing order out of chaos in the creation of the earth, and in protecting the Israelites in times of danger.

Scene 1 (verses 5–8) is set in the heavenly council of the "holy ones." What earlier Israelites might have considered rival gods are now recognized to be angelic servants of Yahweh, to whom no other deity can be compared. Monotheism is emerging in Israel. Yahweh is described as faithful, feared, great, awesome, and mighty.

Scene 2 (verses 9–14) harks back to the chaos that preceded creation (see Genesis 1:1–2). When creation began there was nothing but total darkness and the raging primeval ocean, here personified as "Rahab" (verse 10), a symbol of threat and foreboding (Rahab is the chaotic ocean also in Isaiah 51:9 and Job 26:12). In conquering chaos God brought order, founding the heavens and the earth as a reflection of the quintessential values of divine righteousness, justice, steadfast love, and faithfulness.

The third scene (verses 15–18) brings us to Jerusalem, where we hear a happy festal shout. The worshipers walk "in the light of your countenance," continually exulting in the name of Yahweh and rejoicing in God's favor in strengthening the people and their king.

The concept of God's creation as the establishing of order out of chaos is a powerful image, one that the people of God can emulate. We can continue God's work of creation by bringing order into our own lives and our local societies, and also by protecting our natural world. The governing aim of our efforts would be to reflect the hallmarks of God's creative activity: righteousness, justice, steadfast love, and faithfulness.

*Make me an instrument of your righteousness
and faithfulness, O God. Amen.*

THE DAVIDIC KING

*P*salm 89:19–37 is a royal psalm, a "vision" to the king (verse 19), that concentrates exclusively on David and the Davidic dynasty in Jerusalem. The entire passage is a poetic elaboration of the fount of all "royal theology" in ancient Jerusalem, namely, Nathan's prophecy to David in 2 Samuel 7.

The oldest stratum in 2 Samuel 7 is most likely the assurance of the perpetuity of the Davidic line: "Yahweh will make you a house. . . . Your house and your kingdom shall be made sure for ever before me; your throne shall be established for ever" (verses 11b and 16). David was "chosen from the people" and anointed with holy oil (1 Samuel 16:1–13). God promised him continuous strength to defeat his enemies (overcoming the chaos of "sea" and "rivers," here verse 25). As the chosen king, David is the adopted son of God (verse 26; see 2 Samuel 7:14, "I will be a father to him, and he shall be a son to me" and Psalm 2:7, "You are my son"). The rest of the section reiterates in several ways the promise of the eternal, unchanging, absolute faithfulness of God to the Davidic line of kings—not weakened or changed even if the people break God's commandments. The "divine right of kings" has never been more forcefully articulated.

In point of historical fact, the Davidic line did come to an end with the destruction of Judah in 587 B.C. What, then, became of the repeated promises of Psalm 89? To put it briefly, they were pushed into the future and applied to a new royal figure who would reestablish the kingship in Israel, namely, the "messiah." Christians took up this projection and applied it to Jesus, a Davidic anointed one.

Predictions of perpetuity in history, however, are always shaky at best. History is unstable. There is only One who is "established forever."

Keep me faithful to your truth, Lord God,
in a world of confusing loyalties. Amen.

A FURIOUS CHARGE
OF BROKEN PROMISES

*T*he psalm takes a 180-degree turn with "But now . . ." in verse 38. A horrendous military defeat has occurred during which God failed to come to the aid of the Davidic king (verses 40–45; "you have not supported him in battle," verse 43). The defensive walls of the cities were broken, the strongholds plundered, and the enemies scornfully rejoice that the king's scepter has been thrown to the ground. The king therefore hurls a long string of blunt and almost blasphemous charges against God, speaking of himself in the third person ("You have spurned and rejected him; . . . you have renounced the covenant with your servant" verses 38, 39). In rejecting the Davidic king, Yahweh has rejected David himself—and especially the grandiose promises of the perpetuity of David's line repeated several times in verses 19–37.

Can God be trusted? That was Habakkuk's question when disaster overtook his nation, when "the law becomes slack and justice never prevails" (Habakkuk 1:4): "Why . . . are [you] silent when the wicked swallow those more righteous than they? (Habakkuk 1:13). The psalmist voices the eternal cry of the laments: "How long, O LORD? . . . How long will your wrath burn like fire?" (verse 46). God needs to be reminded of the promises sworn to David (verse 49).

We respond to the anguish of victims of disaster. We understand their cries. But there are times when we must end our accusations and our demands for an easy formula that solves in one stroke the problem of God and human suffering. In the final analysis, we cannot know why there is suffering in this life—and we must realize that no one else does, either. Only then can we move on and find peace.

Through bane and blessing I give thanks for life
and breath and every good thing. Amen.

LIFE IS BUT A DREAM

The superscription ascribes this psalm to "Moses, the man of God," the founder, liberator, and greatest hero in Israelite tradition. Its exquisite poetry is compelling even in translation, and its themes are universal and timeless.

The psalmist acknowledges his debt to the faith of his forebears of all generations (verse 1) and then centers on God, beginning with a glance at creation and before. The God of the forebears was there before the mountains and this God will be there also into the endless future. "You are God" (verse 2), which is to say, You are the source of our strength and salvation beyond the barriers of time.

Human beings, however, are qualitatively different—intentionally so, because of the will and actions of the eternal God. "You sweep them away; they are like a dream" (verse 5). A thousand years in human history might encompass thirty generations but, in the sight of God, it is like yesterday—or like grass that flourishes in the morning dew and then wilts in the heat of the afternoon. And when a ninety-year-old looks back at her life it can seem like a dream of the past night.

The writer of Ecclesiastes makes much of the idea of death as a great equalizer. Death comes to sage and fool, to rich and poor alike. "What happens to the fool will happen to me also"; "the same fate comes to all" (Ecclesiastes 2:15; 9:2). We realize that we are mortal, but we are not quite sure what we should do with this knowledge. For the moment, let us enjoy the gifts that God has given us: "Go, eat your bread with enjoyment. . . . Enjoy life with the wife whom you love. . . . Whatever your hand finds to do, do with your might" (Ecclesiastes 9:7–10).

Lord, you have been our dwelling place in all generations.
Be with me also in the days to come. Amen.

LIFE IS HARD

$\mathcal{V}$erse 7 is a remarkably abrupt change from the previous verses, in which the naturalness of death is the theme—a shift that seems to be a contradiction. Here the psalmist speaks of human frailty as due to the wrath of God, a consuming and overwhelming wrath that keeps hold of iniquities and secret sins (verses 7–8). From this perspective life on earth is nothing but "toil and trouble" and soon vanishes (verse 10). Again we are reminded of the pessimistic realism of another ancient sage: "What do mortals get from all the toil and strain with which they toil under the sun? For all their days are full of pain, and their work is a vexation; even at night their minds do not rest. This also is vanity" (Ecclesiastes 2:22–23). "Who knows what is good for mortals while they live the few days of their vain life, which they pass like a shadow? For who can tell them what will be after them under the sun?" (Ecclesiastes 6:12).

The human life span does not seem to have changed markedly since the psalmist put the average at seventy—"or perhaps eighty, if we are strong" (verse 10). (The figure would no doubt be considerably smaller if the psalmist had included infant mortality and other premature deaths in the calculations.) However one does the figuring, it is not much in the larger sweep of things. "They are soon gone, and we fly away." We are not God, and realism demands that we know our place.

I pray for some joy in my brief time on earth, O God,
and for the strength to bring joy to others. Amen.

WHAT CAN WE LEARN FROM SHORTNESS OF LIFE?

The psalmist continues to complain of God's wrath, but then, in verse 13, suddenly and unexpectedly asks *God* to repent! "Turn, O Lord! How long? Have compassion on your servants!" Indeed, God does occasionally repent (although the English translations tend to soften the statements of the Hebrew Bible): God "was *sorry* that he had made humankind on the earth" and therefore caused the great flood (Genesis 6:6). At the urging of Moses, "the Lord *changed his mind* about the disaster that he planned to bring on his people" after they worshiped the golden calf at Mount Sinai (Exodus 32:14). At the start of the monarchy, God says, "I *regret* that I made Saul king" (1 Samuel 15:11). See also Amos 7:3, 6.

The psalmist prays that God will repent and turn from wrath to compassion. "Make us glad for as many days as you have afflicted us, and as for as many years as we have seen evil" (verse 15). If there was a specific occasion for the lament, we can never know what it was.

A well-known, but curious statement is the psalmist's prayer in verse 12: "So teach us to count our days that we may gain a wise heart." What, we may wonder, can we learn from the fact that our life is short? How can that make our hearts wise? Does this suggest that we should make the most of our brief time on earth, that we should "seize the day"? Or are we to learn our proper place in the cosmos? We cannot live well if we constantly think of death. Much better it is to pray, "Let the favor of the Lord our God be upon us" (verse 17).

Prosper the work of my hands, O Lord, and let it be a blessing to those around me. Amen.

REFUGE UNDER THE WINGS OF GOD

*T*he beauty of this psalm is due to its repeated assurances that God is our shelter, shield, and refuge in time of trouble. This song of trust bears some marks of a wisdom psalm. But who is the "you" in these verses—"You who live in the shelter of the Most High . . . under his wings you will find refuge . . . you will not fear . . ."? Samuel Terrien suggests that this psalm "is apparently destined to be sung for a monarch or a daring man of war who has just escaped violent death and is still exposed to future danger. . . . Several times the psalmist reiterates the certainty that God will intervene in favor of this unknown figure:" The Most High will deliver you from the enemy's snare (verse 3); God will cover you with his wings (verse 4); day and night you will be protected on the bloody battlefield (verses 7–8); no pestilence will afflict you (verses 3, 6, 10); angels will bear you up (verses 11–12); and wild creatures shall not harm you (verse 13).[32]

The variety of names and images used of God is striking. The names are "Most High" (*Elyon*); "Almighty" (*Shaddai*) "Lord" (YHWH); "my God" (*Elohi*). This God provides shelter—a fortress—to those who live in his shadow. God's wings (either the image of a mother hen or an allusion to the wings of the cherubim in the Jerusalem temple) provide refuge. God is shield and buckler and protector.

The psalmist's words speak comfort to the faithful individual of any age and in any condition. How refreshing is this song of joyous trust, with no complaint and no trace of suffering! Positive thinking has its place.

Keep me under the shadow of your wings, Lord God,
and be to me my refuge and strength. Amen.

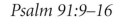
THE CHARGE OF ANGELS

*I*n the conclusion of this psalm, *God* speaks (that is, verses 14–16 are in the form of an oracle), extolling the military hero's piety and God's faithfulness: the warrior loves God, knows God's name, calls to God; God will rescue him, honor him, give him long life, and reveal to him salvation.

In verses 9–13, however, the psalmist (or the temple choir) continues the assurances of God's protection from the previous verses. The hero will experience no evil, no scourge, whether from the enemy or from the lion or the adder, because "he will command his angels concerning you to guard you in all your ways" (verse 11). The concept of guardian angels has persisted from old Babylonian times until today. Here the angels carry the hero like a child, protecting him from even stubbing his toe. But how literally should we take the promise "no evil shall befall you" (verse 10)?

Christian readers recall that, in the story of Jesus' temptations in the desert (Matthew 4:6; Luke 4:10–11), the devil quotes Psalm 91:11–12. The devil taunts Jesus to cast himself from the pinnacle of the temple (as a sign to the people) and to trust the promise made in Psalm 91, "On their hands they will bear you up." Jesus, however, responded by quoting another scripture, "Do not put the Lord your God to the test" (Deuteronomy 6:16). This account—at least in some respects—qualifies the promise of Psalm 91. We are to remember that the psalms reflect the exigencies and pain of earthly life more often and more acutely than they speak of success and victory.

We rejoice in the high points of life and give thanks for times of boundless blessing, but we know that life consists of both blessing and lament.

Be with me, Lord God, in time of trouble, and fill me with thankfulness for your many blessings. Amen.

THE JOY OF MUSIC AND THE GOODNESS OF PRAISE

*T*his psalmist asserts that "It is good [*tob*] to give thanks to the LORD." The Hebrew word *tob* means "good" in both the moral and the esthetic sense, that is, right, pleasing, and beautiful. After the work of creation on the third, fourth, fifth, and sixth days in Genesis 1, God "saw that it was good" (verses 10, 12, 18, 21, and 25). And, when the work of creation was finished, "God saw *everything* that he had made, and indeed, it was *very* good" (Genesis 1:31, emphasis added). God was pleased with the beauty and ethical perfection of creation. The worshiping congregation likewise praises the LORD for "the works of your hands" (verse 4). (The allusion to the days of creation might explain the superscription, "A Song for the Sabbath Day.")

The content of the thankful praise consists of the two fundamental attributes of the Most High: steadfast love and faithfulness, once again revealing the influence of the tradition in Exodus 34:6, "The LORD . . . abounding in steadfast love and faithfulness. . . ." The temple singers praise these innermost qualities of God to an orchestra of different sizes of lyres, some standing on the floor and plucked with the fingers, and smaller, hand-held ones played with a plectrum (verse 3).[33]

Music, the universal language, has been called the speech of angels. Ancient Greeks thought that training in athletics and music was an ideal education. William Congreve (1670–1729) famously remarked that "Music hath charms to soothe the savage breast, / To soften rocks, or bend a knotted oak."[34] Women and men of faith, however, find the greatest joy in making music to the glory of God.

For musicians who lift our spirits by the power of melody
and harmony I give you thanks, O God. Amen.

A PRAYER
FOR THE FLOURISHING
OF THE RIGHTEOUS

*B*eginning with verse 5, Psalm 92 reveals a striking affinity to wisdom literature. References to "the dullard," "the stupid," "the wicked," "your enemies," and "evildoers" in verses 5–9 stand in contrast to the blessings of "the righteous" in verses 12–15. But who is the subject of the intervening verses 10–11, the one who celebrates a military victory? (Verse 9 is reminiscent of the triumphant battle song of Deborah in Judges 5:31.) We can imagine that the guilds of temple singers presented this thanksgiving in celebration of an unnamed battle by the king in Jerusalem.

Fools cannot understand the greatness of the works of the LORD, and, yes, the wicked "sprout like grass, and all evildoers flourish," but they ultimately are "doomed to destruction" (verses 6–7). Their comeuppance awaits the future. The righteous, by contrast, flourish, growing straight and tall like a cedar in Lebanon, flourishing in the courts of God, living in their old age as though they were young—all of which reveals the justice of the LORD (verses 12–15). And yet, the psalm does not deal in any profound way with the question of innocent suffering. The people, gathered at the temple, offer this psalm as a prayer that their king will avert the plots of the evildoers and flourish into a rich old age.

There is no convincing explanation for the success of evildoers in this life, and many are the pious who know sorrow. But we offer our prayers to the God of steadfast love and faithfulness, finding in God the source of our life and our hope.

Reveal to me your righteousness, Lord God,
and let the prayers of those in distress come to you. Amen.

HOLINESS, AWE, AND THE POWER OF THE LORD

*P*salms 47; 93; and 95–99, sometimes called enthronement psalms, celebrate Yahweh's kingship in Israel and over the breadth of the cosmos, a frequent affirmation elsewhere in the psalms as well. The idea of the kingship of God is found even in early texts like Exodus 15:18, "The LORD will reign for ever and ever," and Numbers 23:21, "The LORD their God is with them, acclaimed as a king among them" (see also Judges 8:23; 1 Samuel 8:7; 1 Kings 22:19). Enthronement psalms seem to have been used in the autumnal New Year festival (Rosh Hashanah), at which time the kingship of God was celebrated, along with the renewal of the covenant made at Mount Sinai.

In Psalm 93 the people, gathered at the Jerusalem temple, proclaim, "Yahweh is king, he is robed in majesty!" Without detracting from the prestige of the earthly king, the people acknowledge that Yahweh is the true king over the entire cosmos. So also, at a time when the monarchy in Jerusalem was threatened, the prophet Isaiah had a vision of the King, the LORD of hosts whose glory fills the whole earth (Isaiah 6:3, 5).

Here Yahweh is praised for subduing the roiling, thundering waters of the chaos that preceded creation (Genesis 1:2). God's majesty tames the whelming waves. The psalm ends with a reference to the commandments, "your decrees," given at Mount Sinai (verse 5).

Our images of God reflect the society in which we live. Monarchy in our time seems to have run its course, and now it functions mainly as a national symbol. The image of God as monarch, however, retains its meaning for those who view the divine as the unitary and unifying ground of our being.

Floods both literal and symbolic have overwhelmed the people of earth. Tame the chaos in our lives, O Lord. Amen.

COMEUPPANCE FOR THE ARROGANT

*W*e react negatively to persons who assume an air of "entitlement," who think that the rules do not apply to them, and that they deserve their privilege, their wealth, and the "lifestyle to which they have become accustomed." We are offended when they persuade government officials to give them lucrative contracts and lobby lawmakers to allow tax cuts, all the while scaling back the safety net for those who find themselves, often for no fault of their own, in economic distress.

Our psalmist knew such persons. They were proud, wicked, and—not least—arrogant evildoers who crushed the people and killed the widow, the stranger, and the orphan. Moreover, they did so with callous impunity: "They say, 'The LORD does not see' (verse 7)—as if the only crime would be to get caught.

What does our psalmist say of such folks? They are "dullest of the people"; they are fools (verse 8). There is one who knows their evil plots, their character assassinations, their scheming, and their fostering of injustice in the land: "The LORD knows the thoughts of humankind, that they are but an empty breath" (verse 11), and the entitled ones will eventually get "what they deserve"—their comeuppance (verse 2). To use Christian language, their only hope is that God justifies human beings apart from works of the law—because their works are evil!

It is great comfort to know that the ultimate evaluation of our lives will come from the righteous judge of the whole earth.

Let your justice shine forth, O God, in our world.
Bless those who struggle against the forces of violence
and oppression. Amen.

GOOD CAN COME FROM DISCIPLINE

*T*he psalmist turns from the arrogant to the righteous, the *zaddiq* (verse 15). The righteous person is "disciplined" by the LORD, being taught the law, thereby averting trouble (verse 12). The arrogant ones of the prior verses are undisciplined, paying no attention to the commandments, and seeking only their advantage in any way possible. But the day of reckoning will come, says the psalmist. "Justice will return to the righteous" (verse 15), and a "pit" will be "dug for the wicked" (verse 13). If the scales were not eventually to be balanced, this would amount to God abandoning "his heritage" (verse 14), namely, the covenant made at Sinai, in which promises and commitments were made by each side, God and the people.

Training and discipline are prominent values in the wisdom tradition. The book of Proverbs as a whole centers on wisdom, instruction, and understanding in "wise dealing, righteousness, justice, and equity" (Proverbs 1:3). Proverbs 3:11–12 specifically advises, "My child, do not despise the LORD's discipline . . . for the LORD reproves the one he loves."

Our society rightly places a high value on education; we engage in heated debates over education policies. We realize that children who grow up with no guidance will not learn to curb their innate selfishness. We know also that training and discipline are difficult, never-ending tasks. But we agree also with Ghanaian president Kwame Nkrumah (1909–1972), who said, "Without discipline true freedom cannot survive."[35]

Bless and strengthen those who teach, O God,
that our youth might grow and mature. Amen.

THE SOURCE
OF CONSOLATION

*T*he petitioner was sure that his life had been threatened ("my soul would soon have lived in the land of silence"), and that the evildoers who plotted his death would have succeeded were it not for the help of the LORD (verse 17). He had been beset by torturous thoughts and was subject to fits of anxiety (the translation "cares of my heart," verse 19, does not express the strength of the Hebrew word). But it is striking that the prayer for deliverance is said *after it* has been granted: "Your steadfast love, O LORD, *held* me up" (verse 18); "the LORD *has become* my stronghold, and my God the rock of my refuge" (verse 22). The psalm therefore ends with an expression of trust in the providence of God, albeit with a less-than-lofty sentiment: "The LORD our God will wipe them out," namely, the evildoers (verse 23).

A specific charge against the evildoers emerges in verse 20: wicked rulers contrive mischief by statute, banding together against the righteous, and condemning the innocent to death. The fact that such things still happen today in many parts of the world and that even in Western countries politicians often put their self-interest—especially their greed for money—ahead of the welfare of the people is disheartening. But the psalmist has "consolations" (the Hebrew word occurs only here in the book of Psalms) that cheer his soul (verse 19). It is his trust in "God the rock of my refuge" (verse 22).

In the New Testament, Paul is certain that God "consoles those who are in any affliction" or "downcast" (2 Corinthians 1:4; 7:6).

When my way grows drear, precious Lord, linger near. Amen.

Psalm 95:1–7a

SHEER JOY
IN THE PRESENCE OF GOD

*P*salm 95 has two parts. It begins with a hymn of joy, an invitation to worship God as king (verses 1–7a); it concludes with an oracle regarding the people's rebellion in the past (verses 7b–11). In the first part the flow of thought follows a specific liturgical sequence, suitable for the autumn New Year festival: The congregation is invited to worship the Lord with "joyful noise" (verses 1–2). Yahweh ("the Lord") is revealed as supreme "King above all gods" (verse 3) and as creator of the universe (verse 4), who calls the people to renewed commitment to the commandments of the covenant made at Sinai (verses 7–11). The temple singers repeat the invitation, the introit, in verses 6–7a.

Attributions to and appellations for God are familiar from other psalms: the Lord is like the stability of rock (as an insurance company takes the image of the Rock of Gibraltar). God's kingship reaches to all creation, from the ocean bottom to the highest peak. Most importantly, God is "our Maker," and God remains connected to us as a shepherd to his sheep (verses 6–7).

The exuberance of the psalmist is apparent even today, not least when a worshiping congregation sings these stirring words. There is not yet in these verses any admonition, warning, command, or threat—nor even any mention of God's blessings in the past or present. There is nothing but sheer joy in the presence of God for its own sake. The purest praise comes with no strings attached—no expectation of reward and no bargaining but the expression of elation for no other reason that that the Lord is our God.

Give me a joyful heart, O Lord, remembering that you
are my maker and the shaper of my destiny. Amen.

LESSONS FROM THE PAST

*I*n the middle of verse 7 the tone shifts from exuberant joy to serious admonition. The choir (or perhaps cantor) intones the theme: "O that today you would listen to his voice!" (verse 7b). The examples of not-listening will come from the distant past, but the congregation is to apply the negative lesson to today. What follows is an oracle; God speaks.

The content of the speech of God is the familiar theme of the people's rebellion during the wanderings in the wilderness after the exodus from Egypt (see Jeremiah 2:4–6; Hosea 9:10). According to the story in Exodus 17:1–7, the people hardened their hearts, putting God to the test at Meribah (which means "test" or "contention"; see Numbers 20:13) and quarreling with Moses at Massah (which means "quarrel"). Their question might seem to us a reasonable one: "Is the LORD among us or not?" (Exodus 17:7). But the question reflected a lack of trust that resulted in God loathing that generation for forty years (verse 10) and a solemn promise: "they shall not enter my rest," meaning the promised land (verse 11; see Deuteronomy 12:9, "You have not yet come into the rest and the possession that the LORD your God is giving you").

Verses 7–11 are quoted in the New Testament in Hebrews 3:7–11 with the similar admonition to be faithful to God, but with a subsequent development of the theme of the "sabbath rest . . . for the people of God" (Hebrews 4:1–11). Here the "rest" from struggle and strife that the wilderness generation looked forward to in the land of Canaan becomes the "rest" of the great Sabbath, when all creation breathes a sigh of relief at the end of evil, suffering, tears, and death.

In my passage through life, O Lord, let me learn
from the example of others who have been faithful. Amen.

HONOR, MAJESTY, STRENGTH, AND BEAUTY

*A*s also in Psalms 33:3; 40:3; 98:1; 144:9; and 149:1 the temple singers here urge the gathered congregation to "sing to the LORD a *new* song" (verse 1). This reference to newness seems ironic when we realize that verses 7–13 are almost identical to 1 Chronicles 16:28–33 and have clear echoes also in Psalm 29:1–2—to mention only a few of the parallels. What is the newness? Was it simply a newly composed piece, or was it perhaps used in a renewal of the covenant, in which God is praised as king? Was it a song for a new day?

In any event, the congregation blesses God's name, Yahweh, and proclaims God's glory to the nations (the Gentiles) by recounting God's "marvelous works" of salvation. The LORD is "revered above all gods," which are nothing more than "idols," especially because "the LORD made the heavens" (verses 4–5).

In verse 6 we gain a sense of the emotion of the worshipers in the temple. In the sacred room they experience the royal splendor of the king of the universe whom they worship: honor, majesty, strength, and beauty. Each of these terms is an abstraction and therefore not easy to define. Taken together, however, they convey the essence of reverent awe. Although Psalm 96 associates this sense of sacred otherness with the enthronement of the king, spiritual worship is always closely associated with honor and beauty. From the perspective of human emotion, it is indeed difficult to draw a sharp line between the esthetic experience (of beauty) and the spiritual experience (of the presence of God). Truly, there is beauty in holiness ("holy splendor," verse 9).

Give me voice, O Lord, daily to sing a new song,
and let my voice hearten the lives of others. Amen.

JOYFUL JUDGMENT

*I*t is risky to take poetic parts of the Bible too literally. In the Reformation period John Calvin understood the words "The world is firmly established; it shall never be moved" (Psalm 96:10 and 93:3) as a refutation of Nicolaus Copernicus's theory that the earth revolves around the sun! We read also in Psalm 96 the "all the trees of the forest sing for joy" (verse 12). A proper response to the biblical text requires us to be flexible, open to new understandings and the various ways the ancient writers expressed their convictions and fears.

The exuberance of verses 1–9 leads in verses 10–13 to the joyful proclamation, "The LORD is king!" In these verses the heavenly king is praised as the righteous judge of the universe. Yahweh will ultimately judge not only the Israelites but also "the people"—and all with equity, righteousness, and truth (verses 10, 13b). The thought of this just judgment causes great rejoicing, not only in the Jerusalem temple but also in the heavens and throughout the earth, in fields and forests (verses 11–12). Isaac Watts caught the spirit of the psalmist in his great hymn:

> Joy to the world! the Savior reigns;
> Let all their songs employ;
> While fields and floods, rocks, hills, and plains
> Repeat the sounding joy. . . .

> *O Lord, let me join the hymn of the universe;*
> *open my ears to the harmony of the spheres now*
> *and in the ages to come. Amen.*

REVELATION IN NATURE

*T*heologians have debated whether there is such a thing as "natural" knowledge of God, that is, whether ordinary folk can learn something of the being and character of God by observing the world of nature. (This is different from "intelligent design," which aims specifically at a critique of evolution.) Does a walk in the summer along a stream in a lush forest lead you to faith in a Creator? This might possibly happen to some folks, but, as Martin Luther often pointed out, we can discern only the faint tracks of God in the world of nature, while *who* God is—God's essence of saving grace, redemption, and love for the created world—remains hidden until it is revealed to us.

To perceive even the traces of divine majesty in nature, however, is no small thing. The ancient Israelites celebrated God's "righteousness and justice" in the booms of thunder and the brilliant streaks of lightning that break through the darkness of night (verses 2–4). How would a terrific thunderstorm remind them of "justice" rather than power? The storm reminded them of God's overthrow of "adversaries," which was both an act of power and of justice. It was part of what it meant to call God "king" (verse 1). So "the heavens" literally "proclaim his righteousness" (verse 6), and this is unmistakably evident to "the world" (verse 4) and "the many coastlands" (verse 1), a reference to distant places.

Christians look especially to the teachings of Jesus as revealing the nature and will of God. There we find the core of the matter, a necessary precondition to marveling at the hazy traces of God we see in the natural world.

I thank you, Lord God, for the beauty of the natural world,
but I thank you most of all for the saving word
that brings life and hope. Amen.

NO SHADES OF GRAY?

God's righteousness, revealed in the booming thunderstorm of verses 2–5, brings shame to the idol worshipers. But "Zion hears" the voice of God in the storm, and "the towns of Judah rejoice, because of your judgments, O God" (verse 8). Like a wisdom sage, so also here the psalmist builds a worldview out of contrasts—of the idolaters and the pious, the good and the evil, the righteous and the wicked (verses 10–12).

The twentieth-century theologian Paul Tillich once gave a lecture on the sources of religious thought in which he defined three principles of authority: *autonomy* (the self as foundational principle), *heteronomy* (a source from an outside authority), and *theonomy* (God as revealer). Someone in the audience asked him whether there might be another alternative. He replied in his thick Germanic accent, "Yes there is—ambiguity." Tillich's answer was contrary to the assumption of much of the Bible. Most biblical writers were persons of "primary colors, or rather of black and white, who saw the world always in contour. They were a dogmatic people, despising doubt, our modern crown of thorns. . . . They knew only truth and untruth, belief and unbelief, without our hesitating retinue of finer shades," as T. E. Lawrence wrote of the desert Arabs he encountered.[36] You either worship the Lord or you worship idols that are nonentities. You are either righteous or wicked, wise or foolish.

We who live in the real world know that there are not always simple answers to difficult questions. We know that on some issues there must be shades of gray. Life is often ambiguous. But in the end, we believe, the justice and the mercy of God will prevail over all.

O God, in this world of uncertainty and ambiguity,
show me the right path of righteousness. Amen.

THE UNIVERSAL TRIUMPH OF GOD

*T*he temple singers invite the congregation to sing a "new song" (verse 1; also Psalms 33:3; 40:3; 96:1; 144:9; 149:1), a song about a final victory of God that is inescapably evident to all the nations, even to the ends of the earth. What is this victory?

In the Hebrew language, verbs in the perfect tense usually refer to past actions, but they also can refer to events in the indeterminate future. In Psalm 98 the verbs—"has done . . . have gotten . . . has made known . . . has revealed . . . has remembered . . . have seen"—almost certainly speak of the distant future, when the LORD will have defeated all the forces of evil, a time when God's "vindication," the rightness of God's commands and judgment would be "revealed . . . in the sight of the nations" (verse 2b). It is an ideal picture of the perfecting of all creation. It is, to use technical language, an eschatological picture, an image of the "last things."

God's motivation in this final battle was to remember "his stead-fast love and faithfulness to the house of Israel" a frequent expression in the psalms (for example, 36:6; 88:12; 89:2, 25, 34; 92:3). Although the motivation is directed primarily to Israel, the victory is universal, involving all nations (verses 2–3).

Christians and Jews have traditionally rejected the idea that evil is eternal. The principle of dualism, of two opposing powers for all eternity, is alien to us. We believe that God will ultimately triumph over all the forces that afflict, limit, or destroy life. We believe also that we have a role to play in the struggle against evil in our time. We today sing the new song mainly in anticipation—in the certainty of the final outcome.

Although my way through life is often hard and the way unclear, let me live with the vision of your ultimate overcoming of evil, O God. Amen.

ALIVE WITH THE SOUND OF MUSIC

*P*salm 98:4–9 has two parts: Verses 4–6 describe the music of the new song, while verses 7–9, almost a literal duplicate of Psalm 96:11–13, invite the whole created order to join in this praise of Yahweh, the King (verse 6).

The joyous voices of the temple singers are to be accompanied by the lyre (*kinnor*, a rather high-pitched stringed instrument that was hand-held and plucked with a plectrum), by trumpets, and—the venerable, revered traditional instrument—the horn (*shofar*). (The instruments are named also in Psalms 47:5; 33:2; 71:22; 81:2–3; 150:3–5; see the comments on Psalm 71:17–24, above). All of this is to be praise of "the King, Yahweh" (verse 6b).

As in Joseph Haydn's oratorio *The Creation*, all nature is called on to join the song of triumph. There is poetic alteration: water/land; sea/the world; floods/the hills (verses 7–8). The hills are to be alive with the sound of music (verse 8). Nature rejoices at the imminent coming of the LORD, which will begin the final judgment, a time when righteousness will finally and ultimately become a reality in the entire cosmos.

Images of final judgment in ancient and medieval Christian writings and art often centered on terrifying and horrific punishment of evildoers, with the obvious purpose of scaring people into following the right path. In Psalm 98, by contrast, we have only joy in the ultimate triumph of equity and righteousness for all peoples. There are times in life when it might seem that we live in a hostile environment. In the final analysis, however, the grace that stems from the heart of God will reign supreme over all.

Let me sing a joyful song with all who acknowledge you,
O Lord; let me rejoice in the revelation
of your righteousness. Amen.

THE HOLINESS OF GOD

*I*n Psalm 99 the shout, "Yahweh is king," is followed by three stanzas, each of which ends with the acclamation of God's holiness. Verses 1–3 extol Yahweh's holiness in terms of world rule, while verses 4–5 praise God's establishment of justice. Both end with the shout, "Holy is he!" The third stanza, verses 6–9, lauds Yahweh's holiness in the sweep of history.

Have you ever wondered why so many of the words used in religious piety and in our liturgies are difficult to define? For example, most of us have only a foggy idea of the meaning of the word "holy." The Hebrew word is *qadosh*, which suggests the idea of separation and points to a being or sphere that stands above everyday life. Before revealing the commandments to Moses, Yahweh instructs him to "Set limits around the mountain and keep it holy" (Exodus 19:23). The Old Testament experience of the holy is of something brilliant, overpowering, awe-inspiring, majestic, and exalted. The New Testament term is *hagios*, which means both "holy" and "saint." God—or the things closely associated with God, like the temple—is predominantly the Holy One.

The psalmist senses the holiness of God in the temple, enthroned upon the cherubim (verse 1b). But God's holiness is perceived especially in the rule of justice that God established for the nation. God is "Mighty King, lover of justice" (verse 4). And for this the people sing, "Holy is he!"

Our language of praise must necessarily include abstractions. Indeed, all human words ultimately fail to grasp the essence of absolute truth, which is the heart of God. Nonetheless, in the mysterious presence of the wholly other we can do no better than to confess, "Holy are you, Lord God."

What language shall I borrow to praise you, Lord of heaven and earth? The whole earth is full of your glory. Amen.

MEDIATORS OF THE HOLY

*W*hen Isaiah received his call in the temple, the seraphs sang, "Holy, holy, holy is the LORD of hosts; the whole earth is full of his glory" (the *trisagion* [thrice holy], Isaiah 6:3). In Psalm 99: 3, 5, 9, the temple singers three times acclaim the holiness of God.

Verses 6–9 respond to the confession of God's holiness as involving separation from the everyday life of human beings. Which human beings can speak for God? In ancient Israelite society this was the primary function of the priests and the prophets. Verse 6 names three mediators. *Moses* was the spokesman for God par excellence (see Exodus 33:11, "Yahweh used to speak to Moses face to face, as one speaks to a friend"). He and his brother *Aaron* came from the priestly tribe, Levi. *Samuel* had the prophetic function of communicating God's word to the people at the establishment of the monarchy. Curiously, all three were associated with the Ark of the Covenant, which came to rest in the innermost room of the temple. Moses and Aaron constructed the Ark, and God called the boy Samuel to prophesy in association with the Ark (1 Samuel 3:3). Moreover, the "pillar of cloud" (verse 7) also came to be connected with the innermost room of the temple (see 1 Kings 8:10–11).

The holiness of the LORD was for the psalmists not an obstacle to worship but its very soul. Mediators witnessed to the heart of God, God's core nature—a balance of justice and mercy. "You were a forgiving God to them, but an avenger of their wrongdoings" (verse 8). Because God is steadfast and not capricious, just and not arbitrary, the people could worship with integrity at his holy mountain, the temple hill in Jerusalem (verse 9).

I thank you, O God, for the witness of the saints of old;
give me voice to speak for justice
and forgiveness in my time. Amen.

THE JOY OF WORSHIP

*T*his beloved entrance hymn (an introit or processional) functions as a concluding burst of praise to the preceding enthronement psalms, 93, 95–99, which rejoice in the kingship of Yahweh. The two parts, verses 1–3 and 4–5 have an almost identical form: the invitation to worship is followed by the reason and motivation for praise.

The keynote of the entire Psalm 100 is obvious and emphatic. It is joy—joy in entering the place of the worship of the true God and joy in sensing the presence of God in the worshiping community.

What is the cause and content of this joy? Samuel Terrien hardly exaggerates when he asserts that "the whole catechism of Judaism is already here summed up in four articles: (1) 'The Lord is God'; (2) 'he has made us'; (3) 'we are his people'; (4) 'the Lord is good.'" [37] The starting point of ancient Israel's creed clearly expressed in Deuteronomy 6:4, "Hear O Israel: Yahweh is our God, Yahweh alone." Verse 3a reflects this confession also here: Yahweh is God (verse 3a). Yahweh is not a tribal deity but, in fact, the creator of "all the earth." In spite of this universal dimension, "we are his people," that is, the worshiping community at the temple are the special people of the universal creator. (The fourth emphasis, the goodness of God, is the subject of the reflections for August 24.)

The joy of Psalm 100 has nothing to do with the facile gospel of the preachers of prosperity ("God wants you to succeed"). The psalmists well knew the sufferings of this world, but, above all, they were convinced of the unconditional love of God.

To you, Lord God, my maker and my redeemer,
I lift my voice in joyful praise. Amen.

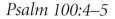

THE GOODNESS OF GOD

*T*he second half of Psalm 100, like the first, begins with the invitation to worship and then provides the rationale for worship. The basic premise is announced in verse 5a: "The Lord is good." Goodness as the inner nature of God is made specific in the two attributes familiar to us from so many hymns in the book of Psalms: God's goodness is manifested in "steadfast love" (we could also translate this term as "grace") and "faithfulness."

God is good. How can such a simple phrase be so difficult for us to absorb as we experience the downside of life? How can we hold together our assertion of the goodness of God in the face of human suffering? We wonder, is God steadfastly good? Is God faithful?

The bedrock of faith—the one essential, the *sine qua non*— remains true through all our earthly experiences. God's goodness, God's grace, and God's faithfulness sustain us in good times and bad. This joyful confidence of Psalm 100 has given us the hymn tune "Old Hundredth," for which authors have provided several texts, including William Kethe (died about 1591):

> All people that on earth do dwell,
>   Sing to the Lord with cheerful voice;
> Him serve with mirth, his praise forth tell;
>   Come ye before him and rejoice.
> For why? The Lord our God is good:
>   His mercy is forever sure;
> His truth at all times firmly stood,
>   And shall from age to age endure.

> *I praise you, O God, for your steadfast love and your*
> *faithfulness through good times and bad. Amen.*

Psalm 101

MARKS OF AN IDEAL RULER

*P*salm 101 includes a list of vices the speaker asserts he will avoid and suppress: baseness, inconstancy, perverseness, evil, slander, haughtiness, arrogance, deceit, lies, wickedness, and evildoing. There is also a list of virtues to be practiced and rewarded: loyalty, justice, blamelessness, integrity, and faithfulness. At first glance this might seem to be the boasting of a proud man who sets himself above his fellows. But then we notice that the speaker has a large house (verses 2, 7). He can pick and choose those who can minister to him (verse 6b), and he wields power sufficient for "cutting off all evildoers from the city of the LORD" (verse 8). The speaker is quite clearly the king or a young man about to become king, and he is a person of admirable qualities.

Some politicians refuse to accept responsibility for the messes they create, piously declining to "play the blame game"! In contrast, this king acknowledges that, like all the inhabitants of his land, he too stands under the moral demands of God. He pledges to the LORD that he will uphold loyalty and justice (verse 1) and aim at blamelessness (verse 2). He will struggle against evil and work for the common good. His court will be marked by honesty and truth, and his assistants and advisors will be trustworthy and free of calumny.

Politics is serious business, and persons of faith have a responsibility to support integrity and justice. No one is above God's laws. No politician can presume to govern by divine right. By the same token, we should support virtuous leaders and thank God for them.

Raise up, O Lord, capable leaders of integrity
who have a passion for justice. Amen.

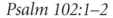

A CRY FROM THE HEART

*T*he superscription of Psalm 102, "A prayer of one afflicted, when faint and pleading before the LORD," is certainly an accurate description of this psalm as a whole. It is, as the French would say, a *cri de coeur*, a cry from the heart, an anguished outburst from the depths of one's being, remarkable for the intensity of grief it displays and especially for a considerable gift at introspection.

The opening lines, verses 1–2, are in the traditional pattern of a prayer from a person afflicted with a terminal illness (later, in verses 23–24, the petitioner expresses the fear of dying prematurely). These verses have three pairs of lines, each pair a desperate plea that God would hear and respond to the afflicted person's prayer.

The psalmist applies two bodily images to God: face and ear. In Old Testament thought the face is the main venue for the expression of a person's attitudes. To "hide your face" (verse 2) is to express displeasure or disinterest, and to "set your face against" something is to express hostility (Jeremiah 21:10). The opposite of this is "to make your face shine on" someone, an indication of blessing and friendship (Numbers 6:25). The "face" of God can mean God's presence, so that the hiding of God's face means the absence of God. Once God acknowledges the suffering petitioner, then "Incline your ear to me" is an appropriate plea for a response.

The fear that God will remain hidden or silent when we suffer can be debilitating and excruciating. The realization that there is no rational way to understand God's silence only compounds the anguish. But, after laying bare his heart in verses 3–11, the psalmist will remember God's faithfulness, and his mood will change to praise.

When my way seems dark, and there are no good answers,
let my cry come to you, O Lord. Amen.

ANATOMY OF ANGUISH

*T*he images of a smoking furnace and burning bones (verse 3) suggest that the psalmist suffered from a fever. These images also convey the feeling that life is slipping away like the dissipation of smoke in the air or "like an evening shadow" (verse 11). The sufferer's heart is shrunk and withered like grass (verses 4, 11). His appetite has gone (verse 9), and he is becoming nothing more than skin and bones (verse 5). He has severe insomnia (verse 7) and feels as deserted and abandoned, like "a little owl of the waste places" (verse 6). To top it off, he has become the object of taunts and curses, no doubt from those who attribute his suffering to some unconfessed sin (verse 8). Is it any wonder that he feels as though God has lifted him up and tossed him aside (verse 10)?

Victims of depression who are able to describe their affliction typically say that they feel "empty inside," reamed out, with nothing left but a shell, their lives totally devoid of meaning. Without intervention, we are at those times in danger of falling into a descending spiral from which it is exceedingly difficult to escape. Counseling is often required, and faithful friends can be a great blessing. Most of all, a vision of the shining face of God is needed for life to return in all its fullness.

The simple act of reading classic hymns can lift our spirits. You would do well to begin with the powerful words of Isaac Watts:

> *O God, our help in ages past, our hope for years to come,*
> *still be our guard while troubles last,*
> *and our eternal home. Amen.*

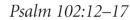

ASSURANCE OF THE COMPASSION OF THE LORD

*A*n abrupt change occurs in verse 12, a transformation from the pits of despair to a hymn of praise for the power and compassion of the LORD (note the change to the second-person pronoun). The hymnic verses, however, are tinged with lament, for the holy city, Zion, Jerusalem, lies in dust (verse 14b), evoking the pity of the inhabitants. This part of the psalm evidently comes from the time after the return from Babylonian exile, which began in 538 B.C., and before the reconstruction of Judah that involved the rebuilding of the temple, dedicated in 515 B.C. The psalmist eagerly anticipates the rebuilding of the city, when the LORD "will appear in his glory [*kabod*]," that is, the presence of the Holy One will again take residence in a new temple in the holy city (verse 16).

The people in Jerusalem "hold its stones dear." At the moment, however, they are "destitute" (verse 17). They therefore can only appeal to the power and compassion of God ("enthroned for ever," verse 12; "You will rise up and have *compassion* on Zion," verse 13). They are sure that this is the right time, the appointed time (verse 13b). When the city is renewed and rebuilt, then the humiliation of defeat and exile will have ended in a transformation that would cause the nations and the kings of the earth to fear the name of Yahweh.

Among the many attributes of God in the Bible, the conviction that God is compassionate can bring despair to an end and usher in a time of hope—both for the nation of old and for individuals today. God, we can say, shares our suffering and therefore we, even on the down days, keep hope alive for renewal and restoration.

Great is your faithfulness, O God my Father.
Your compassions, they fail not. As you have been,
you forever will be. Amen.

A WRITTEN RECORD
OF THE LORD'S DELIVERANCE

Several times the Bible speaks of the writing of records for the sake of posterity. On a large tablet Isaiah wrote the names of his sons, which symbolized his message of destruction and renewal (Isaiah 8:1–4). He later received a command from God to write his more complete message in a book "so that it may be for the time to come as a witness forever" (Isaiah 30:8). Similarly, the LORD commanded Jeremiah to write on a scroll the oracles he had preached for many years (Jeremiah 36:1–3). More famously, Job, in his extreme despair begs that his good name be cleared: "O that my words were written down! O that they were inscribed in a book!" so that even after his death his innocence might be proved and his vindication secured (Job 19:23).

Our psalmist, completely certain of the LORD's restoration of Judah, which had lain in disrepair and ruin for decades, asks that a scribe be appointed to record the anticipated wondrous deliverance. The LORD has heard the groans of the prisoners; God has "looked down from his holy height," and a future generation will be able to read the account and praise the God of heaven. The restoration will magnify the name of Yahweh, and even the foreign nations will gather in the renewed city of Jerusalem to worship.

Some persons keep a spiritual journal, recording their journey of faith through good days and bad. Others do research on their family history, finding there men and women of deep conviction who endured hardship and struggle by virtue of their trust in God. Let us learn from the past, and let us also preserve for our children and their children our witness to the grace of our compassionate God.

I thank you, Lord God, for educators, scholars, and authors
who devote their lives to the search for truth. Amen.

AUGUST 30 *Psalm 102:23–28*

ON DYING BEFORE ONE'S TIME

*A*fter an optimistic appeal to the compassion of God in verses 12–22, the psalmist returns to the pathos of verses 1–11. But now the fear of death looms heavy on his heart: "O my God . . . do not take me away at the mid-point of my life" (verse 24). God, who eons ago laid the foundations of the earth, will have no end, even though the heavens and the earth will eventually disintegrate like a piece of old clothing, after which God will most likely create a new cosmos (verses 25–26). But there is a sense of injustice when someone dies in mid-life. Stephen Foster (1826–1864) captured the melancholy of life and the pathos of death in his plaintive song about the blossoms of the field:

> Sad is my heart for the blighted plants—
>   Its pleasures are aye as brief—
> They bloom at the young year's joyful call,
>   And fade with the autumn leaf.
> Ah! may the red rose live alway,
>   To smile upon earth and sky!
> Why should the beautiful ever weep?
> Why should the beautiful die?[38]

What can you say to someone facing a premature death? How can you comfort a spouse, a child, or a parent who must witness this? And how can you come to terms with your own mortality? Our psalmist ends his reflections with the modest hope that his children will live securely after his passing (verse 28). But we believe in the compassion and grace of God who has power over life and death, and so we can confess, with Paul, that nothing, "neither death, nor life . . . nor things present, nor things to come, nor powers, nor height, nor depth, nor anything else in all creation, will be able to separate us from the love of God in Christ Jesus our Lord" (Romans 8:38–39).

Eternal God, Lord of life, bring comfort to those to whom
death draws near. In my weakness give me strength,
and in my despair give me hope. Amen.

THE BENEFITS OF GOD

$\mathcal{M}$en and women over the centuries have found in the noble words of this great thanksgiving hymn the strength and courage to surmount great difficulties, enabling them to bless God from the core of their being.

Why does the psalmist bless the LORD? Consider the impressive list of benefits accrued. God (1) forgives all your iniquity, (2) heals all your diseases, (3) redeems your life from the Pit, (4) crowns you with steadfast love and mercy, and (5) satisfies you with good as long as you live. What a list of perks! And what a collection of verbs, each one of which we hope and pray to experience! The psalmist has obviously emerged from a severe disorientation to a euphoric new orientation in which an overabundance of gratitude finds expression in an outburst of praise. Guilt is overcome by grace, disease by healing, and fear of death to a new burst of life and well-being. Is there a more beautiful description of salvation?

My soul, now praise your maker!
　Let all within me bless his name
Who makes you full partaker
　Of mercies more than you dare claim.
Forget him not whose meekness
　Still bears with all your sin,
Who heals your ev'ry weakness,
　Renews your life within;
Whose grace and care are endless
　And saved you through the past;
Who leaves no suff'rer friendless,
　But rights the wronged at last.[39]

For the benefits of life, forgiveness, healing, mercy, love,
and strength, O Lord, I bless your name. Amen.

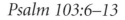

THE CHARACTER OF GOD

*C*ontinuing the outburst of joy, the psalmist turns from God's *benefits* to praise of the *character* of God, specifically justice, mercy, grace, steadfast love, and compassion. These are the qualities that attract and endear, whether found in other human beings or in the heart of God. God was "made known . . . to Moses" as such. The psalmist, like so many others, thinks of the covenant at Sinai, which was itself an act of grace and steadfast love on the part of God. There the LORD gave this self-description, "The LORD, . . . merciful and gracious, slow to anger, and abounding in steadfast love" (Exodus 34:6).

The law of Moses also included the means for forgiveness of transgressions (verses 10–12), namely, the system of sacrifices and other priestly rituals. Although God acts with justice for the oppressed (verse 6), this justice does not trump God's compassion, which removes transgressions "as far as the east is from the west" (verses 10–12). The psalmist twice describes God's love as steadfast (verses 8 and 11). God acts with fatherly compassion toward those who stumble (verse 13).

Both our physical and mental health depends in large part on how we deal with guilt and self-esteem. Negative emotions, especially guilt and shame, can adversely affect our body and create a cloud of doom that hangs over us every minute. Guilt can strangle the life out of us and render us unable to praise. But to trust in God's compassion and steadfast love even as we acknowledge our failings and inadequacies is to live in freedom.

Merciful and gracious God, I confess my failings
and inadequacies; restore to me the joy of salvation
and open my lips in gratitude and praise. Amen.

HUMAN FRAILTY
AND DIVINE SECURITY

*O*nce again we find the contrast between the ephemeral life of human beings and the eternality of God, especially of God's stead-fast love (verses 17–18). Likening the brevity of human life to that of grass—flourishing in the morning dew and withering in the afternoon wind and sun—is commonplace in the Bible (Job 14:1–2; Psalms 37:2; 58:7; 90:5; Isaiah 15:6; 40:6–7; 51:12; 1 Peter 1:24). But the LORD has pity on humankind for the pathos of their existence, for their frailty and mortality: "he knows how we were made; he remembers that we are dust" (verse 14).

One thing remains forever: "The steadfast love of the LORD is from everlasting to everlasting . . . to those who keep his covenant" (verses 17–18). Does the eternality of God's love suggest the hope that our relationship with God will continue beyond our earthly life?

In any case, the rule of God is universal. The temple singers call for the host of heaven to bless the LORD: "angels . . . mighty ones . . . all his hosts . . . his ministers . . . all his works, in all places of his dominion." After all these heavenly beings are urged to bless the LORD, then, finally, I, the individual worshiper, address myself: "Bless the LORD, O my soul" (verse 22b). Verses 20–22 form the closing bookend to verses 1–2, recapitulating the outburst of blessing with which the psalm began.

Psalm 103 depicts God as transcending both time and space. The steadfast love of the LORD is from everlasting to everlasting (verse 17), and the dominion of the LORD extends everywhere and over all (verse 19). The wondrous thing is that I, transient as the grass of the field, am the object of God's steadfast love.

Bless the Lord, O my soul, and all that is within me,
bless his holy name. Amen.

COSMIC MAJESTY

This beautiful hymn praises the majesty of God as it is reflected in the natural world. The first seven stanzas correspond poetically, although not in sequence, to the seven days of creation in Genesis 1:1—2:4: the sky (verses 1–4), the earth (verses 5–9), water (verses 10–13), plants (verses 14–18), moon and sun (verses 19–23), the great sea (verses 24–26), and the sustainer of life (verses 27–30).

The psalmist praises God's greatness and majesty for the first stage in the victory over chaos. God's first creation (see Genesis 1:3) is light, which is God's essence; God is "wrapped in light" (verse 2). God overcomes the ancient terror of total darkness, a symbol of death and primeval chaos.

Construction of the universe then begins. God stretches the canopy of the heavens above the land "like a tent" (verse 2b) and sets pilings in the waters beneath the earth to give the dry land firm support (verse 3). Clouds are chariots of God, winds are the messengers of God, and lightnings God's servant (verses 3–4), as in Psalm 18:9-10, 14: "Thick darkness was under his feet. He rode on a cherub, and flew; he came swiftly upon the wings of the wind. . . . He flashed forth lightnings. . . ."

Ancient Near Easterners had a vastly different conception of the universe from ours. There was water below and above the land, the waters above being prevented from inundating us by the dome or canopy or "firmament" of the sky. It is foolish for us to try to read into the Bible a scientific worldview or to try to find there evidence of a flat earth or of the falsity of evolution. Let us follow the lead of the gifted psalmist of old and marvel at the physical universe, giving thanks all the while to the creator of life.

I marvel, O Lord, at the vastness and majesty
of the starry heaven above, the macrocosm without
and the microcosm within. I bless your name. Amen.

Psalm 104:5–13

WATER IN A THIRSTY LAND

$\mathcal{A}$nyone who lives in a desert or semi-desert knows the value of water. Without water there can be no life. The Colorado River supplies water to five states, and the use of this valuable resource is a matter of intense negotiations among these states, especially Arizona, Nevada, and California, which are experiencing rapid population growth.

Most of Palestine (Canaan, the land of Israel) gets barely enough rain to sustain a dense population (generally the amount of rain increases from the arid southern Negev Desert to the northern hills of Galilee). It is no wonder that there are many references to water and drought in the Bible. Water came to symbolize life itself. The ideal Jerusalem has a gladdening river (Psalm 46:4). Isaiah looks forward to the time when "waters shall break forth in the wilderness, and streams in the desert" (Isaiah 35:6). This might explain why, carved in stone over the entrance to Jewish Theological Seminary in New York City, we see the Hebrew words *tal ve matar*, "dew and rain."

The psalmist refers to the waters above the firmament from which rain falls (verse 6), the streams that flow down from the hills (verse 8), and the waters below the ground that rise up in springs in the valleys (verse 10). All of these give life—to animals, plants, and humans alike.

Jeremiah refers to God as "the fountain of living water" (Jeremiah 2:13; 17:13), and the New Testament speaks of "living water . . . a spring of water gushing up to eternal life" (John 4:10, 14) and of a "river of the water of life, bright as crystal, flowing from the throne of God" in the heavenly city (Revelation 22:1). These words bring hope and comfort to us in the dry periods of our life.

Quench my thirst for health, gladness, and peace, Lord God, and grant me the graciousness to give a cup of water to a fellow pilgrim in need of such. Amen.

EARTHLY BEAUTY

The psalmist here reflects on plants, animals, and the sun and moon. The poet's considerable gifts are evident in easily visualized scenes and vignettes: cattle grazing in a lush pasture, people moistening their skin with olive oil and enjoying a cup of wine, lofty cedars of Lebanon, on top of which you can see a stork's nest, and wild goats frolicking in the high mountains, whose rocks provide a refuge for coneys (rock badger, verses 14–18). These gifts of nature are useful in many ways but they also provide delight and pleasure by their beauty.

As in Genesis 1:14, the moon and sun are God's calendars and clocks. The moon marks the seasons and the sun the times of day (verses 19–23). Ancient Near Eastern religions made the moon a goddess, but for the Israelites it is created by God, and its approximately twenty-nine day cycle served as the basis for the yearly calendar and thus also the date of the annual festivals. (Muslims also follow a lunar calendar.) The sun, by contrast, sets the pattern for the daily alternation of sunrise and sunset, day and night.

The psalmist revels in the beauty of the animate world of plants and animals as well as the inanimate realm of the heavenly bodies— all creatures of the Lord of the cosmos. These creations all reveal orderliness, stability, and regularity and reflect the steadfastness and reliability of the divine being itself. This sense of beauty and wonder inspired Henry van Dyke (1852–1933) to write the hymn "Joyful, Joyful We Adore Thee":

> All thy works with joy surround thee,
>   Earth and heav'n reflect thy rays,
> Stars and angels sing around thee,
>   Center of unbroken praise.
> Field and forest, vale and mountain,
>   Flow'ry meadow, flashing sea,
> Chanting bird and flowing fountain
>   Call us to rejoice in thee.

In the midst of nature's beauty and bounty, O Lord, melt the clouds of sin and sadness and fill me with the light of day. Amen.

THE REFLECTION
OF GOD'S WISDOM

*W*onder at the vastness of the sea and the great variety of creatures in it is the subject of verses 24–26. In the roiling waters are "creeping things innumerable . . . living things both small and great . . . and Leviathan that you formed to sport in it."

Unlike their seafaring neighbors the Phoenicians, who founded colonies throughout the Mediterranean, including Carthage in North Africa and sites on the coast of Spain, the ancient Israelites were not known for their love of travel by sea. Several Old Testament texts mention the symbol of the primordial ocean, the dragon Leviathan (the word means "twisting" or "coiled," Isaiah 27:1; the beast is called Rahab in Job 9:13; 26:12; Psalm 89:10; and Isaiah 51:9). Isaiah 51:9–10 refers to the taming of the "waters of the great deep" at the time of creation (see Genesis 1:2, 6), when Yahweh "cut Rahab in pieces" and "pierced the dragon." In Psalm 104, however, Leviathan is one of God's creations, and the psalmist's whimsy comes through with the statement that God formed the beast "to sport in it," that is, for the pure fun of it.

All of these manifold works reflect God's wisdom (verse 24), which is to say, the created universe reveals order, system, and beauty. In Proverbs 8:22–31 Lady Wisdom speaks, asserting, "Yahweh created me at the beginning of his work . . . before the beginning of the earth. . . .Then I was beside him like a master worker. . . ." Personified wisdom is not a goddess but a poetic expression for the stability and rationality of the created order, an outgrowth of one of the chief attributes of God.

If God created something for self-amusement, how can we humans fail to enjoy the simple pleasures of everyday things?

For fun, for smiles, for humor, and for the curiosities
of nature, I thank you, Lord God. Amen.

GIVER AND SUSTAINER OF LIFE

*I*n Genesis 2:4b–25, "Yahweh, God, formed man [Hebrew: *Adam*] from the dust of the ground [*adamah*] and breathed into his nostrils the breath of life; and the man became a living being." Then God created a garden, in which grew "every tree that is pleasant to the sight and good for food" (verses 5–9).

The psalmist obviously reflects on this "second story of creation." As in the Garden of Eden, God gives all creatures their food in due season. God fills them with good things (verse 28). And, as God breathed life into Adam's body of dust, so also God's "breath" (the same Hebrew word means "spirit") creates life from the ground (*adamah*, verse 30). When God takes away their breath (God's spirit), the living creatures die and "return to their dust" (verse 29).

God is the master of life and none-life. The end of life, according to Psalm 104, is neither accidental nor impersonal nor natural but rather a divine decision. The Creator gives breath and thus can withhold breath. Such a thought must have been in the mind of the storyteller when Job says, "Naked I came from my mother's womb, and naked shall I return there; the LORD gave, and the LORD has taken away; blessed be the name of the LORD" (Job 1:21).

We do not find in Psalm 104 the commonly held idea that our time of death has been foreordained, the common idea that when my time comes, that's it; there's nothing I can do about it. All we know for certain is that we are mortal. But we pray for good health and long life, and we hope also that the God who gave us breath will remain with us beyond the grave (see Psalm 73:24).

*For the breath and spirit of life that you give, and
for sustaining and preserving my life, I thank you,
O Lord. Amen.*

ETERNAL GLORY AND HUMAN PRAISE

Some Christians, not least Lutherans, like to warn themselves against the dangers of a "theology of glory," meaning by that a religion of success and triumph that tries to ignore the glaring evidences of suffering, danger, and evil of all kinds in this life. Our psalmist acknowledges the frailty of life (verse 29b), the dangers of the seafarers (verse 26), the presence of sinners and the wicked (verse 35). But in this final stanza of Psalm 104 we see something transcendent, a

> vision of a God clothed in blinding luminescence [that] evokes the unapproachable sublimity that belongs to the glory of the working Creator. Life, joy, and glory are joined in a symphony of voices, which the temple choir transmutes, thanks to this amazing hymn, into an act of adoration instead of a complaint against adversity. . . ."[40]

The glory (*kabod*) of the LORD is a majestic presence that we sense with fear in earthquake and volcano (verse 32). We experience this glory more gratefully as the Creator of the beautiful universe with its plants and living creatures, and the vast oceans (verses 5–26). But even more do we sense the greatness of God in our own creation, our daily sustenance and our joys in the simple gifts of the day (verses 27–28). There is a time when it is proper for us to sing, "May the glory of the LORD endure for ever," and even to ask that the LORD take time to smell the roses, to "rejoice in his works" (verse 31). This powerful psalm ends with one Hebrew word: "Hallelujah!" Praise the LORD!

I will sing praise to you, O God, while I have being, remembering your gift of life and the joys of each day. Amen.

A PEOPLE'S BLESSING

*T*his hymn extols Yahweh's "deeds," "wonderful works," "miracles," and "judgments" in Israel's past history, from the covenant God made with Abraham up to the conquest of Canaan. Verses 1–15 are identical to the hymn that was sung when the Ark was brought into the temple in 1 Chronicles 16:8–22, showing that this psalm originated in temple liturgy.

Two things are striking in verses 1–11. First, the call to "Glory in his holy name" (verse 3a) combines the "theology of glory," the special presence of God in the temple (see 2 Chronicles 7:2), with the "theology of the name," the personal name Yahweh (the LORD). In Exodus 3:13–15 God indicates that this name means, "I cause to be what I cause to be," namely, historical events. The theology of glory celebrates God's presence in the temple, and the theology of the name celebrates God's actions in the sweep of history.

Second, the psalm emphasizes not the covenant made with Moses but "the covenant [the LORD our God] made with Abraham" (verses 7–11; the making of this covenant is described in Genesis 15:7–21 and 17:1–14). This covenant, unlike that of Moses, is both unconditional and eternal, "an everlasting covenant." The reason for emphasizing Abraham over Moses becomes clear in verse 11, "To you I will give the land of Canaan." It was in the Abrahamic covenant that God made the promise of land (Genesis 15:7, 18–21; 17:8), although the only son of Abraham mentioned is Isaac (not the sons of Keturah, Genesis 25:1–6, or Ishmael, Genesis 16:15; 25:12–14).

God's promise of land to the posterity of Abraham has had a permanent and often contentious influence throughout history. It represents the particularistic streak of the Bible and stands in opposition to the universalistic outlook of the great prophets and parts of the New Testament. The *whole earth* is the Lord's.

Gladden the hearts of those in all the far reaches of the earth
who seek you, O Lord. Amen.

GOD'S HAND IN HISTORY

*T*he psalm continues in verses 12–25 with the Joseph story and the move of Jacob's family to Egypt, setting the stage for the exodus from Egypt under Moses.

The patriarchs (notably Abraham, Isaac, and Jacob) were nomads, living as Bedouins, "wandering from nation to nation" (verse 13). They traveled with the protection of God, who "allowed no one to oppress them" (verse 14). The statement that God "rebuked kings on their account" probably refers to the story of the near violation of Abraham's wife, Sarah (or Sarai), by the king of Egypt (Genesis 12:10–20; doublets of this story are in Genesis 20:3–18 and 26:7–11). More strangely, the ancestors are referred to as "anointed ones" (the Hebrew can be translated "messiahs") and "prophets" (verse 15). Abraham is once called a prophet (Genesis 20:7) but never elsewhere an anointed one.

Verses 16–22 outline the remarkable story of Joseph (Genesis 37–50), that he "was sold as a slave" (but not mentioning that this was done by his brothers) in order that Jacob's family would have connections in Egypt during a famine. The text alludes to Joseph's dreams and his imprisonment by Potiphar (Genesis 39–41), his release and elevation and, finally, the move of Jacob and his family to Egypt, where they became "very fruitful" and "stronger than their foes" (verse 24), creating opposition on the part of Egypt's rulers.

The Joseph story (Genesis 37–50) is one of the most brilliant literary productions of antiquity; it is a pure pleasure to read in one sitting. It is filled with drama, pathos, the pits of despair, the heights of success, and gripping redemption. It reminds us that the Bible deals with the stark realities of earthly life in the context of faith in a just and benevolent God.

From the powers of evil, deliver us, O God, and preserve us
also in times of success and favor. Amen.

REMEMBRANCE OF "SIGNS AND MIRACLES"

$\mathcal{I}$n verse 26 Psalm 105 abruptly introduces "his servant Moses, and Aaron whom he had chosen," who perform "signs . . . and miracles in the land of Ham" (verse 27; Ham is a late Old Testament term for Egypt). Then follows a list of the plagues of the exodus tradition (see also Psalm 78:43–51). Here we have the following sketch:

- darkness, verse 28, the ninth plague (Exodus 10:21)
- water to blood, verse 29, the first plague (Exodus 7:20–24)
- frogs, verse 30, the second plague (Exodus 8:6)
- flies and gnats, verse 31, the fourth and third plagues, respectively (Exodus 8:16, 21)
- hail and thunderstorm, verse 32, the seventh plague (Exodus 9:22–25)
- locusts, verse 34, the eighth plague (Exodus 10:12–20)
- death of the firstborn males, verse 36, the tenth plague (Exodus 11:1–9)
- missing are the fifth plague, of cattle and other herds (Exodus 9:1–7), and the sixth, boils (Exodus 9:8–12).

The ancient Israelites viewed the exodus from Egypt as the quintessential act of redemption. Attention is directed solely to the acts of God—not to the moral character of the Israelites as a whole or to their strenuous efforts to extricate themselves from slavery to the Pharaohs. God is the actor, and Moses and Aaron are but the instruments of God's action. "He sent . . . ; he turned . . . ; he spoke . . . ; he gave . . . ; he struck down. . . ."

On 9/11, remembering a historical disaster, we think of the fragile nature of human life. For Christians as well as for Jews, God is the hope of salvation. We understand differently how this hope operates, but we confess that our security in this world and in the age to come is inextricably linked to the effective grace of God.

In life and in death, O Lord, let your grace shine on me. Amen.

EXODUS, WILDERNESS, CONQUEST

*T*he psalmist continues to extol Yahweh's acts of the exodus period, including (1) Israel taking the Egyptians' silver and gold (Exodus 12:35–36), (2) the "cloud" and "fire" (Exodus 13:21 and elsewhere), (3) the provision of quails and "food from heaven" (manna) in the wilderness (Exodus 16:13–21; Numbers 11), and (4) water from the rock (Exodus 17:6; Numbers 20:11). Then comes the conclusion: "He gave them the lands of the nations, and they took possession of the wealth of the peoples" (verse 44).

There is an astounding omission in this summary—the covenant mediated by Moses at Mount Sinai, an event that is foundational in most of the Old Testament. Instead, the psalmist again reverts to Abraham: "He remembered his holy promise, and Abraham, his servant" (verse 42; see verses 6, 9). How can this be? A possible answer: the Mosaic covenant includes commandments and laws, with punishments for disobedience. The Abrahamic covenant, by contrast, is unconditional, with the exception of the requirement of circumcision (Genesis 17:10–11).

This raises the basic problem of Psalm 105. Unlike the emphasis of the great prophets on social justice and ethical conduct, this psalm reflects a pious nationalism devoid of the moral valuations of the Mosaic covenant and, indeed, of any self-criticism. The possibility of national corruption is far from its purview, the sole purpose of which is to demonstrate divine sanction for the Israelite conquest of the land of Canaan (verses 11, 44). Psalm 105 represents a minority perspective within the Bible. The laws of the Mosaic covenant (Exodus 20–40; Leviticus; and Deuteronomy) and the message of all the great prophets convey the demands of God for ethical behavior and the judgment that comes to those who ignore justice. Yes, God's heart is one of grace, but grace is required only because of human failure.

Lord of the nations, preserve us from jingoism and selfish nationalism and give us a broader view. Amen.

Psalm 106:1–5

LET ME NOT BE LEFT BEHIND

$\mathcal{I}$f Psalm 105 concentrates exclusively on Yahweh's unqualified acts of redemption on behalf of Israel and displays an uncritical nationalism, Psalm 106 offers a corrective. It concentrates on the behavior of the people—not on that of Yahweh—and what it finds is not good. It is a story of rebellion from the exodus to the Babylonian exile, all of which was the operation of the wrath of God.

The psalm begins in a way similar to that of the previous psalm. Yahweh is "good; for his steadfast love endures forever" (verse 1). No human can sufficiently praise God's "mighty doings" (verse 2). But then a new note emerges, the theme of the LORD's requirement of the people: "Happy are those who observe justice, who do righteousness at all times" (verse 3). The demand for justice sets the stage for the story of rebellion and punishment to come.

For the moment, however, the psalmist engages in personal introspection and petition, rare in a hymn: "Remember me, O LORD, when you show favor to your people" (verse 4). The psalmist—along with all those who sing his words—willingly acknowledges that he too is obliged to "observe justice" and "do righteousness." The result of such behavior is joy and gladness (verse 5).

Ancient peoples almost always had a stronger sense of community than do we in the Western world of the twenty-first century. The psalms as a whole reflect this, functioning as they did for communal worship in the Jerusalem temple. And Psalm 106 deals almost entirely with the group, the nation—except for verses 4–5. We learn from this that God makes demands on us as individuals but also on us as a nation. Let us learn to do justice and walk humbly with our God—not only as individuals but also as a people.

Remember me, O Lord when you show favor
to your people. Amen.

REBELLION
AND FORGETFULNESS

The prophet Jeremiah may have inspired this psalm (as perhaps his enemies inspired Psalm 105!). Compare Jeremiah 14:20, "We acknowledge our wickedness, O LORD, the iniquity of our ancestors, for we have sinned against you," with Psalm 106:6, "Both we and our ancestors have sinned; we have committed iniquity, have done wickedly." Both our psalmist and Jeremiah were stamped with the exodus and wilderness traditions, especially with the theme of rebellion in the wilderness.

The first sin of the ancestors is that they "rebelled against the Most High at the Red Sea" (verse 7b), which recalls the complaint of the people in Exodus 14:10–12. "Yet he [Yahweh] saved them for his name's sake" (notice the shift to the third person pronoun) by drying the Red Sea (the Suez isthmus, between the Sinai Peninsula and Egypt proper). With a touch of ghoulish delight, the psalmist exults over the defeat of the Egyptians: "Not one of them was left" (verse 11).

No sooner had the people crossed the sea than they began to complain about hunger and thirst (hardly a "wanton craving," verse 14). Numbers 11 speaks of the LORD satisfying the people's "strong craving" (verse 4) with manna (verses 6–9) and quail (verses 31–32), immediately and strangely accompanied by "a very great plague" (verse 33), called in Psalm 106:15 "a wasting disease."

What starts here is a cyclical pattern of rebellion, restitution, repentance, and rebellion. The people "soon forgot" the works of God (verse 13) and were therefore fated to experience the misery all over again. We might well wonder at times how sane we humans are.

When, O Lord, will we ever learn? Grant us wisdom,
grant us courage for the living of these days. Amen.

REBELLION
AND INTERCESSION

*T*hese verses speak of two instances of rebellion in the wilderness. The first, verses 16–18, is a squabble among the priests, narrated in Numbers 16. Some 250 Levites (the priestly tribe) complained that Moses and Aaron (also from the tribe of Levi) had subordinated them, and they demanded full priestly status. (Korah, the leader of the rebellion, is not mentioned in Psalm 106, possibly because the Korahites came to be a prominent guild in the Jerusalem temple and were credited with authoring Psalms 42; 44—49; 84; 85; 87; and 88.) Psalm 106 mentions two leaders of the revolt, Dathan and Abiram, both of whom met with misfortune. According to Numbers 16:25–35 the earth opened and swallowed the rebels "so they with all that belonged to them went down alive into Sheol; the earth closed over them, and they perished from the midst of the assembly." The fire of Psalm 106:18 is based on Numbers 16:35.

The other rebellion involved the entire people, namely the Golden Calf incident at Horeb (the name for Mount Sinai used by the Israelite tribes that settled in northern Canaan), which is narrated in Exodus 32. The statement that "they exchanged the glory of God for the image of an ox that eats grass" (verse 20) reminds us of Romans 1:23, where Paul finds the primordial sin of the Gentiles that "they exchanged the glory of the immortal God for images resembling a mortal human being or birds of four-footed animals or reptiles." The people escaped annihilation only by Moses' desperate intercession (verse 23).

The Bible often speaks of holy men and women interceding to God on behalf of others. Not only priests but also heroes such as Abraham, Moses, and the servant of Isaiah 53:12, who "made intercession for the transgressors." Christians look to the intercession of Jesus (Hebrews 7:25). All persons of good faith, however, are to be mediators on behalf of the suffering in our midst.

Remove from me the spirit of envy and rebellion, O Lord. Amen.

Psalm 106:24–31

APOSTASY AND ATROCITY

*T*here are more troubles on the way to the promised land. As the people approach Canaan they hesitate to invade; "they despised the pleasant land, having no faith in his promise" (verse 24; Numbers 14:31–33). Then the LORD "swore to them that he would make them fall in the wilderness" (verse 26; Numbers 14:21–23, 28–29).

To make matters worse, as the people went around north and east of the Dead Sea to approach Canaan through the land of Moab, opposite Jericho, they began to be interested in Baal of Peor, a local Moabite version of one of the chief Canaanite gods (verse 28). Such contacts led some Israelite men to become attracted to foreign women (Numbers 25:1). When the priest Phinehas, a grandson of Aaron, came upon a man with a Midianite woman, he ran a spear through both of them (Numbers 25:6–9). We are taken aback to read in Psalm 106:31 that these killings were "reckoned to him as righteousness from generation to generation for ever." The authors of Numbers 25:10–13 have Yahweh announce, "I hereby grant him my covenant of peace. It shall be for him and for his descendants after him a covenant of perpetual priesthood, because he was zealous for his God, and made atonement for the Israelites." Hosea 9:10 recalls the apostasy at Baal-peor but does not mention Phinehas's atrocity.

Readers today have understandable difficulty in coming to terms with brutal acts that are praised in the Bible (another noteworthy example is Samuel's merciless vivisection of the Amalekite king Agag in 1 Samuel 15:33). Can we justify the killing of heretics and apostates? Can we think that the God of the nations would bless such atrocities? The great prophets, in calling us to follow justice and mercy, knew better.

In a world of violence, O God of mercy, let me speak
for the helpless, the victims, the captives, the displaced persons,
and all who suffer unjustly. Amen.

APOSTASY AND BLOODSHED

*V*erses 32–33 mildly criticize the great liberator, Moses, himself. In these verses, reflecting Numbers 20:2–13, the people "contended with Moses" at Meribah (the name means "contention"), complaining that they were about to die of thirst in the wilderness. Moses, just a little piqued, said "Listen, you rebels, shall we bring water for you out of this rock?" But Yahweh thought Moses lacked trust, and the punishment was decreed: "You shall not bring this assembly into the land that I have given them" (Numbers 20:10–12).

The scene abruptly passes over to the time of the conquest of Canaan. Yahweh commanded the extermination of the population of Canaan (verse 34; Numbers 22:50–56; Deuteronomy 7:1–6; 20:16 ["you must not let anything that breathes remain alive"]). They disobeyed this command and "mingled with the nations and learned to do as they did" (verse 35), serving their idols and beginning the obscene practice of child sacrifice (verses 37–38). According to 2 Kings 16:3 and 21:6, Kings Ahaz and Manasseh practiced child sacrifice in Jerusalem. Jeremiah (7:31 and 19:5) refers to the practice, and it is prohibited in Leviticus 18:21 and Deuteronomy 12:31. The practice is an act of prostitution (verse 39; compare Hosea 1:2, "great whoredom").

All sane human beings look with revulsion on child sacrifice. Equally repugnant is the command to exterminate an entire people— and the bizarre idea that people could be punished for not obeying such a command. The teachings of Amos, Jeremiah, Second Isaiah, and Jesus—among others—are the lens through which we must consider such texts. God is the creator of all peoples, and "God shows no partiality, but in every nation anyone who fears him and does what is right is acceptable to him" (Acts 10:34–35).

Lord God of all, save our people from false patriotism; broaden
our horizon and make us sensitive to the suffering
of the world. Amen.

A SEEMINGLY ADDICTIVE CYCLE

$\mathcal{P}$salm 106:40–45 reflects the period of the "judges," that is, the time between Joshua and the rise of monarchy (approximately 1200–1000 B.C.). Judges 2:11–23 finds a cyclical pattern for Israelite life in Canaan during this period: rebellion, retribution, repentance, restoration, rebellion. . . . The people rebel against Yahweh, retribution comes as military defeat and rule by the enemy, the people repent, God restores them by raising up a "judge" (a military leader who overcomes the enemy), the people again repent—and the cycle continues.

The psalmist likewise asserts that people "were rebellious . . . and were brought low through their iniquity." The LORD "gave them into the hand of the nations," who subjected them. "Nevertheless [God] . . . heard their cry. For their sake he remembered his covenant and showed compassion." Can we find a clearer example of the old truth that those who ignore history are condemned to repeat it?

Although Psalm 106 summarizes the beginnings of Israelite history, from Moses to the time of the judges, verses 46–47 suggest that it was written during a time of national disaster, most likely after the destruction of Jerusalem and the exile to Babylon in 587 B.C. The worshipers pray that the LORD God would gather the people who are scattered "among the nations" (predicted in verse 27). The whole of Psalm 106, therefore, functions as a warning to the people to remain faithful to the God of steadfast love.

Individuals also can fall into addictive patterns from which they cannot extricate themselves—perhaps a romantic entanglement, dependence on addictive substances, or some other self-destructive behavior. Intervention then is needed. In such a time let us pray that rescue comes before disaster strikes.

Save us as a nation, O Lord our God, that we may give thanks to your holy name. Amen.

Psalm 107:1–3

ON THANKFULNESS AND REDEMPTION

*T*he esthetically pleasing structure of Psalm 107 suggests that it is the work of a single poet. It has both a prelude (verses 1–3) and a postlude (verse 43). More striking is a refrain that occurs four times: "Then they cried to the LORD in their trouble, / and he delivered them from their distress. / Let them thank the LORD for his steadfast love, / for his wonderful works to humankind" (verses 6 + 8, 13 + 15, 19 + 21, and 28 + 31). The refrain indicates the responsive singing of this psalm. An additional indication of single authorship is the fact that the original Hebrew has basically the same poetic meter (4 + 3).

Not only the structure but also the content points to a single author. This is an appropriate psalm of thanksgiving for protection from various dangers faced by pilgrims traveling to Jerusalem for a festival. It suggests also the dangers of exiles returning from Babylonian captivity in the sixth century B.C.

The prelude, verses 1–3, is sung in the Jerusalem temple by pilgrims who give thanks to the LORD for having traveled safely through dangerous routes. They have come from the four corners of the earth (verse 3).

The worshipers are called "the redeemed of the LORD." The root concept of redemption in the Old Testament is that of payment for freedom, as from slavery or to recover property. Prime examples of the redemption of the people are the exodus from Egypt (see Exodus 6:6; 15:13) and the deliverance of the exiles from Babylon (see Isaiah 43:1; 44:22–23; and often). This usage might support the idea that the psalm reflects the joy of returning exiles from Babylon, but the more likely reading is that the pilgrims, having safely reached Jerusalem, have been delivered or "redeemed" from danger along the way. They are recipients of the steadfast love of the LORD (verse 1).

*I praise your goodness, Lord God, and thank you
for redemption from danger. Keep me in your care all
the days of my life. Amen.*

Psalm 107:4–9

LOST IN THE DESERT

*T*he first group of travelers are a caravan crossing a barren desert. With nothing on the horizon, the leaders become disoriented and are unable to find an inhabited town—a source of water. Westerners can get a sense of the desperation such travelers must have felt by reading T. E. Lawrence's *Seven Pillars of Wisdom* or even by watching the related film, *Lawrence of Arabia*. Careful planning was an absolute necessity for surviving the crossing of a vast desert. Knowing the location of the next water hole or oasis was a matter of life or death.

But then comes the refrain: "they cried to the LORD in their trouble, and he delivered them from their distress; he led them by a straight way, until they reached an inhabited town" (verses 6–7). They ceased going in circles and were led directly to a place of food and water. For that they owe thanks to the LORD "for his steadfast love, for his wonderful works to humankind" (verse 8).

Only a few things are essential to human life. Food and drink are among them. Our psalmist knows that the "God of Jacob . . . gives food to the hungry" (Psalm 146:5, 7), promising those who must cross a threatening desert that "they shall not hunger or thirst" (Isaiah 49:10). Most Westerners can scarcely imagine what it is like to go to bed hungry or to drink water that is obviously contaminated—as many millions of human beings do every day. Our God demands of us that we become aware of human suffering and support the agencies and individuals who seek to overcome starvation and provide clean drinking water to all people. We look forward to the day when the hungry are fed with good things (Luke 1:53).

O Lord, help me to see the hungry and give food,
and the thirsty and give something to drink. Amen.

PRISONERS IN IRONS

*I*mprisonment is often mentioned in the Bible. Sometimes an offender was confined until the leaders could decide the appropriate judgment. In Leviticus 24:10–12 a man who had blasphemed the divine name, Yahweh, was put "in custody, until the decision of Yahweh should be made clear." And in Numbers 15:32–36 a man who gathered sticks on the Sabbath was put "in custody, because it was not clear what should be done to him." Custody sometimes involved life imprisonment with no chance of parole (as for David's concubines in 2 Samuel 20:3), and in all cases it was a great humiliation.

The prisoners in Psalm 107:10 sit "in darkness and in gloom . . . in misery and in irons," images that suggest something like the experience of Jeremiah. Because he predicted the fall of Judah and Jerusalem, he was thrown into a cistern where "there was no water . . . but only mud, and Jeremiah sank in the mud" (Jeremiah 38:6).

Freedom of prisoners is a recurring image in Second Isaiah. The author uses it to express joy over the edict of the Persian emperor Cyrus the Great in 538 B.C., which allowed the Jews to return to Judah from the captivity in Babylon (Isaiah 42:7; 45:13; 49:9). Psalm 107:16 recurs in almost identical words in Isaiah 45:2. Jesus also spoke about compassion for prisoners (Matthew 25:36, 39, 43).

It is an outrage that even today many countries still engage in the torture and killing of prisoners. To treat human beings humanely is not being "soft on crime." The prisoners in Psalm 107 deserved their fate ("they had rebelled against the words of God"). But they "cried to the LORD in their trouble, and he saved them from their distress" (verse 13). Freeing the prisoners is one of the results of the steadfast love of the LORD, who "shatters the doors of bronze, and cuts in two the bars of iron" (verse 16).

Teach me, Lord God, to refrain from returning evil for evil;
help me to learn justice. Amen.

ILLNESS AND DISTRESS

Sickness is another threat to life that scarcely anyone can completely avoid. Illness can be debilitating and make the thought of eating food entirely repulsive. Severe illness can sap the body of strength, so that the sufferer feels death drawing near (verse 18).

The belief that sickness is the result of sin is widespread in the Bible, reaching into New Testament times. It is reflected (among other places) in the question put to Jesus in John 9:2 regarding a blind man: "Rabbi, who sinned, this man or his parents, that he was born blind?" Most biblical writers believed that if God is powerful and just, then what happens in this world must be caused or at least allowed by God. The poetic body of the book of Job is a classic protest against this assumption, and Jesus at least on one occasion refused to find a simple link between disasters and the will of God (Luke 13:1–5; see also Matthew 5:45).

The Hebrew text of verse 17 literally translated reads: "Some were fools through their sinful ways." Was the psalmist thinking of mental illness, something that involved anorexia ("they loathed any kind of food")? Although we cannot be certain of the original wording, we do know that illness of mind can be even more destructive of life than bodily ailments are.

The sick persons also "cried to the Lord in their trouble," and "he sent out his word and healed them, and delivered them from destruction" (verses 19–20). How was this word sent? Did it come through a human comforter, a kind and solicitous soul who functioned as the instrument of the God of steadfast love? Those who bring hope and healing to children, women, and men in times of deathly distress are—without a doubt—the shining face of God.

Send out your word of comfort, O God, to the sick of body or mind, and to those who draw near to the end of life. Amen.

DANGERS OF THE DEEP

*T*he first chapter of the book of Jonah vividly depicts the terror of life-threatening storms on the high seas, as does Acts 27 in the New Testament. Ancient Israelites originated as a nomadic people, and the glorification of the Bedouin style of living endured for centuries ("Ask for the ancient paths," the prophet says in Jeremiah 6:16; see also chapter 34). In striking contrast, their seafaring neighbors the Phoenicians sailed the entire Mediterranean Sea, establishing colonies as far away as Spain. They, indeed, did "business on the mighty waters" (verse 23).

Our psalmist devotes more lines to the dangers of the deep than to the other parts of the psalm. A fierce wind raised huge waves that dropped the ship into the depths, causing the sailors to stagger and reel. Just as the sailors on Jonah's ship cried to their gods, so these men cried to the LORD. Then "he made the storm be still, and the waves of the sea were hushed. Then they were glad because they had quiet, and he brought them to their desired haven" (verse 29).

Christians will reflexively think of the story of Jesus stilling the storm on the Sea of Galilee (Matthew 8:23–27; Mark 4:35–41; Luke 8:22–25). A great wind whipped up high waves that threatened to swamp the boat. Jesus rebuked the wind; "the wind ceased, and there was a dead calm." The disciples "were filled with great awe" (Mark 4:39–41). Is there a literary relationship between the psalm and the Gospels?

Some persons might call the sailors' experience a desperation faith, the prayer of persons in a life-threatening situation. But, like the others in this psalm, the sailors belonged to a faith community, "the congregation," who "thank the LORD for his steadfast love, for his wonderful works to humankind" (verses 31–32). When we feel as though we are sinking into the deep, let us also cry to the Lord, remembering that we also belong to the community of faith.

Let my life be one of praise for your wonderful works, O Lord,
in good times and bad. Amen.

WATER IS LIFE

*A*lthough the waters of the great deep are foreboding and often life-threatening, water in the desert is life-giving and life-sustaining. The psalmist here departs from the stanza-and-refrain pattern of verses 1–32 and praises the goodness of God as life-giver in a noble hymn.

The psalmist knows the precarious nature of farming. He is aware also of the unpredictability of climate changes. Fertile land can become a desert, a salty waste (verses 33–34; "By my rebuke I dry up the sea, I make the rivers a desert," Isaiah 50:2b). And—perhaps less often—a parched land can become a fruitful oasis with fields, vineyards, cattle, and a village (verses 35–38; "I will make the wilderness a pool of water, and the dry land springs of water," "rivers in the desert," Isaiah 41:18; 43:19).

Our generation is witnessing rapid global warming, which threatens animal and human life from the Arctic regions to the southern edge of the Sahara Desert in Africa, the region known as the Sahel. The Sahara is noticeably growing southward as rainfall declines. This only adds to ethnic tensions and extreme desperation in the region, not least in the Darfur area of western Sudan. Decent persons throughout the world have an obligation to care and to act to save human life and to deal with the larger factors that cause such major tragedies.

Advances in agricultural production in the past century have been astounding, not least in the creation of new species of cereal grains. We admire also those who feed the hungry and those who struggle for peace in the ravaged areas. These also are the hands of God at work in our world.

O Lord, bless those who work to increase the food supply
of the earth; bless those who feed the hungry, and bless those
who struggle for peace in a war-ravaged world. Amen.

PREFERENCE FOR THE NEEDY

*T*hose who insist that the Bible has a preference for the poor can find support here. The "they" of verse 39 are unidentified, but we may assume that they are the ones endangered "through oppression, trouble, and sorrow" of prior parts of the psalm.

Unlike earlier parts of Psalm 107, these final verses have a closer relationship to the wisdom writers than to the prophets. Verse 40 reminds us of Job 12:21, 24: "He pours contempt on princes . . . and makes them wander in a pathless waste." And compare verse 42 with Job 22:19, "The righteous see it and are glad; the innocent laugh them to scorn" (see also Job 5:16). Here we have some contrasts typical of wisdom literature, princes/needy, upright/wicked, and the words are addressed to "those who are wise" (verse 43).

The Bible as a whole does not condemn wealth as such. From the stories of the large flocks of the Hebrew patriarchs in Genesis to the idea of wealth as a blessing from God in the wisdom literature, we learn that the good things of life are not to be despised. The wisdom writer, after seeing everything, puts it this way: "It is fitting to eat and drink and find enjoyment in all the toil with which one toils under the sun. . . . Likewise all to whom God gives wealth and possessions and whom he enables to enjoy them, and to accept their lot and find enjoyment in their toil—this is the gift of God" (Ecclesiastes 5:18–19). Nonetheless, God's compassion is especially directed to the needy, the oppressed, and the sorrowing of humankind. Goodness, grace, and steadfast love are the quintessential qualities of God, the veritable definition of God.

Bountiful God, I thank you for the simple pleasures of life;
let me receive them as your gifts. Amen.

Psalm 108:1–5

GOD'S FAITHFULNESS AND HUMAN STEADFASTNESS

*A*ncient editors have been at work here. Verses 1–5 of this psalm are almost identical to Psalm 57:7–11, and verses 6–13 to Psalm 60:5–12. There were no copyright laws in Old Testament times, and good texts could be recycled (as happens with some sermons in our time).

The first stanza, verses 1–5, is a joyful outburst of praise of God, who is exalted above the heavens and whose glory covers the whole earth (verse 5). The psalmist is a musician, skilled both with the harp and lyre and in singing (verses 1–3). Apparently a morning person, he begins the day at dawn by lifting his voice in praise (verse 2). The sole reason given for this joyous song is God's steadfast love and faithfulness (verse 4). Humans can depend on the promises of God and not wonder what God might do next. The singer responds in like manner: "My heart is steadfast, O God, my heart is steadfast" (verse 1).

Theologians debate the question whether God is perfectly and absolutely free in action and will. At first glance it seems reasonable to think so. But God has willed a self-limitation by entering into covenant and making binding, unconditional promises to humankind. God first made such a promise to Noah after the flood: "I establish my covenant with you, that . . . never again shall there be a flood to destroy the earth" (Genesis 9:11). The covenant made with Moses (Exodus 24) includes not only numerous commandments for the people but also unchangeable promises made by God.

God is not capricious or unpredictable or subject to human fits of emotion. We need not wonder what God wills for us. God is faithful and just, abounding in steadfast love. For this our heart, too, is steadfast.

Let me sing and make melody in praise of your faithfulness,
O God, all the days of my life. Amen.

A WASHBASIN AND A THROWN SHOE

*T*hese verses have their origin in an otherwise unknown military catastrophe. The community's prayer (verse 6) is followed by an oracle of promised victory (speech of God, verses 7–9). But something seems to have gone wrong; the psalm ends with a communal lament that suggests defeat (verses 10–13).

We have here a kind of territorial theology. To God belong not only the core areas of Judah and the northern hill country of Ephraim and Manasseh but also the neighboring lands of Moab, Edom, Philistia, and the area east of the Jordan River (Gilead). The military battle that prompted these verses apparently was fought against the Edomites (verse 10), a battle that went badly for the Israelites.

We can learn much from the way a specific culture makes insults. This psalm includes two. First, "Moab is my wash-basin" (verse 9) is an oblique reference to the Dead Sea, the lowest place on the surface of the earth. The washbasin is a depository of washed-off residue, like the sea with no outlet.

Second, God throws a shoe at Edom (verse 9). Shoes and sandals had symbolic meaning in Old Testament times. If a man refused to enter into a levirate marriage (that is, to beget a child with the wife of his childless, deceased brother), the woman, in public, would "pull his sandal off his foot, spit in his face, and declare, 'This is what is done to the man who does not build up his brother's house'" (Deuteronomy 25:9; see also Ruth 4:7–8). Shoes were legal symbols and, when God hurls a shoe at Edom it indicates possession.

Military expansionism is repugnant to all thinking persons. As a reflection of military disaster, we might understand the venting in this psalm. Better it is, however, to seek peace and try to understand those who differ from us.

Lord God, cure you children's warring madness
and bend our pride to your control. Amen.

BAD THINGS HAPPEN TO GOOD PEOPLE

$\mathcal{H}$ere we have another lament of the individual. This poet speaks eloquently and intimately of God, "O God of my praise," which suggests a long life of piety and therefore also perhaps a slight claim on God to help the sufferer in the current crisis: "Do not be silent."

As is typical in psalms of this type, the psalmist protests his innocence. He is being attacked without cause (verse 3b). To make matters worse, he earlier had expressed love for these persons, and even (if we follow the Greek translation of verse 4) had made intercessory prayer for them. This might have involved going to the temple to beseech God when the others were unable to do so. And what was the result? They spoke lies and deceit, words of hate, returning evil for good and hatred for love.

Betrayal by someone we considered to be a close friend causes great anguish. In *The Divine Comedy* Dante reserved the lowest place in hell for such. And yet such betrayal does happen. Personal relationships are almost always more complex than either side realizes, and we do not know the motivations and thoughts of the enemies. Yet it is true that bad things do happen to good people.

The age-old question, "Why is this happening to me?" will never have a satisfactory answer, at least on this side of the grave. We need to be wary of those who offer simple explanations, finding God at work in tragedies large and small. We cannot believe that God causes evil to happen. But we can turn to God in time of deep distress, and we can rest assured that God's steadfast love will never end.

Stir up your power, O Lord, and come to the aid of those who face mortal danger. Give me strength to do my part. Amen.

PRAYER IN REVERSE

*T*hese remarkable verses are as impressive a collection of curses as you can find in the Bible. But who uttered them? Here we come up against a puzzle. The New Revised Standard Version introduces these verses with the words, "They say," interpreting them as the enemies' curses of the psalmist. But the original Hebrew text lacks these words, suggesting that here the psalmist is cursing *his* enemies. It is true that the prophet Jeremiah was able to curse his enemies in similarly embarrassing, vehement language (see Jeremiah 18:21–23). But it is most significant that the enemies are referred to in the plural in verses 2–5, while in verses 6–19 only one person is cursed. This supports the idea that this is a collection of insults and curses leveled against the psalmist by his enemies.

If verses 6–19 are a summary of the enemies' curses, the content is all the more astounding. The accusers drag him to court and insist on a guilty verdict (verses 6–7). They pray that he will die prematurely (verse 8). They curse the psalmist's parents, his children, his property, and his posterity (verses 9–15). They accuse him of oppressing the poor and needy and of driving "the broken-hearted to their death" (verse 16; is this a charge of murder?). Finally, they refer to the psalmist's love of cursing, and they pray that the curses would revert back to him, wrapping his body with them like a coat (verses 17–19).

Whichever way you read these verses, it is abundantly clear that what had been a close relationship (verse 4) has been irrevocably broken. Bridges are burned, and there is no possibility of reconciliation. At our distance from this estrangement it is almost impossible to determine justice in this situation. But we see what is desperately needed: healing, mercy, forgiveness, and reconciliation.

Keep me, O God, from debilitating hatred. As you reveal your grace to me, help me to grow in grace to others. Amen.

DRAINED OF STRENGTH AND AT GOD'S MERCY

Whoever originally spoke the words of verses 6–19, the psalmist prays that they be turned back against his enemies (verse 20). His situation has become even more urgent: His "heart is pierced," he has become gaunt and his "knees are weak from fasting," he is almost gone, "like a shadow at evening," and he has become "an object of scorn" and sees people shaking their heads when he appears (verses 22–25).

With increasing desperation, he throws himself at the mercy of God: "Because your steadfast love is good, deliver me. For I am poor and needy" (verses 21–22). The frequently occurring word *hesed*, here translated "steadfast love" has a wide range of meanings: faithfulness, compassion, fidelity, pity, and mercy. As Samuel Terrien puts it, "Mercy is the divine reality in which the psalmist is living. He now begs for this mercy with an unprecedented intensity. . . . He now places in balance God's mercy, which is goodness, and his own poverty, his need, his pierced heart."[42]

To throw yourself at the mercy of someone is to realize that you have hit bottom. Jeremiah graphically described his experience of this in passages known as his "confessions," especially in 15:15–20, which speaks of a kind of rebirth in the midst of severe depression. Like Jeremiah, our psalmist has no power to wield against his enemies. He turns to the only sure source of consolation, "Yahweh his Lord" (verse 21).

There are times in life when all we can say is, "Where can I go but to the Lord?"

Help me grow and develop into mature faith,
Lord God. Preserve me from pettiness
and give me a more generous heart. Amen.

OCTOBER 1   *Psalm 109:26–31*

A PLEA AND A VOW

A long series of charges and countercharges here comes to an end with a plea and a vow. The Hebrew word translated "Save me" in verse 26 is related to the word *Hosanna*, and the cry is connected to an appeal to God's reputation: "Let them know that this is your hand; you, O LORD, have done it" (verses 26–27). The plea is for a reversal, that the shame being experienced by the psalmist be turned back onto the enemies. The petitioner prays that the enemies—not he—be "wrapped in their own shame as in a mantle" (verse 29). In short, the psalmist wants vindication, the restoration of his good name.

The vow is a promise made to the LORD. He will "give great thanks to the LORD," praising God in the midst of the gathered multitude, thereby proclaiming God's steadfast love for the needy and those threatened with capital punishment (verses 30–31).

Psalm 109 as a whole is a graphic example of the dangers of making accusations and charges against someone or of engaging in gossip. How often can we be sure of the truth when we repeat destructive words? How can we know what is in the heart of the accused? How can we be sure that God is on our side and that we are completely innocent of the damage that has been done in a relationship? Are we aware of the destructive power of angry exchanges?

When you are the victim of slander, how can you best respond? Christians can well think of the words of Paul: "Who will bring any charge against God's elect? It is God who justifies. Who is to condemn? It is Christ Jesus, who died, yes, who was raised, who is at the right hand of God, who indeed intercedes for us" (Romans 8:33–34).

May my words, Lord God, be fitly spoken; may they work
to heal and not hurt, to save and not destroy. Amen.

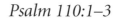

A ROYAL INVITATION

*T*his royal psalm is the most quoted of all psalms in the New Testament. It originally functioned, however, as a liturgy of enthronement of the king in Jerusalem, probably from the early period of the monarchy, that is, any time after 1000 B.C.

The first three words of the Hebrew text can be translated, "An oracle of Yahweh to my lord. . . ." This means that *God* speaks the following words to *the king*: "Sit at my right hand until I make your enemies your footstool." Here a prophet attached to the royal court communicates God's invitation to the king to be God's right-hand man and to lead his people in successful battle against his foes. The king will have the strength of a young man, fresh as the morning dew (verse 3b).

New Testament writers assume from the superscription, "Of David," that David wrote Psalm 110. On this assumption, David announces that God is saying something to "his lord," namely, the Messiah. In a strangely complex passage, Jesus himself is said to have posed a conundrum on this basis to "the scribes": If David calls the Messiah lord, how can the Messiah be the son of David? No one calls a son his "lord" (Mark 12:35–37; there are parallels in Matthew 22:41–45 and Luke 20:41–44). That the crowd responded "with delight" indicates that this was probably no more than a clever riddle (Mark 12:37), and not a disclaimer on Jesus' part of messianic dignity.

Verse 1 is cited also in Matthew 26:64; Acts 2:34; 7:55; Romans 8:34; 1 Corinthians 15:21–27; Ephesians 1:20; Colossians 3:1; Hebrews 1:13; 8:1; 10:12; and 1 Peter 3:22, always in reference to Jesus' ascension to the right hand of God. Early Christians followed Jewish tradition, which, after the fall of the monarchy, interpreted the royal psalms as messianic.

Bless us with just rulers, O God, who follow the example
of your servant Jesus. Amen.

A PRIESTLY KING

$\mathcal{V}$erse 4 is striking in several respects. Yahweh swears a solemn oath to the king: "You are a priest for ever according to the order of Melchizedek." The king is also to be a priest. This is exceptional, even if we read that in the early period of the monarchy that both Saul and David offered sacrifices (1 Samuel 13:9; 2 Samuel 6:13, 17–19), as did Solomon at the dedication of the temple (1 Kings 8:62–63).

But, if the Jerusalem kings were from the tribe of Judah rather than the priestly tribe of Levi, how could they be designated priests? Here the court poet draws on an obscure statement in Genesis 14:18: "King Melchizedek of Salem [Jerusalem] brought out bread and wine; he was priest of God Most High [*El Elyon*]," and he gave Abram a priestly blessing. This king was not a Hebrew—to say nothing of belonging to the tribe of Levi, which did not even exist at that time— but he was nonetheless a priest. So also the Davidic king in Jerusalem is a priest, made so by the irrevocable oath of God. And this time *God* is at *the king's* right hand (contrast verse 1) to give victory in exceedingly bloody battles with the nations "over the wide earth."

The New Testament Epistle to the Hebrews applies the saying about Melchizedek to the exalted Jesus (Hebrews 5:5–10; 6:13–20; 7:1–28). According to early Christian tradition, Jesus, like the Old Testament kings was from the tribe of Judah (Matthew 1:1–17; Luke 3:23–38; and several references to Jesus as "son of David"). Nonetheless, some early Christians venerated Jesus as a priestly intercessor before God. They found a rationale for this function in the tradition of Melchizedek, the non-Israelite who made sacrifices and gave a priestly blessing to Abraham, the father of the Jews.

Let us give thanks for all who intercede for us at the throne of mercy.

I offer prayer to you, God Most High, seeking your blessing
and giving thanks for intercessors through the ages. Amen.

GLORY AND GRACIOUSNESS

*H*ere begins a series of three "Hallelujah hymns," so called from the first words, *hallelu yah*, "Praise Yahweh." In the original Hebrew, Psalm 111 is an acrostic poem: After the opening "Hallelujah," each line begins with the successive letter of the Hebrew alphabet, a somewhat artificial form that imposes restrictions on the poet.

The psalmist is aware of the traditions of Israel's early history. The introductory line, "I will give thanks to the LORD with my whole heart," is an echo of the old liturgical call, "You shall love the LORD your God with all your heart, and with all your soul, and with all your might" (Deuteronomy 6:5). Mentioned also, however, is "his covenant," presumably the covenant mediated by Moses at Mount Sinai (instead of the covenant with Abraham [Genesis 17] or with David). Then the food provided "for those who fear him" would be the manna and quails of the wilderness period (Exodus 16).

In this first stanza of the psalm, God is described in striking, complementary terms. On the one hand, God's mighty acts are "great," "full of honor and majesty," "righteous," and "wonderful." On the other hand, "the LORD is gracious and merciful," as exemplified in his provision of food in the wilderness. We worship a God of glory and grace.

Infinite glory, if it were unmixed with grace, would be intolerable to us finite humans. When God's face shines on us, we know that it is a glance of graciousness. We therefore approach with confidence.

I give thanks to you, O Lord, with my whole heart.
Let me respond to your graciousness with generosity
toward those around me. Amen.

POWER AND JUSTICE

*T*he psalmist praises God for the conquest of Canaan by his ancestors. It was the LORD who gave them "the heritage of nations," which is one of the "works of his hands" that "are faithful and just." As was typical of international relations in the ancient Near East—and, unfortunately among even major powers today—there is no hint of the moral issues associated with bloody conflict. Instead, says the psalmist, the conquest displays both the *power* and the *justice* of the LORD (verses 6–7).

According to our psalmist, the justice and faithfulness of the LORD are forever set forth in the "precepts" of "his covenant" (verses 7b, 9), namely, the law of Moses. This law was given during the greatest act of redemption in Old Testament history—the exodus from Egypt (verse 9a). The word *redemption* means to be set free, as the Hebrews were delivered from Egyptian slavery. The exodus as an act of redemption reveals God's power, justice, and faithfulness.

Power, without checks, corrupts, and absolute power corrupts absolutely. Justice is a necessary counterbalance and guide for the proper use of power.

To complete the acrostic, the psalmist appends verse 10, quoting a familiar adage from the wisdom literature: "The fear of the LORD is the beginning of wisdom" (also in Proverbs 1:7; 9:10; Job 28:28). The thought nonetheless summarizes the thrust of the psalm as a whole: Proper knowledge of God is to praise God's glory, graciousness, power, and justice.

God of grace and God of glory, on your people pour your power. Grant us wisdom, grant us courage for the living of these days. Amen.

Psalm 112:1–5

GOOD THINGS CAN HAPPEN TO GOOD PEOPLE

*P*salm 112—another acrostic poem—outlines the virtues and values of the wisdom tradition in ancient Israel. The reference to the fear of the Lord in verse 1 creates a link with the final verse of the preceding psalm. The two psalms form a diptych: Psalm 111 is a praise of *God* and Psalm 112 praises the *godly person.*

The godly, those who "fear the Lord, who delight in his commandments," will see many blessings. Their numerous descendants will be movers and shakers in society. They will become wealthy and live in magnificent houses. More significantly, they will be known for their righteousness as well as for graciousness, mercy, generosity, and honest business practices. In short, they will be "happy" (verse 1a). The psalmist, like the wisdom writers, the compilers of proverbs, are sure that good things happen to good people.

We who live so many centuries after this psalm was written and sung might think that the psalmist is simplistic, promulgating a theology of reward. But the ancients knew as well as we do that not everything in this life makes sense; justice does not always prevail. In spite of this, the fact remains that anyone who cultivates righteousness, graciousness, mercy, honesty, and generosity is almost certain to find more enjoyment in life than the curmudgeon who grovels in cynicism, vengefulness, and callousness to those in need. We read this psalm best when we practice the virtues it inculcates.

Give me grace, Lord God, to grow in grace
and generosity. Amen.

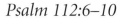

PHILANTHROPY
AND MISANTHROPY

*T*he psalmist ventures into matters of psychology, displaying keen insight, especially into the advantages of a healthy self-esteem. "The righteous will never be moved. . . . They are not afraid of evil tidings; their hearts are firm, secure in the LORD" (verses 6–7). This self-confidence is quite different from the boastings of the insecure. It is the self-assurance that allows one to be outgoing and generous. A steady heart (verse 8) has control over negative emotions and the inner strength necessary for clarity of judgment. The resulting freedom enables the righteous to engage in philanthropy, particularly by helping the poor (verse 9). His reputation for generosity will endure long past his death. What is missing here, however, is the awareness that riches and success, like political power, can degenerate into smugness and self-satisfaction.

The opposite of philanthropy is misanthropy. The wicked, lacking inner security, can react only with envy and bitterness at the success of others. But their own plans come to nothing (verse 10).

The psalmist was on the verge of the significant insight that much of what we call wickedness or sin with respect to the behavior of others actually stems from deep-seated feelings of inadequacy. Emotional insecurity can cause carping, gossip, and many other destructive, negative actions. Each generation needs to take care that children grow to maturity with a healthy self-esteem.

Lord God, I pray for the health of our children and youth,
that they may develop into self-confident
and generous adults. Amen.

GREATNESS AS ACTS OF COMPASSION

*I*n modern Judaism, Psalms 113–118 are known as the "Hallel" psalms and are chanted or read at the Passover meal. Originally, however, these psalms were probably sung by pilgrims on their way to the Jerusalem temple.

Two themes jump out from Psalm 113. First, the worshipers are repeatedly called to praise the glory of the name Yahweh (verses 1–6). This is the sacred and ineffable name of God, the name not to be taken in vain (Exodus 20:7), the name revealed personally to Moses. According to Exodus 33:19, God announces to Moses, "I . . . will proclaim before you the name, 'Yahweh'; and I will be gracious to whom I will be gracious, and will show mercy on whom I will show mercy." For our psalmist this name suggests the incomparable majesty of God, "high above the nations, and his glory above the heavens" (verse 4).

The second theme comes as a surprise. The greatness of Yahweh, the utterly transcendent God, finds expression not in displays of worldly power or the conquests of nations but in acts such as Mother Teresa might have done: "He raises the poor from the dust, and lifts the needy from the ash heap. . . . He gives the barren woman a home, making her the joyous mother of children" (verses 7–9). Psalm 113 echoes the Song of Hannah in 1 Samuel 2:1–9. Hannah struggled with infertility and praised the name Yahweh, who "raises up the poor from the dust; he lifts the needy from the ash heap, to make them sit with princes" (verses 2, 3, 8).

With our mass-market forms of worship, many modern Westerners have lost the sense of transcendent majesty. This is regrettable because the experience of the holy rejuvenates us to tend to the world's woes and bring hope to the hopeless.

Let me experience the beauty of holiness, and let the wonder
of your sacred name impel me to bring justice
to the downtrodden. Amen.

THE EARTH TREMBLES

*I*n Israelite memory the heart of the exodus from Egypt was the crossing of the sea in the area of what is now the Suez Canal. Four texts in the book of Exodus celebrate this great act of redemption, listed here in the order of their composition: the Song of Miriam (15:21); the Song of Moses (15:1–18); the older narrative, "J," which says that "Yahweh drove the sea back by a strong east wind all night, and turned the sea into dry land" (14:19–25); and the later narrative, "P," which speaks of the waters of the sea "forming a wall for them on their right and on their left" (14:26–29).

In Psalm 114 Israel left "a people of strange language," a people who were different and into which the Hebrews had not assimilated. (Similarly, Isaiah 33:19 refers to Assyrians as "the insolent people, the people of an obscure speech . . . , stammering in a language that you cannot understand.") The result of the deliverance at the sea was the eventual founding of the two kingdoms, Judah in southern Palestine and Israel in the north (verse 2). In mocking irony the poet personifies the Red Sea. It "fled" (past tense). The poet refers to the similar story of the crossing of the Jordan River as the conquest began. Joshua 4:23 explicitly links these two traditions. Then, obliquely referring to the conquest of the watery chaos at creation, the poet directly addresses the sea and the hills: "Why is it, O sea, that you flee?" (present tense, verses 5–6).

In the presence of "the God of Jacob" the very earth trembles. The tsunami turns back, the mountains quake, and water flows from the rock. This language certainly reflects the ancients' awe of nature. But *we* also marvel at the mysterious and sometimes violent forces of nature and the indescribable power of the atom. The God we worship stands behind both.

O God of storm and quiet, of the trembling earth and the con-
fident heart, be my strength in time of danger. Amen.

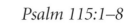

GLORY TO WHOM GLORY IS DUE

*A*lthough Psalm 115 does not quite fit any of the typical forms of psalms, it is a liturgy for public worship that combines elements of the hymn and the song of trust.

Verses 1–8 contrast Israel's worship with that of "the nations," namely, the Gentiles. The nations taunt Israel for worshiping an invisible God: "Where is their God?" (verse 2). The worshipers in the temple have two responses. First, "Our God is in the heavens; he does whatever he pleases" (verse 3). The true God is not contained in a shrine on a hilltop or in a grove of trees and cannot be controlled or coerced to act in a certain way by praying to an image.

Second, the worshipers intone a satire on idol worship. The Gentiles make idols of silver and gold, but they cannot speak, see, hear, smell, walk, or make sounds (verses 4–7). These verses echo several Old Testament passages. Deuteronomy 4:28 warns, "You will serve other gods made by human hands, objects of wood and stone that neither see, not hear, nor eat, nor smell." Jeremiah 10:3–5 mocks, "Their idols are like scarecrows in a cucumber field, and they cannot speak." The classic parody of idol worship is Isaiah 40:19–20 (see also 44:9–20; 46:5–8).

The issue, however, is greater than an inter-religious squabble. To whom is glory due? The worshiping congregation confesses, "Not to us, O LORD, not to us, but to your name give glory" (verse 1). The universe does not center around our individual or corporate selves. Nor are we to give glory to the idols of our culture. The essential spiritual task for all human beings of all times and of all places is to separate the multitude of our penultimate concerns from the one ultimate concern, which we identify as the God in the heavens, the God of steadfast love and faithfulness.

Not to us, O Lord, not to us, but to your name
we give glory. Amen.

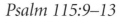

GOD-FEARERS AND THE PEOPLE OF GOD

 $\mathcal{T}$ he mention in verse 8 of those who trust in idols leads the congregation to encourage three groups to "trust in the LORD" (verse 9). The first is the whole congregation of "Israel." The second is the "house of Aaron," the privileged priesthood of the temple. And the third are "You who fear the Lord," apparently the proselytes, converts to the God of Israel (in the book of Acts 10:22 the Roman centurion Cornelius is called a "God-fearing man"). These three groups are mentioned in the same order again in verse 12, this time as the recipients of the blessing of God.

Incorporation of non-Israelites into the people of Yahweh was a reality throughout Israel's history. According to Genesis 12:3, God already promised Abram (Abraham) that in him "all the families of the earth shall be blessed." At the conquest of Canaan the Gibeonites and others joined the tribal federation (Joshua 9). Also, during the monarchy, foreigners would come to worship (1 Kings 8:41–43; 1 Kings 5:17). Although such receptivity was severely curtailed under the leadership of Ezra and Nehemiah after the exile, the Maccabees, who ruled Palestine in the second and first centuries B.C., incorporated a large Gentile population into the Jewish people. The early church viewed itself as part of Israel, and the question of who belongs, and who doesn't, and on what basis, convulsed the early followers of Jesus for several decades.

The opposing tendencies toward particularism and inclusiveness (or universalism) involve on-going debates within both Judaism and Christianity. Texts on both sides can easily be found in both Testaments. The bottom line for God, however, might well be Peter's words in Acts 10:35, "In every nation anyone who fears [God] and does what is right is acceptable to him."

Give me an open and generous heart, O God, toward those
outside of my community. Amen.

"THE DEAD DO NOT PRAISE THE LORD"

*T*he psalmist concludes by contrasting the heavens and the earth and also the living and the dead. To Yahweh belong eternity and the heavens, and to human beings mortality on the earth. Thus what mere mortals can hope for is the increase of progeny and blessings from God.

In the oldest Old Testament texts the dead linger on in Sheol, where the memory of God has faded and where praise of God is therefore impossible. "The dead do not praise the LORD" (verse 17). Isaiah 38:18-19 tersely expresses this view: "Sheol cannot thank you [God], death cannot praise you. . . . The living, the living, they thank you." Death here is the disappearance of the life force, the *nephesh* (often translated "soul").

As the generations passed, however, the conviction that God has power even over death emerged. The idea that the dead "sleep a perpetual sleep" (Jeremiah 51:39, 57) developed into the assurance that God would one day awaken "many of those who sleep in the dust of the earth" and bring them into "everlasting life" (Daniel 12:2). Then God's victory would be complete: "The LORD of hosts . . . will destroy on this mountain the shroud that is cast over all peoples . . . ; he will swallow up death for ever. Then the Lord GOD will wipe away the tears from all faces" (Isaiah 25:6-8).

The early Christians unanimously found in the resurrection of Jesus the certain hope for new life after death. Readily acknowledging that this new life is beyond all human description—or even comprehension—they were certain that "when this perishable body puts on imperishability . . . then the saying that is written will be fulfilled: 'Death has been swallowed up in victory.' 'Where, O death, is your victory? Where, O death is your sting?'" (1 Corinthians 15:54-55).

O Lord of heaven and earth, of life and death, I will bless your
name from this time on and forever, in this life and the next.
Amen.

A NEAR-DEATH EXPERIENCE

*A*n individual here expresses thanks and love to the LORD for rescue from a near-death experience. In deep distress and anguish, the "snares of death" and the "pangs of Sheol laid hold on [him]" (verse 3). The experience of terminal illness—or any life-threatening situation—can be described as being bound with cords. David's hymn of praise for victory in past battles is so similar to the words of the psalmist that a literary dependence might be assumed: "The waves of death encompassed me . . . , the cords of Sheol entangled me, the snares of death confronted me" (2 Samuel 22:5–6; also Psalm 18:4–5). Extreme anguish is often experienced as the feeling of pressure on the chest, causing difficulty in breathing.

In the depths of anguish and pain, the psalmist appealed to the source of life: "Then I called on the name of the LORD." The experience is so firmly etched on his mind that he remembers the exact words he used, "O LORD, I pray, save my life!" (verse 4b). The LORD did hear.

No one completely escapes the experience of anguish such as that of this psalmist. We are able to grieve with those whose end draws near, and we can minister to those in the pits of despair. In such cases, however, let us remember to take it to the LORD in prayer.

> *O Joy that seekest me through pain, I cannot close my heart*
> *to thee; I trace the rainbow through the rain, and feel the*
> *promise is not vain that morn shall tearless be.*[43] *Amen.*

 *Psalm 116:5–11*

THE JOY OF RECOVERY

*T*he psalmist first blesses the LORD for his recovery (verses 5–7) and then reflects on his suffering (verses 8–11): the sequence, new orientation ⟶ disorientation, is the reverse of the psalmist's experience.

Again we read of the near-death experience, characterized by tears and weakness. The suffering was so intense and unceasing that his gait was uncertain and tottering (verse 8). But now he rejoices, "I walk before the LORD in the land of the living." He contrasts his own words, "I am greatly afflicted," with those of his acquaintances: "I said in my consternation, 'Everyone is a liar'" (verses 10–11). It is typical of the lament that the petitioner speaks of being the object of slander and lies and of being forsaken by former friends and even family members. We can imagine questions such as were hurled at Job by his "friends": "What have you done to deserve this? Examine your heart." Through it all, however, the sufferer kept faith in the steadfast love of God (verse 10a), and his faith was vindicated. In Romans 3:4, Paul reflects the psalmist's words: "Although everyone is a liar, let God be proved true."

In his new orientation, the psalmist grasps the true heart of God: "Gracious is the LORD, and righteous; our God is merciful" (verse 5). Contrary to the accusations and innuendoes of the onlookers, God is not vindictive. God's wrath is not the final word. In grace, righteousness, and mercy, God deals bountifully, saving and restoring. The "simple" in verse 6 who are protected by the LORD are not the foolish, as in Proverbs, but instead are like the "poor" in the psalms: those who have nowhere else to turn but to the God of mercy and justice. And so the agitated soul can now return to its rest, rejoicing in the bounty of the LORD.

I would keep faith in you, Lord God, in your graciousness,
righteousness, and mercy. Amen.

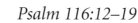

"PRECIOUS IN THE SIGHT OF THE LORD"

*W*hat is the proper response to an astounding reversal of fortune, a complete restoration of health after a near-death experience? Verses 13–14 are a doublet of verses 17–18. The "cup of salvation" (verse 13) is therefore a complement to "a thanksgiving sacrifice" (verse 17), indicating that the cup is a libation, a liquid offering that might be drunk in a ceremony in the temple. The opposite of the "cup of salvation" is the "cup of wrath" (Isaiah 51:17, 22; Lamentations 4:21; Ezekiel 23:31–33). In addition to offering a libation and a thanksgiving sacrifice, the restored man will pay his vows to the LORD in public at the temple (verses 14, 18; for the laws on vows see Leviticus 7:16–17; 22:17–25; 27; Numbers 6; 15:1–10; 30; Deuteronomy 12).

Verse 15 is one of the most beautiful in the book of Psalms: "Precious in the sight of the LORD is the death of his faithful ones." In the first instance, this might simply refer to the psalmist's rescue from his near-death experience. God shares the sorrow of humans at the death of someone dearly loved. Ultimately, however, these words raise the hope of eternal life with God. The anguish that God feels at the death of those who keep faith in God must lead to rescue also from death, the final enemy of human life.

O Lord, I am your servant; you have loosed my bonds. I will
lift up the cup of salvation and call on your name. Amen.

UNIVERSAL PRAISE

*W*e have come to the shortest psalm, a simple and unpretentious song of praise. Although its brevity has led some to speculate that it originally was the final stanza of Psalm 116 or the opening stanza of Psalm 118, it serves exquisitely as an introit, a call to worship, that brings together several bedrock affirmations of ancient Israelite worship.

The temple singers invite all nations and all peoples to praise the Lord, the God of Israel (an invitation found also in Psalms 22:27; 72:11; 96:7; 100:1). The celebration of the holy name of God was especially associated with temple worship. (Paul in Romans 15:11 quotes verse 1 to refer to the inclusion of the Gentiles in the people of God.)

Praise is due from all peoples of earth because of Yahweh's "steadfast love . . . and faithfulness," "grace and truth" (*hesed* and *emeth*). These two terms occur several dozen times in the psalms, often linked together. They are the two central and essential attributes of God, celebrated in a confession of faith traced back to the time of Moses: "The Lord, the Lord, a God merciful and gracious, slow to anger, and abounding in steadfast love and faithfulness, keeping steadfast love for the thousandth generation, forgiving iniquity and transgression and sin" (Exodus 34:6–7). Steadfast love and faithfulness are two self-limitations on the power of God. God is—so to speak—not free to act capriciously but is bound to the promise to act with justice and mercy. God is faithful. Praise the Lord!

> *As you, O God, have dealt with me in steadfast love and*
> *faithfulness, give me strength to deal with grace*
> *and mercy to others. Amen.*

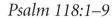

DELIVERANCE FROM DESPERATION

*A*s in Psalm 115, three groups are invited to participate exuberantly in a liturgical ceremony at the temple, giving "thanks to the LORD, for . . . his steadfast love." First is the general congregation of Israelites (verse 2), then the ranks of priests, "the house of Aaron" (verse 3), and finally "those who fear the LORD," the proselytes (converts, verse 4). (According to another interpretation, the God-fearers are the elite pious ones who have outstanding devotion to Yahweh.) Then, in the presence of the great assembly in the temple, an individual, presumably the king, gives thanks to God for deliverance from a perilous situation. Priestly assurances and blessings conclude this thanksgiving psalm.

Beginning in verse 5, the king describes a difficult battle. When he found himself in "distress" and hemmed in from all sides he "called on the LORD; the LORD answered me and set me in a broad place" (verse 5). He took courage from the thought that the LORD was on his side (verse 7), and he came to the conviction that "it is better to take refuge in the LORD than to put confidence in princes" (verse 9).

The king's testimony can encourage anyone who is squeezed in a tight place. In his heated struggles with pope and princes, Martin Luther often turned to Psalm 118. In a preface to his sixty-three page commentary on this psalm, he wrote, "This is my own beloved psalm. . . . I call it my own. When emperors and kings, the wise and the learned, and even saints could not aid me, this psalm proved a friend and helped me out of many great troubles."[44]

In distress we too can make a claim on God's steadfast love, acknowledging that the one "who trusts in God's unchanging love builds on the Rock that cannot move" (George Neumark, 1627–1681).

Though human comfort fail, let me take refuge
in your steadfast love, O Lord. Amen.

GLAD TO BE ALIVE

Life and death hung in the balance for the king. With some exaggeration, he describes how he was surrounded by "all nations" (verse 10), as if by a swarm of bees or by a brush fire (verse 12). He was pushed hard, he was falling (verse 13). He was almost gone. But, as he shouts three times, "In the name of Yahweh I cut them off!" (verses 10, 11, 12). No details are given of the carnage, but the king assures us that "The Lord is my strength and my might; he has become my salvation" (verse 14). Therefore, "there are glad songs of victory in the tents of the righteous," songs that repeat over and over again, "the right hand of the Lord does valiantly" (verses 15–16).

God had severely tested the king, but God did not hand him over to death. "I shall not die, but I shall live" (verse 17).

We are shocked and grieved when a family member or friend dies, especially when death strikes someone prematurely. But, when a person recovers from a life-threatening crisis, we almost reflexively rejoice. Survival is our ultimate objective. When asked how he was, a middle-aged man who recovered fully from a heart attack said simply, "I'm glad to be here." That is an affirmation of the gift of life, a gift we all are obliged to treasure.

When my way grows dark and I am hemmed in,
be my strength and my salvation, Lord God. Amen.

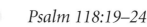

THE GATES, THE STONE, THE DAY

*T*he king, rescued from death in a fierce battle, now enters the sanctuary to give thanks to God: "Open to me the gates of righteousness . . . the gate of the LORD . . . I thank you that you . . . have become my salvation" (verses 19–21).

In verse 22 the congregation applies to the king a proverb: "The stone that the builders rejected has become the chief cornerstone." Why had this king made the nation's leaders uneasy? Was it his age (several of Jerusalem's kings ascended to the throne in their teen years)? Was it a physical illness? Was it his personality? In any case, like a stone that was mistakenly cut or that cracked and yet became the foundation stone of the entire building, the king has almost miraculously defended and preserved the nation. The congregation gives credit to God: "This is the LORD's doing; it is marvelous in our eyes" (verse 23). "This is the day that the LORD has made; let us rejoice and be glad in it" (verse 24).

In Judaism the rejected stone came to be interpreted of David and thus of the coming messiah. It is therefore not surprising that early Christians found here a parallel to their experience of Jesus, who was rejected and crucified but then exalted to the right hand of God. Such is the use of Psalm 118:22 in Mark 12:10–11; Matthew 21:42; Luke 20:17; and 1 Peter 2:7.

The work of God is done in this world by folks great and small. An average student can quickly blossom and accomplish marvelous things. A humble person can surprise us with consistent and unpretentious work that brings comfort and health to a broken community. The saints of God are not always the "beautiful people" of society, but they are beautiful in the sight of God.

You have made this day, O Lord;
let me rejoice and be glad in it. Amen.

ENTERING WITH EXUBERANT JOY

*T*he congregation cries to God for continued protection: "Save us . . . O Lord!" (verse 25; *hoshi'a na*, "Hosanna!" but translated as "Help" in 2 Samuel 14:4; 2 Kings 6:26; Psalms 12:1; 28:9; and as "Give victory" in Psalms 20:9; 60:5; 108:6). The crowd welcomes the king as the agent of God: "Blessed is the one who comes in the name of Yahweh" (verse 26). The people exhort one another to arrange a glorious procession to the main altar of the "house of Yahweh," carrying lights and strewing the entire way with branches (verses 26–27). The king then speaks final words of thanks to God (verse 28), and the psalm ends with the same words with which it began (verses 1, 29).

The authors of the New Testament Gospels found in these verses a parallel to Jesus' entry into Jerusalem on the Sunday before his crucifixion. He came "in the name of the Lord," and the crowds shouted "Hosanna!" (Mark 11:9; Matthew 21:9, 15). Luke 19:38 omits "Hosanna!" but interprets the psalm verse as referring to a king: "Blessed is the king who comes in the name of the Lord!" John 12:12–13 takes up the cry, follows Luke regarding kingship, and also brings in the branches from Psalm 118:27. Moreover, Matthew 23:39 and Luke 13:35 have Jesus himself cite Psalm 118:26: "For I tell you, you will not see me again until you say, 'Blessed is the one who comes in the name of the Lord.'"

The biblical writers were not automatons, writing as if in some woozy *Twilight Zone* trance. They wrote for specific purposes, fully aware of what they were writing. Christians have nothing to gain by pretending that the New Testament's use of psalm texts is the same as their function in the liturgy of the Jerusalem temple in Old Testament times. Integrity and truth are virtues to be treasured and preserved.

I bless all who come in the name of the Lord, testifying to God's steadfast love. Amen.

AIMING AT PERFECTION

$\mathcal{P}$salm 119 is by far the longest in the entire Psalter, and it has an unusually artificial acrostic form. All eight lines of each stanza begin with the same letter, and the twenty-two stanzas follow the order of the Hebrew alphabet (they are so labeled here). The content is widely diverse, including wisdom sayings, praise, lament, thanksgiving, affirmations of faith, and songs of trust. But the basic emphasis throughout is love and veneration for God's law.

א (*alef*), verses 1–8, make clear the major thrust of the entire psalm. "Happy are those . . . who walk in the law of the LORD" and keep its "decrees . . . precepts . . . statutes . . . commandments . . . ordinances" (the psalmist uses eight synonyms for "laws"). The word translated "happy" is often rendered "blessed." It corresponds to the Greek word in Jesus' Beatitudes, "*Blessed* are the . . . for they shall . . ." (Matthew 5:1–12). The book of Proverbs also promises happiness to those who followed good counsel and who trust in the LORD (8:32; 16:20). But the closest parallel to this *alef* stanza is the linkage between blessedness and keeping the commandments that we find in Deuteronomy 28:1–6: "If you will only obey the LORD your God, by diligently observing all his commandments . . . all these blessings shall come upon you . . . : Blessed shall you be in the city, and blessed shall you be in the field. Blessed shall be the fruit of your womb. . . . Blessed shall be your basket and your kneading-bowl. Blessed shall you be when you come in, and blessed shall you be when you go out."

Our psalmist expresses self-interest in this law-piety. He hopes by diligent keeping of the law to avoid shame (verse 6a) and not to be forsaken by God (verse 8b). In this opening verse he thinks of personal morality rather then his obligations to others. But we can admire his desire to walk in the ways of God, and can try to do likewise.

Be a light to my path, O Lord, and give me the strength
to grow to a mature lifestyle. Amen.

YOUTHFUL PURITY

ב (*beth*): In the original Hebrew text, all eight lines of this stanza begin with this second letter of the Hebrew alphabet.

The psalmist introduces himself as a youth reaching adulthood: "How can a young man keep his way pure?" (RSV; NRSV: "young people"). The transition from youth to mature adulthood is often difficult. It is a testosterone time, especially in the life of young men, when emotions are strong and permanent patterns are not yet established. We can assume that our psalmist was not yet married and that he struggled with strong sexual urges, a subject that occupied the attention of the wisdom writers (Proverbs 7:6–27 is a classic example). Several Old Testament writers refer to the passions and failings of young adults ("the sins of my youth," Psalm 25:7; "the shame of your youth," Isaiah 54:4; "the disgrace of my youth," Jeremiah 31:19b). What young man has not struggled with such passions?

Religious passion can help in dealing with hormonal passion. Our psalmist knows this, and he seeks God with his "whole heart" (verse 10), treasuring God's words "so that I may not sin against you" (verse 11). He fixes his eyes on the ways of God (verse 15) in extraordinary concentration, all the while finding delight in doing so (verse 16).

Spiritual advisers walk a fine line in counseling young people. Sexual urges are natural; they cannot be abolished, and they must not be condemned for being what they are. But this drive is also dangerous in that it can lead a person into destructive behavior. Those who seek to do God's will are certainly on the right track.

Help me, Lord God, to seek to do your will in a time
of confusion. Amen.

"A STRANGER UPON THE EARTH"

ג (*gimel*): In the original Hebrew text, all eight lines of this stanza begin with this third letter of the Hebrew alphabet.

The psalmist declares that he has been the object of "scorn and contempt" from "the insolent, accursed ones, who wander from your commandments" (verses 21–22) and that "princes sit plotting against me" (verse 23). These vague feelings of persecution (whether real or imagined) have created in him *weltschmerz*, depression and fatigue at the gaping chasm between the world as it is and the world as it should be. He makes a sad confession, with a touch of self-pity: "I am a sojourner on earth" (verse 19, RSV; NRSV: "alien").

The "sojourner"—an outsider, an alien, a stranger who has no claim to the land—is a familiar figure in the Old Testament. Abraham was a sojourner in Egypt and in Canaan (Genesis 12:10; 19:9; 21:23, 34). According to ancient Near Eastern custom, hospitality was to be given to sojourners. "Love the sojourners . . . for you were sojourners in the land of Egypt" (Deuteronomy 10:19; 23:7; 27:19; also Psalm 39:12 and elsewhere).

Our psalmist has spiritualized this concept; he lives as a sojourner, an outsider, on the earth. He is isolated and alone, scorned and insulted by those around him. He takes comfort in God's commandments and statutes and decrees, which are his delight and his counselors (verse 24). And he petitions God to remove the ostracism and "take away from me their scorn and contempt" (verse 22).

But has he been honest in assessing the breakdown of personal relationships? Before we blame others for our isolation, we should engage in introspection and perhaps seek counsel from disinterested observers. Let us not return insult for insult, but let us respond to others with goodwill and humor. Life is too short for anything else.

Open my eyes, O Lord, that I may discern the right path. Amen.

MELTING IN SORROW

ד (*daleth*): In the original Hebrew text, all eight lines of this stanza begin with this fourth letter of the Hebrew alphabet.

This stanza continues the lament of the previous verses. There is a bit of wallowing in self-pity: "My soul [*nephesh*] clings to the dust. . . . My soul melts away for sorrow" (verses 25, 28). The *nephesh* is broader than the Greek or modern concept of the human psyche. It designates the life force, the totality of consciousness, the breath of life that the LORD breathed into the first human being (Genesis 2:7). When the soul "melts away for sorrow" and "clings to the dust," there is shortness of breath, a feeling of suffocation, and a sense of death.

Again the psalmist reveals his strong Torah-piety. He appeals to God's "word . . . statutes . . . precepts . . . wondrous works . . . law . . . ordinances . . . decrees . . . commandments." Because he has rejected "false ways" and has "chosen the way of faithfulness" (verses 29–30), he lays claim on God's "word" of salvation, which will "revive" and "strengthen" him (verses 25, 28).

It is remarkable how often the psalmists express psychological and spiritual depression. We might assume that relatively happy and content persons are less likely to write spiritual poetry. But it is also true that persons who most strongly strive to follow lofty ideals can become disillusioned with the realities of life in this world. When we become discouraged at human foibles and follies, and when we become weary of the world, let us remember the wondrous works that God had done for us. Let us give thanks for the gifts of music, the fresh autumn air, healthy physical activity, good conversation, and the privileged life we live in the Western world.

Forgive me, merciful God, for my complaining;
revive me according to your word. Amen.

THE VANITIES OF LIFE

ה (*hĕ*): In the original Hebrew text, all eight lines of this stanza begin with this fifth letter of the Hebrew alphabet.

This stanza consists mainly of petitions, and they center on requests for ways to observe the "statutes . . . law . . . commandments . . . decrees [and] . . . ordinances" ever more completely. To turn aside from these would be to seek "selfish gain" (verse 36) and to bring upon oneself "disgrace" (verse 39). By contrast, the "servant" (verse 38) who delights (verse 35) in the law will receive the promises of God (verse 38) and find true life (verses 37, 40b).

The heart of this stanza is verse 37: "Turn my eyes from looking at vanities; give me life in your ways." The psalmist prays to have the right priorities in life. All of us eventually learn the wisdom of this petition, although for some this knowledge comes too late. We need to separate the penultimate concerns of our earthly strivings from the ultimate concern: to honor God, to trust in God's eternal and steadfast love for us, and to respond properly to God's demand for justice and lovingkindness in our daily lives.

The entire book of Ecclesiastes is a reflection on this theme: "Vanity of vanities, says the Teacher, . . . All is vanity. What do people gain from all the toil at which they toil under the sun?" (Ecclesiastes 1:2–3). The book ends with the thought of our psalmist: "The end of the matter; all has been heard. Fear God, and keep his commandments; for that is the whole duty of everyone" (12:13).

When we are disappointed or embarrassed, or when we are overcome with anxiety, we should pray to be able to distinguish the penultimate from the ultimate. We can ask ourselves, will this matter one hundred years from now?

Straighten my priorities, O God, and keep me focused
on the right path. Amen.

WALKING IN LIBERTY

ו (*waw* or *vav*): In the original Hebrew text, all eight lines of this stanza begin with this sixth letter of the Hebrew alphabet.

Here again we find the psalmist praying about God's "word of truth . . . ordinances . . . law . . . precepts . . . decrees . . . commandments . . . [and] statutes." But now other motifs emerge as well. He prays for Yahweh's "steadfast love" in his life, which is promised "salvation" (verse 41). Allowing his ego to come to the fore, he refers to persons who taunt him (verse 42, as in verses 21–22) while he also looks forward to testifying of God's decrees before kings (verse 45; compare verse 23).

Readers today might be struck by what seems to be a contradiction. We tend to assume that the concept of "law" is antithetical to "freedom." The psalmist, however, while repeatedly emphasizing his love for and delight in God's commandments (verses 47–48), says that God's "precepts" will enable him to "walk at liberty" (verse 45, literally, "a broad place"). Can law lead to liberty? Is this thought related to the reference in James 1:25 to "the perfect law, the law of liberty"?

Perhaps there is insight in the psalmist's assertion. We are not free when we are addicted or habituated to destructive behavior. Nor are we complete human beings when we deny justice to others or fail to show mercy. Even if not all their details are applicable to life today, the basic principles of biblical commandments and prophetic demands for justice can lead to a "roomy" walk through life, a life of liberty.

I claim your promises and your steadfast love, O Lord;
let me walk in liberty following your path. Amen.

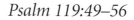

REMEMBERING

ז (*zayin*): In the original Hebrew text, all eight lines of this stanza begin with this seventh letter of the Hebrew alphabet. It is not as easy to begin sentences with the letter *zayin* as with many others, and this stanza consequently is perhaps more disjointed than most others in this psalm. We nonetheless find here, as in earlier stanzas, references to God's "word . . . promise . . . ordinances . . . statutes . . . law . . . [and] precepts."

Motifs from earlier parts of the psalm recur here. (1) The psalmist is in personal distress (verse 50; compare verses 25, 28). (2) He is derided (verse 51; compare verse 22). (3) The wicked forsake the law (verse 53; compare verse 21). (4) The psalmist lives on earth as a sojourner (verse 54; "wherever I make my home" literally translated is "in the house of my sojourning"; compare verse 19).

Noteworthy here is that both God and the psalmist are to remember something. "Remember your word to your servant, in which you have made me hope" (verse 49). What word is this? Is it a mystical revelation that came at night (see verse 55)? More likely the psalmist is thinking of the many promises of God recorded in the various law codes, promises of long life (for example, Exodus 20:12) and of a variety of blessings (among many examples, see Deuteronomy 28:1–6). The psalmist knows these blessings (verse 56). God's promises are a kind of self-limitation. God is bound to these promises; they are "steadfast."

The psalmist also remembers. "I remember your name in the night, O Yahweh, and keep your law" (verse 55), and "I think of your ordinances from of old" (verse 52). Remembering can be destructive, as when a person is debilitated by guilt or regret. But remembering God's promises is a form of faithfulness, and it leads to blessing.

*Your word is a comfort in my distress, and your promise gives
me life. For this I thank you, Lord God. Amen.*

GRACE AND OBEDIENCE

ח (*heth*): In the original Hebrew text, all eight lines of this stanza begin with this eighth letter of the Hebrew alphabet.

We hear yet again of "words ... promise ... decrees ... commandments ... law ... ordinances ... precepts ... [and] statutes," and the psalmist lets a touch of paranoia emerge in verse 61. But there is now a refreshing addition of more positive motifs. First is the confession, "The LORD is my portion" (verse 57), which suggests that the psalmist was from the priestly tribe, Levi, which had no "portion" in the allotment of the land of Canaan. "Levi has no allotment or inheritance with his kindred; the LORD is his inheritance, as the LORD your God promised him" (Deuteronomy 10:9; see also Numbers 18:20; Joshua 13:14).

Second, in spite of endlessly repeated assertions of his delight in God's commandments, the poet pleads with all his heart for God's favor and grace (verse 58). Everyone, no matter how mature or pious, needs the experience of grace, because to err is human. Human perfectibility will always remain just out of reach in this world.

Finally, along with numerous voices throughout the Bible, the poet moves from his individual life to a cosmic purview: "The earth, O LORD, is full of your steadfast love" (verse 64). He can only pray that his personal life will be brought into harmony with the universal grace of all creation.

After all our striving after virtue and all our efforts at good works, we find ourselves admitting, "We have done only what we ought to have done" (Luke 17:10). Nonetheless, doing our duty is not to be denigrated.

Be gracious to me, Lord God,
according to your promise. Amen.

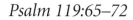
GOOD JUDGMENT FOLLOWING A STUMBLE

ט (*teth*): In the original Hebrew text, all eight lines of this stanza begin with this ninth letter of the Hebrew alphabet.

The psalmist several times has expressed inner despair (verses 27, 28) and has also referred to his rectitude ("I have chosen the way of faithfulness," verse 30). But not until now have we sensed a hint of a confession of sin: "Before I was humbled I went astray" (verse 67). It would be fascinating to know more about this—if, indeed, it was a real experience and not merely a literary allusion. Was that the time when "the arrogant"—those whose "hearts are fat and gross"— smeared him with lies (verse 69a)? In any case he twice admits that he "was humbled" and now perceives that it was good (verses 67, 71). His humiliation led to "good judgment and knowledge" (verse 66), so that henceforth he keeps God's word and values God's law "bet- ter . . . than thousands of gold and silver pieces" (verse 72).

Even through the rather artificial form of acrostic we can sense a personal transformation in these verses. Although it has become a cliché to refer to "hitting bottom" before we can move back up, that does sometimes happen in real life. Life can be difficult and con- fusing, and we might have to go through severe difficulties in order to learn to "Let go, and let God." Then we can praise God with the psalmist, "You are good and do good" (verse 68).

You have dealt well with me, O Lord,
and I have experienced your goodness. Amen.

BLAME AND SHAME

˒ (*yod*): In the original Hebrew text, all eight lines of this stanza begin with this tenth letter of the Hebrew alphabet.

In verse 75 we read again of an experience of humiliation in the psalmist's past, which he attributes to the just action of God: " I know, O Lord, that your judgments are right, and that in faithfulness you have humbled me." We have no particulars, but in verses 78 and 80 there are subtle hints that the psalmist was "shamed" by "arrogant" people. He prays for two things: (1) "May *my heart* be blameless . . . so that *I* may not be put to shame," but (2) "Let *the arrogant* be put to shame, because they have subverted me with guile." Ancient Semites dreaded the thought of losing face: "A good name is to be chosen rather than great riches" (Proverbs 22:1). The opprobrium of others—and especially social ostracism—was one of the worst fates that could befall you. Shunning of someone—an evil and heinous practice—happened then, and it does still today.

Somebody here is playing the blame and shame game—an exercise well known in present-day politics. How much easier it is to blame someone in the opposing political party instead of accepting responsibility for the disastrous results of your own ill-considered policies. And how much easier it is to seek to shame someone else rather than admit our own failings—even to hurl accusations of treason against a politician who lost three limbs in a war while fighting for his country.

The psalmist is on his way toward purity of heart. He admits that he deserved his humiliation. The next step is to avoid slandering the enemies. We cannot control our emotional response to others, but we most certainly are responsible for our words and actions. When we stop playing the blame and shame game, we might be able to break the vicious circle that perpetuates hatred.

Let your steadfast love fill my life, Lord God, that I may
respond in maturity toward others. Amen.

THE WORD OF GOD

un): In the original Hebrew text, all eight lines of this stanza begin th this fourteenth letter of the Hebrew alphabet.

Verse 105 is both beloved and familiar: "Your word is a lamp to feet and a light to my path." God's commandments guide the thful person through life on a path that is just, gracious, and mer- ul. In severe affliction, in times of danger, and in life-threatening uations, this word sustains life (verses 107, 109–110).

The word of God has a fascinating history in the Bible. We counter it first at creation, when God speaks, and order emerges at of chaos (Genesis 1). Then, however—strange as it seems to oderns—God literally speaks words of promise to Noah, Abraham, d the other patriarchs. (We would like to know how the ancients nderstood this to have happened.) The word of God par excellence the Old Testament, however, is expressed in the covenant God ade with Moses, especially in the "law" (Torah). This word is what he psalmist delights in: the revelation of God's will in the form of ommandments, ordinances, and so forth. God then continues to peak, but during the period of monarchy this occurs mainly through he medium of the prophets, who receive the word in the form of racles ("Thus says the LORD . . ."). In the time after the Babylonian xile (the sixth century B.C.), however, God does not speak directly nd personally to individual humans but only through the mediation of angels or dreams. And finally, some of the early Christians found he word (*logos*) of God revealed in the person of Jesus, the "Word ecame flesh" (John 1:14).

In all its manifestations, the word of God is God's self-revelation. The Bible bears witness to this word—in creation, as promise, as the lamp of guidance, and as the teachings of Jesus.

Lighten my path through the dark stretches of life, O Lord,
and lead me to true life. Amen.

"HOW LONG?"

כ (*kaph*): In the original Hebrew text, all eight lines of this stanza begin with this eleventh letter of the Hebrew alphabet.

This stanza stands out from the others in Psalm 119 in that its content is that of an individual lament throughout. The psalmist is being persecuted without cause (verses 84b, 86b), almost to the point of death (verse 87). His arrogant enemies have arranged pitfalls for him (verse 85), and he feels "like a wineskin in the smoke" (verse 83), a symbol of life-threatening danger. "The wine, . . . exposed to heat as improvement, also risks destruction. The heat of the flames may burn out the skin and lose the wine."[45]

The victim lays bare his soul, begging for salvation. "My eyes fail with watching for your promise; I ask, 'When will you comfort me?'" (verse 82). He begs that God, in steadfast love, would spare his life (verse 88). Then come the most pathetic words that sufferers of all times utter when undergoing tragedy and deep despair: "How long?" (verse 84).

How long must I suffer? When will it ever end? Will I ever again see the shining face of God? Such are the desperate questions of the psalms of lament. Yes, "the mills of God grind slowly."[46] And yes, there are times in life when we cannot help but ask unanswerable questions. "Why is this happening to me?" "What have I done to deserve this?" "How long?"

Perhaps the underlying question is, What can I do when my questions have no answer? All we can do—answer or no answer—is what the psalmist did. We keep looking to God's mercy, steadfast love, trusting that the universe, in the final analysis, operates on the principle of grace.

My soul languishes for your salvation, O Lord;
I trust in your promise. Amen.

UNIVERSAL AND ETERNAL

ל (*lamed*): In the original Hebrew text, all eight lines of this stanza begin with this twelfth letter of the Hebrew alphabet.

The psalmist acknowledges that, just as "the LORD exists forever," so God's word is "firmly fixed in the heaven" (verse 89), an affirmation seconded by a great prophet: "The word of our God will stand for ever" (Isaiah 40:8). God's word—God's speech—is universally valid, because, as the psalmist confesses, "You have established the earth," and everything in it "stands" by God's appointment (verses 90b, 91).

God's universal and eternal word sustains the entire earth. But our psalmist sings praise because this stabilizing word has been his salvation: "If your law had not been my delight, I would have perished in my misery" (verse 92). The cosmic has become the personal, and the eternal has become the temporal. The uncreated God cares for the creatures.

Literalists have stumbled at such statements as "You have established the earth, and it stands fast" (verse 90b). Does the sun revolve around the earth? Nicolaus Copernicus's treatise on the "revolution of the heavenly orbs" was published in 1543, showing that the earth revolves around the sun. Martin Luther responded by asserting that Joshua commanded the sun, not the earth to stand still (Joshua 10:12–13), John Calvin quoted Psalm 93:1, "He has established the world; it shall never be moved," and the pope complained that Copernicus contradicted Aristotle! How is it that everyone can read most poetry as it was intended—except *biblical* poetry?

Let us rejoice that, although all else in this life is temporal and falls short of perfection (verse 96), the universe as a whole reveals the stability of our uncreated, eternal, and universal God.

Your faithfulness, O God, endures to all generations;
all things are your servants. Amen.

BOASTING IN PIET

מ (*mem*): In the original Hebrew text, all eight line begin with this thirteenth letter of the Hebrew alphab

Can we detect an overly robust ego in this stanza than a hint of boasting in the psalmist's piety? He m long, leaving others to do the chores (verse 97). He i non-stop reflection has made him wiser than his enen and more understanding than his wisdom teachers and (verses 99, 100). He informs almighty God that he ha cepts (verse 100b) and ordinances (verse 102), avoids (verse 101) and hates "every false way" (verse 104).

All of this expended energy, however, has been fo delight. "How sweet are your words to my taste, sweete to my mouth!" (verse 103). The image of eating words r the similar experience of the prophets. "Your words wer I ate them, and your words became to me a joy and the d heart," says Jeremiah (15:16). And God commanded Eze scroll on which the prophet had written the words of C mouth it was as sweet as honey" (Ezekiel 3:3).

We should not too harshly judge a person who has fo in meditation. Such exercises can strengthen our inner b us for the work at hand and making us useful in a world healing.

Lord God, you know my faults and my failings;
I rely on your steadfast and unfailing love. Amen.

SPIRITUALITY AND FANATICISM

ס (*samek*): In the original Hebrew text, all eight lines of this stanza begin with this fifteenth letter of the Hebrew alphabet.

Many persons, most especially modern Westerners, are not quite certain how to balance commitment to a set of beliefs, on the one hand, and our strongly cherished freedom to voice our dissent, on the other. How can we steer a course that values both convictions and toleration?

Fanatic devotion can be exceedingly evil. No one ever accused Josef Stalin, Adolf Hitler, Pol Pot, Saddam Hussein, or any other dictator of flip-flopping. True believerism is not to be admired, no matter how many times we are warned against blowing "neither hot nor cold." Fanaticism is no virtue, and the ends most certainly do not justify the means. You cannot save a nation by killing its citizens. You cannot lead people on the right path by approaching them in hatred. Moreover, "in every age, hypocrisy is always but a stone's throw away from religious zeal."[47]

Mature persons, however, know that it is not a virtue to be "double-minded" (verse 113). They seek out the basic, most humane principles of biblical teachings and find ways to incorporate these in their daily living. They shun the practice of putting a "spin" on deceptive behavior, and they aim at inner integrity. They know what the prophet meant, "What does the Lᴏʀᴅ require of you but to do justice, and to love kindness, and to walk humbly with your God?" (Micah 6:8).

You are my hiding place and my shield, O God;
I hope in your word. Amen.

WAITING

ע (*ayin*): In the original Hebrew text, all eight lines of this stanza begin with this sixteenth letter of the Hebrew alphabet.

Much of our time is spent waiting. We wait for the traffic to move during rush hour. We wait in line at the grocery store. We wait in the "waiting room." We wait for the mortgage to be paid. We wait for good news. The psalmist is waiting, and he is desperately tired of waiting. The object of his waiting is rather vague: he waits "for your salvation, and for the fulfillment of your righteous promise" (verse 123). But there are hints at what lies behind this. He is oppressed by "the godless" (verses 121b, 122b), those who have broken the law of the LORD (verse 126b).

The psalmist waits for the LORD, but his patience is reaching its limit. He knows what the Argentinean writer Luisa Valenzuela (b. 1938) meant when she said, "Waiting is the most uninspired form of death." He cries out in frustration, "It is time for the LORD to act" (verse 126). It is the cry of throngs of faithful ones through the ages, "Where is God in my suffering? How long? When?" If the petitioner sounds harsh, we know that prayer in the Bible "may at times contradict the rules of elegant politeness. Prayer may then sound like a military command. . . . Such is . . . pathos in its extremity."[48]

In such a situation we need to remember the words of another psalmist: "I believe that I shall see the goodness of the LORD in the land of the living. Wait for the LORD; be strong, and let your heart take courage; wait for the LORD!" (Psalm 27:13–14).

Lift my vision, heal my spirits, and give me a heart of joy and gratitude, Lord God. Amen.

UNFOLDING OF WORDS AND GOD'S SHINING FACE

פ (*peh*): In the original Hebrew text, all eight lines of this stanza begin with this seventeenth letter of the Hebrew alphabet.

Several motifs of earlier stanzas appear here: the synonyms for "commandments," the appeal to God's promises, the request for help in keeping them, the psalmist's persecution, and his grief over the transgressions of God's law by others. Assertions that the petitioner keeps God's decrees and loves God's name (verse 132b) while he informs God how upset he is over the transgressions of others might strike readers today as self-serving. It probably is. But, if he is in mortal danger, as previous stanzas have indicated, then it is understandable that he prays for redemption (verse 134) and appeals to God's grace (verse 132).

Two motifs stand out in these verses. First, in order to find "light" in his distress, the psalmist is engaged in "the unfolding of your words" (verse 130). He apparently spends much of his time in textual biblical interpretation, poring over the law codes that were stored in the temple in Jerusalem and finding in them guidance for his personal life. This might well be the beginning of technical biblical studies!

The second motif is the plea for a living experience of God's grace: "Make your face shine upon your servant" (verse 135). The "face" is often shorthand for someone's presence. To behold God's face is to be certain of God's presence, and to see God's *shining* face is to be certain of God's gracious presence that comforts, assures, and strengthens us. The founder of Israel's priesthood, Moses' brother Aaron, gave this motif its classic expression: "The Lord bless you and keep you; the Lord make his face to shine upon you, and be gracious to you; the Lord lift up his countenance upon you, and give you peace" (Numbers 6:24–26).

O Lord, in the rough patches of my life
let your shining face be my strength. Amen.

RIGHTEOUSNESS

צ (*tsadeh*): In the original Hebrew text, all lines of this stanza begin with this letter of the Hebrew alphabet. If it were not for the various forms of the Hebrew term *tsedeq* (or *zedeq*), "righteous" or "just," this could be a challenge.

One theme is dominant here, the everlasting righteousness of God (verses 137, 142) and of God's decrees (verses 138, 144). Righteousness is a central motif throughout the Bible, and it has many facets. Humans are righteous when they work for the well-being of the community and treat others fairly and generously. Behavior can then be judged legally as righteous or unrighteous. But, above all, God is righteous (not once in the Bible is God held to be unrighteous). Abraham's question is rhetorical, "Shall not the Judge of all the earth do what is just?" (Genesis 18:25). God is not capricious or unpredictable but is bound to standards of justice and to the promises of the covenant.

God reckons human behavior as righteous or unrighteous. Abraham (Abram) believed Yahweh's promises of posterity, and God "reckoned it to him as righteousness" (Genesis 15:6). Ethical standards are typically based on the demands of the law codes; so our psalmist declares God's judgments and decrees to be righteous forever (verses 137b, 138, 144). When Amos exhorts, "Let justice roll down like waters, and righteousness like an ever-flowing stream" (Amos 5:24), he thinks of the demands of God for social justice.

In a remarkable development, a prophet of the sixth century B.C. equated God's righteousness with salvation: "I bring near my *righteousness*, it is not far off, and my salvation will not tarry" (Isaiah 46:13).[49] This thought becomes a major theme in the writings of the apostle Paul, who insists that God bestows righteousness on undeserving human beings "as a gift" to those who believe in the redemption wrought by God in Jesus (Romans 3:21–26 and elsewhere).

Lord God, with all my faults I appeal to your steadfast love
and look for your gift of righteousness. Amen.

INSOMNIA

ק (*qoph*): All eight lines of this stanza begin with this nineteenth letter of the Hebrew alphabet.

Many psalmists complain about insomnia, and especially about weeping through the night (for example, Psalms 6:6; 16:7; 22:2; 30:5; 42:3; 77:2; 88:1). Another poet graphically described their experience: "Nights of misery are apportioned to me. When I lie down I say, 'When shall I rise?' But the night is long, and I am full of tossing until dawn" (Job 7:3–4). Anxiety, dread, worry, and almost any profound emotion can disturb and prevent sleep.

Our psalmist complains that his persecutors, lawless ones, draw near (verse 150), threatening his life (verse 149). His eyes are wide open "before each watch of the night" (verse 148; the night was divided into three watches), and he rises before dawn, crying for help (verse 147). The darkness of night could evoke terror and foreboding, and many waited for the dawn. (It is possible, however, that the petitioner spent the night in vigil at a shrine, waiting for the LORD to answer. Both ordinary folk and prophets would sometimes "sleep on it" before the word of the LORD came.)

Many modern Westerners struggle with insomnia, and many more in our hectic way of living try to get along with insufficient sleep, with the result that the enjoyment of life is diminished. Those who are able to find refreshment in several hours of sound sleep each night are truly blessed. Insomnia can be difficult to overcome. Better than drugs is meditation on God's promises (verse 148b), finding hope in the source of all life.

> *Oh, may my soul in thee repose, and may sweet sleep mine*
> *eyelids close, sleep that shall me more vigorous make*
> *to serve my God when I awake.*[50] *Amen.*

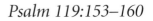
DISGUST OVER LAWLESSNESS

ר (*resh*): In the original Hebrew text, all eight lines of this stanza begin with this twentieth letter of the Hebrew alphabet.

Legal disputes are a frequent topic in the Old Testament. From the earliest period, the "patriarchs" would function as judges in their own families (Genesis 21–22 and elsewhere). Abraham entered into lengthy negotiations with the Hittites to purchase a burying place for his wife Sarah (Genesis 23). Moses appointed judges (Exodus 18:15) and personally oversaw many disputes, and city elders could serve as judges at the gate (Ruth 4:1–6). Later, the kings served as the court of final appeal.

Our psalmist, however, knows that Yahweh is the supreme judge and also his personal attorney: "Plead my cause and redeem me," "rescue me," "give me life" (verses 153a, 154). The "adversaries" are "persecutors" and "the wicked" (verses 155, 157), although we do not learn here the specific nature of their actions. What jumps out at us, however, is the assertion, "I look at the faithless with disgust, because they do not keep your commands" (verse 158).

Once again the psalmist enters tricky and complicated waters. We have learned in recent years that religious indignation is not always righteous. The name "Christian" has often been taken over by those who link it almost exclusively to sexual and reproductive issues while ignoring the "weightier matters of the law: justice and mercy and faith" (Matthew 23:23). Severe, punitive, and even ugly forms of piety have emerged simultaneously in Islam and in Christendom, and justice, mercy, and faith have been their victims. But let the final word here be verse 160: "The sum of your word is truth." After all our contentions and disputes, truth remains.

Great is your mercy, O Lord; give me life according
to your justice. Amen.

"HOW LONG?"

ב (*kaph*): In the original Hebrew text, all eight lines of this stanza begin with this eleventh letter of the Hebrew alphabet.

This stanza stands out from the others in Psalm 119 in that its content is that of an individual lament throughout. The psalmist is being persecuted without cause (verses 84b, 86b), almost to the point of death (verse 87). His arrogant enemies have arranged pitfalls for him (verse 85), and he feels "like a wineskin in the smoke" (verse 83), a symbol of life-threatening danger. "The wine, . . . exposed to heat as improvement, also risks destruction. The heat of the flames may burn out the skin and lose the wine."[45]

The victim lays bare his soul, begging for salvation. "My eyes fail with watching for your promise; I ask, 'When will you comfort me?'" (verse 82). He begs that God, in steadfast love, would spare his life (verse 88). Then come the most pathetic words that sufferers of all times utter when undergoing tragedy and deep despair: "How long?" (verse 84).

How long must I suffer? When will it ever end? Will I ever again see the shining face of God? Such are the desperate questions of the psalms of lament. Yes, "the mills of God grind slowly."[46] And yes, there are times in life when we cannot help but ask unanswerable questions. "Why is this happening to me?" "What have I done to deserve this?" "How long?"

Perhaps the underlying question is, What can I do when my questions have no answer? All we can do—answer or no answer—is what the psalmist did. We keep looking to God's mercy, steadfast love, trusting that the universe, in the final analysis, operates on the principle of grace.

My soul languishes for your salvation, O Lord;
I trust in your promise. Amen.

UNIVERSAL AND ETERNAL

ל (*lamed*): In the original Hebrew text, all eight lines of this stanza begin with this twelfth letter of the Hebrew alphabet.

The psalmist acknowledges that, just as "the LORD exists forever," so God's word is "firmly fixed in the heaven" (verse 89), an affirmation seconded by a great prophet: "The word of our God will stand for ever" (Isaiah 40:8). God's word—God's speech—is universally valid, because, as the psalmist confesses, "You have established the earth," and everything in it "stands" by God's appointment (verses 90b, 91).

God's universal and eternal word sustains the entire earth. But our psalmist sings praise because this stabilizing word has been his salvation: "If your law had not been my delight, I would have perished in my misery" (verse 92). The cosmic has become the personal, and the eternal has become the temporal. The uncreated God cares for the creatures.

Literalists have stumbled at such statements as "You have established the earth, and it stands fast" (verse 90b). Does the sun revolve around the earth? Nicolaus Copernicus's treatise on the "revolution of the heavenly orbs" was published in 1543, showing that the earth revolves around the sun. Martin Luther responded by asserting that Joshua commanded the sun, not the earth to stand still (Joshua 10:12–13), John Calvin quoted Psalm 93:1, "He has established the world; it shall never be moved," and the pope complained that Copernicus contradicted Aristotle! How is it that everyone can read most poetry as it was intended—except *biblical* poetry?

Let us rejoice that, although all else in this life is temporal and falls short of perfection (verse 96), the universe as a whole reveals the stability of our uncreated, eternal, and universal God.

Your faithfulness, O God, endures to all generations;
all things are your servants. Amen.

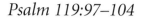

BOASTING IN PIETY

מ (*mem*): In the original Hebrew text, all eight lines of this stanza begin with this thirteenth letter of the Hebrew alphabet.

Can we detect an overly robust ego in this stanza? Is there more than a hint of boasting in the psalmist's piety? He meditates all day long, leaving others to do the chores (verse 97). He is sure that his non-stop reflection has made him wiser than his enemies (verse 98) and more understanding than his wisdom teachers and the old sages (verses 99, 100). He informs almighty God that he has kept all precepts (verse 100b) and ordinances (verse 102), avoids every evil way (verse 101) and hates "every false way" (verse 104).

All of this expended energy, however, has been for him a great delight. "How sweet are your words to my taste, sweeter than honey to my mouth!" (verse 103). The image of eating words reminds us of the similar experience of the prophets. "Your words were found, and I ate them, and your words became to me a joy and the delight of my heart," says Jeremiah (15:16). And God commanded Ezekiel to eat a scroll on which the prophet had written the words of God; "in my mouth it was as sweet as honey" (Ezekiel 3:3).

We should not too harshly judge a person who has found delight in meditation. Such exercises can strengthen our inner being, fitting us for the work at hand and making us useful in a world that needs healing.

Lord God, you know my faults and my failings;
I rely on your steadfast and unfailing love. Amen.

THE WORD OF GOD

נ (*nun*): In the original Hebrew text, all eight lines of this stanza begin with this fourteenth letter of the Hebrew alphabet.

Verse 105 is both beloved and familiar: "Your word is a lamp to my feet and a light to my path." God's commandments guide the faithful person through life on a path that is just, gracious, and merciful. In severe affliction, in times of danger, and in life-threatening situations, this word sustains life (verses 107, 109–110).

The word of God has a fascinating history in the Bible. We encounter it first at creation, when God speaks, and order emerges out of chaos (Genesis 1). Then, however—strange as it seems to moderns—God literally speaks words of promise to Noah, Abraham, and the other patriarchs. (We would like to know how the ancients understood this to have happened.) The word of God par excellence in the Old Testament, however, is expressed in the covenant God made with Moses, especially in the "law" (Torah). This word is what the psalmist delights in: the revelation of God's will in the form of commandments, ordinances, and so forth. God then continues to speak, but during the period of monarchy this occurs mainly through the medium of the prophets, who receive the word in the form of oracles ("Thus says the LORD . . ."). In the time after the Babylonian exile (the sixth century B.C.), however, God does not speak directly and personally to individual humans but only through the mediation of angels or dreams. And finally, some of the early Christians found the word (*logos*) of God revealed in the person of Jesus, the "Word became flesh" (John 1:14).

In all its manifestations, the word of God is God's self-revelation. The Bible bears witness to this word—in creation, as promise, as the lamp of guidance, and as the teachings of Jesus.

Lighten my path through the dark stretches of life, O Lord,
and lead me to true life. Amen.

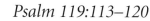

SPIRITUALITY AND FANATICISM

ס (*samek*): In the original Hebrew text, all eight lines of this stanza begin with this fifteenth letter of the Hebrew alphabet.

Many persons, most especially modern Westerners, are not quite certain how to balance commitment to a set of beliefs, on the one hand, and our strongly cherished freedom to voice our dissent, on the other. How can we steer a course that values both convictions and toleration?

Fanatic devotion can be exceedingly evil. No one ever accused Josef Stalin, Adolf Hitler, Pol Pot, Saddam Hussein, or any other dictator of flip-flopping. True believerism is not to be admired, no matter how many times we are warned against blowing "neither hot nor cold." Fanaticism is no virtue, and the ends most certainly do not justify the means. You cannot save a nation by killing its citizens. You cannot lead people on the right path by approaching them in hatred. Moreover, "in every age, hypocrisy is always but a stone's throw away from religious zeal."[47]

Mature persons, however, know that it is not a virtue to be "double-minded" (verse 113). They seek out the basic, most humane principles of biblical teachings and find ways to incorporate these in their daily living. They shun the practice of putting a "spin" on deceptive behavior, and they aim at inner integrity. They know what the prophet meant, "What does the LORD require of you but to do justice, and to love kindness, and to walk humbly with your God?" (Micah 6:8).

You are my hiding place and my shield, O God;
I hope in your word. Amen.

WAITING

ע (*ayin*): In the original Hebrew text, all eight lines of this stanza begin with this sixteenth letter of the Hebrew alphabet.

Much of our time is spent waiting. We wait for the traffic to move during rush hour. We wait in line at the grocery store. We wait in the "waiting room." We wait for the mortgage to be paid. We wait for good news. The psalmist is waiting, and he is desperately tired of waiting. The object of his waiting is rather vague: he waits "for your salvation, and for the fulfillment of your righteous promise" (verse 123). But there are hints at what lies behind this. He is oppressed by "the godless" (verses 121b, 122b), those who have broken the law of the LORD (verse 126b).

The psalmist waits for the LORD, but his patience is reaching its limit. He knows what the Argentinean writer Luisa Valenzuela (b. 1938) meant when she said, "Waiting is the most uninspired form of death." He cries out in frustration, "It is time for the LORD to act" (verse 126). It is the cry of throngs of faithful ones through the ages, "Where is God in my suffering? How long? When?" If the petitioner sounds harsh, we know that prayer in the Bible "may at times contradict the rules of elegant politeness. Prayer may then sound like a military command. . . . Such is . . . pathos in its extremity."[48]

In such a situation we need to remember the words of another psalmist: "I believe that I shall see the goodness of the LORD in the land of the living. Wait for the LORD; be strong, and let your heart take courage; wait for the LORD!" (Psalm 27:13–14).

Lift my vision, heal my spirits, and give me a heart of joy
and gratitude, Lord God. Amen.

UNFOLDING OF WORDS AND GOD'S SHINING FACE

פ (*peh*): In the original Hebrew text, all eight lines of this stanza begin with this seventeenth letter of the Hebrew alphabet.

Several motifs of earlier stanzas appear here: the synonyms for "commandments," the appeal to God's promises, the request for help in keeping them, the psalmist's persecution, and his grief over the transgressions of God's law by others. Assertions that the petitioner keeps God's decrees and loves God's name (verse 132b) while he informs God how upset he is over the transgressions of others might strike readers today as self-serving. It probably is. But, if he is in mortal danger, as previous stanzas have indicated, then it is understandable that he prays for redemption (verse 134) and appeals to God's grace (verse 132).

Two motifs stand out in these verses. First, in order to find "light" in his distress, the psalmist is engaged in "the unfolding of your words" (verse 130). He apparently spends much of his time in textual biblical interpretation, poring over the law codes that were stored in the temple in Jerusalem and finding in them guidance for his personal life. This might well be the beginning of technical biblical studies!

The second motif is the plea for a living experience of God's grace: "Make your face shine upon your servant" (verse 135). The "face" is often shorthand for someone's presence. To behold God's face is to be certain of God's presence, and to see God's *shining* face is to be certain of God's gracious presence that comforts, assures, and strengthens us. The founder of Israel's priesthood, Moses' brother Aaron, gave this motif its classic expression: "The Lord bless you and keep you; the Lord make his face to shine upon you, and be gracious to you; the Lord lift up his countenance upon you, and give you peace" (Numbers 6:24–26).

O Lord, in the rough patches of my life
let your shining face be my strength. Amen.

RIGHTEOUSNESS

צ (*tsadeh*): In the original Hebrew text, all lines of this stanza begin with this letter of the Hebrew alphabet. If it were not for the various forms of the Hebrew term *tsedeq* (or *zedeq*), "righteous" or "just," this could be a challenge.

One theme is dominant here, the everlasting righteousness of God (verses 137, 142) and of God's decrees (verses 138, 144). Righteousness is a central motif throughout the Bible, and it has many facets. Humans are righteous when they work for the well-being of the community and treat others fairly and generously. Behavior can then be judged legally as righteous or unrighteous. But, above all, God is righteous (not once in the Bible is God held to be unrighteous). Abraham's question is rhetorical, "Shall not the Judge of all the earth do what is just?" (Genesis 18:25). God is not capricious or unpredictable but is bound to standards of justice and to the promises of the covenant.

God reckons human behavior as righteous or unrighteous. Abraham (Abram) believed Yahweh's promises of posterity, and God "reckoned it to him as righteousness" (Genesis 15:6). Ethical standards are typically based on the demands of the law codes; so our psalmist declares God's judgments and decrees to be righteous forever (verses 137b, 138, 144). When Amos exhorts, "Let justice roll down like waters, and righteousness like an ever-flowing stream" (Amos 5:24), he thinks of the demands of God for social justice.

In a remarkable development, a prophet of the sixth century B.C. equated God's righteousness with salvation: "I bring near my *righteousness*, it is not far off, and my salvation will not tarry" (Isaiah 46:13).[49] This thought becomes a major theme in the writings of the apostle Paul, who insists that God bestows righteousness on undeserving human beings "as a gift" to those who believe in the redemption wrought by God in Jesus (Romans 3:21–26 and elsewhere).

Lord God, with all my faults I appeal to your steadfast love
and look for your gift of righteousness. Amen.

NOVEMBER 8 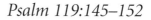 *Psalm 119:145–152*

INSOMNIA

ק (*qoph*): All eight lines of this stanza begin with this nineteenth letter of the Hebrew alphabet.

Many psalmists complain about insomnia, and especially about weeping through the night (for example, Psalms 6:6; 16:7; 22:2; 30:5; 42:3; 77:2; 88:1). Another poet graphically described their experience: "Nights of misery are apportioned to me. When I lie down I say, 'When shall I rise?' But the night is long, and I am full of tossing until dawn" (Job 7:3–4). Anxiety, dread, worry, and almost any profound emotion can disturb and prevent sleep.

Our psalmist complains that his persecutors, lawless ones, draw near (verse 150), threatening his life (verse 149). His eyes are wide open "before each watch of the night" (verse 148; the night was divided into three watches), and he rises before dawn, crying for help (verse 147). The darkness of night could evoke terror and foreboding, and many waited for the dawn. (It is possible, however, that the petitioner spent the night in vigil at a shrine, waiting for the LORD to answer. Both ordinary folk and prophets would sometimes "sleep on it" before the word of the LORD came.)

Many modern Westerners struggle with insomnia, and many more in our hectic way of living try to get along with insufficient sleep, with the result that the enjoyment of life is diminished. Those who are able to find refreshment in several hours of sound sleep each night are truly blessed. Insomnia can be difficult to overcome. Better than drugs is meditation on God's promises (verse 148b), finding hope in the source of all life.

> *Oh, may my soul in thee repose, and may sweet sleep mine*
> *eyelids close, sleep that shall me more vigorous make*
> *to serve my God when I awake.*[50] *Amen.*

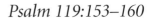 *Psalm 119:153–160*

DISGUST OVER LAWLESSNESS

ר (*resh*): In the original Hebrew text, all eight lines of this stanza begin with this twentieth letter of the Hebrew alphabet.

Legal disputes are a frequent topic in the Old Testament. From the earliest period, the "patriarchs" would function as judges in their own families (Genesis 21–22 and elsewhere). Abraham entered into lengthy negotiations with the Hittites to purchase a burying place for his wife Sarah (Genesis 23). Moses appointed judges (Exodus 18:15) and personally oversaw many disputes, and city elders could serve as judges at the gate (Ruth 4:1–6). Later, the kings served as the court of final appeal.

Our psalmist, however, knows that Yahweh is the supreme judge and also his personal attorney: "Plead my cause and redeem me," "rescue me," "give me life" (verses 153a, 154). The "adversaries" are "persecutors" and "the wicked" (verses 155, 157), although we do not learn here the specific nature of their actions. What jumps out at us, however, is the assertion, "I look at the faithless with disgust, because they do not keep your commands" (verse 158).

Once again the psalmist enters tricky and complicated waters. We have learned in recent years that religious indignation is not always righteous. The name "Christian" has often been taken over by those who link it almost exclusively to sexual and reproductive issues while ignoring the "weightier matters of the law: justice and mercy and faith" (Matthew 23:23). Severe, punitive, and even ugly forms of piety have emerged simultaneously in Islam and in Christendom, and justice, mercy, and faith have been their victims. But let the final word here be verse 160: "The sum of your word is truth." After all our contentions and disputes, truth remains.

Great is your mercy, O Lord; give me life according
to your justice. Amen.

REMINDING GOD
OF YOUR PIETY

שׁ (*shin*): In the original Hebrew text, all eight lines of this stanza begin with this twenty-first letter of the Hebrew alphabet.

The psalmist again accuses princes of persecuting him "without cause" (verse 161). If this is an autobiographical reflection, is it related to his past experience of going astray and being "humbled" (verse 67)? How would the princes have described this incident? We will never know but, as the classic Japanese film *Rashomon* illustrated, there sometimes are even more than two sides to one story.

The petitioner reminds God that he gives praise "seven times a day" (verse 164). If this is not a symbolic use of the "perfect number," it probably includes "each watch of the night" (verse 148), of which there were three. A late Old Testament writing refers to the practice of prayer three times a day (Daniel 6:10); in praying seven times a day, our psalmist goes much further than did others of his time.

We all have heard public prayers that inform God of things that God probably already knew, and we suspect that the one who prays in such a way has the audience in mind rather than God. Our psalmist's descriptions of his super piety give us the same impression. "My heart stands in awe of your words. . . . I hate and abhor falsehood. . . . I fulfill your commandments. My soul keeps your decrees; I love them exceedingly. I keep your precepts and decrees" (verses 161–167).

Spirituality does require an individual's commitment to God and God's will as we know it from the ethical principles of the Bible, especially from its great prophets and teachers. But spiritual maturity also includes a dose of humility about our place in the sweep of things—and especially in our bearing toward our Creator. Let us cultivate the higher virtues and forgo reminding God of our piety.

Oh, let your mighty love prevail to purge us of our pride, that we may stand before your throne by mercy purified.[51] *Amen.*

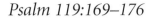

POURING FORTH PRAISE

ת (*taw* or *tav*): In the original Hebrew text, all eight lines of this stanza begin with this last letter of the Hebrew alphabet.

The final stanza of Psalm 119 sums up the preceding petitions. The danger and the anxiety it brings are still here, and the psalmist raises a supplication for deliverance, help, and salvation. And again we find references to God's "word . . . statutes . . . promise . . . commandments . . . precepts . . . law . . . [and] ordinances." But the last verse comes as a shock, seemingly at odds with almost all that has gone before: "I have gone astray like a lost sheep; seek out your servant . . ." (verse 176). Is this a blanket confession of imperfection? Is it a reference to the going astray of verse 67? Or is it a general statement of the endemic confusion of life in this world? It could be all of these together.

Considering its acrostic form and other stylistic features, Psalm 119 is a thoroughly crafted poem. The poet borrows motifs and language from the whole range of Israel's traditions, but especially from the speech style of the prophet Jeremiah. In content, its overriding theme is love of God's law. The long list of synonyms for "law" and of phrases expressing delight in the law shows that the psalmist is thinking not of a specific law code but of God's primordial will for human life. The word of God is a dynamic that impels us to good living (verse 175). It cannot be frozen for all time but becomes active in the lives of the faithful in the evolving course of history. And yet, ironically, after all our striving and all of God's urging, our final petition is a confession and a plea for God to be our Good Shepherd: "I have gone astray like a lost sheep; seek out your servant" (verse 176).

Help me, Lord God, to live the life I sing about in my song,
to grow in integrity, and to seek your will in my thoughts
and actions. Amen.

A SOJOURNER ON A PILGRIMAGE

The superscriptions of Psalms 120–134 all include the phrase "Song of Ascents," indicating that they were sung by pilgrims on their way to worship at the Jerusalem temple. But the double complaint of false accusations from "a deceitful tongue" (verses 2b, 3b) and "lying lips" (verse 2) marks this as an individual lament.

The three stanzas are curious. If we translate verse 1 in the past tense, "I cried to the LORD, and he answered me," verse 2 would be the words of the psalmist's desperate plea, which was answered. In that case, however, we can scarcely make sense of the vehement curse in verses 3–4. Therefore, the first stanza must be the psalmist's still-unanswered distress cry.

No reason is given for the heated curse in the second stanza, verses 3–4. A rhetorical question, "What shall be given to you?" gets a specific answer: "A warrior's sharp arrows, with glowing coals of the broom tree!" The broom bush, a kind of juniper, maintains a hot fire for a long time. Here it is a curse, a symbol of judgment (compare the more beneficent thrust of the "burning coals" in Romans 12:20)

Most puzzling is the third stanza (verses 5–7). Meshech, a son of Japheth (Genesis 10:2) lies far north of Palestine, while Kedar, a son of Ishmael (Genesis 25:13), is in the other direction, northern Arabia. Was the psalmist literally a sojourner in either place? Or is this a symbolic reference to living among pagans? In either case, the psalmist has lived away from his own for too long (verse 6), and he has discovered, much to his regret, that his offers of peace and friendship were returned by bellicose, lying lips (verse 7). Pilgrims leaving hostile pagan areas for the wonders of the worship of God in the holy city might well have chanted this strange psalm.

Guide me ever, great Redeemer,
pilgrim through this barren land. Amen.

"FROM WHERE WILL MY HELP COME?"

*T*his beautiful psalm expresses supreme confidence in Yahweh's protection of the pilgrims moving toward Jerusalem. Their feet will not move onto the wrong path because, although the pilgrims will take their rest on the way, Yahweh "will neither slumber nor sleep" (verse 4). Yahweh is not a fertility god, like Baal, whose priests Elijah taunted at the contest on Mount Carmel: "Cry aloud! . . . either he is meditating, or he has wandered away, or he is on a journey, or perhaps he is asleep and must be awakened" (1 Kings 18:27; Felix Mendelssohn used the text of Psalm 121 in his oratorio *Elijah*). Fertility gods usually went dormant at the end of the growing season. Yahweh, the one who made heaven and earth (verse 2b), not Baal, controls the earth, and it is this God who guards and keeps the pilgrims and all Israel.

There are two ways to read the second line of this psalm. Most translations today take it as a question: "From where will my help come?" According to this reading, the pilgrims travel through hilly areas where dangers lurk from wild animals or difficult terrain. Through treacherous regions the pilgrims sing of their confidence in Yahweh.

Others, however, follow Martin Luther's translation of line two as a statement: "I lift up my eyes to the hills, from where my help comes." The pilgrims are moving toward Jerusalem, and that city is nestled in hills that rise from all sides, especially from the east and west. Yahweh's "glory" is located in the holy of holies in the Jerusalem temple, and there is the earthly localization of Yahweh's help.

Paul Gerhardt (1607–1676) expressed the confidence of this psalmist in his hymn "Befiehl du deine Weg" (Entrust Your Way):

Who points the clouds their course
Whom winds and seas obey,
He shall direct your wandering feet,
He shall prepare your way.

Guide my feet on the right path, O Lord,
my maker and redeemer. Amen.

NOVEMBER 14 *Psalm 121:5–8*

BLESSED ASSURANCE

*E*ach line of the second half of this psalm is a benediction. On their way to Jerusalem, the LORD's protection follows the pilgrims both day and night. Through the blazing midday heat they are shielded from sunstroke, and by night they are protected from the baleful effects of the moon, widely regarded in antiquity as the cause of various illnesses, including fever, leprosy, and being "moonstruck" (the word "lunacy" comes from the Latin *luna*, "moon"). The pilgrims' lives are safe on this journey; no evil will befall them (verse 7). Indeed, Yahweh will "keep" their going out and their coming in—not only going to and returning from the sanctuary in Jerusalem but also "from this time on and for evermore" (verse 8).

The name Yahweh ("the LORD") occurs often in this brief psalm. The LORD, as creator of heaven and earth (verse 2), can protect the pilgrims from destructive powers of nature. Yahweh protects all Israel (verse 4) and also is the keeper of the individual who walks a difficult way in worry and doubt. The psalmist uses the image of a long and hazardous journey as an image of our journey through life. The whole of life, every going out and coming in, are under the protection of the one who made heaven and earth. And this blessing, says the psalmist, will never cease.

> If you but trust in God to guide you
> > And place your confidence in him,
> You'll find him always there beside you
> > To give you hope and strength within.
> For those who trust God's changeless love
> > Build on the rock that will not move.[52]

Lord God, be with me through the hard passages of life;
keep me from evil through your great mercy. Amen.

THE BEAUTIFUL CITY

We can hear a pilgrim singing this song while returning from the joyful events of a festival in Jerusalem. He begins by remembering the excited anticipation of going to "the house of Yahweh" (verse 1); he then finds himself "standing within your gates, O Jerusalem" (verse 2). He looks around at the city, observing its firm construction, its fortified walls (verse 3), watching the pilgrims moving into it (verse 4), and standing in awe at the magnificent government buildings (verse 5).

The emotion of the pilgrim breaks through in his blessing of the holy city. He prays "for the peace [*shalom*] of Jerusalem" (verse 6; "Jerusalem" means "foundation of Shalem" or, less probably, "foundation of peace"). May the fortifications of the city preserve his relatives and friends there. But especially he prays for peace because of the temple there, "the house of Yahweh our God" (verse 9).

Jerusalem, located on the backbone of hills in central Palestine, was an ancient city, named in documents about 3900 years ago, but settled much earlier than that. David (verse 5b) first captured the city for the Israelites in about 1000 B.C. and made it the capital of the "United Monarchy" of the twelve tribes. By bringing the Ark of the Covenant into the city he also made Jerusalem the permanent religious center for his people.

Even today, pilgrims to Jerusalem might experience the thrill of the psalmist. Yes, we pray for the peace of Jerusalem and of all the region around it. We recognize, however, that God is the lord of heaven and earth and of all the tribes of the whole world. This city is still enthralling to pilgrims, but we look forward to a new Jerusalem, the symbol of renewed life on earth, the end of strife and bitterness and weeping—a city of peace.

Lord God, I pray that your rule might become effective over all
the earth; bring an end to human strife and make
our world a city of peace. Amen.

A PLEA FOR MERCY

*H*ere a lament is placed within the group of pilgrimage songs. Although the psalmist speaks in the first person singular in verse 1, the plural pronouns in the rest of the psalm demonstrate its form as that of a communal lament.

The psalmist lifts his eyes to the LORD (verse 1; also Psalms 25:15; 121:1; 141:8; 145:15) in supplication for his people. It is a posture of deep yearning and longing, a plea for help directed to the one who is "enthroned in the heavens," the transcendent one. The psalmist and his people take on the pleading stance of slaves before their master and of a maid before her mistress (verse 2). The psalm thus centers on the contrast of the powerless and the powerful, a contrast is not only between humans and God but also between "the proud" and those who are the objects of their contempt (verses 3–4). There is a class struggle behind this lament, one that involves domination and oppression.

We can imagine either of two backgrounds for this lament. The psalm might reflect the haughty attitude of a group of the power elite in the psalmist's own community who respond with contempt to the less fortunate. Or the background might be that of foreign oppression, as of the Persian governors of Judah in the post-exilic period (that is, after 538 B.C.), with pilgrims traveling to Jerusalem expressing their grief over the despoiling of the holy city.

We can learn something from a psalmist who prays for mercy not for himself but for his people. We should be concerned that the leaders of our country act respectfully to leaders of other nations and that they deal justly both with our citizens and with human beings in other countries. And it is appropriate that we turn to God in a plea for mercy for all who are victims of the proud and scornful.

O Lord, lead my country on paths of justice for all. Amen.

MORTAL DANGER
AND TRUE PROTECTION

*T*his thanksgiving psalm is remarkable for its graphic images of national catastrophe and deliverance. The unidentified enemies are like a devouring beast about to swallow its prey whole. In the background might be the image of Sheol, which opens wide its maw and draws in its victim alive (Numbers 16:32–33; Psalm 55:15; Proverbs 1:12). Then, in verse 6b, the beast is a wild animal with threatening fangs, and in verse 7 the people are like a bird caught in a fowler's net.

In verses 4–5 a different image emerges. The threat is like a flash flood, a torrent in a gorge during the rainy season that suddenly fills the valley and carries everything away, a phenomenon that can happen yet today in Palestine. In the background here might be the image of the primeval waters of chaos that preceded creation (Genesis 1:2).

Although we cannot know what specific historical situation is reflected here, it is clear that this was a dire threat, a matter of the actual survival of the people. But help came. Four times the singers identify the source of help: the LORD (Yahweh; verses 1, 2, 6, 8), and specifically, "the *name* of Yahweh, who made heaven and earth" (verse 8). This, the personal name of Israel's God, means in Hebrew something like, "The one who causes to be," namely, the God who oversees events and who therefore can determine the outcome of a critical battle. No wonder the pilgrims repeat their words, "If it had not been Yahweh who was on our side . . ." (verse 1, 2).

Human beings are frail, and our lives are tenuous. Where can we find security in uncertain times? The apostle Paul points to the same answer we find in the psalm: "If God is for us, who is against us?" (Romans 8:31).

Blessed are you, O Lord, the true source of life
and strength. Amen.

JUST DESSERTS
AND MY GOODNESS

*H*ere is another marching song for pilgrims anticipating their arrival in Jerusalem. These *zadiqim* ("the righteous," verse 3b) "trust in the LORD" (verse 1); they "are good" and "upright in their hearts" (verse 4). They are not a sect but rather the faithful of the entire community—such as persons who would make the arduous journey to attend a festival at the temple in Jerusalem. They are Yahweh's people (verse 2b).

In contrast to the *zadiqim* are the wicked—apparently foreign rulers—who, at the moment, have control of the land. During the monarchy, Assyria controlled events in Judah during most of the sixth century and Babylon did after 612 B.C. After the exile Judah (Judea) was governed by the Persians. In such a time, the pilgrims express their trust that Mount Zion (the holy hill in Jerusalem) "cannot be moved" (verse 1). They are confident that the LORD surrounds the people with protection, just as the mountains surround Jerusalem (verse 2; the city is situated on the ridge of hills that runs between and parallel to the Mediterranean and the Jordan valley). The evildoers will certainly be led away (verse 5).

The "righteous" are those who are good (verse 4). Samuel Terrien aptly observes:

> The anthropology of "goodness" persists both in Judaism and Christianity, in spite of a bold retort attributed to Jesus. When a certain ruler asked him, saying, "Good teacher, what must I do to inherit eternal life?" Jesus is remembered as having said, "Why do you call me good? No one is good but God alone" (Mark 10:17–18; Luke 18:19). Another Gospel corrected the logion into the following, "Why do you ask me about what is good?" (Matt 19:17). Some manuscripts do not accept the humility attributed to Jesus. Perhaps they argued the theology of Psalm 125.[53]

Peace be upon Israel, O Lord, and upon all its neighbors.
And may peace be upon us. Amen.

SOWING IN TEARS, REAPING IN JOY

$\mathcal{P}$salm 126 presupposes a time not long after the initial return of Judahite (Jewish) exiles from Babylon (present-day southern Iraq). After defeating Babylon, the Persian king Cyrus (Persia is present-day Iran) issued in 538 B.C. a decree that allowed the exiles to return to Judah (Judea) and rebuild the temple (the edict is preserved in Ezra 1:2–4). Leaders of the return and rebuilding efforts were Zerubbabel, Ezra the scribe, Nehemiah, Joshua the priest, and the prophets Haggai and Zechariah. The reconstruction of Judea was a long, slow process, but by 515 B.C. a rather modest temple was standing in Jerusalem.

"When the LORD brought back those who returned to Zion, we were like those who dream" (verse 1, New Revised Standard Version, note). It was a time of laughter and joy, and an occasion for the Gentiles to marvel at the works of the God in Zion (verse 2b). But the work was far from complete. There was yet much sowing to be done, but the prophetic voice promises, "Those who go out weeping, bearing the seed for sowing, shall come home with shouts of joy, carrying their sheaves" (verse 6).

An old German proverb advises, "Do not laugh when you sow; otherwise you must weep when you reap."[54] The thought of weeping when sowing goes back to ancient fertility cults, in which the deity descends into the underworld when the ground goes barren and then ascends during the growing season. It is an apt image for the danger, toil, and sweat of the returned exiles trying to rebuild their land after years of despoliation. It is a reminder also to us that good things often require strenuous efforts and the investment of scarce resources. The promise of reaping good things from what we sow, however, spurs us on (see Mark 4:1–8).

Refresh my soul, O Lord, like water in the desert,
that I may do what needs to be done. Amen.

A SAFE AND NURTURING HOME

*T*his wisdom psalm is a compilation of proverbs on a single theme: Human labor and our striving to establish a safe and nurturing home can be successful only with the help and protection of the LORD. The superscription ascribes the psalm to King Solomon, patron of wisdom literature and also the builder of God's "house," the temple in Jerusalem (verse 1a).

The psalmist develops the theme both in negative and in positive assertions. First come three enterprises that are "in vain" without the LORD: (1) building a house, verse 1a; (2) guarding a city, verse 1b; and (3) toiling the entire day and suffering insomnia at night, verse 2. These three activities are the necessary prerequisites for establishing and maintaining healthy families.

The positive assertions relate to siring many sons. The image is of a young family ("sons of one's youth," verse 4b), the father of which is rewarded by God with a goodly heritage—a quiver full of sons (verses 4–5). The many sons provide to the father two things. First, they assured protection of the father from "enemies at the gate," where legal decisions were made by the elders of the city (Deuteronomy 21:19; 22:15; Ruth 4:11; Isaiah 29:21; Amos 5: 12, 15). Second, they were for the father a source of pride: "He shall not be put to shame" (verse 5).

Psalm 127, like much of the Bible, is thoroughly male-oriented. There is no denigration of women, but the psalmist speaks to those who establish a home and try to provide for it. We live today in a vastly different culture. The ancients could scarcely imagine a time when the world would be overpopulated. Large families in our time are no longer a necessity. But to build a home where God is reverenced and children grow up in emotional security is just as important today as it was in the time of the psalmists.

Bless my home, O Lord, I pray. Make it safe by night and day. Amen.

FAMILY VALUES

*T*his wisdom psalm is a benediction on the family that "fears the Lord" (verses 1, 4). The fear of God in the psalms generally does not denote terror at the prospect of divine wrath or judgment but rather the awe that accompanies the sense of divine presence. Those who fear the Lord are the righteous, the pious who "walk in his ways."

Temple singers and priests pray for the happiness of family relationships. The husband is "happy" because he enjoys the fruit of his labor and is prosperous (verse 2). The wife, the master of the household, is as "fruitful" as a healthy grapevine or olive trees (verse 3), the chief symbols of successful agriculture in Palestine. Together, the couple produce numerous children, who complete the picture of the model family gathered around the dinner table (verse 3c). The temple singers add a final blessing on this family, directed to the husband (women and men were separated at temple liturgies). They pray for the prosperity of Jerusalem "all the days of your life" and also for the married couple, that they will see their children's children (verses 5–6).

The nuclear family has been a source of security, satisfaction, and joy for many millennia. Positive "Norman Rockwell" images of the family at work, at play, at meals, and at worship have left an indelible imprint on many Americans. But neither can we deny that this image is an ideal that few actual families can maintain—or even attain. Marriages fail, and single parent families are common. Many young persons now avoid marriage altogether. The definition of "family" is rapidly changing. And all parents know first-hand how difficult it is to raise children in twenty-first-century Western culture. In spite of our struggles and failures, however, we know that there is true joy to be had in positive human relationships, and it is appropriate for us to seek God's blessing on our family.

O Lord, protect my home, and make it a haven for all who
come and go in it. Amen.

ON DEALING WITH ENEMIES

*I*n this communal lament the nation of Israel surveys its history: "Often have they attacked me from my youth" (verses 1–2). "My youth" is the exodus from Egypt, the original military threat, when Israel became God's son (Exodus 4:22–23; Hosea 11:1).

Israel would know continual, intermittent military threats over the centuries. These came from the neighboring small states, Philistia, Edom, Moab, Ammon, and Phoenicia. They came much more ominously from the world empires: Egypt, Assyria, Babylon, Persia, the Greeks, and the Romans. As the plow makes furrows in the field, so they left their marks on the land. But—astoundingly—throughout it all, the nation survived. It was conquered more than once, its cities razed, its people deported, but it was never exterminated. There were haters of Zion aplenty. But on them the psalm singers place a curse: Let them be like wheat that withers before it produces grain (verses 6–7). And, when they try to reap a harvest, let no passersby pronounce the customary blessing, "Yahweh bless you" (verse 8).

The ambiguity of war lies beneath the purview of the psalmist. "It is difficult, if not humanly impossible, even for devout religionists, to acknowledge or discern their own responsibility in the bellicose conflicts that accompanied the conquests of the Holy Land. . . . Religious wars are the most cruel and inhuman of all international conflicts."[55] Psalm 129 retained its relevance in post-biblical times when the Jews experienced exile, massacres, expulsions, and pogroms from various sides (including Christendom), and—in world-historical proportions—the Holocaust of the twentieth century.

When will we ever learn? When will we study war no more? When will be beat our swords into plowshares? When will lay down our burdens?

From war's alarms, from deadly pestilence, be your strong
arm, O Lord, our ever sure defense. Amen.

A CRY FROM THE DEPTHS

This profound expression of despair is one of the seven "penitential laments" of the early church (Psalms 6, 32, 38, 51, 102, 130, 143). Well-known from the first two words of its Latin translation, *De profundis*, it is often read at funerals. Because it is one of the few psalms in which sin is confessed and forgiveness sought, Martin Luther included it in his list of "Pauline psalms" (Psalms 32, 51, 130, 143).

The pathos of the psalmist is unmistakable. He cries "out of the depths"—the abode of the dead or as one sinking in deep waters (both images occur in Psalm 69:15; see also Psalms 18:4, 15; 69:2; Genesis 1:2; Isaiah 51:10; and elsewhere). God has not yet heard his desperate cries (verse 2), and God's absence is like the separation of death. The psalmist has nothing left to lose, and he therefore throws himself with no conditions whatever at the mercy of the Lord.

The man in grief has only one argument to set before God: "If you, O LORD, should mark iniquities, Lord, who could stand?" (verse 3). Could God find even one perfectly righteous person in that generation? No one could pass that final inspection without comment. And so the psalmist makes only one appeal—to divine forgiveness. We learn nothing about a specific sin for which he appeals for forgiveness nor of the nature of his suffering. We learn only that he has hit bottom and presents himself totally vulnerable before the Lord of forgiveness.

In one important respect, the New Revised Standard Version is better than earlier translations: "There is forgiveness with you, so that you may be revered" (not, "that thou mayest be *feared*"). All human beings experience despair. And most of us have known guilt. But we need to be reminded that the heart of the God we worship is not wrath but mercy.

When I am in the depths, I appeal to your eternal mercy,
Lord God. Amen.

WAITING AND HOPING

*T*he psalm changes from a prayer to that of a confession or witness to the congregation. Three verbs are dominant. The first verb, three times repeated, is "wait." "Wait for the LORD." The psalmist anxiously waits for God to answer, even more than watchmen at the city gates wait for the morning light and the lessening of danger. This is like Francis Scott Key's "The Star-Spangled Banner," in which the soldiers strain to determine whether, after a night of heavy fighting with the British in the War of 1812, the nation's flag is still waving over Fort McHenry in Baltimore.

The second verb is "hope." Without hope—the prospect of a resolution—waiting would be futile. But we must be clear about the object of our hope. The psalmist hopes in "his word" (verse 5), presumably a word of promise from God, an oracle communicated by a priest in the temple. The temple singers then encourage the entire congregation to "hope in the LORD!" (verse 7), because the heart of God is "steadfast love," the motivation for forgiveness.

The third verb is "redeem" (verses 7b, 8). The LORD has "great power to redeem," and "he . . . will redeem Israel from all its iniquities." The word "redemption" originally referred to gaining freedom, usually by purchase. Israel was redeemed from Egyptian slavery (Exodus 6:6; 15:13) and from exile in Babylon (Isaiah 48:20; Micah 4:10). But the word was often used for freedom from any kind of oppression, including moral and spiritual slavery (Jeremiah 15:21) and even from death (Hosea 13:14).

In a real sense, all humanity waits and hopes for redemption, for freedom from everything that thwarts the fullness of life. We wait for the fullness of God's reign, the time when God's will is done in all the earth.

My soul waits for you, O Lord, more than watchmen waiting
for the light of morning. Amen.

MODEST CONTENTMENT

*T*his song of trust is a modest statement from a person who informs God about his modesty. Coming amid the emotional outbursts of numerous psalms that are laden with complaints, boastful statements, protestations of innocence, and bellicose attitudes toward neighboring peoples, it is a breath of fresh air—at least at first glance.

The psalmist claims that he does not put on airs, but has an honest self-appraisal: "My heart is not lifted up." And he has not condescended toward his peers: "My eyes are not raised too high" (verse 1a). He has not aimed too high nor taken on himself grandiose projects that were beyond his abilities and reach (verse 1b). Instead, like the apostle Paul, he has "learned to be content in whatever I have" (Philippians 4:11).

An ancient Egyptian (about 2000 B.C.) once wrote a dialogue between his soul (*ka*) and himself about whether he should commit suicide.[56] Our psalmist's dialogue with himself was different. He has taught his "soul" to be content, just as a weaned child has learned to sit contentedly in his mother's lap without crying for the breast. By introspection he has "calmed and quieted" his soul (verse 2).

The quest for humility, however, can be tricky. Is this paragon of modesty engaged in an "egocentric display of humility"?[57] Does this explain the attribution of the psalm to David—a man who combined pride and humility, belligerence and compassion? Or is this a statement from someone who, like the writer of Ecclesiastes, has seen the futility of proud ambition and the desperate yearning for ego-stroking?

We encourage our children to reach for the stars. We hope that they will develop a healthy self-confidence. But they—and all of us—need to learn also that contentment has its place, and the calm and quiet soul is a thing of beauty. Through it all, we need to learn to "hope in the LORD" (verse 3).

Help me to use my talents and gifts wisely and justly,
Lord God. Amen.

THE LORD'S PROMISE TO DAVID

*T*his royal liturgy celebrates (1) King David's choice of Jerusalem as the religious center for the tribes of Israel, (2) the bringing of the Ark of the Covenant into the city, and (3) the promise of the perpetuity of David's dynasty, all of which are narrated in 2 Samuel 6–7. Verses 8–10 are part of Solomon's prayer at the dedication of the temple in 1 Chronicles 6:41–42.

David swore to Yahweh that he would "find a place for Yahweh" (verses 2–5), a vow obliquely hinted at in 2 Samuel 7:1–2. The reference to the northern tribes' traditional designation of Yahweh as the "Mighty One of Jacob" (verse 5; Genesis 49:24; Isaiah 49:26; 60:16) is an attempt to transfer loyalty from local shrines to the new religious center, Jerusalem.

Verses 6–10, the only explicit mention of the Ark in the book of Psalms, recount the bringing of the Ark into Jerusalem (2 Samuel 7). David, in Bethlehem (here called Ephrathah, as in Ruth 4:11; Micah 5:2), hears about the Ark being in Jaar (another name for Kiriath-Jearim; 1 Samuel 7:1–2) and arranges for its transfer to Jerusalem with great pomp, ceremony, and rejoicing. The exclamation, "Rise up, O Yahweh, and go to your resting-place, you and the ark of your might" (verse 8), is a variant of an ancient military shout (Number 10:35).

In verses 11–12 Yahweh swears an oath to David, a solemn promise that David's son will succeed him as king and that his descendants will "for evermore" sit on his throne, if only they keep Yahweh's covenant.

This psalm refers to a specific people, a unique religious system, and a historical line of kings. The temple singers rejoice at the establishment of peace and security in their nation. But they confess also that God's promise of security is contingent: the *justice* encoded in the covenant is required for their king—as it is for the rulers of all nations.

O God, establish justice in our land, from sea to shining sea. Amen.

THE NATIONAL SHRINE AND CIVIL RELIGION

$\mathcal{V}$erses 13–18 continue the twin themes of Zion and David. In verses 1–5 it is David who chooses Jerusalem as "the dwelling place" for the Lord. Here "*the* Lord has chosen Zion" as "my resting place for ever" (verses 13–14). According to the "Zion theology" of the Jerusalem priests, the "glory" (*kabod*) of Yahweh was situated over the outstretched wings of the cherubim (winged sphinxes) that covered the Ark of the Covenant. The Ark was, in effect, the "seat" or throne of Yahweh (Isaiah 6:1–3). In the earliest period of Israel's story, the Ark, virtually identified with Yahweh, was carried into battle, much as the Crusaders reportedly carried the original cross of Jesus into battle in the eleventh century A.D.

God promises prosperity to the holy city, so that even the poor are amply fed (verse 15). There the priests have a place of prominence, and the Davidic king reigns with the light of God in splendid regalia (verses 17–18).

Among the great prophets it is mainly Isaiah of Jerusalem who supported this form of civil religion, often called "Zion theology." Isaiah was a court prophet, and he unfailingly brought God's word of comfort and assurance to the king, proclaiming the inviolability of Jerusalem when the nation was critically threatened by military invasion.

Americans have a difficult time with civil religion. Can we really believe that God favors one country over all the rest? Is the creator of the universe behind all of our military adventures? Or is God the Lord of *all* the nations, the one before whom all, both mighty and powerless, rich and poor, must give account?

*God of justice, save our people from the clash of race
and creed; from the strife of class and faction, make
our nation free indeed.*[58] *Amen.*

NOVEMBER 28 *Psalm 133*

PEACEFUL RELATIVES

*T*his wisdom psalm gives us an attractive glimpse into family relationships, quite the opposite of the Hatfields and McCoys. It might well have been sung in joyful camaraderie by pilgrims journeying to worship in Jerusalem, as the superscription suggests.

Kinship, especially the relationship of brothers ("kindred," verse 1) is frequently mentioned throughout the Bible. Think of Cain and Abel, Esau and Jacob, Amnon and Absalom, and the two sons in Jesus' parable of the "prodigal son." Inheritance squabbles could erupt, and male relatives might have to learn to live together in peace in order to keep the land in the family.

The psalmist uses two images that suggest the beauty of brotherly love. First, "it is like the precious oil on the head, running down" (verse 2). Oil mixed with spices was poured over the hair (see Psalm 23:5), not as an official anointing or ordination but as a luxury, a soothing cosmetic for the care of hair and skin. Second, it is like "the dew of Mount Hermon" (verse 3), the 9000-foot mountain on the northeastern corner of Palestine.

To witness a family spat in public is repugnant. But to see a group of family and friends conversing, joshing, laughing, and enjoying one another is a thing of beauty.

How good it is for brothers who know each other well,
    In unity together on this fair earth to dwell.
As dew from lofty Hermon into the valley flows,
    So God upon the brothers his choicest gifts bestows.[59]

O Lord, bless my home; make it a haven, a place of joy
and comfort. Amen.

A CALL TO BLESSING

$\mathcal{I}$n this last of the series of "Songs of Ascent" (see the superscription), the pilgrims are finally within sight of Jerusalem and its sanctuary. The time is already late ("by night"; Isaiah 30:29 refers to a temple service at night), and they excitedly sing of their welcome to the city and especially to the "house of the Lord," the temple. They encourage "the servants of the Lord" to "bless the Lord!" (verse 1). The divine name Yahweh, "the Lord," occurs five times in this brief psalm, pointing to the central object of their pilgrimage.

In verse 2 the pilgrims address one another: "Lift up your hands to the holy place, and bless the Lord." They refer to the posture of prayer, uplifted hands, as often depicted in early Christian art in the catacombs of Rome. And they face the "holy place," the sanctuary grounds—or perhaps the building, the shrine itself.

The final verse is a blessing on the pilgrims by the priest. The tradition of priestly blessing of the people is ancient, traced back to the time of Moses and Aaron, the ancestor of the priesthood: "The Lord spoke to Moses, saying: Speak to Aaron and his son, saying, Thus you shall bless the Israelites: You shall say to them, The Lord bless you and keep you; the Lord make his face to shine upon you, and be gracious to you; the Lord lift up his countenance upon you, and give you peace" (Numbers 6:22–26).

Every one of us needs blessings, and every one of us should try to be a blessing to others. Thus Ira B. Wilson (1880–1950) urged in his gospel song "Make Me a Blessing," "Out in the highways and byways of life, many are weary and sad. Carry the sunshine where darkness is rife, making the sorrowing glad. Make me a blessing, O Savior, I pray, make me a blessing today."

O Lord, maker of heaven and earth,
I bless your holy name. Amen.

GOD'S HAND IN NATURE AND HISTORY

*L*ike Psalms 111–113, this hymn begins with the shout "Hallelujah!" Praise Yahweh! Its contents are a kind of a mosaic of quotations from various biblical books, which makes it a summary of several major motifs of the Old Testament.

The temple singers praise the name of Yahweh (verses 1, 3), first, because "the LORD has chosen Jacob for himself, Israel as his own possession" (verse 4). The psalmist links the "election" of Israel the personal name of God and sees this as an act of grace (verse 3). Yahweh, however, is more than Israel's tribal deity: "the LORD is great ... above all gods" (verse 5), for it is Yahweh who has control over the entire cosmos, all heaven and earth, including the seas and the watery depths and the forces of nature (verses 6–7).

Yahweh also is the one who delivered the people from Egyptian slavery and, in a bloody series of events, gave them the land of Canaan (verses 8–12). On the death of the firstborn see Exodus 12:29, on the other "signs and wonders," see Exodus 7:8—11:10, and on Sihon and Og see Numbers 21:21–24, 33–35; Deuteronomy 3:1–11; Joshua 12:2, 4. The reference to Canaan as "a heritage" or inheritance is based on Joshua 11:23.

The ancients saw the actions of the gods or God in the forces of nature. The Israelites saw God at work also in their history. For moderns, both of these categories are ambiguous as sources of revelation. We know more about the physical world than did the ancients, and history is seldom "holy" in any sense of the word. Even biblical history, with its rapes, mass slaughters, and assorted human foibles can be confusing when we try to find there the hand of God. Let us turn our attention instead to God's greatest spokespersons, the classical prophets and the teachings of Jesus as found in Matthew, Mark, and Luke.

Be my light and life, Lord God, in a world of confusion
and ambiguity. Amen.

AVOIDING IDOLATRY

The name Yahweh dominates Psalm 135, and the psalmist praises this name again in the hymnic interlude of verses 13–14. This name and its fame will endure forever, especially when the LORD's compassion on Israel becomes apparent to all.

Reflecting on the name Yahweh causes the psalmist to think of the competition, "the idols of the nations" (verse 15), and to write a parody of them and the idol worshipers (verses 15–18; for a close parallel see Psalm 115:4–8). The idols are made of silver and gold, with care and at great expense. "They have mouths, but they do not speak; . . . eyes, but they do not see; . . . ears, but they do not hear, and there is no breath in their mouths." The idol makers and the idol worshipers will become like the objects of their worship: mute, blind, deaf, and dead (verse 18).

As in Psalm 115:9–11, so also here the mocking of idolatry is followed by a call to the constituents of the temple community to worship the true God. The "house of Israel" are the non-priestly groups; the "house of Aaron" are the priests; the "house of Levi" (mentioned nowhere else in the book of Psalms) are the temple singers and assistants to the priests, and "you that fear the LORD" are possibly non-Israelites who worship the true God.

In our society, as in ancient Israel, it would not be easy to find anyone who would speak a good word for idols or their worshipers. But do we detect a trace of chauvinism in parodies of them? And do we think to engage in self-examination before lampooning someone else's religion? Your god is what you devote your life to. How many persons today worship false gods, and how can I avoid doing so in my life?

Lead me, O God, on the path of truth and justice. Amen.

THANKFULNESS FOR STABILITY IN NATURE

*E*very other line of the twenty-six verses of this psalm has exactly the same words, "for his steadfast love endures for ever." The priest or the temple singers probably intoned the first line, and the worshiping assembly responded with the refrain.

The story of Solomon's dedication of the temple in 2 Chronicles 7:1–3 affords a glimpse as to how Psalm 136 might have been performed. After Solomon finished his prayer, "fire came down from heaven and consumed the burnt-offering and the sacrifices; and the glory [*kabod*] of Yahweh filled the temple. . . . When all the people of Israel saw the fire come down and the glory of the LORD on the temple, they bowed down on the pavement with their faces to the ground, and worshiped and gave thanks to the LORD, saying, 'For he is good, for his steadfast love endures forever.'"

The psalm singers give thanks to Yahweh as the "God of gods" and "Lord of lords" (verses 2–3), phrases that might reflect a polytheistic background—or that simply refer to the heavenly council. Verses 4–9 praise the "great wonders" of God's acts in creation, following the sequence of Genesis 1:6–19. The heavens are separated from the earth, then the water on the earth is separated from the dry land (although waters remain under the dry land, verse 6). Then come the luminaries, the sun, moon, and stars. All of this was the working of divine "understanding" (verse 5), which points to the stability and regularity of the natural world.

The ancients marveled at the patterns of the natural world, and scientists even today continue to explore its workings and "laws." Although we have learned much, we have made hardly a dent in grasping the extent and mystery of the universe—or of the relation of matter and energy in subatomic reality. It truly is a marvel.

I thank you, Lord God, for the beauty of the earth,
for the beauty of the skies, and for the love that from
my birth over and around me lies. Amen.

Psalm 136:10–22

THANKFULNESS FOR GOD'S ACTS IN HISTORY

*T*his summary of the mighty acts of God in Israel's history includes the mention of the miraculous crossing of the sea at the exodus and the wilderness wanderings (verses 13–15; compare Psalm 135:8–12). The historical overview begins in Egypt with the tenth plague, the death of the firstborn of the Egyptians and their cattle (Exodus 12:29). The psalm singers depict Yahweh as a muscled strongman who, "with a strong hand and an outstretched arm," brought Israel out from Egypt (verses 11–12). In referring to the crossing of the sea (verses 13–15) the psalmist adds an image unique to this psalm, asserting that Yahweh "divided the Red Sea in two" (verse 13). (The splitting of the sea apparently reflects awareness of a Canaanite tradition about a primeval battle with the sea dragon.)

After a passing mention of the wilderness wanderings (verse 16), the temple singers, as in Psalm 135:10–11, refer to the killing of "famous kings," "Sihon, king of the Amorites" in the area of Moab, and "Og, king of Bashan," north of Moab, both on the east side of the Jordan River. These actions are narrated in Numbers 21:21–24, 33 –35; and Deuteronomy 3:1–11. As in Psalm 135:12, Yahweh gave the land of these kings as "a heritage to his servant Israel" (verses 21–22).

All nations have stories and legends about their founding—stories that provide a sense of identity and character. Because nations are typically forged in military struggle, it is not surprising that such traditions and legends often center on battles. It is nonetheless jarring, after hearing that Yahweh "killed famous kings," to sing, "for his steadfast love endures for ever" (verse 18). We in North America are unspeakably fortunate to live where and when we do. Let us give thanks for our good fortune, and let us use our blessings wisely.

O Lord, I am blessed beyond measure. Make me mindful
of those who yearn for justice. Amen.

THANKFULNESS FOR GOD'S EVERLASTING STEADFAST LOVE

*T*his impressive litany concludes with two reasons for the twenty-six repetitions of its antiphonal responses, "his steadfast love endures for ever." The first is the LORD's rescue of the people. The psalmist recalls the origin of the nation in Egyptian slavery and the many critical threats to their survival in the land of Canaan. "It is he who remembered us in our low estate . . . and rescued us from our foes" (verses 23–24). God protects and rescues.

The second reason is that God "gives food to all flesh" (verse 25), all creatures of the earth. The pervasive nationalism of the psalm here gives way to concern for all peoples—and other creatures as well. God provides—without considering race or creed.

It is now time to ask: what, exactly is "steadfast love"? The Hebrew word is *hesed*, and it is variously translated as "goodness," "mercy," "grace," "fidelity," "faithfulness," "kindness," "devotion," "beauty," "compassionate love," and in other ways. The word encompasses all these nuances, and it thus points to the beneficent heart of God. The divine essence is not ultimately wrath and judgment, and not even unmitigated justice. Grace and mercy lie at the heart of the universe, and we would do well to strive to imitate *hesed* in all our doings during our brief time on earth.

Lord God, I give you praise. Mercy and truth are all your ways. Your mercies ever shall endure when lords and kings are known no more. Amen.

THE EMOTIONS OF EXILE

*A*ll readers sense the power, pathos, and strange beauty of this communal lament. It expresses in terse images the utter despair of a people in exile, and it concludes with two violent curses. This psalm is the only one that can be dated reliably. Jewish exiles in Babylon weep over the greatest disaster in Old Testament history, the destruction of Jerusalem in 587 B.C. The destroyer, Babylon, remained in power (verse 8) until it was destroyed by the Persians in 539 B.C. We can therefore safely date the writing of this psalm between those two dates.

Exiles from Judah sit and weep "by the rivers of Babylon," the many canals and waterways that crisscrossed the area between the Tigris and Euphrates Rivers ("Mesopotamia" means "between the rivers"). Their tormenting captors, either mockingly or simply wanting to hear a good tune, asked the captives for a song (verse 3). But how can you sing when your heart is full of grief and your voice chokes with tears? "How could we sing Yahweh's song in a foreign land?" (verse 4).

Instead of a song, the psalmist vents his hatred. "Remember, O Yahweh, against the Edomites the day of Jerusalem's fall, how they said, 'Tear it down! Tear it down'" (verse 7). Apparently, some Edomites were mercenaries in Nebuchadnezzar's army. More gruesome is the call to slaughter babies (verse 9), which aims at the annihilation of the Babylonians (the same thought occurs in 2 Kings 8:12; Hosea 10:14; and Nahum 3:10). There is no thought of the anguish that would be caused to innocent bystanders, just as nations even today are accustomed to count only their own dead soldiers, giving little thought to the "collateral damage" of the enemy.

Can we give vent to our tears without calling for more violence? Can we learn to study war no more? Can we emulate Yahweh's steadfast love?

Lord God, have mercy, I pray, on all who suffer violence;
give them hope and lead them to safety. Amen.

HUMBLE THANKFULNESS

*T*he scene is the courtyard before the sanctuary in Jerusalem. In front of the shrine stands the altar of burnt offering. Here a grateful man takes a typical ancient posture for prayer, facing the temple building and prostrating himself (verse 2a). In this posture of grateful reverence, he composes a song of thanksgiving for answered prayer (verse 3), a hymn-like praise of the name of Yahweh (verse 2).

What was the prayer that had been answered? The poet speaks of walking "in the midst of trouble" and refers to "the wrath of my enemies" (verse 7), which might point to slander or even physical danger. But he also says that when the LORD answered his prayer, "you increased my strength of soul" (*nephesh*, the life force, verse 3b), which suggests a serious illness. In any case, his "whole heart" (verse 1a) is filled with praise.

The theme of the psalmist's thanksgiving is the greatness of the LORD (verse 5), whose name is praised "before the gods" (perhaps the gods of the surrounding nations have now become ministering spirits, verse 1b). The two prime attributes of God, steadfast love and faithfulness, evoke praise. And the LORD will be praised by "all the kings of the earth" (verse 4).

Primarily, however, the poet gives thanks because Yahweh, although resplendent with glory, "regards the lowly," while observing the haughty from afar (verse 6). The humble posture of the worshiper, lying face down before the gates of the temple, is itself a visual communication to the LORD of profound gratitude. The humble thankfulness of the poet ends with a plea that the LORD, whose steadfast love endures forever, will continue to work in his life.

To observe someone giving thanks from the bottom of the heart is a thing of beauty. Thanksgiving cannot be fulfilled in one day out of the year. It is a habit to be cultivated, and this habit can add much joy to our lives.

I give thanks to you, O Lord,
for your steadfast love to me. Amen.

GOD KNOWS

*T*his curious and marvelous poem defies classification. It combines elements of hymns, wisdom psalms, songs of trust, and laments (especially the outburst in verses 19–22). Its content likewise is distinctive, reflecting an almost mystical sense of being enveloped in the all-knowing, everywhere present, and eternal God. This poet is in an "I-Thou" relationship with the deity, and Psalm 139 is an intimate exchange between the worshiper and the worshiped.

We might have a clue to the setting of this psalm from its final verses (19–24). The psalmist faces violent enemies, and he begs God to search his heart and "see if there is any wicked way in me." God is to judge between the petitioner and his enemies, a situation precisely the same as the prophet Jeremiah faced (Jeremiah 12:3; also 23:23–24). Ancient Israelites believed that "Yahweh is a God of knowledge, and by him actions are weighed" (1 Samuel 2:3; also 16:7, "Yahweh looks on the heart," not the outward appearance). And so the first stanza stresses the omniscience of God: God knows. God has searched and known the plaintiff and can defend his case.

The psalmist emphasizes and re-emphasizes Yahweh's total, unconditional scrutiny of him wherever he goes and whatever he does. The LORD knows what he will say before he says it (verses 2–4; also Jeremiah 17:16b). Like Job, he feels somewhat hemmed in (verse 5), but he nonetheless appeals to this omniscience in his defense.

Believers respond differently to the thought that God knows. For some, it exacerbates the feeling of guilt. Such a thought can impel others to escape God's scrutiny (as in Job 7:16–21). For others, however, like our psalmist, the conviction that God knows is a comfort. God will take up his case in vindication.

Lord God, you know my thoughts, and you search my ways;
let your grace shine on me. Amen.

GOD IS THERE

The theme of the psalm moves from "God knows" to "God is there," from omniscience to omnipresence. "Where can I go from your spirit?" (verse 7). To heaven? To Sheol? To the farthest limits of the sea? Into darkness? The answer is the same: nowhere.

The neighbors of Israel considered that different gods oversaw things in the heavens and in Sheol; they had distinctive functions. But here the one God permeates every place in the universe—God is omnipresent, ubiquitous. The classical prophets had reached this monotheistic thought. In about 750 B.C. Amos proclaimed this oracle about those seeking to flee from foreign invaders: "Though they dig into Sheol, from there shall my hand take them; though they climb up to heaven, from there I will bring them down" (Amos 9:2). Another prophet spoke similar words: "Who can hide in secret places so that I cannot see them? says the LORD" (Jeremiah 23:24).

The wording of the question in verse 7b, however, is curious: "Where can I flee from your presence?" This might be an expression of wonder at the comforting thought that the LORD stands by the psalmist everywhere and always. The use of the verb "flee," however, suggests unease or even irritation at unrelenting scrutiny from the LORD. Such a thought emerges unmistakably in the poem of Job: "Will you not look away from me for a while, let me alone until I swallow my spittle? . . . Why have you made me your target? Why have I become a burden to you?" (Job 7:17–21).

When we are anxious, when we face the tragedies of life, and when the burdens of life threaten to overwhelm us, then the poetic gifts of this great psalmist can speak directly to our situation. Come what may, God is there.

In the darkness, be thou near me, O Lord, my God. Amen.

FOREKNOWLEDGE AND EMBRYOLOGY

*T*he psalmist now considers the origin and creation of his own physical existence—his body, God's "works" (verse 14b)—here not God's works in history but in the creation of the human individual. The human being is an intricately formed network, "knit together," "fearfully and wonderfully made" (verses 13–14). The LORD formed the psalmist's "inward parts" (verse 13a, literally, the kidneys, the seat of the will and the inmost feelings). God formed the embryo in the mother's womb and watched it grow (verse 13, 16a), even as the fetus was "woven in the depths of the earth" (verse 15b), a mythic expression of Mother Earth that was common in the ancient Near East and also among the Greeks.[60] Human life is precious, and the drive to protect new life is innate to us all.

Convinced of the absolute knowledge and universal presence of God, the psalmist speaks of God's "book," in which "were written all the days that were formed for me" (verse 16). God's book of life (Exodus 32:32–33; Psalms 56:8; 69:28) is here a record of God's foreknowledge of all the days of one's life—even prior to that person's birth. Neither this poetic statement nor the prophet's retrospective glance, "Before I formed you in the womb I knew you" (Jeremiah 1:5), however, should be confused with later Christian theories of predestination. The psalmist's utterances are the natural result of the conception of God as beyond the human categories of space and time (past, present, and future).

Philosophical arguments over determinism and fate have little relevance for our lives. A fatalistic attitude that our destiny is predetermined and written in stone cannot nullify our responsibility for our actions. We cannot know what lies ahead in our course through life. It is best to end with the psalmist: "I come to the end" (or, "Even when I awake")—I am still with you" (verse 18b).

Through life and even in death, O Lord, I am in your hands. Amen.

"SEARCH ME, O GOD"

*A*fter eighteen verses of lofty reflections on the marvelous attributes of God, readers are rudely jolted by the abrupt call to "kill the wicked, O God" and the psalmist's vituperation, "I hate them with perfect hatred" (verses 19a, 22a). What is going on?

This stanza actually lays bare the occasion and purpose of the entire psalm. The petitioner is attacked by "the wicked," "the bloodthirsty," "those who speak of you maliciously," persons who hate the LORD. These enemies have slandered the psalmist, and the psalmist appeals to Yahweh as judge. This explains the repeated references to God's omniscience, omnipresence, and works of creation. God knows the truth of the matter, who stands in the right, and the psalmist now—so to speak—calls for God's lie-detector test: "Search me, O God . . . test me . . . see if there is any wicked way in me" (verses 23–24). He has little doubt as to the outcome of this examination. Psalm 139 is thus an articulate plea for vindication, one of the more elegant "prayers of the falsely accused."

The author of Psalm 139 displays exceptional boldness in his conversation with God, an intimacy that points to the later development of mysticism in the great religions of the world. For this poet, God, our maker and judge, is not limited by time and space nor by the finitude of human thoughts. James C. Wallace (1793–1841) expressed this psalmist's praise of God:

There is an eye that never sleeps
    Beneath the wing of night;
There is an ear that never shuts,
    When sink the beams of light.
There is an arm that never tires,
    When human strength gives way;
There is a love that never fails,
    When earthly loves decay.[61]

Look on me with mercy, O Lord,
and lead me in the way everlasting. Amen.

EVIL PLOTTERS

*P*salm 140 has several typical features of the lament of the individual. The evildoers, the violent ones, have tongues "sharp as a snake's," slandering with "the venom of vipers" (verse 3). These wicked persons plot the psalmist's downfall, hiding traps and (like the "improvised explosive devices," IEDs, used by insurgents) setting snares along the road (verse 5).

The two military allusions are somewhat less common in a lament. The violent ones "stir up wars continually" (verse 2b), and the petitioner testifies that Yahweh has "covered my head in the day of battle" (verse 7b). Although most references to war in the psalms are to be taken literally, and although the poet in this case might have had military experience, the strife in this psalm is apparently of a domestic sort, as in Psalm 55:21. He is the object of personal attack, and the attack centers on slander. The enemies' goal is the downfall of the petitioner (verse 4b).

The psalmist's appeal to the LORD (verse 6) is also couched in the familiar language of the lament. He pleads to be delivered, and—what seems strange to readers today—he prays also that Yahweh will not "further their evil plot" (verse 8b). Is this a lack of trust, a hint of uncertainty as to which side the LORD will defend?

The psalmist feels as though he is walking through a minefield. There are pitfalls on every side. This nearly universal human experience has spawned many expressions: "out on a limb"; "up a tree"; "at the end of my rope"; "between a rock and a hard place"—to name only a few. When we find ourselves in such a situation, do we, like the psalmist, have a place of appeal? Can we pray to one who is "my strong deliverer," who has been our fortress in years past (verse 7)?

Give ear, O Lord, to the voice of my supplications. Amen.

BURNING COALS AND THE CAUSE OF THE NEEDY

*T*he psalmist confirms that he is the victim of a slanderer (the singular noun is used in verse 11a), and that he is surrounded by the "mischief of [the] lips" of the haughty (verse 9). Apparently, several persons found one person's slander to be credible; together, they constitute a serious threat to the lamenter.

What should be done to these arrogant ones? In verse 10 the psalmist prays for judgment from above and also judgment below. "Let burning coals fall on them!" as "Yahweh rained on Sodom and Gomorrah sulfur and fire . . . out of heaven" (Genesis 19:24; see Psalm 11:6, "On the wicked he will rain coals of fire and sulfur"; also 7:16; 120:4). "Let them be flung into pits, no more to rise!" as with the household of Korah during the exodus wanderings: "the ground under them was split apart. The earth opened its mouth and swallowed them up, . . . everyone who belonged to Korah. . . . They . . . went down alive into Sheol; the earth closed over them, and they perished from the midst of the assembly" (Numbers 16:31–33).

The book of Proverbs suggests a different use of burning coals. "If your enemies are hungry, give them bread to eat; and if they are thirsty, give them water to drink; for you will heap coals of fire on their heads, and the LORD will reward you" (Proverbs 25:21–22; quoted by Paul in Romans 12:20). The psalmist, however, is certain that justice is on his side: "The LORD . . . executes justice for the poor," presumably himself. But, just as the steadfast love of the LORD is without limit, so our beneficence cannot be directed exclusively to those of our circle.

I thank you, Lord God, that you maintain the cause
of the needy and execute justice for the poor. Amen.

DECEMBER 13   *Psalm 141:1–4*

"A GUARD OVER MY MOUTH"

$\mathcal{I}$f the previous psalm spoke of enemies with snake's tongues, full of slander, the lamenter here prays that the LORD would guard his mouth and "keep watch over the door of my lips" (verse 3). The psalmist, familiar with temple liturgies, asks that his prayer be "counted as incense . . . and the lifting up of my hands as an evening sacrifice" (verse 2), in other words, as a substitute for, or possibly a spiritualization of an animal sacrifice. (Similarly, in Protestant churches, Sunday worship might alternate between a communion service and a service of prayer, singing, and a homily.)

The petitioner is acquainted "with those who work iniquity" (verse 4b), an expression that might refer to deviant religious practices—perhaps like those of the idolatrous priests whom Josiah drove out of the temple in about 620 B.C. (2 Kings 23:5–9). In any case, these workers of iniquity had tempting "delicacies" (verse 4c), which can be taken either literally or symbolically (referring to luxury and conspicuous consumption).

The wisdom writers warned against careless speech: "Those who open wide their lips come to ruin" (Proverbs 13:3b). A later sage asked, "Who will set a guard over my mouth, and an effective seal over my lips, so that I may not fall because of them, and my tongue may not destroy me?" (Sirach 22:27). But this psalmist goes further, praying for protection against himself, for strength to withstand the allure of the enticing but destructive speech and deeds of the worldly wise.

Words have power to do lasting harm. Gossip, "the sin of the pious," is but one of its hurtful potentials. But our words also have the power to heal, to overcome the barriers of race and class, and to reduce the suspicions of long-standing enemies. "A word fitly spoken is like apples of gold in a setting of silver" (Proverbs 25:11).

Set a guard over my mouth, O Lord, and let my words lead
to healing and hope. Amen.

ACCEPTING CORRECTION

*T*he willingness to stand corrected is by no means a universal human characteristic. "Advice is seldom welcome; and those who want it the most always like it the least" (Lord Chesterfield, in a letter to his son, January 29, 1748). "Advice would always be more acceptable if it didn't always conflict with our plans" (anonymous). "No one wants advice—only corroboration" (John Steinbeck, *The Winter of Our Discontent*, 1961).

The petitioner's prayer that God would guard his speech (verse 3) apparently was a serious response to some kind of lapse on his part. Out of friendship, his friends, "the righteous" (*zaddiqim*), have taken it upon themselves to rebuke him (verse 5). He is able to accept their correction—but not the words of the wicked, those whose bones should be broken into pieces and "strewn at the mouth of Sheol" (verse 7, an image similar to the "enlarged appetite" of Sheol in Isaiah 5:14).

The psalmist is in an ambiguous situation. He is not entirely guilt-free in the breakdown of his personal relationships. He has said some ill-considered things, and he has broken the informal code of the *zaddiqim*, namely, regular prayer, careful speech, cautious conduct, avoiding ostentatious displays, and good judgment.

But he has one redeeming virtue: he is willing to accept correction from those he respects. His friends have redirected his attention to his God (verse 8), and there is where he finds his refuge. Can we accept and appreciate well-intentioned criticism?

O God of mercy, open my heart to accept correction,
and let me find refuge in you. Amen.

"NO ONE CARES"

*T*he mention of being in prison (or a dungeon) in verse 7a has led editors to ascribe this lament to David, who took refuge in a cave on more than one occasion (1 Samuel 22:1–2; 24:1–7). Israelite custom provided that, in legal cases difficult to judge, transgressors could be incarcerated until a verdict of God could be determined (Leviticus 24:12; Numbers 25:34). Could a prisoner's prayer find its way into a collection of temple liturgies? The imprisonment here is more like the despair of Lamentations 3:6–9: "He has made me sit in darkness. . . . He has walled me about so that I cannot escape; he has put heavy chains on me; though I call and cry for help; . . . he has blocked my ways with hewn stones." So also the psalmist prays, "Bring my *nephesh* [life force] out of prison" (verse 7).

The persecutors are strong (verse 6b). They have driven their victim to mental exhaustion (verse 3). Even worse, they have convinced all of the victim's acquaintances to stand aside. There is no one at his right hand, "no one who takes notice of me; . . . no one cares for me" (verse 4). He stands utterly alone, without refuge, accused. His inner being is in solitary confinement.

Loneliness is a hallmark of American culture, with its emphasis on rugged individualism and self-sufficiency. For many, this problem increases as we become more vulnerable with age, and new relationships are more difficult to form. Even worse than loneliness itself is the feeling of being deserted and forsaken when we need friends the most. When that happens we have only one recourse, and that is to pray with the psalmist:

> *You O Lord, are my refuge, my portion in the land*
> *of the living; give heed to my cry. Amen.*

Psalm 143:1–6

APPEALING TO THE GOD OF RIGHTEOUSNESS

*A*gain we have the lament of a man persecuted by enemies. They pursue him and crush him to the ground; his spirit (or breath) faints within and his heart becomes numb ("appalled," verse 4). The complaint in verse 3b about the persecutors "making me sit in darkness like those long dead" is almost identical to Lamentations 3:6. The supplicant clearly is near the end of hope; he is like a land in which life is dying in a severe drought.

This is the last of the seven penitential psalms of the liturgy of the ancient church (Psalms 6; 32; 38; 51; 102; 130; 143), and appropriately so. The psalmist appeals to the LORD's faithfulness and righteousness (verse 1), but then makes an astonishing plea, "Do not enter into judgment with your servant, for no one living is righteous before you" (verse 2). Aware of his failures, he wants not God's verdict on his life but simply God's answer. Unlike the many other psalmists who issue strong protestations of their innocence, this poet makes no legal claim on God. So also Isaiah, in the presence of the holy God, was acutely aware of being inextricably involved with human frailty: "Woe is me! I am lost, for I am a man of unclean lips, and I live among a people of unclean lips" (Isaiah 6:5).

The psalmist appeals to a God who transcends human standards and even the dictates of sacral law. He knows that God's righteousness might not be identical with the "moral values" of believers. God's mercy covers a multitude of sins and a horde of human foibles. Even in our darkest moments we can do no better than to appeal to God's steadfast love, which is evident in many deeds in "the days of old" (verse 5a), when God's mercy trumped all human expectations.

Care for me, O God of grace, help me that I never anxious look to future days but may trust you ever.[62] *Amen.*

DIVINE ABSENCE

*T*hrough the night (verse 8a) the psalmist confesses his inadequacies and failures: "Teach me the way I should go. . . . Teach me to do your will. . . . Let your good spirit lead me on a level path" (verses 8b, 10). He mentions no specific sin, but he is keenly aware of the contrast between the righteousness of God and his lack of it: "No one living is righteous before you" (verse 2b). This is the recognition of guilt.

Divine absence is the cause of the psalmist's anguish. If this persists it will be like death: "Do not hide your face from me, or I shall be like those who go down to the Pit" (that is, Sheol; verse 7b). He pleads in all the varieties of language he can muster: "Answer me quickly," "Let me hear of your steadfast love," "Save me," "Preserve my life," "In your righteousness bring me out of trouble." The enemies continue to threaten him, and he flees for refuge to the LORD, basing his plea on God's righteousness, steadfast love, and the honor of the name Yahweh (verses 11–12).

The absence of God in a time of trouble is an excruciating experience for every person of piety, from biblical times to the present day. "Why do you hide your face, and count me as your enemy?" (Job 13:24). "How long will you hide your face from me?" (Psalm 13:1b). "Do not hide your face from your servant" (Psalm 69:17a). A psychological black hole, however, comes when we face not only the absence of God but even the feeling of abandonment: "My God, my God, why have you forsaken me?" (Psalm 22:1; quoted by Jesus, the last words before his death, Mark 15:34).

From the depths we can appeal to God's "good spirit," a new "breath" of life that sets us on a level path (verse 10b). There we seek refuge (verse 9b).

Bless and keep, O Lord, your creatures; reveal to us your gracious features; turn to us your face with peace. Amen.

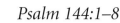

VICTORIES, HUMAN FINITUDE, AND A PRAYER FOR DIVINE DISPLAYS

$\mathcal{I}$n this royal psalm the king in Jerusalem, preparing for battle, reflects on the fleetingness of human life and prays for the assistance of Yahweh in spectacular displays of power. His prayer was most probably uttered in a temple liturgy. The king readily confesses Yahweh as his "rock," "fortress," "stronghold," "deliverer," and "shield." It is this God who trains the king for war. The king has had several previous military triumphs (verses 1–2).

As he goes to battle, the king acknowledges to God that he also is mortal, and that the outcome of battle is never guaranteed. His words, "What are human beings that you regard them, or mortals that you think of them?" are used in another psalm in a quite different context (Psalm 8:4). The king knows that war brings death, but we read nothing here about the wives, parents, and orphans of the dead soldiers—and certainly nothing of the "collateral damage" of battle, the inadvertent killing of civilians who happen to be in the wrong place at the wrong time.

The king prays for assistance from the God who controls nature. He asks for a tremendous display of power in the coming battle, as of an erupting volcano (verse 5b, a rarity in the Bible) and flashes of lightning—God's arrows—that scatter the foe. He would be rescued "from the mighty waters," a frequent image of the dangers of primeval chaos (verses 5–7).

From Sumerian sagas to Homer and the Bible, all the ancients glorified war and cultivated military "virtues." War was not something abnormal but expected: "In the spring of the year, the time when kings go out to battle . . ." (2 Samuel 11:1). But the prophets knew better (Micah 4:3; Isaiah 2:4), and our generals today all seem to agree that war—literally—is hell.

Lord God, from war's alarms, from deadly pestilence, be your strong arm our ever sure defense. Amen.

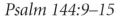

A KING'S PRAYER
FOR HIS NATION

*T*his happy warrior (verse 15), gifted in voice and with the "ten-stringed harp" (verse 9), reminds us of King David, the musician-warrior whose prayers were heartfelt and elegant. The Jerusalem kings, all of them descended from David, looked back to the great hero of their ancestry (see the superscription and verse 10b). David's many battles brought the nation complete security from foreign intervention. His diplomacy led to a 400-year dynasty in Jerusalem. And, in spite of his political machinations, his adultery, and his political murders, he was remembered as a great psalm writer and the pious king who could repent of his sins, and with whom God made an eternal covenant.

Before a critical battle, the king prays for his personal deliverance (verse 11) and also for the welfare of his people and the entire nation, which was dependent on his success. He prays for the increase of the nation's population (verse 12) and for barns full of produce and pastures overflowing with flocks of sheep and cattle (verses 13–14). And, especially before the imminent battle, he prays that the walls of the city not be breached and that no cry of distress be heard in its streets (verse 14). Such a people—those whose God is Yahweh—know true happiness (verse 15).

As the earliest Israelites suspected, the monarchy was both bane and blessing (see Judges 21:25; 1 Samuel 8:4–18). It was necessary for self-preservation, but it required violence and brought oppression. Christianity began as a counter-cultural movement, and it took centuries before it became comfortable with secular rule. The history of the resulting Christendom, however, shows that this was also a mixed blessing. Suspicion of worldly power should be a virtue of the pious.

Judge eternal, throned in splendor, Lord of lords and King
of kings, with your living fire of judgment, purge our land
of bitter things. Solace all its wide dominion with the healing
of your wings.[63] *Amen.*

CEASELESS PRAISE
OF THE HEAVENLY KING

*T*he psalms from here to the end of the collection are all hymns. These majestic poems praise the LORD from a variety of perspectives and gradually build up to the last verse in the book, which is a call to praise God by "everything that breathes" (150:6). Psalm 145 is in acrostic form, like Psalms 9–10; 25; 34; 37; 111; 112; 119; 145; each verse begins with the successive letter of the Hebrew alphabet.

The congregation at the Jerusalem temple praises Yahweh as King (verse 1a). Neighbors of the ancient Israelites believed that each people had their own god or gods, who were thought of as sovereign over their own territory. Among many other places, this is seen in the strange story of Naaman the Syrian, who moved two mule-loads of Israelite soil to Syria so that he could worship Yahweh in a land overseen by the god Rimmon (or Hadad, 2 Kings 5:15–17). But to call God "King" was unusual in other parts of the ancient Near East. "Yahweh their God is with them, acclaimed as a king among them" (Numbers 23:21b). Just before 1000 B.C., the Philistine threat to the survival of the Israelite tribes in Canaan led to the establishment of the monarchy. This created tension between the idea of the kingship of Yahweh and that of an earthly monarch (Judges 8:23; 1 Samuel 8:7). Although this unease persisted (Hosea 8:4), most Israelites came to terms with the idea of the earthly king, who ruled as sovereign over his people but as a vassal of the heavenly King.

The temple singers praise Yahweh in royal terms: unsearchable greatness, majesty replete with "glorious splendor" and wondrous and mighty works. No politician, no matter how loud and stringent his claims of divine right, can avoid vassalage to the God of righteousness (verse 7b). The kingship of God is eternal (verse 1b).

Holy God, I praise your name; Lord of all, I bow before you!
Infinite your vast domain, everlasting is your reign.[64] *Amen.*

"SLOW TO ANGER AND ABOUNDING IN STEADFAST LOVE"

*W*e worship a God of glory, power, mighty deeds, and glorious splendor (verses 11–12), but these attributions of glory are not in themselves the heart of God. What more comforting and beautiful words can we hear than these: "The LORD is gracious and merciful, slow to anger and abounding in steadfast love. The LORD is good to all, and his compassion is over all that he has made" (verse 8–9). Once again the psalmist harks back to the formative description of God in Exodus 34:6, as "merciful and gracious, slow to anger, and abounding in steadfast love and faithfulness." The "mighty deeds" of the LORD, ironically, are those done out of steadfast love and compassion.

To judge from the incessant holy wars of antiquity we can imagine that it took a long time for the biblical writers to perceive God's mercy, grace, steadfast love, and faithfulness. Many today find it equally difficult to latch onto the inner heart of God, finding it easier to believe that God will rain down hellfire and brimstone on those who have different political views or lifestyles. Is God as vindictive as some believers are? Can we believe in the pettiness of God? Let us rejoice that the ultimate verdict on each one of us will come not from presumptuous pretenders but from the God of grace, mercy, and compassion.

God is King, and the psalmist assures us that "Your kingdom is an everlasting kingdom . . . throughout all generations" (verse 13a). The compassionate heart of God remains steadfast forever. Thank God.

O God of mercy, God of might, in love and pity infinite,
teach us as ever in your sight to live our lives to you.[65] *Amen.*

THE TENDER MERCIES OF OUR GOD

*E*arlier, in verses 8–9, the psalmist described the gracious qualities of God (here summarized as justice and kindness, verse 17). Now we read about the actions that stream from these attributes. It is a beautiful list of the tender mercies of our God, which are directed to "all flesh" (verse 21b). We could enrich our lives by a regular reading of these verses.

According to our psalmist, God gives special attention to those who are "bowed down" (verse 14b), hungry (verse 15), or in need of rescue (verse 19). These verses remind us of other great texts of the Bible. In the Song of Hannah God "raises up the poor from the dust; he lifts the needy from the ash heap" (1 Samuel 2:8). Mary, in the "Magnificat," testifies that God "has brought down the powerful from their thrones, and lifted up the lowly; he has filled the hungry with good things, and sent the rich away empty" (Luke 1:52–53). And Jesus in the Beatitudes, pronounces blessings on the poor, the hungry, mourners, and those who are persecuted (Luke 6:20–22; compare Matthew 5:1–11).

Because of verse 15, "The eyes of all look to you, and you give them their food in due season," this psalm was used by early Christians as a prayer at midday meals, and it is used as a table prayer by some families still today.

Psalm 145 moves from the affirmation of God as King (verse 1) to a kind of universalism: "*All flesh* will bless his holy name forever and ever" (verse 21). The LORD is not a tribal God but the one who gives life and all good things to "all your works" (verse 10).

For your bounties and blessings beyond number,
I thank you, Lord God. Amen.

PRAISE TO WHOM PRAISE IS DUE

*T*he last five psalms in our collection—all hymns—each begin with the word "Hallelujah!" ("Praise Yahweh"). In Psalm 146 the psalmist engages in a psychological dialogue with his own soul (*nephesh*, "inner being"), exhorting it to praise the LORD. His inner being responds, "I will praise the LORD as long as I live" (verses 1–2).

The psalmist then gives advice, both negative and positive. First we learn whom *not* to rely on: "Do not put your trust in princes. . . . When their breath departs, they return to the earth; on that very day their plans perish" (verses 3 –4). This is not necessarily a political attack on the princes (or aristocracy or "excellent ones") but simply a reminder of the universality of death, which brings an end to the "best-laid plans of mice and men."

Then comes the positive advice: Put your ultimate trust in "the God of Jacob," the LORD (verse 5). Why? There are two reasons. First, the LORD is the one "who made heaven and earth, the sea, and all that is in them" (verse 6), and therefore holds sway over all that is. Second, unlike even the best of politicians, all of whom come to an end, the God of Jacob "keeps faith for ever" (verse 6b):

> Praise the Almighty, my soul, adore him!
> > Yes, I will laud him until death;
> With songs and anthems I come before him
> > As long as he allows me breath.
> From him my life and all things came;
> > Bless, O my soul, his holy name.
> Trust not in rulers; they are but mortal;
> > Earthborn they are and soon decay.
> Vain are their counsels at life's last portal,
> > When the dark grave engulfs its prey.
> Since mortals can no help afford,
> > Place all your trust in Christ, our Lord. [66]

I will praise you, O Lord, as long as I live, with a thankful heart. Amen.

DIVINE COMPASSION

On this day of expectation and celebration for Christians, we read in Psalm 146 of the compassionate acts of the God who made heaven and earth. It is one of the most beautiful, hopeful, and encouraging texts in the entire Bible. In verses 7–9, God

- executes justice for the oppressed
- gives food to the hungry
- sets the prisoners free
- lifts up those who are bowed down
- loves the righteous
- watches over the strangers
- upholds the orphan and the widow

Unlike the actions of the most benevolent politicians, the kindness of God is not limited in time, because "the LORD will reign for ever, your God, O Zion, for all generations" (verse 10).

Early Christians unanimously testified that Jesus, the "Prince of Peace," worked with precisely the values that our psalmist attributes to the Almighty. Jesus spoke on behalf of all the oppressed mentioned in our psalm as well as those who suffered illness or disability. According to one writer, at the beginning of his ministry he suggested that the Lord had anointed him "to bring good news to the poor . . . to proclaim release to the captives and recovery of sight to the blind, to let the oppressed go free" (Luke 4:18–19, 21, a paraphrase of Isaiah 58:6; 61:1–2). And, according to another early Christian, in his final parable he spoke of our need to show compassion to the hungry, strangers, the poor, the sick, and the prisoners (Matthew 25:35–47). Such is the heart of God's demand of the pious.

With hearts and hands uplifted, we plead, O Lord, to see the day of earth's redemption that brings us unto thee.[67] *Amen.*

LIFTING UP THE LOWLY

On this Christmas Day our psalm text exults over the second great act of redemption in Old Testament history (the exodus from Egypt was the first), the end of Babylonian exile and the beginning of the restoration of Judea (formerly "Judah"). It was a kind of new exodus. Jerusalem was being rebuilt and the exiles were returning (verse 2). In light of the fact that the second temple was dedicated in 515 B.C., this suggests that the psalm was written a few years later.

The greatness and power of God that led to the redemption of Israel are reflected in the vastness of the starry heavens. God has not only created them all but also given them names (verses 4–5). But God's greatness is experienced by earthlings in acts of compassion: God "heals the broken-hearted, and binds up their wounds" (verse 3). "The LORD lifts up the downtrodden" (verse 6a). Salvation is restoration to wholeness.

According to Luke, when Mary became pregnant she praised God for lifting up the lowly and filling the hungry with good things (Luke 1:52–53). Her child was blessed by Simeon, a "righteous and devout" man, in the Jerusalem temple. He said, "Lord, now let your servant depart in peace, according to your word. For my eyes have seen your salvation, which you have prepared in the presence of all peoples, a light for revelation to the Gentiles, and for glory to your people Israel" (Luke 2:29–32). This child grew up to work for the healing of a broken humanity. Let us rejoice.

> Joy comes to all the world today,
> To halls and cottage hasting.
> Come, sparrow and dove, from roof tree tall,
> And share our Christmas feasting.[68]

Almighty God, you made this day shine with true light.
Help us to walk as children of the light all the days of our lives. Amen.

WHAT GOD DELIGHTS IN

Stanza 2 of Psalm 147 centers on thanksgiving for God's providence. As the ancient Israelites settled in the land of Canaan in the late second millennium B.C., many of them faced a transition from the nomadic life of Bedouins to settled agricultural life. Their Canaanite neighbors were familiar with the annual cycle of rain and drought, and this was reflected in their worship of the Baals, who controlled the fertility of the land. The temple singers, however, assert that it is Yahweh, not Baal, who brings the clouds and rain that cause grass to grow, providing food for the flocks. It is this God who feeds all creatures, including the ravens (see Job 38:41). Although ravens were widely considered ill omens in the ancient world, in 1 Kings 17:4 they are servants of the LORD; God commands them to feed Elijah.

If humans delight in God's providence, what does God delight in? In earlier centuries the psalmists might praise the war horse and the infantry. Now, however, in the difficult days of reconstruction after the Babylonian exile, the temple singers perceive that God takes no delight in such measures of military strength or athletic prowess. "The LORD takes pleasure in those who fear him, in those who hope in his steadfast love" (verse 11). To "fear" God is not to respond in terror, but to respond with respect to God's will and to "hope in his steadfast love."

On December 26, Saint Stephen's Day, good King Wenceslas (tenth century, Bohemia) reportedly looked out on a frosty day and saw a poor man gathering winter fuel. He summoned his page and ordered food and drink to provide a feast for the man. The carol concludes: "Therefore, Christian men, be sure, / Wealth or rank possessing, / Ye who now will bless the poor, / Shall yourself find blessing."[69] We can be sure that God takes delight in such.

You have blessed me, Lord God; make me a blessing
to those around me. Amen.

PEACE AND PROSPERITY

This third stanza centers on *shalom*: "peace," "prosperity," "security" (verse 14). Hopes for such stability were growing in Jerusalem after the dedication of the second temple in 515 B.C. and the rebuilding of the city walls and gates by Nehemiah around 445 B.C. (verse 13 attributes this to Yahweh). Jerusalem now was secure and prosperous (verse 14). Optimism was growing.

God also creates stability in nature. God's word comes to earth, ordering snow to fall on the central hills, and frost and hail (verses 16–17). The beauty of the winter is mixed with the suffering of the cold. But God again sends out the word, and the snow, frost, and hail melt into spring, causing the waters to flow and life to be refreshed. The word of the LORD is powerful (see Psalm 29) and effective. It comes not only to the mind of the prophets but also into the world of nature. To Israel it comes also in the form of "statutes and ordinances" (verse 19).   This psalmist, however, adds the unnecessary verse 20, that God has not so favored any other nation with these ordinances.

At the end of December in many parts of North America, "as the days begin to lengthen, the cold begins to strengthen." Ancient persons of faith found the hand of God behind events both in history and in nature. Everyone knew that Nehemiah oversaw the rebuilding of the walls and gates of Jerusalem, but God was the effective cause. Meteorologists might describe the natural causes of the change of seasons, but this comes because God sends the word. Knowledge and faith are companions.

Let your word, O Lord, bring peace and security to the far corners of the world, and let it begin with me. Amen.

ALL THINGS IN HEAVEN AND ON EARTH GIVE PRAISE

*A*s we near the end of the Psalter, the praise of God begins a crescendo that culminates in Psalm 150. In their call to worship, the psalmists were careful to include all that they knew of the entire cosmos, from the starry heavens to the depths of the sea, from the heavenly host to the ranks of earthly creatures. This call to praise the glory of God cannot be set aside as a "theology of glory" that ignores the suffering of the universe. The focus is not on the inner life of man or beast but on the primal duty of all creatures—to praise God. There are numerous psalms of complaint and lament, but they are penultimate; praise is ultimate.

The grand symphony of praise begins in the heavens. Sentient beings there, the angels and all the host of heaven, praise the Lord. Inanimate creations, the luminaries as well as the oceans that lie above the firmament (verse 4, as in Genesis 1:6–7) praise the holy name, Yahweh (verse 5). All these are God's creations, and they are "fixed" and unchangeable, remaining stable as God intended.

The temple singers then call on the sea monsters in the great deeps, and also fire, hail, snow, frost, and windstorm to play their parts. The next section consists of the hills covered with varieties of flora and fauna, fruit trees, cedars, wild and domestic animals, "creeping things" (always abhorrent in the Old Testament), and birds of the air (verses 7–10).

Numerous hymns, canticles, and other sacred poetry call on the world of nature to praise God. The music of the spheres (the idea that the heavenly bodies move in predetermined, transparent spheres) joins the melody of earthly creatures in a grand symphony of praise.

Thou reignest in glory; thou dwellest in light;
Thine angels adore thee, all veiling their sight; All laud
we would render; oh, help us to see 'tis only the splendor
of light hideth thee![70] *Amen.*

ALL RANKS OF PEOPLE
GIVE PRAISE

*T*he temple singers now call on *human beings* to add their voices to the cosmic symphony. The hallmark of the appeal is inclusivity. First mentioned are the classes of ancient society that wield power: kings, princes, and judges ("rulers") of all peoples of the earth (verse 11), not only in Judah. Then come gender divisions: "young men and women alike" (verse 12a) are invited to give praise, worthy of note in a male culture that separated the genders in public worship. Finally, the barriers of age are removed: "old and young together" will "praise the name of the LORD," whose "glory" transcends both earth and heaven (verse 12b).

From the music of the universe and all its creatures, the temple singers turn their attention back to the worshiping community. Yahweh has "raised up a horn," a symbol of strength, new vitality, and *shalom*, for the faithful people of Israel, "who are close to him" (verse 14).

In societies of all ages, not least of today, there is often tension between particularism and inclusiveness. Should we draw lines around our group? If so, where? Should our churches welcome all persons as full participants in the worship of God? Can classes of people be excluded from ordination to the ministry of Christian congregations? These are ongoing questions, on which practice will differ. But all Christians will agree on the principle enunciated by Paul: "There is no longer Jew or Greek, there is no longer slave or free, there is no longer male and female; for all of you are one in Christ Jesus" (Galatians 3:28).

Eternal are thy mercies, Lord! Eternal truth attends thy word.
Thy praise shall sound from shore to shore, till suns shall rise
and set no more.[71] *Amen.*

DECEMBER 30 *Psalm 149*

MUSIC, DANCING, AND VENGEANCE

*T*he psalm seems to be a hymn with a war dance. Salvation and judgment are juxtaposed. The congregation at the temple sings a "new song" (or "a song for renewal") of victory accompanied by instruments and dancing (verses 1–5)—a praise of God for victory in battle. The obverse follows—an invitation to execute military judgment on the nations who were threatening "the faithful ones" (verses 6–9).

Dancing and instrumental music, along with singing, were well-known in religious practices of the ancient Near East. Rhythmic and plucked instruments, "tambourine and lyre," are used here in preference to flutes and trumpets (were the latter considered too sensual for this occasion?).

The judgment is accomplished by men with two-edged swords who shriek war cries (verse 6). They bind the kings and nobles of the enemy with iron chains, a practice well known from the Assyrian Empire. Vengeance on the nations is "glory for all his faithful ones" (verse 9b).

Many readers are astounded that this psalm would morph from praise of the LORD to a song of vengeance after a cruel war. (The theme of the destruction of the enemies is found both in this second-to-last psalm and also in Psalm 2. Is this a coincidence?) Should we read this psalm as a symbol of God's own sword bringing human evil to its final end? Given the realities of war in the ancient Near East and the bloody invasions of Israel by Assyria, Egypt, and Babylon, we need not look beyond the text. If the nation has survived a critical threat, the assembly of the pious would most certainly celebrate in Jerusalem. Others have been known to "Praise the Lord and pass the ammunition." Nonetheless, it is taking the human race far, far too long to study war no more.

I pray for the peace of Jerusalem and all the victims of war,
Lord God. Show us a better way. Amen.

EVERYTHING THAT BREATHES GIVES PRAISE

*T*his doxology to the entire collection of psalms is a glorious paean of praise. The performers pull out all the strings as well as the horns and percussion instruments: trumpet, lute, harp, various strings, pipe (flute?), and different kinds of cymbals (some have been found in excavations in the area). The celebration at the temple has its parallel celebration in the "mighty firmament," the dome that separates the earth from the heavens above (verse 1).

As the temple courtyard fills with unrestrained joy, the singers cry out, "Let everything that breathes praise the LORD!" (verse 6). They conclude their song with the shout "Hallelujah!" "Praise the LORD!"

This magnificent poem is fitting also for the close of another year. We praise God for the blessings of the past months and for the simple gift of the breath of life. In the words of the great hymn writer Isaac Watts (1674–1748), we give thanks for what has been, and we look forward to what is to come:

O God, our help in ages past, / Our hope for years to come,
    Our shelter from the stormy blast, / And our eternal home!
A thousand ages in thy sight / Are like an ev'ning gone;
    Short as the watch that ends the night / Before the rising sun.
Our God, our help in ages past, / Our hope for years to come,
    Be Thou our guard while life shall last, / And our eternal home.[72]

I praise you, O God, your name I bless; you, Lord of all,
I do confess. The whole creation worships you, the Father
of eternity. Amen.

POSTSCRIPT

You have now gone through each line of the longest book in the Bible. I hope that for you it has been instructive and enriching. You have no doubt been startled at the frankness of the psalmists and the extent to which some of them wear their hearts on their sleeves. You have been amazed at the variety of human emotions expressed—objective praise of God, nationalistic chauvinism, bitter cries for vengeance and vindication, and thanksgiving for God's protection. A close reading of the book of Psalms leaves the impression that, as a whole, it is human—all too human.

Theologians debate the question whether we should think that God takes the initiative in reaching out to us or whether our spiritual life proceeds in the other direction—from us to God. There is much to be said for the image of the faithful and compassionate God seeking a relationship with us flawed human beings. But—for the most part—the psalms go the other way. They are the voices of human beings desperately pleading for God to act on their behalf. They are also the voices of men and women blessing God for acts of grace and redemption. Less often, the psalmists submit their own transgressions to the judgment of the merciful God. At other times, however, we do hear the voice of God encouraging us in our despair and urging us forward on the path of justice and truth.

Our journey of faith in this life takes many twists and turns, and we cannot see far along the road ahead. Whatever we meet along the way, we can find in the psalms a word fitly spoken, a word that helps us to lay bare our inner self to the Lord of heaven and earth.

A SHORT INTRODUCTION
TO THE PSALMS

Christians have always found that the Psalms provide encouragement in times of despair, compassionate voices in times of anger and self-pity, examples of repentance in times of guilt, and words of thanksgiving in times of rejoicing. Martin Luther reflected the view of believers throughout the ages when he wrote of the uniqueness of the Old Testament Psalms:

> The book of Psalms . . . preserves not the trivial and ordinary things said by the saints but their deepest and noblest utterances, those that they used when speaking in full earnestness and all urgency to God. It not only tells what they say about their work and conduct but also lays bare their hearts and the deepest treasures hidden in their souls. . . .
>
> The human heart is like a ship on a stormy sea driven about by winds blowing from all four corners of heaven. One person has fear and anxiety about impending disaster; another groans and moans at all the surrounding evil. One person mingles hope and presumption out of anticipated good fortune; . . . and another is puffed up with confidence and pleasure in present possessions. Such storms, however, teach us to speak sincerely and frankly and make a clean breast. . . . The book of Psalms is full of heartfelt utterances made during storms of this kind. Where can one find nobler words to express joy than in the psalms of praise or gratitude? . . . Or where can one find more profound, more penitent, more sorrowful words in which to express grief than in the psalms of lamentation?
>
> It is therefore easy to understand why the book of Psalms is the favorite book of all the saints. For everyone on every occasion can find in it psalms that fit one's special needs, . . . as if they had been set there just for our sake.[73]

The psalms are indeed a record of men and women wrestling with God, pleading, thanking, lamenting, cursing, blessing—and much more. Whatever your situation in life and whatever your mood at the moment, you will find in the Psalter a voice that speaks to you.

The Origin of the Psalms and Their Major Types[74]

Until the twentieth century, most readers assumed that the Psalms were written by David and other Israelite heroes and that these poems reflected crucial episodes in their individual lives. This view was based on the titles or superscriptions found at the beginning of many of the psalms. But there is good evidence that the superscriptions were added by ancient editors and were not an original component of the psalms. Thus we cannot assume that the superscriptions accurately indicate the origin or function of a given psalm.[75]

In the first half of the twentieth century a new approach was pioneered by European scholars who showed that most psalms were composed as liturgies—for public worship in the temple at Jerusalem or for individual prayer.[76] (Commentators differ on the question of whether more psalms were originally composed in the time of the first temple, built by Solomon around 950 B.C. and destroyed by the Babylonians in 587 B.C., or for the second temple, begun around 515 B.C.) This means that the 150 psalms in our Old Testament book were written over a period of almost 1000 years—from before the time of David (1000 B.C.) to the period of Jewish independence under the Maccabees (165 B.C. and later). According to the pioneering scholars of the psalms, there are at least five major types of psalms, labeled according to their probable original function:

1. The *hymn* is a poem the sole purpose of which is to extol the glory and wonders of God. The emotional state of the worshiper is not suggested. Hymns might focus on the majesty of God as seen in nature (Psalms 8; 24), in history (Psalms 113–118, especially Psalm 114), in the temple at Jerusalem (Psalms 84; 122), or of the LORD[77] as enthroned as king of Zion (Psalms 24; 47; 93–99). Psalm 29, possibly derived from a Canaanite poem, is a good example of a hymn. Between a symmetrical prologue (verses 1–2) and epilogue (verses 10–11) are four strophes (stanzas) that describe a powerful thunderstorm, with lightning, thunder, and hail moving from the Mediterranean (verse 3) south to the wilderness of Kadesh (verse 8) where it dies. The writer's

focus, however, is on the response of the worshipers in the temple, who, sensing the power of God in the storm, cry, "Glory!" (*kabod*).

2. The *community lament* (national lament) has a typical form: the occasion for the lament is followed by the plea, "How long, O Lord?" or "Why?" An appeal to the blessings of God in the past and an oracle of comfort or assurance conclude the lament. The purpose of the lament is to move God to pity and to action.

Laments are found in the Bible apart from the Psalms. The book of Joel is a national lament occasioned by a devastating plague of locusts, while the book of Lamentations mourns over the fall of Jerusalem to the Babylonians on the ninth of Ab (Jewish calendar) in 587 B.C. Lamentations combines intense emotion with a highly developed poetic structure. The poems convey a harsh reality: carnage, destruction, cannibalism, slaughter, and almost unspeakable anguish. How could the fall of Jerusalem be reconciled with faith in the God who had entered into covenant with Moses? Can God be the source of horror? Had God deserted the people? In spite of this anguish, the whole poem is a kind of prayer aimed at evoking God's mercy and intervention.

Within the Psalter, Psalm 137 ("By the waters of Babylon—there we sat down and there we wept / when we remembered Zion . . .") expresses all the extreme emotion of this genre in recalling the beginning of exile. Quite different is the mood in the masterful Psalm 90, which reflects on the brevity and harshness of life:

> Lord, you have been our dwelling place
> > in all generations.
> Before the mountains were brought forth,
> > or ever you had formed the earth and the world,
> > from everlasting to everlasting you are God.
> You turn us back to dust,
> > and say, "Turn back, you mortals,
> For a thousand years in your sight
> > are like yesterday when it is past,
> > or like a watch in the night.
> You sweep them away; they are like a dream,
> > like grass that is renewed in the morning;

In the morning it flourishes and is renewed;
    in the evening it fades and withers.

3. Most numerous in the book of Psalms are the *individual laments*, which are similar in form to the community laments and in content to the speeches of Job. The large number of individual laments in comparison to the number of hymns is typical of the human tendency to beg and complain more than to praise.

While the occasions for laments vary, a significant group stems from those who see themselves as falsely accused. Most of these psalm writers convey no consciousness of sin, guilt, or shortcoming. Like Job, they were proud of their integrity and certain that they were suffering unjustly. They therefore appealed to the justice of God, at times leaving room for curses and prayers for vengeance (see below, "The 'Cursing Psalms'"). A few, like 42 and 43, are noble supplications in which the occasion for the lament is not clearly indicated.

In some respects, the most impressive of the individual laments are two that most explicitly center on repentance, Psalms 51 and 130, both of which continue to be in liturgical use to the present day.

Psalm 22, a vivid account of an individual who appears to have been tortured, is cited by New Testament writers in their descriptions of Jesus' crucifixion. This use of the psalms involves the finding of parallels rather than the fulfillment of predictions (see below, "Christological Interpretation").

Songs of trust can be understood as a development of one component of the lament, namely, the statement of assurance in the Lord's willingness and ability to help the sufferer. Such psalms, like Psalms 11; 16; 23; 26:1–6; 27; and 62 have affinities also to the hymn type.

4. *Royal psalms* center on the king and were used as enthronement liturgies. The king in Jerusalem could be called the "son" of the Almighty (2:7), and his rule could be said to make amends for the injustices and weaknesses of society, bringing life and prosperity to the earth.

Psalm 2 opens with the plotting of Judah's neighbors, who are intent on taking advantage of the uncertainty between the death of the king and the accession of his successor. The psalmist, however, looks to heaven, where the Lord laughs derisively, announcing the new king in Zion. The king then speaks of his commission from God, promising sudden destruction of the plotters.

Psalm 110 likewise refers to the LORD's commissioning and the king's military prowess:

> Yahweh says to my lord,
>> "Sit at my right hand
> until I make your enemies your footstool."
>> Yahweh is at your right hand;
>> he will shatter kings on the day of his wrath.

After the Israelite monarchies were brought to an end in 587 B.C., these magnificent poems gradually came to be interpreted as referring to the future restoration of the Davidic monarchy, that is, to a royal messiah. These psalms, especially Psalm 110, are cited in this sense in the New Testament.

5. *Thanksgivings* are liturgies for personal or communal use. Included here are some familiar texts, like Psalms 23 ("The LORD is my shepherd, I shall not want") and 103 ("Bless the LORD, O my soul, and all that is within me, bless his holy name"). Other examples of thanksgivings are Psalms 30; 32; 34; 65; 66; 107.

There also are several "minor" types, those that occur less frequently. Among these are *wisdom psalms*, which deal with the same topics and assumptions as the material in the books of Proverbs and Ecclesiastes (examples are Psalms 1; 37; 49; 53; 112; and 128). *Pilgrimage songs* were sung by worshipers on their way to a festival in Jerusalem (examples are Psalm 84, "How lovely is your dwelling place, O LORD of hosts"; Psalm 121, "I lift up my eyes to the hills [i.e., Jerusalem], from where my help comes"; and Psalm 122, "I was glad when they said to me, 'Let us go to the house of the LORD'"). Finally, *songs of Zion*, like Psalms 46; 48; 76; and 87, praise God's glory—or presence—in the holy city, Jerusalem.

Walter Brueggemann has proposed an alternative way to classify the psalms, an intriguing model that is based on the flow of actual human life, thereby linking the life experience of the ancient psalm writers with ours. He arranges the psalms in three categories:[78]

1. Psalms of *orientation* reflect "seasons of well-being that evoke gratitude for the constancy of blessing." Such psalms "articulate the

joy, delight, goodness, coherence, and reliability of God, God's creation, God's governing law." Examples are psalms of creation (145; 104; 33; 8), poems of the law (1; 119; 15; 24), and wisdom psalms (37; 14).

2. Psalms of *disorientation* reflect "seasons of hurt, alienation, suffering, and death" that cause emotions of rage, resentment, self-pity, and hatred to arise in the human heart. These are psalms of personal lament (13; 86; 35) or community lament (74; 79; 137; 50; 81) and the seven "penitential psalms" of the early church (6; 32; 38; 51; 102; 130; 143).

3. Psalms of *new orientation* reflect "turns of surprise when we are overwhelmed with the new gifts of God, when joy breaks through the despair." These psalms speak boldly about a fresh intrusion that makes all things new. They "affirm a sovereign God who puts humankind in a new situation." These include psalms of thanksgiving (27; 23; 30; 40; 91; 138; 34; 65; 66; 124), songs celebrating the kingship of God (114; 29; 96; 93; 97; 98; 99; 47), and hymns of praise (117; 135; 103; 113; 146; 147; 148; 100; 149; 150).

This model resonates not only with recurring human experience but also with traditional understandings of stages in spiritual experience: paradise, paradise lost, paradise regained—the garden, the fall, redemption. Brueggemann's schema has the added advantage of linking the results of scholarly study of the psalms to the devotional reading of them.

The Psalms as Hebrew Poetry[79]

Roughly one-third of the Old Testament and parts of the New Testament are poetic in form. This includes the Psalms, most of the wisdom literature, and much of the prophetic books. Only seven Old Testament books have no poetic lines (Leviticus, Ruth, Esther, Ezra, Nehemiah, Haggai, and Malachi). Moreover, much of the earliest literature that came to be included in the Old Testament is poetic: the Song of Lamech (Genesis 4:23–24), the Song of Miriam (Exodus 15:21), the Song of the Ark (Numbers 10:35–36), the Book of Jashar (Joshua 10:13; 2 Samuel 1:18), the Book of the Wars of the LORD (Numbers 21:14), the Song of Deborah (Judges 5), and others.

For centuries the formal characteristics of Hebrew poetry had been forgotten and unobserved. Although in most Hebrew manuscripts of the Old Testament three books—the Psalms, Proverbs, and Job—are arranged in poetic form, the Greek and Latin manuscripts paid no attention at all to the differences between prose and poetry. Among English translations, the Revised Standard Version (1952) was the first to make this distinction consistently. The reading of prose and poetry without distinguishing between them often led to eccentric and fanciful interpretations of the text. For example, it is possible that in the account of Jesus' entry into Jerusalem in Matthew 21:7 there is a misreading or overly literal interpretation of the quotation from Zechariah 9:9:

> ^{A1}Lo, your king comes to you;
>> ^{A2}triumphant and victorious is he,
> ^{B1}humble and riding on a donkey,
>> ^{B2}on a colt, the foal of a donkey.

Mark 11:7 and Luke 19:30–35 mention only one animal, but Matthew thinks there were two, possibly because of the synonymous parallelism of the two B lines in Zechariah 9:9.

Robert Lowth of Oxford, England, made a lasting contribution to biblical studies in 1753 with the publication of *Lectures on the Sacred Poetry of the Hebrews,* which was followed in 1787 by a translation of the book of Isaiah. Lowth identified the essential feature of ancient Hebrew poetry, "parallelism of members," the placing of two or three lines in parallel position with each other, and he tried to classify the various types of parallelism used in the poetry of the Old Testament. There are two basic types:

1. *Internal parallelism* involves two or three lines within one stanza. Typical is Psalm 24:1–4:

> ^{A1}The earth is the LORD's and all that is in it,
>> ^{A2}the world, and those who live in it;
> ^{B1}for he has founded it on the seas,
>> ^{B2}and established it on the rivers.
> ^{C1}Who shall ascend the hill of the LORD?
>> ^{C2}And who shall stand in his holy place?

^{D1}Those who have clean hands and pure hearts,
  ^{D2}who do not lift up their souls to what is false,
    ^{D3}and do not swear deceitfully.

There are several kinds of internal parallelism. In *synonymous parallelism* the same thought is conveyed in successive lines, as in Psalm 24; there is no change of meaning or purpose from A1 to A2, although the second line can echo the first completely or only in part.

Antithetic parallelism displays an opposition or contrast of thought, which was especially fitting for the contrasts of proverbs:

^{A1}The poor are disliked even by their neighbors,
  ^{A2}but the rich have many friends.

(Proverbs 14:20)

^{A1}For the LORD watches over the way of the righteous,
  ^{A2}but the way of the wicked will perish.

(Psalm 1:6)

In *synthetic parallelism* the second line advances the thought of the first, a formal pattern that involves rhythm and meter:

^{A1}The fool says in his heart,
  ^{A2}"There is no God."
^{B1}They are corrupt, they do abominable deeds;
  ^{B2}there is none that does good.
^{C1}The LORD looks down from heaven
  ^{C2}upon the children of men
^{D1}to see if there are any that act wisely,
  ^{D2}that seek after God.

(Psalm 14:1–2 = Psalm 53, RSV)

The A and C lines here are in synthetic parallelism, while B and D are synonymous.

There are other kinds of *miscellaneous* internal parallelism, including similes and metaphors:

^{A1}Like the partridge hatching what it did not lay,
  ^{A2}so are all who amass wealth unjustly. . . .

(Jeremiah 17:11);

stairlike or "climactic" parallelism, with a partial repetition combined with an advance (recapitulation plus extension):

> ^{A1}Ascribe to Yahweh, O heavenly beings,
>> ^{A2}ascribe to Yahweh glory and strength.
> ^{B1}Ascribe to Yahweh the glory of his name;
>> ^{B2}Worship Yahweh in holy splendor.

(Psalm 29:1);

inverted parallelism:

> ^{A1}Ephraim shall not be jealous of Judah,
>> ^{A2}and Judah shall not be hostile towards Ephraim.

(Isaiah 11:13);

2. *External parallelism* is a correspondence between or among groups of lines. A simple example that has four lines is Isaiah 1:10:

> ^{A1}Hear the word of the LORD
>> ^{A2}you rulers of Sodom!
> ^{B1}Listen to the teaching of our God,
>> ^{B2}you people of Gomorrah!

The two A lines are in synonymous parallel position to the B lines. *Other techniques of Hebrew poetry* can most often be seen only in the original Hebrew text:

- meter (the rhythm of accented syllables). Technical commentaries on the Psalms analyze the meter of the Hebrew text of each psalm.
- alliteration (similar sounds in the beginnings of the words)
- assonance (similar sounds in the vowels of the words)
- paronomasia or puns, found especially in the poetry of the prophets
- acrostic (the first letters of stichs follow the sequence of the Hebrew alphabet). Examples are Psalms 9–10; 25; 34; 37; 111; 112; 119; 145; Proverbs 31:10–31; Lamentations 1–4; and Nahum 1:2–8.
- onomatopoeia (the aping of actual sounds in the words)

Because most English translations of the Bible of the past several decades distinguish between prose and poetry in the way the text is laid out on the page, readers today should have little difficulty in identifying a specific text as poetry—or at least to observe the translators' decision on the matter.

The Present Edition of the Book of Psalms

Many commentaries of the past two decades have concentrated not only on the form and content of the individual psalms but also on the arrangements of the psalms in groups and as the entire collection. For example, some have found a balance between the first two and the last two psalms in the collection, Psalm 1 finding its counterpart in Psalm 150 and Psalm 2 with Psalm 149. Practitioners of this kind of "canonical criticism" aim at discovering the intentions of the editors or compilers of large or small groupings (see below for some examples of groups as indicated by their superscriptions). In this book, however, I focus more on the testimony of the individual psalmists than on the motivations of later arrangers of their material.

The book of Psalms as we have it is divided into five "books," a pattern that might be influenced by the fivefold division of the Pentateuch:

1. Psalms 1–41
2. Psalms 42–72
3. Psalms 73–89
4. Psalms 90–106
5. Psalms 107–150

Each of these sections, although consisting of mixed types, ends with a blessing or doxology (41:13; 72:20; 89:52; 106:48), and Psalm 150 is a benediction for the entire collection. The final collection of the whole into a group of 150 was completed by about 100 B.C.[80]

In addition to the fivefold sectioning, many psalms have superscriptions, which, in English translation are frequently printed before the first verse.[81]

Psalms 3–41, which are attributed to David (many are prefaced by the Hebrew phrase *l'David*, which can mean "to David" or "for David" or, possibly, "of David"), deserve special mention. The superscriptions of thirteen psalms actually purport to identify the occasion at which David composed them. The fact that in the original Hebrew these psalms prefer "YHWH" (Yahweh) to "Elohim" as a designation for God suggests that they were a separate collection prior to the editing of the present book.

In 2 Samuel and 1 Chronicles, David is credited with planning the building of the temple in Jerusalem and organizing the worship there

(2 Samuel 7; 1 Chronicles 15; 28). Moreover, he is said to have written numerous psalms and other poems (for example, 2 Samuel 1:17–27; 3:34; 22; 23:1–7; 1 Chronicles 16:7–36). It is therefore not surprising that "the time of David in the Psalter is among the fundamental historical events to which reference is made again and again."[82]

But does the attribution to David reflect historical reality? There is little doubt that David was a psalm writer, among which are some of those in our book of Psalms. But the editors of collections of psalms over the centuries certainly added details and attributions. Although we cannot assume that any given superscription reflects the actual origin of the psalm, the large number of psalms attributed to David reflect the powerful influence of the great biblical hero of the psalms as a whole. In this book I do not assume that the superscriptions provide historically accurate information about the origin of any given psalm.

Beyond the "psalms of David," most of the other superscriptions of psalms point to their connection to temple worship:

- Psalms 43–49 are attributed to the Korahites, a clan that originally lived around Hebron in southern Palestine but which later was one of the two great guilds of temple singers.
- Psalms 73–83 are attributed to another priestly group, the Asaphites.
- Psalms 120–135 are titled "Songs of Ascent," songs used by pilgrims on their way to worship in Jerusalem.
- Groups of "Hallelujah" ("praise Yah") psalms are found in Psalms 104–106; 111–118; and 146–150.

The numbering of our 150 psalms in the ancient Greek translation (the Septuagint) differs from that of the original Hebrew (and English translations). For example, our Psalms 9–10 in the Greek version are Psalm 9, and our Psalms 11–113 are Psalms 10–112. Moreover, the Greek translation includes a Psalm 151, which has the superscription, "beyond the number."

Two Ongoing Issues of Interpretation

Two basic problems of interpretation confront the reader almost immediately: (1) Can there be or should there be a specifically Christian way of reading these ancient Israelite poems, for example, as if many of them refer by way of prediction to Jesus or the Christian church? (2) How can we understand the frequent calls for the destruction of the enemy?

1. Christological Interpretation

In line with the majority of the church fathers and major Christian theologians throughout history, including those of the Protestant Reformation, the twentieth-century Christian martyr Dietrich Bonhoeffer straightforwardly read the psalms from the perspective of his faith in Jesus Christ.[83] "Jesus himself prayed the beginning of Psalm 22 on the cross [Mark 15:34; Matthew 27:46], and thus clearly made it his prayer. . . . If David himself once prayed this psalm in his own suffering, he did it as the king anointed by God and therefore persecuted by men. From this king, Christ was to come. We can pray this psalm only in community with Jesus Christ as those who have participated in the suffering of Christ." Bonhoeffer knew that the original psalmists did not intend this kind of reading, and he also acknowledged that some passages seem at odds with a christological interpretation. For example, he noted that the words in Psalm 69:5, "O God, you know my folly; the wrongs I have done are not hidden from you," when put into the mouth of Jesus "present certain difficulties."[84]

I believe that Christians need to recognize that the psalms were written by Israelites long before the advent of Christianity. To be sure, many of them are timeless models of spirituality for Jews and Christians alike. But many also reflect the specific contexts of ancient Israel—worship in the Jerusalem temple, popular attitudes of the time toward the king in Judah, the system of sacrifices, the conquest of the land, and much else that has little to do with Christianity either of the early periods or of today. It is important that we allow these ancient texts to retain their integrity and original authenticity. The very act of reading the text with an open or seeking mind, however, initiates a dialogue between the text and our own life situation, and this process can lead to personal growth.

Most early Christians interpreted many psalms—especially the royal psalms—as messianic or as specifically referring to Jesus, and many took individual words or phrases to be symbols of "spiritual" truths (the "allegorical method") in order to read the text in that way. A few voices from the Christian past, however, allowed the psalms to retain their historical context and integrity. A prime example is Theodore of Mopsuestia (approximately 350–428 A.D.),[85] who consciously strove to understand the Scriptures in a historical way. Theodore interpreted as nonmessianic several psalms—like Psalms 67, 69, 71, and 108—that were interpreted by almost all other church fathers as messianic references to Jesus. Theodore was not convinced otherwise even when the New Testament explained psalm passages as predictions. Regarding Psalm 68:18, he commented that the author of Ephesians 4:8–10 simply used the verse as though it referred to Christ and altered the psalm text to suit his purpose. (Theodore himself interpreted the verse in its historical context.) And since the superscriptions attached to the psalms often did not agree with the content of the psalm, he took them to be the work of editors. Theodore thereby proceeded consistently as a historian—and his results therefore often seem quite contemporary to us. Theodore refers nineteen psalms to David and his time (about 1000–960 B.C.), twenty-four to the Assyrian period (about 750–612 B.C.), sixty-six to the Babylonian period and the return from exile (about 612–400 B.C.), seventeen to the time of the Maccabees (about 170–63 B.C.), one to anonymous Israelites without designation of time, and one to Jeremiah (about 620–580 B.C.). His interpretation of the psalms he thought came from the Maccabean period (second century B.C.) are especially perceptive and exhibit keen historical insight. Even today, for example, commentators view his judgment about the origin of Psalms 43; 68; 73; 78; and 82 as correct.

Christians who read the psalms reflectively will often be reminded of similar details in the story of Jesus in the New Testament Gospels. They will especially find links between the psalms of lament and the story of Jesus' passion, death, and resurrection. But all such cases are parallels and not predictions; they are *our* reading and not that of the worshipers of ancient Israel.

2. The "Cursing Psalms" (Imprecatory Psalms, Psalms of Vengeance)

Every reader of the psalms has wondered about the passionate calls for vengeance on personal enemies that we find in a large number of psalms, including Psalms 5; 7; 9; 10; 13; 16; 21; 23; 28; 31; 35; 36; 40; 41; 44; 52; 54; 55; 58; 59; 68; 69; 70; 71; 109; 137; and others. C. S. Lewis wrote, "In some of the Psalms the spirit of hatred which strikes us in the face is like the heat from a furnace mouth. In others the same spirit ceases to be frightful only by becoming (to a modern mind) almost comic in its naivete."[86]

Dietrich Bonhoeffer presented the issue of these psalms succinctly:

> No part of the Psalter causes us greater difficulty today than the so-called psalms of vengeance. With shocking frequency their thoughts penetrate the entire Psalter. . . . All attempts to pray these psalms seem doomed to failure. . . . Christ prays on the cross for his enemies and teaches us to do the same. How can we call down God's vengeance upon our enemies with these psalms? The question is therefore: Can the imprecatory psalms be understood as the Word of God for us and as the prayer of Jesus Christ? Can we pray these psalms as Christians?[87]

Bonhoeffer nonetheless struggled toward a Christian and christological approach to these psalms. He asserted (without providing evidence) that the enemies in these psalms are not personal enemies but enemies of God. "God's vengeance" falls not on the sinners but "on the only sinless Son of God, who stood in the place of sinners. . . . Even today I can believe God's love and forgive enemies only through the cross of Christ, through the carrying out of God's vengeance." [88]

Samuel Terrien pointed to the vastly different culture of the ancient Near East compared to that of twenty-first century America: "The tone of certain psalms . . . repulses the sensibility of our age. Let one recall the poverty and oppression endured, and the violence of wars. This might explain, without excusing, the terror, the despair, and at times the spirit of vengeance in which some of the poets wallowed."[89] He noted also that the wrongfully accused—the poor, the humble, the pious, the oppressed—do not, as a rule, take matters into their own hands but rather appeal to God for redress.[90]

Walter Brueggemann wrestled with this issue in his treatment of Psalm 109, parts of which are "a raw undisciplined song of hate and wish for vengeance by someone who has suffered deep hurt and humiliation" from a powerful person who brought only misery.[91] The psalmist hands his utter rage over to God for judgment. The psalm therefore can be read as an "act of liberation" and "an affirmation of God's governance.... The very address to the throne is an act of hope that disorder is not the last word. Such prayers must be prayed until the full order of God's kingdom comes among us."[92]

Erich Zenger called us to reconsider these psalms, especially because of an historic tendency to contrast them with the supposedly higher morality of the New Testament.[93] Zenger insists that these psalms should be read as the authentic prayers of people who appealed to the absolute justice of God, the ultimate judge of all humanity. These poems "are a form of struggle against chaos—a struggle simultaneously *against* and *with* God. . . . [They] are the expression of a longing that evil, and evil people, may not have the last word in history, for this world and its history belong to God.... These psalms are contextually legitimate on the lips of the victims, but a blasphemy in the mouths of the executioners, except as an expression of willingness to submit oneself . . . to God's judgment."[94]

James L. Crenshaw finds all attempts to justify the prayers for vengeance wanting, and the force of his remarks cannot be gainsaid. These psalms "cannot be justified theologically, whether in terms of an altruistic concern for victims of injustice, or defense of divine honor. Perhaps the strongest objection to such efforts is the failure to recognize the extent to which religious people tend to identify their own enemies with God's adversaries. The arrogance of such thinking is conceived in pride, possibly a more grievous sin than those offenses that have earned 'evildoers' a sentence of death in the prayers of the proud.... The use of Psalms for daily devotion and as a model of prayer therefore runs the risk of infecting religious people with harmful attitudes."[95] I have kept such thoughts in mind when writing this book.

Some aspects of the book of Psalms must be interpreted from the perspective of the witness of the Bible as a whole. Although the problem of the "cursing psalms" can never be explained to the satisfaction of all readers, the witness of the Old Testament prophets and the teachings of Jesus in Matthew, Mark, and Luke on the themes of justice and mercy can go far to put the issue in proper perspective.

Major Motifs of the Psalms

All varieties of psalms presuppose the centrality of worship as the basic purpose of human life. The ultimate good for human beings is "to glorify God and to enjoy him forever," as the Shorter Westminster Catechism puts it. The whole of creation is brought into the perspective of worship and the objectivity of praise. The psalmists had a strong sense of the presence of God—alternating between the praise of God's transcendence and yet acknowledging God's imminence in the sanctuary.

The psalms are models of prayer par excellence, exhibiting boldness in the presence of the divine and also persistence in spite of the silence of God. With a few notable exceptions, they prayed with an admirable lack of hypocrisy and with utter realism about human suffering. From our point of view their major failing was the occasional display of malignant joy at the prospect of the humiliation of their enemies.

The psalmists display an awareness of the moral and social obligations that are involved in true worship. Purity of heart is required of the worshiper, and the one who experiences the blessings of the Almighty receives an obligation to give witness to salvation and to seek justice for the oppressed in the community.

Especially common in the laments is the appeal to God's justice. The psalmists do not explicitly deal with the issue of innocent suffering from a theoretical point of view, but neither do they rest in the face of false accusations and other forms of injustice. They assume that God is just and that justice will ultimately prevail.

The Psalms represent all major religious and cultural traditions of all historical periods of biblical Israel. Some psalms speak of God's actions in past *history*, perhaps most often referring to the exodus from Egypt or the reign of David. Other psalms are good examples of the assumptions and language of *wisdom* literature. Many psalms reflect the values and concerns for social justice that we find in the major *prophets*. And even the hope for the eventual triumph of God's will that is so typical of *apocalyptic* literature can be found in some of the psalms. Finally, and most obviously, because they were written and collected basically for liturgical use, the psalms reflect the *priestly* traditions of ancient Israel.

Most of the psalms originated in the formal worship of ancient Israel, but seldom do they ignore the inward life of reverence and awe. Free of hypocrisy and empty phrases, they lay bare a wide range of human emotion and provide a voice for the suffering, the anxious, the grateful, and the exuberant of all ages. In powerful and majestic language they celebrate history, nature, and the possibilities of the healing of human life. Most significantly, they reflect a wide variety of human experiences and emotions. That is why, whatever your situation in life, there is a psalm for you.

FOR FURTHER READING

Bonhoeffer, Dietrich. *Prayerbook of the Bible: An Introduction to the Psalms*. Translated by J. Burtness. In *Life Together/Prayerbook of the Bible*, pages 155–177. Dietrich Bonhoeffer Works 5. Minneapolis: Fortress Press, 1996.

Brueggemann, Walter. *The Message of the Psalms*. Minneapolis: Augsburg, 1984.

Crenshaw, James L. *The Psalms: An Introduction*. Grand Rapids: Eerdmans, 2001.

Holladay, William. *The Psalms through Three Thousand Years: Prayerbook of a Cloud of Witnesses*. Minneapolis: Fortress Press, 1993.

Hossfeld, Frank-Lothar, and Erich Zenger. *Psalms 2: A Commentary on Psalms 51–100*. Translated by Linda M. Maloney. Hermeneia. Minneapolis: Fortress Press, 2005.

Kraus, Hans-Joachim. *Psalms 1–59. Psalms 60–150. Theology of the Psalms*. Translated by H. Oswald. Minneapolis: Augsburg, 1986, 1988, 1989.

Limburg, James. *Psalms*. Westminster Bible Commentary. Louisville: Westminster John Knox, 2000.

Mays, James Luther. *Psalms*. Interpretation. Louisville: John Knox, 1994.

Terrien, Samuel. *The Psalms: Strophic Structure and Theological Commentary*. Grand Rapids: Eerdmans, 2003.

Weiser, Artur. *The Psalms: A Commentary*. Translated by H. Hartwell. Philadelphia: Westminster, 1962.

Zenger, Erich. *A God of Vengeance? Understanding the Psalms of Divine Wrath*. Translated by Linda M. Maloney. Louisville: Westminster John Knox, 1996.

NOTES

1. Patrick D. Miller, *They Cried to the Lord: The Form and Theology of Biblical Prayer* (Minneapolis: Fortress Press, 1994), provides the list on page 413, note 2; he discusses "Prayers Women Prayed" on pp. 233–243.

2. Thomas Moore (1779–1852), "Come, Ye Disconsolate," *Service Book and Hymnal* (Minneapolis: Augsburg, and various Lutheran publishers, 1958), hymn 569, verse 2.

3. Adapted from words attributed to Mrs. M. B. S. Dana, in *Cantate Domino: A Selected Collection of Sacred Songs for Three and Four-Part Treble Voices,*" arranged and edited by Leland B. Sateren (Minneapolis: Augsburg, 1942), 10.

4. Jules Renard, *Journal* (1877–1910), for December 1906. Cited from *Encarta Book of Quotations*, edited by Bill Swanson (New York: St. Martin's, 2000), 790.

5. Martin Luther King Jr., *Where Do We Go from Here? Chaos or Community?* (Boston: Beacon, 1968), 37.

6. Kraus, *Psalms 1–59*, 276.

7. Weimar edition of Luther's works 5:569, 8, cited by Kraus, *Psalms 1–59*, 282.

8. Jefferson expressed his thoughts on religion most clearly in his private correspondence. I included one such letter of his, written June 26, 1822, in *The Evolution of Christianity* (New York: Continuum, 2005), 155–156.

9. Composite translation, *The Concordia Hymnal* (Minneapolis: Augsburg, 1932), hymn 285.

10. See Terrien, *The Psalms*, 362.

11. Isaac Watts (1674–1748), "God Is the Refuge of His Saints," *The Concordia Hymnal*, hymn 290.

12. Terrien, *The Psalms*, 435.

13. Ibid., 432.

14. Ibid., 450.

15. *Chicago Tribune*, May 25, 1916.

16. "Authority," in *Nomos I*, edited by Carl J. Friedrich and John W. Chapman; cited from *Encarta*, page 31.

17. See the structure of his *Theology of the Old Testament* (Minneapolis: Fortress Press, 1997).

18. Artur Weiser, *The Psalms* (Philadelphia: Westminster, 1962), 493.

19. Frank-Lothar Hossfeld, "Psalm 71," in Hossfeld and Erich Zenger,

Psalms 2: A Commentary on Psalms 51–100; translated by Linda M. Maloney; Hermeneia (Minneapolis: Fortress Press, 2005), 192.

20. See on this Erich Zenger's comments on Psalm 92:4 in *Psalms 2*, page 437; ancient drawings of these instruments are reproduced on page 438.

21. Zenger, in *Psalms 2*, 220.

22. H. Schmidt, quoted by Kraus, *Psalms 60–150*; translated by H. C. Oswald (Minneapolis: Augsburg, 1989), 117.

23. In *The Psalms*, page 564, Terrien writes, "Psalm 78 is perhaps unique in the hymnology of ancient Israel. Its form is neither that of individual complaints, prayers of supplication, or hymns of praise. . . . Partly influence by wisdom poetry, the poet recites, with prolixity and redundancy, a legendary history of Israel, from the exodus to David."

24. Other possibilities are the defeat of the northerners that resulted in King Saul's death on Mount Gilboa (1 Samuel 31) and the "Syro-Ephraimitic War" (2 Kings 16:1–20; Isaiah 7).

25. Søren Kierkegaard, *Purity of Heart Is to Will One Thing*, translated by Douglas V. Steere (New York: Harper, 1938).

26. Charles T. Brooks, 1834, "God Bless Our Native Land," *Concordia Hymnal*, hymn 411.

27. Erich Zenger gives a complete list in *Psalms 2*, page 305. He comments, "Overall the psalm is in an intertextual conversation with the book of Jeremiah."

28. Josephus, *Antiquities of the Jews* 3.12.2.

29. Gerhard von Rad, *God at Work in Israel*, page 202; cited by Kraus, *Psalms 60–150*, 195.

30. Cited in *Encarta Book of Quotations*, 885.

31. Verse 52 is a concluding doxology to Book III of the final edition of the book of Psalms. See "The Present Edition of the Book of Psalms," page 377, above.

32. Terrien, *The Psalms*, 652.

33. See note 20.

34. William Congreve, *The Mourning Bride*, Act I, Scene 1.

35. From his autobiography of 1959.

36. T. E. Lawrence, *Seven Pillars of Wisdom: A Triumph* (New York: Anchor, 1991; original, 1926), 38.

37. Terrien, *The Psalms*, 690.

38. The text is from "Songs by Stephen Foster," recorded at the Smithsonian Institution (New York: Nonesuch Records, H-71268, 1972).

39. Johann Gramann (1487–1541), "My Soul, Now Praise Your Maker!" translated by Catherine Winkworth (1829–1878); *Lutheran Book of Worship*

(Minneapolis: Augsburg; Philadelphia: Board of Publication, 1978), hymn 519, verse 1.

40. Terrien, *The Psalms*, 718.

41. Verse 48, found also in 1 Chronicles 16:36, is the concluding benediction of Book IV of the Psalter.

42. Terrien, *The Psalms*, 747.

43. George Matheson (1842–1906), "O Love That Will Not Let Me Go," *Lutheran Book of Worship*, hymn 324, verse 3.

44. "Psalm 118," translated by George Beto, in *Luther's Works*, American Edition (St. Louis: Concordia, 1958), 45; the commentary is on pages 43–106.

45. Terrien, *The Psalms*, 801.

46. This phrase appears to have originated in a writing of the ancient Hellenistic scholar Sextus Empiricus (about 200 A.D.). It was used by Friedrich von Logau (1604–55), whose poem was, in turn, taken up by Henry Wadsworth Longfellow (1807–1882) in "Retribution": "Though the mills of God grind slowly, yet they grind exceeding small; / Though with patience He stands waiting, with exactness grinds He all."

47. Allen Dwight Callahan, "The Gospel of John," in *True to Our Native Land: An African American New Testament Commentary* (Minneapolis: Fortress Press, 2007), comments on John 7:53—8:11.

48. Terrien, *The Psalms*, 803.

49. The Revised Standard Version and New Revised Standard Version translate the form of *zedek* here as "deliverance."

50. Thomas Ken (1637–1711), "All Praise to Thee, My God, This Night," *Lutheran Book of Worship*, hymn 278, verse 4.

51. From a Latin hymn of the eighth century, "O Christ, Our Hope," translated by John Chandler (1806–1876); *Lutheran Book of Worship*, hymn 300, verse 4.

52. Georg Neumark (1621–1681), "If You But Trust in God to Guide You," composite translation, hymn 453, *Lutheran Book of Worship*.

53. Terrien, *The Psalms*, 824; quotations from Mark and Matthew are changed to the New Revised Standard Version.

54. Weiser, *The Psalms*, 762.

55. Terrien, *The Psalms*, 836.

56. "A Dispute over Suicide," in *Documents from Old Testament Times*, translated and edited by D. Winton Thomas (New York: Harper and Row, 1958), pages 162–167. The Egyptian *ka* corresponds to the Hebrew *nephesh*, the life force, anima, or consciousness of an individual that, according to Genesis 2:7, Yahweh breathed into the first man.

57. Terrien, *The Psalms*, 843.

58. James Montgomery (1771–1854), "Not Alone for Mighty Empire," *Service Book and Hymnal*, verse 4a.

59. F. G. Wetzel, "How Good It Is for Brethren," *The Concordia Hymnal*, hymn 408, adapted.

60. Plato, *Republic* 3.414.c–e; Genesis 2:7; Terrien, *The Psalms*, 877.

61. James Wallace (1793–1841), "There Is an Eye that Never Sleeps," *Concordia Hymnal*, hymn 25, verses 1–2.

62. Laudamille Elisabeth (1640–1672), "Care for Me, O God of Grace," *Concordia Hymnal*, hymn 302, adapted.

63. Henry Scott Holland (1847–1918), "Judge Eternal, Throned in Splendor," *Service Book and Hymnal*, hymn 343, adapted.

64. Anonymous, eighteenth-century Germany, "Holy God, We Praise Thy Name," translated by Clarence A. Walworth, *Service Book and Hymnal*, hymn 167, verse 1, adapted.

65. Godfrey Thring (1823–1903), "O God of Mercy, God of Might," *Concordia Hymnal*, hymn 405, adapted.

66. Paraphrase of Psalm 146 by Johann David Herrnschmidt (1675–1723), "Praise the Almighty," translated by Alfred E. R. Brauer (1866–1949), *Lutheran Book of Worship*, hymn 539, verses 1–2.

67. Laurentius Laurentii (1660–1722), "Rejoice, All Ye Believers," translated by Sarah Findlater (1823–1907), *Concordia Hymnal*, hymn 113, verse 4b.

68. Bernard Severen Ingemann (1789–1862), "Christmas Brings Joy to Every Heart," *Service Book and Hymnal*, hymn 46, verse 2.

69. Translated by John Mason Neale (1818–1866), *The International Book of Christmas Carols*, edited by Walter Ehret and George K. Evans (Englewood Cliffs, N.J.: Prentice-Hall, 1963), 17.

70. W. Chalmers Smith (1824–1908), "Immortal, Invisible, God Only Wise," *Lutheran Book of Worship*, hymn 526, verse 4.

71. Isaac Watts (1674–1748), "From All that Dwell below the Skies," *Concordia Hymnal*, hymn 35, verse 2.

72. "O God, Our Help in Ages Past" is found in most hymnals. I have cited verses 1, 2, and 4 from *The Concordia Hymnal*, hymn 142.

73. Martin Luther, "Preface to the Psalms," translation adapted from Bertram Lee Woolf, *The Spirit of the Protestant Reformation* (London: Lutterworth, 1956), 2:267–71; cited by John Dillenberger, *Martin Luther: Selections from His Writings*; Anchor Books (Garden City, N.Y.: Doubleday, 1961), 37–41. Another translation, by C. M. Jacobs, is in *Luther's Works,* American Edition (Philadelphia: Muhlenberg [Fortress Press], 1960) 35:253–255.

74. The following paragraphs are based on comments in my book *Making Sense of the Bible* (Grand Rapids: Eerdmans, 2002), 26–30.

75. Hans-Joachim Kraus, *Psalms 1–59*, translated by Hilton C. Oswald (Minneapolis: Augsburg, 1988), page 65, asserts that "originally all of the psalm poetry was transmitted anonymously," a widely held opinion. On the origin and meaning of the 101 superscriptions in the book of Psalms, see Kraus, pages 21–32, and James Luther Mays, *Psalms*; Interpretation (Louisville: John Knox, 1994), 11–14.

76. Among these pioneering scholars were Hermann Gunkel (1862–1932) of Germany and Sigmund Mowinckel (1884–1965) of Norway.

77. An interesting linguistic and religious problem is the rendition in English of the various Hebrew terms for God, especially the personal name indicated by the consonants YHWH (the Hebrew alphabet has no vowels). Pious Jews from late antiquity until today have considered this name of God so holy that it must not be pronounced. English translations of the Bible usually render this term "Lord" (initial capital followed by small caps), reflecting the Jewish tradition of pronouncing the Hebrew word *Adonai* (Lord) where these four letters occur in the text. In this book I indicate the occurrence of this term alternately by "YHWH," "the Lord," or "Yahweh" (the presumed pronunciation of the term in antiquity). See *Making Sense of the Bible*, 6.

78. Walter Brueggemann, *The Message of the Psalms* (Minneapolis: Augsburg, 1984). A summary of this model is on page 19. With the exception of three of the "penitential psalms," lists of psalms in the following paragraphs are those on which Brueggemann comments in this book.

79. See *Making Sense of the Bible*, 144–148.

80. The ancient Greek translation of the Hebrew Bible, the Septuagint, has 151 psalms. The last psalm has the superscription "outside the number." Moreover, the Luke 24:44 refers to "the law of Moses, the prophets, and the psalms," suggesting that the first two divisions of the Hebrew Bible, but not entirely the third, were in place as collections at that time.

81. In the Hebrew Bible and in many translations into languages other than English, the superscription is listed as verse 1. The tradition of the English translations, therefore, creates a discrepancy in verse numbering between the Hebrew and the English. In this book I follow the versification of the New Revised Standard Version.

82. Kraus, *Psalms 1–59*, 64.

83. Dietrich Bonhoeffer, *Prayerbook of the Bible: An Introduction to the Psalms*; ed. G. Kelly; translated by J. Burtness; in Dietrich Bonhoeffer Works 5 (Minneapolis: Fortress Press, 1996), 165–167.

84. Bonhoeffer, *Prayerbook*, 166.

85. My comments on Theodore are based on Rudolf Bultmann, *Die Exegese des Theodor von Mopsuestia* (Stuttgart: Kohlhammer, 1984), 99–102. See also Rowan A. Greer, *Theodore of Mopsuestia: Exegete and Theologian* (London: Faith Press, 1961), 101–102.

86. C. S. Lewis, "The Cursings," in *Reflections on the Psalms* (New York: Harvest Books, 1958), page 20, cited by Samuel Terrien, *The Psalms: Strophic Structure and Theological Commentary* (Grand Rapids: Eerdmans, 2003), 52.

87. Bonhoeffer, *Prayerbook*, 174.

88. Bonhoeffer, *Prayerbook*, 175–176.

89. Terrien, *The Psalms*, xiv.

90. Terrien, *The Psalms*, 52–53.

91. Brueggemann, *Message of the Psalms*, 83. Brueggemann's comments on the psalm are on pages 81–88.

92. Brueggemann, *Message of the Psalms*, 87–88.

93. Erich Zenger, *A God of Vengeance? Understanding the Psalms of Divine Wrath*; translated by Linda M. Maloney (Louisville: Westminster John Knox, 1996). Negative reactions to these psalms are summarized on pages 13–23.

94. Zenger, *A God of Vengeance?* 74, 85.

95. James L. Crenshaw, *The Psalms: An Introduction* (Grand Rapids: Eerdmans, 2001), 68.

INDEX OF MOTIFS